Science and Technology
in World History
Volume 2

Science and Technology in World History

Volume 2: Early Christianity, the Rise of Islam and the Middle Ages

David Deming

McFarland & Company, Inc., Publishers

Jefferson, North Carolina, and London

The history of science is the history of mankind's unity,
of its sublime purpose, of its gradual redemption.
— George Sarton (1884–1956)

LIBRARY OF CONGRESS CATALOGUING-IN-PUBLICATION DATA

Deming, David, 1954–
Science and technology in world history / David Deming.
v.   cm.
v. 1. The ancient world and classical civilization — v. 2. Early
Christianity, the rise of Islam and the Middle Ages.
Includes bibliographical references and index.

ISBN 978-0-7864-3932-4 (v. 1 : softcover : 50# alk. paper) — ∞
ISBN 978-0-7864-5839-4 (v. 2 : softcover : 50# alk. paper)

1. Science — History.   2. Technology — History.   3. World history.   I. Title
Q125.D334   2010   509 — dc22   2010008935

British Library cataloguing data are available

On the cover: Illustrated plate from *L'atmosphere: meteorologie populaire*,
Camille Flammarion, 1888; (background) Plate 1 of the *Harmonia
Macrocosmica*, Andreas Cellarius, 1661

Manufactured in the United States of America

McFarland & Company, Inc., Publishers
Box 611, Jefferson, North Carolina 28640
www.mcfarlandpub.com

Table of Contents

Preface

In the preface to the first book of this series, *The Ancient World and Classical Civilization*, I discussed many pertinent topics that apply to this tome as well. These include my purpose, approach, and sources.

There remains little to be said that is unique to this volume, with the exception of some rationale for the extended treatment of Christianity and Islam. Some readers may wonder why religion has received so much space in a history of science.

For a long time, students of the history of science have recognized that religion cannot be separated from science in any historical treatment, especially one that deals with the Middle Ages in Europe. If we are to understand the history of science, we must understand science as the people who constructed it understood it.

In the Middle Ages, science in Europe largely meant natural philosophy, and philosophy was subjugated to theology. In 1277, the Christian Church cracked down on heretical teachings at the University of Paris. The condemned articles consisted of a list of 219 specific propositions, many of which were derived from Aristotle's natural philosophy. Pierre Duhem (1861–1916) proposed the idea that the ecclesiastical proclamation of 1277 promoted the growth of science in Europe by separating philosophy from science. By essentially outlawing metaphysical speculation, the Church left philosophers nowhere to turn but to empiricism.

Whatever one thinks of Duhem's thesis, it serves as an example of the intertwined histories of religion, science, and philosophy. Each of these fields was related to the other. If we are to understand, for example, why the Christian Church condemned the thesis that the world is eternal, we must have some knowledge and appreciation for their doctrines and for the historical development of Christianity. In the Middle Ages, Europe was permeated and dominated by Christianity to a degree that a modern European would find difficult to comprehend. Compare, for example, the themes of modern artistic works with those created in the thirteenth century.

Despite the fact that there is nearly universal recognition of the necessity of treating religion in any history of science, the extant histories of science known to me are largely silent on the origins and doctrines of the major religions. In part this is because Europe and the Americas have been so strongly influenced by Christianity that authors assume readers are already acquainted with both the historical foundations and doctrines of this faith. I have made no such assumption in this book. Writers may have also avoided the discussion of religion due to the intrinsically emotional and controversial nature of the subject. I have tried to set such prejudices aside and present a brief history of both Christianity and Islam from an objective, scholarly standpoint. Having no personal access to God, I make no judgments concerning the validity of any religious belief. In such matters, it is always my goal to understand and describe, not make value judgments.

1

CHAPTER 1

Christianity

Jesus Christ (c. 4 B.C.–A.D. 30)

SOURCES

Jesus of Nazareth was born, lived, and died in near total obscurity. In his early thirties, he was put to death in a cruel manner reserved for the meanest and lowest of criminals. During his short life, he wrote not a single word, teaching only in the oral tradition. His followers gave him the title of *Christ*, meaning "anointed one." As late as fifty years after his death, hardly any historian or person of importance considered Jesus' life or teachings to have been significant. He was an itinerant preacher who wandered about the countryside working miracles and exorcising demons. But Jesus Christ would eventually become the single most influential person in the history of Western Civilization.

With all historical figures of such early times, we have the problem of knowing whether they really existed. The evidence for Jesus' historical existence is not strong, but then neither is that of innumerable other figures whose existence goes unquestioned.

The primary documentary sources for Jesus' life are the letters of Paul the Apostle and the gospels of Mark, Luke, Matthew, and John. Paul's epistles are the earliest sources, having been written in A.D. 50–56.[1] The first three gospels are referred to as the *synoptic* gospels, reflecting the fact that they essentially offer similar or parallel versions of the same story. The earliest of these is *Mark*, finalized by A.D. 79.[2] *Mark* is notable for its "directness and simplicity ... the narrative appears to be a mere transcript of remembered facts."[3]

Luke and *Matthew* are believed to have been written c. A.D. 90, and *John* "very early in the second century" A.D.[4] The text of *Luke* and *Matthew* closely follows, and is apparently derived from, *Mark*. "So much of St. Mark's gospel has been taken over word for word in the gospels of St. Luke and St. Matthew that, if every copy of it had perished, we could still reconstruct large portions of it by carefully comparing their narratives."[5]

In attempting to reconstruct Jesus as a historical figure, it should be kept in mind that "the gospels are neither histories nor biographies ... [but] good newses."[6] In other words, the gospels were written for the purpose of proselytizing. The author of *John* stated plainly why he wrote. "These are written that you may believe that Jesus is the Christ, the Son of God, and that by believing you may have life in his name."[7] Although the gospels are not objective historical documents, Christianity is not based on the historical Jesus, but the Christ portrayed in the gospels. If Christianity is to be understood it is the gospels that must be studied.

There are some references to either Jesus or to Christians in a few documents of non–Christian origin. The earliest of these is by Flavius Josephus (c. A.D. 37–101), a Jewish historian who became a Roman citizen. Josephus' *Antiquities of the Jews* is a comprehensive history of the Jews; his chronology runs from the Creation to the beginning of the revolt against Rome in A.D. 66. In Chapter 18, Josephus mentioned Jesus.

> Now there was about this time Jesus, a wise man, if it be lawful to call him a man; for he was a doer of wonderful works, a teacher of such men as receive the truth with pleasure. He drew over to him both many of the Jews and many of the Gentiles. He was [the] Christ. And when Pilate, at the suggestion of the principal men amongst us, had condemned him to the cross, those that loved him at the first did not forsake him; for he appeared to them alive again the third day; as the divine prophets had foretold these and ten thousand other wonderful things concerning him. And the tribe of Christians, so named from him, are not extinct at this day.[8]

There are references in Roman sources as well. Tacitus (c. A.D. 56–117) recorded that in A.D. 64, Nero made Christians scapegoats for the great fire in Rome.[9] Around A.D. 110, Pliny the Younger (c. A.D. 61–113) wrote to the Emperor Trajan (A.D. 52–117) asking his advice on how to deal with Christians. Pliny described the Christians he interrogated as "people [who] were actuated by an absurd and excessive superstition."[10] He warned that "this contagious superstition [Christianity] is not confined to the cities only, but has spread its infection among the neighboring villages and country."[11]

Pliny confessed that he was not sure how to deal with the problem. "Having never been present at any trials concerning those persons who are Christians, I am unacquainted, not only with the nature of their crimes, or the measure of their punishment, but how far it is proper to enter into an examination concerning them."[12] Pliny stated that his method had been to punish those who confessed. But accused persons who denied being Christians, and would consent to make a token gesture of paganism, were released.[13]

In his reply to Pliny, Trajan advised "if the crime [of Christianity] should be proved, they must be punished."[14] But Trajan counseled Pliny to not enter into any active persecution of Christians. "I would not have you officiously enter into any inquiries concerning them [Christians]."[15] Anyone who denied the crime and accepted the Roman gods was to "be pardoned upon his repentance."[16] Furthermore, Trajan admonished Pliny to not prosecute anyone on the basis of an anonymous accusation. "Informations without the accuser's name subscribed, ought not to be received in prosecutions of any sort; as it is introducing a very dangerous precedent, and by no means agreeable to the equity of my government."[17]

In consideration of the importance of Jesus, a critical and skeptical examination of the historical evidence seems prudent. However there can be little doubt that Jesus Christ was an actual historical figure. If, as Tacitus implies, Christianity was already a strong movement throughout the Roman Empire as early as A.D. 64, it would require a marked degree of credulity to conclude that such a creed could have been founded upon a person who never lived.

EARLY LIFE

According to the gospels, Jesus' mother, Mary, was a virgin impregnated by the Holy Ghost, and thus literally the son of God.[18] Virgin-birth stories and legends were common in pagan mythology. "In Greek mythology virgin-birth ... in later times ... was asserted of anyone who seemed, by his exalted position, to have had a divine origin.... It was felt that those who were to be of superior rank, or either divine or semi-divine beings, in assuming an earthly form, should not do so in an ordinary way."[19] These myths were not confined to Western Civilization. Virgin-birth stories were also found among the Chinese, Aztecs, and Iroquois.[20]

The child Jesus was born in a manger in his father's ancestral city of Bethlehem,[21] the birth being heralded by the appearance of a new star in the sky.* Astrologers told Herod the Great (73–4 B.C.), King of Judea, that the omen in the sky represented the birth of a man who would be King of the Jews.[22] Herod responded by ordering that all male infants living in Bethlehem who were less than two years of age should be killed.[23] Jesus' father, Joseph, was warned in a dream, and took the family to sanctuary in Egypt.[24]

After the death of Herod (c. 4 B.C.), Jesus' family returned to Nazareth.[25] Nazareth was an agricultural village, "but its peasants lived in the shadow of a major administrative city, in the middle of a densely populated urban network, and in continuity with its hellenized cultural traditions."[26]

Joseph's profession was carpentry, and Jesus was one child in a large family. "Is not this the carpenter, the son of Mary, the brother of James, and Joses, and of Juda, and Simon? and are not his sisters here with us? Aren't all his sisters with us?"[27] It seems likely that Jesus would have been trained in his father's trade.

We may surmise that the youth also was educated, perhaps not in Greek philosophy, but certainly in the religious texts of his people.[28] He was an exceptional student, for when he was twelve years of age his parents found him in the temple in Jerusalem taking part in scholarly discussions. "And it came to pass, that after three days they found him in the temple, sitting in the midst of the doctors, both hearing them, and asking them questions. And all that heard him were astonished at his understanding and answers."[29]

As Jesus came of age in his twenties, he was influenced by the most controversial religious figure of his time, John the Baptist. John was a wild man who lived in the desert. He "was clothed with camel's hair, and with a girdle of a skin about his loins; and he did eat locusts and wild honey."[30]

John was not subtle in his message. He preached repentance and baptized. But when he thought people were insincere, he denounced them as hypocrites. "Then said he [John the Baptist] to the multitude that came forth to be baptized of him, O generation of vipers, who hath warned you to flee from the wrath to come? Bring forth therefore fruits worthy of repentance, and begin not to say within yourselves, We have Abraham to our father: for I say unto you, That God is able of these stones to raise up children unto Abraham. And now also the axe is laid unto the root of the trees: every tree therefore which bringeth not forth good fruit is hewn down, and cast into the fire."[31]

Fearless, John denounced Herod Antipas (son of Herod the Great) for marrying his brother's wife.[32] Herod had John arrested and imprisoned, but was afraid to execute him for fear of arousing the prophet's followers. Herod's wife, Herodias, resented John even more than Herod did. She arranged to have her daughter dance for Herod. In return, Herod promised to give the daughter whatever she requested. At her mother's urging, the daughter asked for the head of John the Baptist. "And the king was sorry: nevertheless for the oath's sake, and them which sat with him at meat, he commanded it to be given her. And he sent, and beheaded John in the prison. And his head was brought in a charger, and given to the damsel: and she brought it to her mother. And his disciples came, and took up the body, and buried it, and went and told Jesus."[33]

---

*I follow here the account given in the gospels, keeping in mind all the previously stated caveats concerning their historical accuracy and objectivity.

Doctrine and Teachings

After Jesus had been baptized by John,[34] he went into the desert, fasting and meditating for forty days. It was there that he confronted his fate: was he to devote his life to a spiritual quest, or was he to seek success and fame in the material world? The Nazarene wrestled with temptation.

"Then was Jesus led up of the Spirit into the wilderness to be tempted of the devil. And when he had fasted forty days and forty nights, he was afterward an hungred. And when the tempter came to him, he said, If thou be the Son of God, command that these stones be made bread. But he answered and said, It is written, Man shall not live by bread alone, but by every word that proceedeth out of the mouth of God."[35]

"Again, the devil taketh him up into an exceeding high mountain, and sheweth him all the kingdoms of the world, and the glory of them; And saith unto him, All these things will I give thee, if thou wilt fall down and worship me. Then saith Jesus unto him, Get thee hence, Satan: for it is written, Thou shalt worship the Lord thy God, and him only shalt thou serve."[36]

Jesus passed the test and decided to become a prophet in the tradition of John the Baptist. He began teaching in his home town of Nazareth but was poorly received. Having known Jesus his entire life, his friends and neighbors could not accept the son of the carpenter as a prophet of God. Jesus left town, noting that his neighbors could not accept him as a prophet because of their familiarity with him. "No prophet is accepted in his own country."[37]

The gospels depict a man who was a mass of unresolved contradictions. Jesus advised that evil should not be resisted. If anyone struck you on the cheek, you were to turn the other cheek to them.[38] He also preached that the meek would inherit the earth.[39]

But after preaching forbearance to his followers, Jesus drove moneychangers out of the Temple in Jerusalem in a fit of righteous rage.[40] When one of his disciples pulled a sword to defend him, Jesus told him to put it away, "for all they that take the sword shall perish with the sword."[41] Yet moments earlier, he had advised that anyone who did not own a sword should sell the clothes off their back to buy one.[42]

Jesus said, "blessed are the peacemakers: for they shall be called the children of God,"[43] but warned his disciples "think not that I am come to send peace on earth: I came not to send peace, but a sword."[44] When Simon Peter called him the Messiah, the Son of the Living God,[45] he received Jesus' approbation. But when someone called him "good master," Jesus reproached him, and said "why callest thou me good? there is none good but one, that is, God."[46]

Jesus preached "judge not, and ye shall not be judged,"[47] but ominously warned any city that did not receive his disciples would be worse off than Sodom and Gomorra,[48] the cities that God had destroyed with "brimstone and fire."[49]

The presence of these apparent unresolved contradictions add to the historical authenticity of the gospels. Fictional narratives are more cohesive and lack internal contradictions.

Jesus brought a message of hope and love. His exemplary teaching was the Sermon on the Mount.

> Blessed are the poor in spirit: for theirs is the kingdom of heaven.
> Blessed are they that mourn: for they shall be comforted.
> Blessed are the meek: for they shall inherit the earth.
> Blessed are they which do hunger and thirst after righteousness: for they
>   shall be filled.

> Blessed are the merciful: for they shall obtain mercy.
> Blessed are the pure in heart: for they shall see God.
> Blessed are the peacemakers: for they shall be called the children of God.
> Blessed are they which are persecuted for righteousness' sake: for theirs
>   is the kingdom of heaven.[50]

However, Jesus was uncompromising in his theology; he offered the *only* way to salvation. "I am the way and the truth and the life. No one comes to the Father except through me."[51] And his message of hope, peace, and love was accompanied by warnings of death, damnation, and unending torment in hell. In *Mark* 9:43, Jesus warned of eternal fire in hell. "And if thy hand offend thee, cut it off: it is better for thee to enter into life maimed, than having two hands to go into hell, into the fire that never shall be quenched."[52] The soul survived the death of the body, but it was not immortal. Jesus warned that God could destroy the soul in hell. "And fear not them which kill the body, but are not able to kill the soul: but rather fear him which is able to destroy both soul and body in hell."[53]

The fact that Jesus' teaching included unending torment in hell is manifest in the story of Lazarus. "And it came to pass, that the beggar died, and was carried by the angels into Abraham's bosom: the rich man also died, and was buried; And in hell he lift up his eyes, being in torments, and seeth Abraham afar off, and Lazarus in his bosom. And he cried and said, Father Abraham, have mercy on me, and send Lazarus, that he may dip the tip of his finger in water, and cool my tongue; for I am tormented in this flame."[54]

Jesus' cosmology was apocalyptic. The world was not evolving progressively; it was predestined for doom from the moment of its creation. The last days would be marked by the "abomination of desolation,"[55] "signs and wonders,"[56] and "false prophets."[57] At the end of the age, Jesus himself would return. "And the stars of heaven shall fall, and the powers that are in heaven shall be shaken. And then shall they see the Son of man coming in the clouds with great power and glory. And then shall he send his angels, and shall gather together his elect from the four winds, from the uttermost part of the earth to the uttermost part of heaven."[58] When would this happen? Jesus said that he didn't know. "Of that day and that hour knoweth no man, no, not the angels which are in heaven, neither the Son, but the Father."[59]

Nowhere is the apocalyptic nature of Jesus' doctrine revealed with greater clarity than in the parable of the wheat and the tares (weeds).[60] He told the story to his disciples. A farmer went out and sowed wheat seeds in his field. But while the farmer slept one night, an enemy came and sowed tare seeds amongst the wheat. The farmer saw the weeds growing amongst the wheat, but did not rip them up because he did not want to disturb or injure the fruitful crop. At the harvest the wheat was saved in the barn, but the weeds were gathered and burned.

Jesus explained the true — and chilling — meaning of the parable to his disciples.

> He that soweth the good seed is the Son of man; The field is the world; the good seed are the children of the kingdom; but the tares are the children of the wicked one; The enemy that sowed them is the devil; the harvest is the end of the world; and the reapers are the angels. As therefore the tares are gathered and burned in the fire; so shall it be in the end of this world. The Son of man shall send forth his angels, and they shall gather out of his kingdom all things that offend, and them which do iniquity; And shall cast them into a furnace of fire: there shall be wailing and gnashing of teeth.[61]

CRUCIFIXION AND RESURRECTION

Jesus' public career as a teacher and prophet lasted no more than two or three years. He ultimately ran afoul not so much of the Roman authorities as his own people. According to Josephus, "there were three sects among the Jews, who had different opinions concerning human actions; the one was called the sect of the Pharisees, another the sect of the Sadducees, and the other the sect of the Essenes."[62]

The most influential of these groups were the Pharisees. After A.D. 70, "they moulded the religion of the [Jewish] people."[63] The Pharisees were conservative, insisting upon "the strict observance of the [religious] law."[64]

Jesus clashed with the Pharisees. They questioned as to why he would mingle with disreputable people. "And when the scribes and Pharisees saw him eat with publicans and sinners, they said unto his disciples, How is it that he eateth and drinketh with publicans and sinners?"[65]

A special point of contention was the failure to observe the Sabbath. "The sacred badge of the Jew's religion, which marked them from other men all the world over, was their observance of the Sabbath."[66] As Jesus walked through a field of corn on the Sabbath day, "his disciples began, as they went, to pluck the ears of corn."[67] According to the strict interpretation of the Pharisees, "plucking and rubbing the ears of corn was counted a form of reaping and threshing,"[68] and therefore forbidden by Jewish law. One of Moses' Ten Commandments forbade work on the Sabbath. "Six days shalt thou labor, and do all thy work. But the seventh day is the sabbath of the Lord thy God: in it thou shalt not do any work."[69]

The Pharisees tried to entrap Jesus. They asked him if it were legal to pay tribute to Rome. If he had answered "no," he would have been in trouble with the Roman authorities. If he had answered "yes," he would have been guilty of betraying the Jews.

> Then went the Pharisees, and took counsel how they might entangle him in his talk. And they sent out unto him their disciples with the Herodians, saying, Master, we know that thou art true, and teachest the way of God in truth, neither carest thou for any man: for thou regardest not the person of men. Tell us therefore, What thinkest thou? Is it lawful to give tribute unto Caesar, or not? But Jesus perceived their wickedness, and said, Why tempt ye me, ye hypocrites? Show me the tribute money. And they brought unto him a penny. And he saith unto them, Whose is this image and superscription? They say unto him, Caesar's. Then saith he unto them, Render therefore unto Caesar the things which are Caesar's; and unto God the things that are God's.[70]

Jesus' declaration of separating religious and secular duties was a factor in the eventual development of the separation of church and state in Western Civilization.

On another occasion, the Pharisees brought a woman accused of adultery before Jesus and asked him to pronounce judgment.[71] There was no question as to her guilt, as she had been caught "in the very act."[72] The Mosaic Law proscribed the death penalty for adultery. "And the man that committeth adultery with another man's wife, even he that committeth adultery with his neighbor's wife, the adulterer and the adulteress shall surely be put to death."[73]

If Jesus had let the woman go he would have been guilty of not following the law. But if he followed the law, he would have demonstrated that his teachings of love and mercy were hollow and that he was a hypocrite. Again, he proved himself master of the situation.

> And the scribes and Pharisees brought unto him a woman taken in adultery; and when they had set her in the midst, They say unto him, Master, this woman was taken in adultery, in the very act. Now Moses in the law commanded us, that such should be stoned: but what sayest thou? This they said, tempting him, that they might have to accuse him. But Jesus stooped down, and with his finger wrote on the ground, as though he heard them not.* So when they continued asking him, he lifted up himself, and said unto them, He that is without sin among you, let him first cast a stone at her.[74]

---

*a marvelous detail that suggests the incident actually happened as described.

If the Pharisees were jealous of Jesus' popularity, and resentful of his outwitting them at every turn, his own denunciations of them made peace impossible. In explicit language, Jesus publicly denounced the religious authorities as "serpents,"[75] "vipers,"[76] children of hell,[77] and "blind guides, which strain at a gnat, and swallow a camel."[78] "Woe unto you, Scribes and Pharisees, hypocrites! for ye are like unto whited sepulchres, which indeed appear beautiful outward, but are within full of dead men's bones, and of all uncleanness. Even so ye also outwardly appear righteous unto men, but within ye are full of hypocrisy and iniquity."[79]

It is likely that Jesus' accusations were not meant to be a wholesale condemnation of the Pharisees as a group. "The Pharisees were never a homogeneous body," and Jesus "denounced not all the Pharisees but the hypocrites only."[80]

A significant faction of the Pharisees wanted Jesus dead, and they found someone who would help them: one of Jesus' own disciples, Judas Iscariot. "One of the twelve [disciples], called Judas Iscariot, went unto the chief priests, And said unto them, What will ye give me, and I will deliver him [Jesus] unto you? And they covenanted with him for thirty pieces of silver. And from that time he [Judas] sought opportunity to betray him [Jesus]."[81]

In Jerusalem for the Passover celebration, Jesus and his disciples met for the Last Supper.[82] After eating, they went to the garden of Gesthemane to spend the night.[83] Jesus was arrested surreptitiously in the middle of the night. Judas identified him with a kiss,[84] and "they laid their hands on him, and took him [Jesus]."[85] Jesus' disciples "all forsook him, and fled."[86]

Jesus was brought before the high court of the Jews.[87] The high priest asked him, "Art thou the Christ, the Son of the Blessed?"[88] Jesus answered, "I am: and ye shall see the Son of man sitting on the right hand of power, and coming in the clouds of heaven."[89]

In referring to himself as the "Son of man sitting on the right hand of power," Jesus was fulfilling a prophecy in the Book of *Daniel*. "I saw in the night visions, and, behold, one like the Son of man came with the clouds of heaven, and came to the Ancient of days, and they brought him near before him. And there was given him dominion, and glory, and a kingdom, that all people, nations, and languages, should serve him: his dominion is an everlasting dominion, which shall not pass away, and his kingdom that which shall not be destroyed."[90]

"Thereupon he [Jesus] was condemned to death for manifest blasphemy."[91] However Israel was an occupied country. The Jews had no authority to put a man to death; that power resided in the Roman procurator [governor], Pontius Pilate.

The next "morning the chief priests held a consultation with the elders and scribes and the whole council, and bound Jesus, and carried him away, and delivered him to Pilate." Pontius Pilate likely had little to no interest in the internal religious squabbles of the Jews. However he was also obliged to maintain good relations with the local religious authorities, as it only made governance that much easier.

Pilate was described by Philo (20 B.C.–A.D. 50) as "inflexible, merciless, and obstinate."[92] "The Jews hated him and his administration, for he was not only very severe, but showed little consideration for their susceptibilities."[93] However, Pilate searched for a way to absolve Jesus.

It was the Jewish Passover, and there was a tradition that a prisoner be granted clemency in honor of the occasion. Pilate went to the balcony over his courtyard and asked the crowd, "Whom will ye that I release unto you? Barabbas, or Jesus which is called Christ?"[94]

"The chief priests and elders persuaded the multitude that they should ask Barabbas, and destroy Jesus."[95] Pilate asked the crowd what he should do with Jesus. They responded, "let him be crucified."[96] Pilate was unhappy at being compelled to order the execution of man over a Jewish religious quarrel that meant nothing to him. He asked, "Why, what evil hath he done? But they cried out the more, saying, Let him be crucified."[97]

Seeing that the Jews were adamant, Pilate acquiesced to their demands. But he quite literally washed his hands of the matter, seeking to absolve himself of any guilt. "When Pilate saw that he could prevail nothing, but that rather a tumult was made, he took water, and washed his hands before the multitude, saying, I am innocent of the blood of this just person: see ye to it."[98]

The sentence was carried out immediately. Informed that Jesus was accused of being "King of the Jews," the Roman soldiers charged with enforcing his punishment cruelly mocked him. "The soldiers led him [Jesus] away into the hall, called Praetorium; and they call together the whole band. And they clothed him with purple, and platted a crown of thorns, and put it about his head, And began to salute him, Hail, King of the Jews! And they smote him on the head with a reed, and did spit upon him, and bowing their knees worshipped him. And when they had mocked him, they took off the purple from him, and put his own clothes on him, and led him out to crucify him."[99]

Jesus' crucifixion was preceded by scourging.[100] Scourgings that preceded crucifixions were intensely brutal. "The criminal was first of all usually stripped naked, and bound to an upright stake, where he was so cruelly scourged with an implement, formed of strips of leather having pieces of iron, or some other hard material, at their ends, that not merely was the flesh often stripped from the bones, but even the entrails partly protruded, and the anatomy of the body was disclosed."[101]

"After the scourging at the stake, the criminal was made to carry a gibbet, formed of two transverse bars of wood, to the place of execution, and he was then fastened to it by iron nails driven through the outstretched arms and through the ankles."[102] Jesus may have been too weak to carry the cross. The gospel of *Mark* states that "they [the Romans] compel[led] one Simon a Cyrenian, who passed by, coming out of the country, the father of Alexander and Rufus, to bear his [Jesus'] cross."[103]

As Jesus hung on the cross, the Romans threw dice to decide who would get his garments.[104] The Jewish priests and Pharisees mocked Jesus, saying "Save thyself, and come down from the cross,"[105] and "Let Christ the King of Israel descend now from the cross, that we may see and believe."[106]

Jesus died after only six hours on the cross. Pontius Pilate expressed surprise that he had succumbed so quickly.[107] A wealthy follower, Joseph of Arimathea, asked Pilate for the body. After being assured that Jesus was really dead, Pilate gave his consent.[108] Jesus' body was laid in a tomb hewn out of solid rock, and sealed by a stone rolled in front of the entrance.[109]

Knowing that Jesus had prophesized his own resurrection from the dead after three days, the Pharisees went to Pontius Pilate and asked that the tomb be guarded for the next three days. "Command therefore that the sepulchre be made sure until the third day, lest his disciples come by night, and steal him away, and say unto the people, He is risen from the dead."[110]

The following Sunday morning, Mary Magdalene and two other women went to the tomb to anoint Jesus' body and found that the blocking stone had been rolled out from the entrance. "They saw that the stone was rolled away: for it was very great."[111] "Entering into the sepulchre, they [the women] saw a young man sitting on the right side, clothed in a long white garment; and they were affrighted."[112] The man, identified in *Matthew* as an angel whose "countenance was like lightning,"[113] told the women "he [Jesus] is risen."[114]

The resurrected Jesus "appeared first to Mary Magdalene,"[115] and later to his disciples. "When the doors were shut where the disciples were assembled for fear of the Jews, came Jesus and stood in the midst, and saith unto them, Peace be unto you."[116] Not being present when Jesus appeared, one of the twelve disciples, Thomas, doubted the reality of the apparition. "Except I shall see in his hands the print of the nails, and put my finger into the print of the nails, and thrust my hand into his side, I will not believe."[117]

Eight days later, Jesus appeared when Thomas was present. "And Thomas ... said unto him [Jesus], My Lord and my God."[118] Jesus replied, "Thomas, because thou hast seen me, thou hast believed: blessed are they that have not seen, and yet have believed."[119]

The Resurrection of Jesus is the central element in Christianity. It gives credence to Jesus' supernatural status and authority to the Christian religion. Historical analysis is of little help in verifying or falsifying the reality of the Resurrection. There are "literary, historical and theological"[120] problems in the reports of the Resurrection found in the gospels. For example, the earliest documents in the history of Christianity, the epistles of Paul the Apostle, make no mention of the empty tomb described in the gospels.

Resurrection of a god was a common theme in pagan mythology.[121] The god Adonis was a beautiful youth whose worship originated in Phoenicia. By the fifth century B.C., festivals honoring Adonis were celebrated in Greece.[122] "At Byblus* the death of Adonis was annually mourned with weeping, wailing, and beating of the breast; but next day he was believed to come to life again and ascend up to heaven in the presence of his worshippers."[123]

In *The Golden Bough*, J. G. Frazer speculated that the myth of resurrection may have been derived from the common observation in temperate climates of the annual death and rebirth of vegetation.

> Under the names of Osiris, Adonis, Tammuz, Attis, and Dionysus, the Egyptians, Syrians, Babylonians, Phrygians, and Greeks represented the decay and revival of vegetation with rites.... The annual death and revival of vegetation is a conception which readily presents itself to men in every stage of savagery and civilization; and the vastness of the scale on which this yearly decay and regeneration takes place, together with man's intimate dependence on it for subsistence, combine to render it the most striking annual phenomenon in nature, at least within the temperate zones.[124]

Crucifixion was a common punishment in Jerusalem. Josephus records that in A.D. 70, the Romans crucified "five hundred Jews" a day.[125] Nor was it unheard for a person to be taken down from the cross before the punishment had culminated in their death. Josephus wrote, "I saw many captives crucified; and remembered three of them as my former acquaintance. I was very sorry at this in my mind, and went with tears in my eyes to Titus, and told him of them; so he immediately commanded them to be taken down, and to have the greatest care taken of them, in order to their recovery; yet two of them died under the physician's hands, while the third recovered."[126]

If the gospel accounts can be believed, Pontius Pilate was unhappy about ordering the crucifixion of Jesus. By acquiescing to Jesus' removal from the cross before death, Pilate may have simultaneously assuaged his conscience and bought political favor with Jesus' followers. Pilate may have felt that the scourging and crucifixion of Jesus had discharged his obligation to the Jews who sought Jesus' execution.

---

*a Phoenician city located in present day Lebanon

The most that can be offered for historical evidence of a miraculous Resurrection is the argument that if it had not occurred, the Christian Church would not have grown as rapidly as it did. Jesus' own disciples were relatively fickle and faithless. Judas sold him out for a handful of coins. Peter said that he would die before he denied Jesus, but hours later he fled in fear and claimed that he never knew him.[127] After Jesus' death, "the disciples ... made a recovery so rapid that it puzzles the historians."[128]

THE MONOTHEISTIC BREAKTHROUGH

Whatever the case may be for Jesus' Resurrection and divinity, his life and teachings had a profound effect upon Western Civilization. It was Jesus Christ who finally killed polytheism and reconciled Western Civilization to monotheism.

The appearance of both monotheism and science in the 6th century B.C. was not a coincidence. Both are manifestations of the abandonment of supernaturalism and a new realization of understanding the world in terms of abstract and natural principles. Monotheism was not just a simplification of reducing a multiplicity of gods to one god; it was a spiritual breakthrough.

The pagan gods in the ancient polytheistic systems were anthropomorphic. They possessed human qualities and emotions; both positive and negative. They fought with each other, had enmities, jealousies, and passions. Monotheism, in contrast, is the concept of a superior spiritual principle; a greater reality that human beings can strive for. It is not a matter of degree or number, but a genuine difference of kind.

The First Commandment of the Israelites was "Thou shalt have no other gods before me."[129] In polytheism, it was always possible to add another god to the multitude. But the monotheistic God is a jealous god, because it is not another god, but a greater spiritual reality.

Monotheism in Judaism developed gradually. "In the early period the Hebrew religion was of the ordinary Semitic type. In its ancient stories were remnants of primitive religion, of tabu, of anthropomorphic gods, of native forms of worship, of magic and divination, of local and tribal cults. Out of these developed, by the labors of the prophets, a religion of high spirituality and exalted ethical ideals."[130]

Similarly, Greek science was not just another set of empirical rules: it was an entirely different way of viewing the world. Polytheism offered superstitious explanations for natural phenomena, but naturalism supposed that the world could be understood by human reason comprehending the sequence of cause and effect dictated by invariant natural law.

But the natural philosophers did little to nothing to improve the moral condition of the human race. Moral philosophy was of no assistance. Epicureanism and Stoicism probably had little appeal to the average person who was uneducated and illiterate. Neither did they offer much hope. The best advice that could be offered to the Stoic was to accept fate and suffer the adversities of life without complaint. Thomas Babington Macaulay (1800–1859) noted the moral failings of Greek philosophy when he noted that "[the philosophers] filled the world with long words and long beards; and they left it as wicked and ignorant as they found it."[131]

The great civilizations of the future would require cooperation on a continental scale. Christianity provided this by instilling an ethic of universal human brotherhood. The Greeks had intelligence and courage, but couldn't get along with each other or unify on a national level.[132] The Romans united the entire Mediterranean region, but this was accomplished rather by brute force than cooperation. Three mass slave revolts in Italy between 139 and 71 B.C. illustrated the need to maintain Roman social order through a strong central authority.[133] It would prove impossible to maintain this order forever.

The Greek philosophers were monotheists, but their monotheism failed to replace polytheism among the general population of either Greece or Rome. There were two problems with monotheism. First, how should God be understood? The paradox of God is that as soon as it is reduced to human terms, it is no longer God, but something less. The minute that God is comprehended it ceases to be God.

The second difficulty with monotheism was obtaining a practical benefit from it. The polytheistic gods offered practical explanations; they assuaged people's curiosities, fears, and concerns. Of what good was a God that was beyond apprehension? People turn to religion for answers to existential questions: Why am I here? What is the purpose of my life? How should I act in life? What is good and what is bad? The exalted monotheism of the philosophers failed to answer these questions. God as an abstract principle was all right for Plato and Aristotle, but it wasn't providing practical guidance for ordinary people.

Jesus Christ solved these problems, and thus fully realized the monotheistic breakthrough. First, he answered that God was to be understood through *Him*; he was both the Son of Man and the Son of God. God was intangible; but Christ was here and now, he lived and provided an example for men to follow. In this sense, the physical reality of the Resurrection was irrelevant. Christ was a spiritual principle, not an individual person.

Second, Jesus gave people guidance for living their lives that was simple and straightforward. "You shall love the Lord your God with all your heart, with all your soul, and with all your mind. This is the first and great commandment. And the second is like it: You shall love your neighbor as yourself."[134]

Love one another: it was the most obvious lesson possible, and the people who heard it knew intuitively that it was correct. The God of Jesus Christ was not the abstract deity of the philosophers, it was a principle that could be understood by everyone, even by children. And Christianity provided hope in the form of salvation and eternal life. This life might be hard, but the Christian was assured that this was temporary, to be replaced by eternal life.

"[Jesus] set forth communion with God as the most certain fact of man's experience and as simple reality made it accessible to every one. Thus his teaching contains the note of universality — not in terms and proclamations but as plain matter of fact. His way for others to this reality is likewise plain and level to the comprehension of the unlearned and of children."[135] Ironically, in the centuries to follow, atrocities would be committed in Jesus' name.

It was the author of the gospel *John* who wrote the eulogy for Jesus. "And there are also many other things which Jesus did, the which, if they should be written every one, I suppose that even the world itself could not contain the books that should be written. Amen."[136]

Paul the Apostle (c. A.D. 0–60)

CONVERSION TO CHRISTIANITY

Although Jesus Christ is regarded by Christians as the resurrected Messiah, he may not have been the most important founder of Christianity. Neither were any of his apostles. Strangely enough, that distinction goes to a man who was simultaneously a Jew, a Pharisee, and a Roman citizen.

Paul, the missionary to the gentiles, was born Saul in the city of Tarsus in present day Turkey, on the northern shore of the eastern Mediterranean. His family was Jewish, but from his father he inherited Roman citizenship. In the first century A.D., Jewish communities were already widespread throughout the Roman Empire. Jews constituted about seven percent of the Empire's population. Outside of Palestine, they largely lived in Egypt and Syria including the great cities of Alexandria, Antioch, and Damascus.[137]

As respected members of the Roman Empire, Jews enjoyed religious freedom and a certain amount of self-government. Paul was educated in Jerusalem. Following tradition, he learned both Jewish Law and the craft of tent-making. Conservative in his leanings, Paul was attracted to the teachings of the Pharisees and became zealous in his devotion to the Jewish Law.

Ironically, it was persecution by the Jewish authorities that caused early Christians to migrate and thereby fostered the spread of Christianity. The first martyr of the Church was Stephen. "And Stephen, full of faith and power, did great wonders and miracles among the people."[138] Stephen was brought before the Jewish authorities and charged with blasphemy.[139] He responded, "Which of the prophets have not your fathers persecuted?"[140] and then said, "Behold, I see the heavens opened, and the Son of man [Jesus] standing on the right hand of God."[141] Stephen was stoned to death.[142] Among Stephen's persecutors was Paul the Apostle, then a young man named Saul.[143]

Paul was zealous in his persecution of Christians. He searched for blasphemers everywhere, even to the extent of entering private homes and arresting the guilty. "As for Saul, he made havoc of the [Christian] Church, entering into every house, and hauling [off] men and women committed them to prison."[144] Paul's zeal betrayed his own inner doubts. He must have been a man tormented by a hunger for the truth. No other explanation is plausible for Paul's overly zealous defense of the Jewish Law against Christian blasphemy.

So fervent was Paul in his pursuit of Christians that it was not enough to confine his activities to Jerusalem. Around A.D. 32, he asked for permission travel to the city of Damascus to prosecute Christians there. "Saul, yet breathing out threatenings and slaughter against the disciples of the Lord, went unto the high priest, And desired of him letters to Damascus to the synagogues."[145]

En route to Damascus, Saul was interrupted by an ecstatic experience. "And as he journeyed, he [Saul] came near Damascus: and suddenly there shined round about him a light from heaven: And he fell to the earth, and heard a voice saying unto him, Saul, Saul, why persecutest thou me? And he said, Who art thou, Lord? And the Lord said, I am Jesus whom thou persecutest.... And Saul arose from the earth; and when his eyes were opened, he saw no man: but they led him by the hand, and brought him into Damascus. And he was three days without sight, and neither did [he] eat nor drink."[146]

Paul believed he had received a new mission directly from Jesus Christ. In Paul's mind, his experience with Christ was every bit as authentic as those of the Apostles who had lived with Jesus in the flesh. In *1 Corinthians*, Paul wrote "He [Jesus] was seen of [by] me also, as of one born out of due time."[147]

Paul immediately converted to Christianity. "And immediately there fell from his [Paul's] eyes as it had been scales: and he received sight forthwith, and arose, and was baptized.... And straightway he preached Christ in the synagogues, that he is the Son of God."[148]

SALVATION THROUGH FAITH

Along with Paul's mystic experience, there was a new intellectual comprehension. In an instantaneous flash of cognition, Paul saw that the Jewish Law would never provide him with salvation.[149] The Law only proscribed how one should act, it did not control the inner life. As his obeisance to the Law had increased, Paul had found that his heart had become darker. Man was not saved by acts—it wasn't enough to live the good life. The only salvation was to find a change of heart through faith in Jesus Christ.

Paul later wrote that faith alone would provide salvation. "Knowing that a man is not justified by the works of the law, but by the faith of Jesus Christ, even we have believed in Jesus Christ, that we might be justified by the faith of Christ, and not by the works of the law: for by the works of the law shall no flesh be justified."[150]

In *Galatians*, Paul summed up the heart of his doctrine. "I came to realize that I could never find God's favor by trying—and failing—to obey the laws.... Acceptance with God comes by believing in Christ."[151] Paul concluded that by studying the Scriptures and obeying them he could never come to know God. Salvation was only possible by naive faith in Jesus Christ.

The Law of Moses and the Prophets was no longer the mediator between God and man. The new mediator was Jesus Christ. It was a complete break from the past. "Paul first perceived and set forth the principle of inspiration to God-likeness by a personal ideal in place of obedience to an impersonal Law, as a condition of salvation.... [He] was the pioneer who secured mankind for ever against bondage to religious legalism."[152]

To the Apostles, Jesus Christ had been the Jewish Messiah, the man who would lead Israel and her people to new glories. To Paul, Jesus Christ was much more than that. Christ was a universal spiritual principle, the pathway to God for all people, not a national leader sent to restore the power of Israel and the Jews. "Paul saw in Jesus ... the divine Spirit, who had come down from heaven to transform the lives of men, all of whom are sinners."[153] Paul envisaged Christianity as the new universal religion, not just a variant or extension of Judaism.

The doctrines of original sin and redemption through Christ began with Paul. Adam, the first man, had sinned and brought death and corruption upon the entire human race. All men from the time of their birth were doomed by Adam's sin. "Wherefore, as by one man [Adam] sin entered into the world, and death by sin; and so death passed upon all men, for that all have sinned."[154]

Adam had brought sin and death, but Jesus brought redemption and life. The death of Jesus Christ was the sacrifice that redeemed humanity to God. "Therefore as by the offence of one [man] judgment came upon all men to condemnation; even so by the righteousness of one [Jesus] the free gift came upon all men unto justification of life."[155]

Salvation was to be obtained by faith in Jesus Christ. Paul's concept of salvation was quite literally a resurrection of the physical body. "We, too, wait anxiously for that day when God will give us our full rights as his children, including the new bodies he has promised us."[156]

Although the Christian Church eventually absorbed Hellenistic principles, Greek philosophy was alien to Paul's theology. Paul had likely studied a certain amount of Hellenistic philosophy. His "letters bear traces of Hellenistic culture up to the level of a man of liberal education."[157] But Paul considered philosophy inadequate to "meet the deeper longings of the human spirit."[158]

The speculations, ruminations, and hypotheses of philosophers paled in comparison to Paul's ecstatic epiphany. "Metaphysics and speculative theories were valueless for Paul; he was conscious of a mighty power transforming his own life and filling him with joy, and that this power was identical with Jesus of Nazareth he knew."[159] Mystic communion, providing direct experience of God, made every other form of knowledge trivial and mute. In *2 Corinthians*, Paul wrote, "fourteen years ago I was taken up to heaven for a visit. Don't ask me whether my body was there or just my spirit, for I don't know; only God can answer that ... I was in paradise, and heard things so astounding that they are beyond a man's power to describe or put in words."[160]

From irrelevance, Greek philosophy passed into foolishness. "For it is written, I will destroy the wisdom of the wise, and will bring to nothing the understanding of the prudent. Where is the wise? where is the scribe? where is the disputer of this world? hath not God made foolish the wisdom of this world?"[161]

In Paul's view, philosophy was not only irrelevant and foolish, but could also be dangerous. What good could come of it, other than the destruction of faith? The only knowledge that anyone needed was knowledge of Jesus Christ. "Beware lest any man spoil you through philosophy and vain deceit, after the tradition of men, after the rudiments of the world, and not after Christ. For in him dwelleth all the fullness of the Godhead bodily. And ye are complete in him, which is the head of all principality and power."[162]

MISSIONARY TO THE GENTILES

Paul was a relentless and tireless missionary. Immediately following his epiphany on the road, he began his proselytizing in Damascus. From there, he journeyed directly to Arabia, not bothering to consult with any of the original Apostles in Jerusalem. "Neither went I up to Jerusalem to them which were apostles before me; but I went into Arabia, and returned again unto Damascus."[163] Paul did not feel the need to consult with Jesus' disciples, because he believed he had received his mission and authority directly from Jesus Christ. "But I certify you, brethren, that the gospel which was preached of me is not after man. For I neither received it of man, neither was I taught it, but by the revelation of Jesus Christ."[164]

Three years after his conversion, Paul met with Peter in Jerusalem. "After three years I went up to Jerusalem to see Peter, and abode with him fifteen days."[165] We can presume the meeting was cordial; there is no record of any dissension on doctrine or strategy. Presumably the understanding that was reached was that Paul would continue his missionary work to the gentiles and the diaspora Jews.

For approximately the next twelve years, Paul preached in Syria, the Roman province of Cilicia, Cyprus, and Asia Minor. He was not always well received, especially by the Jews. In *2 Corinthians*, Paul wrote that he had been whipped five times by the Jews, beaten with rods three times, stoned, and repeatedly shipwrecked. On the road, he was often beset by robbers, and suffered from cold, pain, and hunger.[166]

Eventually, matters came to a head. Paul's abrogation of the Jewish law was leading to a schism in the new religion. Did Christians have to follow the Jewish Law and code of conduct or not? The crux of the matter centered around a most personal obligation: circumcision. The requisite of circumcision had been given to Abraham, the father of the Jews, by God himself. "And God said unto Abraham, Thou shalt keep my covenant therefore, thou, and thy seed after thee in their generations. This is my covenant, which ye shall keep, between me and you and thy seed after thee; Every man child among you shall be circumcised."[167]

The Jews circumcised male children a few days after birth. But adults were naturally reluctant to submit to the operation. Paul realized that if the requirement were kept Christianity would never be anything but a Jewish sect, perhaps one that would eventually fade into obscurity. For a universal church to become a reality, the Jewish Law had to be abandoned. Paul took the viewpoint that what mattered was a man's heart, not a ritual of the flesh. "For he is not a Jew, which is one outwardly; neither is that circumcision, which is outward in the flesh: But he is a Jew, which is one inwardly; and circumcision is that of the heart, in the spirit, and not in the letter; whose praise is not of men, but of God."[168]

The question was decided at an apostolic assembly held in Jerusalem around A.D. 48 Although the conference's decision can be officially described as a compromise, in effect it was a complete victory for Paul's doctrine. The requirement of circumcision was waived, and the assembly held that Gentiles converted to Christianity only had to obey the Jewish Law in some inconsequential respects. "For it seemed good to the Holy Ghost, and to us, to lay upon you no greater burden than these necessary things; That ye abstain from meats offered to idols, and from blood, and from things strangled, and from fornication: from which if ye keep yourselves, ye shall do well. Fare ye well."[169]

Triumphant in the establishment of his doctrine, Paul resumed his missionary work. Around A.D. 49–56, he made his greatest contribution to Christianity by writing epistles (letters) to Christian congregations in various locations around the Empire. Thirteen of these letters became incorporated into the Christian *Bible* as Books of the *New Testament*, including *Romans*, *1* and *2 Corinthians*, and *Galatians*.

DEATH IN ROME

Paul's final days in some ways mirrored those of Jesus. Around A.D. 56 or 57, he was arrested in Jerusalem. His accusers were again the Jews, angry at his apostasy and heresy. "The Jews which were of Asia, when they saw him in the temple, stirred up all the people, and laid hands on him, Crying out, Men of Israel, help: This is the man, that teacheth all men every where against the people, and the law, and this place: and further brought Greeks also into the temple, and hath polluted this holy place."[170]

Roman soldiers literally had to pull Paul out of a crowd that was in the process of beating him to death. The Romans took Paul into custody but were generally unhappy about being caught in the middle of a Jewish dispute. They wanted to remain on good terms with the populace, but really could not care less about the fine points of the Jewish religion.

Neither was Paul so easily dealt with. More than twenty years on the road had made him a difficult and wily character. The Roman commander decided to deal with the situation through the expedient of having Paul lashed and released. However, Paul surprised him by announcing his Roman citizenship. "And as they bound him with thongs, Paul said unto the centurion that stood by, Is it lawful for you to scourge a man that is a Roman, and uncondemned?"[171] The local commander lacked the authority to whip a Roman citizen without a trial, so he ordered a meeting between himself, Paul, and the Jewish Council.

The Jewish Council was composed of both Pharisees and Sadducees, two groups who were not entirely in agreement on Jewish doctrine. Paul saw an opportunity to divide his opposition. He stood up and declared himself to be a Pharisee who believed in the resurrection of the dead, a belief to which the Sadducees did not ascribe. He then said that he was being persecuted because of his belief in resurrection.[172]

The Jews started arguing amongst themselves. The meeting quickly degenerated into a shouting match and the Romans took Paul back to prison. The local Roman commander washed his hands of the entire affair the next day by sending Paul to the Roman governor.[173] The Roman governor simply left Paul in prison for two years, hoping that he could profit from the situation by obtaining a bribe in return for Paul's release. He also continued Paul's imprisonment to gain political favor with the Jews.[174]

Two years passed, and a new Roman governor arrived in Judea, Porcius Festus. Festus asked Paul if he was willing to be tried in Jerusalem. "Wilt thou go up to Jerusalem, and there be judged of these things before me?"[175] At this point, Paul made a fatal mistake. He answered "no," and demanded as a Roman citizen his right to be tried by the Emperor himself. "I appeal unto Caesar."[176]

Festus summoned Paul for a hearing before himself and the Judean king, Agrippa II. Paul told his story, of his ecstatic vision of Jesus, and of his belief in bodily resurrection. After listening patiently, Festus told Paul that he thought he was mad. "Festus said with a loud voice, Paul, thou art beside thyself; much learning doth make thee mad."[177] When Paul had left the hearing room, Festus and Agrippa II concluded that Paul might have been simply released if he had not invoked his right to trial at Rome. "This man doeth nothing worthy of death or of bonds. Then said Agrippa unto Festus, This man might have been set at liberty, if he had not appealed unto Caesar."[178]

Paul arrived in Rome around A.D. 58–60; it was his misfortune to arrive in Rome at a time when Nero was emperor. Paul's last days are lost in obscurity. He lived there for two years under house arrest.[179] Evidently, he was subsequently executed.[180]

Growth of the Christian Church

SACRAMENTS AND PRIESTS

If Paul had founded the Christian Church, he didn't solve all of its problems. For a long time, it wasn't the sort of faith that would attract the upper classes. No Roman or Greek in his right mind would consider worshipping a Jew who had been crucified by a Roman Governor a few years hence. A respectable person worshipped a proper god, such as Zeus or Apollo.

Faith in Jesus wasn't enough, especially in an age when most people could not read and did not have access to the Scriptures. The Christian Church responded by instituting a priesthood and sacraments, physical rituals designed to bring God's grace to man. The seven sacraments are baptism, confirmation, the Eucharist, penance, anointing, ordination, and matrimony.

Eventually, the Christian Church did not so much replace paganism as it absorbed it. The practice of worshipping idols was accommodated by placing figures representing the crucified Jesus and the saints in the churches. The worship of the Great Mother, embodiment of earthly fertility, was transferred to adulation of the Virgin Mary, as was the cult of the Egyptian goddess Isis. "Ancient Egypt may have contributed its share to the gorgeous symbolism of the Catholic Church as well as to the pale abstractions of her theology. Certainly in art the figure of Isis suckling the infant Horus is so like that of the Madonna and child that it has sometimes received the adoration of ignorant Christians."[181]

The Roman festival of Saturnalia and the pagan celebration of the winter solstice became Christmas, a celebration of the birth of Jesus. "On the whole, the evidence goes to show that the great Christian festivals were arbitrarily timed by the church so as to coincide with previously existing pagan festivals for the sake of weaning the heathen from their old faith and bringing them over to the new religion."[182]

Even the central theme of Christianity, the death and rebirth of Jesus, struck a chord in the pagan heart.

> All over Western Asia from time immemorial the mournful death and happy resurrection of a divine being appear to have been annually celebrated with alternate rites of bitter lamentation and exultant joy; and through the veil which mythic fancy has woven round this tragic figure we can still detect the features of those great yearly changes in earth and sky which, under all distinctions of race and religion, must always touch the natural human heart with alternate emotions of gladness and regret, because they exhibit on the vastest scale open to our observation the mysterious struggle between life and death.[183]

As time passed, the Church became more dogmatic. In effect, Christians instituted a new law to replace the Jewish law they had abrogated. By the third century A.D., it was widely accepted that no man could achieve salvation unless he were a member of the Church and received the grace of God through its sacraments. Cyprian, bishop of Carthage who died in A.D. 258, maintained "salvation is not without the Church.... They cannot by any means attain to the true promise of divine grace, unless they first come to the truth of the Church."[184]

The gospels of the *New Testament* taught "the universal priesthood" of all believers.[185] But to administer the sacraments, the Church had to institute a priesthood. The priesthood appeared circa A.D. 200,[186] and "we find, so early as the third century, the foundation of a complete hierarchy."[187] However the Christian priesthood of the third century A.D. was not yet the priesthood of the modern Catholic Church. "Tertullian, Gregory of Nyssa, and other distinguished church leaders, lived in wedlock, though theoretically preferring the unmarried state."[188]

ROMAN PERSECUTIONS

From the time of Nero's execution of Christians in Rome in A.D. 64, the practice of Christianity in the Roman Empire was officially a crime. "So soon as it [Christianity] was understood as a *new* religion, and as, in fact, claiming universal validity and acceptance, it was set down as unlawful and treasonable."[189] "The conscientious refusal of the Christians to pay divine honors to the emperor and his statue, and to take part in any idolatrous ceremonies at public festivities, their aversion to the imperial military service, their disregard for politics and depreciation of all civil and temporal affairs as compared with the spiritual and eternal interests of man, their close brotherly union and frequent meetings, drew upon them the suspicion of hostility to the Caesars and the Roman people, and the unpardonable crime of conspiracy against the state."[190]

The Emperor Domitian (A.D. 51–96) "treated the embracing of Christianity as a crime against the state, and condemned to death many Christians, even his own cousin."[191] But Pliny the Younger's correspondence with Trajan shows that by A.D. 110, the de facto Roman policy was one of tolerance. No one looked for Christians. If they were publicly accused all they had to do was deny their Christian faith and they would be released. But anyone who refused to deny Christ had to be prosecuted. Such was the case with Ignatius, bishop of Antioch. In A.D. 107, Trajan "condemned him to be thrown to the lions at Rome."[192]

Christians were also generally unpopular with the common people. "At every inundation, or drought, or famine, or pestilence, the fanatical populace cried: 'Away with the atheists! To the lions with the Christians!'"[193]

In reference to their apparent "enthusiasm for martyrdom,"[194] the Emperor Marcus Aurelius Antoninus (A.D. 121–180) referred to Christians as "obstinate."[195] Edward Gibbon concluded, "the behavior of the Christians was too remarkable to escape the notice of the ancient philosophers; but ... they treated such an eagerness to die as the strange result of obstinate despair, of stupid insensibility, or of superstitious frenzy."[196]

The first systematic attempt to seek out and punish Christians was done in A.D. 250 by the Emperor Decius, who made a belated attempt to restore paganism. Decius ordered the execution of all Christian Bishops and Priests. Rank and file Christians were required to renounce their faith, and make a token gesture of pagan faith such as the sacrifice of an animal or the burning of incense before an idol. It was "a persecution which, in extent, consistency, and cruelty, exceeded all before it."[197]

Decius was killed in a military campaign in A.D. 251, and in the period A.D. 260–303, "the church rose rapidly in numbers and outward prosperity."[198] "Christians ... flourished in peace and prosperity."[199] The persecution of Christians was renewed in A.D. 303 by Diocletian, who was Emperor from A.D. 284 to 305. It "was the last desperate struggle of Roman heathenism for its life. It was the crisis of utter extinction or absolute supremacy for each of the two religions. At the close of the contest the old Roman state religion was exhausted."[200]

Diocletian's decision to suppress Christianity was perhaps influenced by acts of the following sort: Marcellus, a Roman centurion, "threw away his belt, his arms, and the ensigns of his office, and exclaimed with a loud voice that he would obey none but Jesus Christ the eternal King, and that he renounced forever the use of carnal weapons and the service of an idolatrous master."[201] The centurion was "was condemned and beheaded for the crime of desertion."[202]

On the 24th day of February, A.D. 303, Diocletian issued an official edict against Christians:

> It was enacted that their churches, in all the provinces of the empire, should be demolished to their foundations; and the punishment of death was denounced against all who should presume to hold any secret assemblies for the purpose of religious worship ... [it was ordered] that the bishops and presbyters [priests] should deliver all their sacred books into the hands of the magistrates; who were commanded, under the severest penalties, to burn them in a public and solemn manner. By the same edict, the property of the church was at once confiscated.[203]

The Diocletian persecution was documented by Eusebius of Caesarea (c. A.D. 260–340), author of *Ecclesiastical History*, the first history of the Christian Church. Eusebius's accounts should be read with the understanding that he was an Christian apologist who "had no pretensions whatever to impartiality."[204]

Eusebius described how one Christian was tortured for refusing to renounce his faith and make a token sacrifice to pagan deities:

> He was then commanded to sacrifice, but as he refused, he was ordered to be stripped, and lifted on high, and to be scourged with rods over his whole body, until he should be subdued in his resolution and forced to do what he was commanded. But as he was unmovable amid all these sufferings, his bones already appearing bared of the flesh, they mixed vinegar with salt, and poured it upon the mangled parts of the body. But as he bore these tortures, a gridiron and fire was produced, and the remnants of his body, like pieces of meat for roasting and eating, were placed in the fire, not at once, so that he might not expire soon, but taken by little and little,

whilst his torturers were not permitted to let him alone, unless after these sufferings he breathed his last before they had completed their task.[205]

Throughout the Roman Empire, Christians who refused to renounce their religion were tortured:

> Some beat them [Christians] with clubs, some with rods, some with scourges, others again with thongs, others with ropes. And the sight of these torments was varied and multiplied, exhibiting excessive malignity. For some had their hands tied behind them and were suspended on the rack, and every limb was stretched by machines. Then the torturers, according to their orders, applied the pincers to the whole body, not merely as in the case of murderers, to the sides, but also to the stomach and knees and cheeks.[206]
>
> Some had their fingers pierced with sharp reeds thrust under their nails. Others, having masses of melted lead, bubbling and boiling with heat, poured down their backs, and roasted, especially in the most sensitive parts of their body. Others, also, endured insufferable torments on their bowels and other parts, such as decency forbids to describe, which those generous and equitable judges, with a view to display their own cruelty, devised as some pre-eminence in wisdom, worthy their ambition. Thus constantly inventing new tortures, they vied with one another, as if there were prizes proposed in the contest, who should invent the greatest cruelties.[207]

The persecution started by Diocletian lasted for nearly ten years. However Eusebius sarcastically noted that the severity of the tortures was eventually reduced. "We were liberated from this punishment [death] by the great clemency of the emperors. After this, therefore, they were ordered only to tear out our eyes, or to deprive us of one of our legs. Such was their kindness, and such the lightest kind of punishment against us; so that in consequence of this humanity of theirs, it was impossible to tell the great and incalculable number of those that had their right eye dug out with the sword first, and after this seared with a red-hot iron."[208]

STATE RELIGION

In A.D. 305 the Emperor Diocletian retired, and in A.D. 312 civil war broke out in the Roman Empire between Maxentius and Constantine I (c. 280–337). Constantine I left Gaul with his troops and marched on Italy. Maxentius and his troops waited for them at the Milvian Bridge, about 10 miles (16 kilometers) north of Rome.

Maxentius enjoyed superiority in numbers, but Constantine's army was better trained and more experienced.[209] "Maxentius ... was utterly defeated.... It was a battle of annihilation ... [and] Maxentius himself drowned."[210]

In his panegyric *Life of Constantine*, Eusebius, who had personal acquaintance with Constantine, claimed that Constantine had been inspired to victory by a vision of the Christian cross. Reflecting on the fact that those who had prayed to pagan gods in the past had lost, Constantine "began to seek for divine assistance," and decided to pray to "the one supreme God."[211]

While Constantine was praying, he had a vision. "A most marvelous sign appeared to him from heaven ... he [Constantine I] said that about mid-day, when the sun was beginning to decline, he saw with his own eyes the trophy of a cross of light in the heavens, above the sun, and bearing the inscription, CONQUER BY THIS."[212]

The significance of the vision was explained to Constantine in a dream. "In his sleep the Christ of God appeared to him with the same sign which he had seen in the heavens, and commanded him to procure a standard made in the likeness of that sign, and to use it as a safeguard in all engagements with his enemies."[213]

Constantin's vision is "one of the most noted miracles in [Christian] church history

... [but] the occurrence is variously described and is not without serious difficulties. Lactantius, the earliest witness, some three years after the battle, speaks only of a dream by night."[214]

In *The Outline of History*, H. G. Wells (1866–1946) suggested that Constantine's decision to adopt Christianity may have been inspired more by practical politics than by a divine miracle.

> If Christianity was a rebellious and destructive force towards a pagan Rome, it was a unifying and organizing force within its own communion. This fact the genius of Constantine grasped. The spirit of Jesus, for all the doctrinal dissensions that prevailed, made a great freemasonry throughout and even beyond the limits of the empire. The faith was spreading among the barbarians beyond the border; it had extended into Persia and Central Asia. It provided the only hope of moral solidarity he could discern in the great welter of narrow views and self-seeking over which he had to rule. It, and it alone, had the facilities for organizing will, for the need of which the empire was falling to pieces like a piece of rotten cloth.[215]

In A.D. 313, Constantine issued an edict establishing toleration for Christianity. The Edict of Milan was "a decisive step from hostile neutrality to friendly neutrality and protection, and prepared the way for the legal recognition of Christianity, as the religion of the empire."[216] Not only was Christianity to be tolerated, but Constantine also ordered the restoration of Church property that had been seized under the persecution of Diocletian.

In A.D. 337, Constantine fell ill. With death imminent, he decided to be baptized as a Christian.[217] "There is no reason to doubt the sincerity of Constantin's conversion to Christianity, although we may not attribute to him the fervent piety which Eusebius ascribes to him ... the moral precepts of the new religion were not without influence upon his life, and he caused his sons to receive a Christian education."[218]

As the power and influence of the Roman Catholic Church grew, so did the necessity of enforcing a uniform doctrine and suppressing all heresies. The most significant controversy erupted around A.D. 320; it was the inevitable result of trying to reconcile the divinity of Jesus Christ with monotheism.

Jesus Christ had said he was the Son of God — but what did that imply? Was he the same as God, or was he a created being? How could Christianity be a monotheistic religion if it had two or more gods? The dispute was touched off by an Alexandrian priest named Arius. Arius "taught that Christ, while he was indeed the creator of the world, was himself a creature of God, therefore not truly divine."[219] In effect, Jesus, the Son of God, was a lesser god than God the Father.

"The controversy soon involved, through the importance of the subject and the zeal of the parties, the entire church, and transformed the whole Christian East into a theological battle-field."[220] The question was important, as the nature of Jesus as Christ defined the very nature of the relationship between God and man in Christianity.[221]

Constantine I called a conference to resolve the controversy. The first Ecumenical Council was convened at Nicaea on May 20, A.D. 325. In attendance were 318 Christian bishops, about one-sixth of the total number in Constantine's empire.[222]

The Council of Nicaea repudiated Arius and declared the doctrine of the Trinity: one God with three natures. The Council adopted a profession of faith that became known as the *Nicene Creed*. "We believe in one God, the Father Almighty, maker of all things, both visible and invisible; and in one Lord, Jesus Christ, the Son of God, begotten of the Father, only begotten, that is to say of the substance of the Father, God of God and Light of Light, very God of very God, begotten, not made, being of one substance with the Father."[223]

The solution, relying upon metaphysical and theological arguments, smacked of Greek philosophy. Thus "we have a peculiar combination—the religious doctrines of the *Bible*, as culminating in the person of Jesus, run through the forms of an alien philosophy."[224] "Justice is done to all the factors of our problem—God remains as Father, the infinitely remote and absolute source of us all; as Son, the Word who is revealed to man and incarnate in him; as Spirit, who dwells even in our souls and by his substance unites us to God."[225]

The ascension of Christianity as the official state religion of the Roman empire was secured under the reign of Theodosius (A.D. 379–395).[226] Theodosius "gave it [Christianity] all the privileges of the state religion, and issued a series of rigid laws against all heretics and schismatics.... In the year 391 he prohibited, under heavy fine, the visiting of a heathen temple for a religious purpose; in the following year, even the private performance of libations and other pagan rites. The practice of idolatry was therefore henceforth a political offense ... and was subjected to the severest penalties."[227]

The factors that led to the rise and triumph of Christianity were assessed by W. E. H. Lecky in *History of European Morals*:

> By the beauty of its moral precepts, by the systematic skill with which it governed the imagination and habits of its worshippers, by the strong religious motives to which it could appeal, by its admirable ecclesiastical organization and, ... by its unsparing use of the arm of power, Christianity soon eclipsed or destroyed all other sects, and became ... the supreme ruler of the moral world [in Western Civilization]. Combining the Stoical doctrine of universal brotherhood, the Greek predilection for the amiable qualities, and the Egyptian spirit of reverence and religious awe, it acquired from the first an intensity and universality of influence which none of the philosophies it had superseded had approached.[228]

Monasticism

EASTERN ASCETICISM

The early Christian Church was sanctimonious, ascetic, and intolerant of other systems of thought and belief. The intolerance was not so much a calculated malfeasance as it was a natural outgrowth of the strong belief that Christians possessed the one true creed. From nearly the beginning, the Christian Church adopted a tone that was moralistic. The Doctrine of Original Sin implied that the world was an evil place and all men were born sinners, redeemed only by the grace of Jesus Christ. Eusebius (A.D. 260–340) said that Christianity had not appeared on Earth earlier because men were too wicked to deserve redemption:

> The life of men, in ancient times, was not in a situation to receive the doctrine of Christ, in the ... fullness of its wisdom and its virtue. For immediately ... after that happy state [the Garden of Eden], the first man [Adam], neglecting the Divine commands, fell into the present mortal and afflicted condition, and exchanged his former divine enjoyment for the present earth, subject to the curse [original sin]. The descendants of this one ... proved themselves much worse, ... [and] commenced a certain brutal and disorderly mode of life. They had neither city nor state, no arts or sciences, even in contemplation. Laws and justice, virtue and philosophy, they knew not, even in name. They wandered lawless through the desert ... destroying the intellectual facility of man, and exterminating the very seeds of reason and culture of the human mind by the excesses of determined wickedness, and by a total surrender of themselves to every species of iniquity.[229]

In his essay *Ad Martyras* (*To the Martyrs*) Tertullian (c. A.D. 155–220) sought to console Christian martyrs by comparing the world to a prison:

> If we reflect that the world is more really the prison, we shall see that you have gone out of a prison rather than into one. The world has the greater darkness, blinding men's hearts. The world imposes the more grievous fetters, binding men's very souls. The world breathes out the worst impurities—human lusts. The world contains the larger number of criminals, even the whole human race.... The Christian outside the prison has renounced the world, but in the prison he has renounced a prison too. It is of no consequence where you are in the world—you who are not of it.[230]

The early Christians saw themselves as morally superior to the rest of the world. Tertullian asserted Christian superiority as a simple matter of fact. "We [Christians], then, alone are without crime."[231] Tertullian went on to explain that this was not so much an egotistical boast, as an inevitable corollary to Christianity. Christians had been instructed on the nature of goodness by God, while pagans derived their moral concepts from fallible human authority. "Is there ought wonderful in that, if it be a very necessity with us? For a necessity indeed it is. Taught of God himself what goodness is, we have both a perfect knowledge of it as revealed to us by a perfect Master.... But your ideas of virtue you have got from mere human opinion; on human authority, too, its obligation rests; hence your system of practical morality is deficient."[232]

In *The Refutation of All Heresies*, Hippolytus (c. A.D. 165–235) admonished pagans and heretics that they should regard him as their humane advisor. "And to you I am become an adviser, inasmuch as I am a disciple of the benevolent Logos, and hence humane, in order that you may hasten and by us may be taught who the true God is, and what is His well-ordered creation."[233]

Patiently, Hippolytus explained to pagans that because of his beneficent proselytizing they would escape damnation. "You shall escape the boiling flood of hell's eternal lake of fire and the eye ever fixed in menacing glare of fallen angels chained in Tartarus as punishment for their sins; and you shall escape the worm that ceaselessly coils for food around the body whose scum has bred it. Now such (torments) as these shall thou avoid by being instructed in a knowledge of the true God."[234]

With all men corruptible and damned by original sin, is it any wonder that Christians fled to the monastic life? Gregory of Nazianzen (c. 329–388) explained his desire to flee from the world:

> For nothing seemed to me so desirable as to close the doors of my senses, and, escaping from the flesh and the world, collected within myself, having no further connection than was absolutely necessary with human affairs, and speaking to myself and to God, to live superior to visible things, ever preserving in myself the divine impressions pure and unmixed with the erring tokens of this lower world.... If any of you has been possessed by this longing, he knows what I mean and will sympathize with my feelings at that time.[235]

The first Christian monastics were hermits who lived in the Egyptian desert in the third century A.D.[236] "There is something in the very climate of the land of the Pharaohs, in its striking contrast between the solitude of the desert and the fertility of the banks of the Nile, so closely bordering on each other, and in the sepulchral sadness of the people, which induces men to withdraw from the busy turmoil and the active duties of life. It is certain that the first Christian hermits and monks were Egyptians."[237]

The life of these early Eastern monastics was patterned after the Hebrew prophet Elijah and John the Baptist. In *History of the Christian Church*, Philip Schaff (1819–1893), offered this picture of the typical ascetic. "His clothing is a hair shirt and a wild beast's skin; his food, bread and salt; his dwelling a cave; his employment, prayer, affliction of the body, and conflict with satanic powers and wild images of fancy."[238]

By the end of the fourth century A.D., the number of Christian monks who had withdrawn from the world numbered in the tens of thousands. The life of these men was ascetic in the extreme. In *History of European Morals*, W. E. H. Lecky (1838–1903), described the excesses of the movement.

> There is, perhaps, no phase in the moral history of mankind of a deeper or more painful interest than this ascetic epidemic. A hideous, sordid, and emaciated maniac ... quailing before the ghastly phantoms of his delirious brain, had become the ideal of the nations which had known the writings of Plato and Cicero and the lives of Socrates and Cato. For ... St. Jerome declares, with a thrill of admiration, how he had seen a monk, who for thirty years had lived exclusively on a small portion of barley bread and of muddy water; another, who lived in a hole and never ate more than five figs for his daily repast; a third, who cut his hair only on Easter Sunday, who never washed his clothes, who never changed his tunic till it fell to pieces, who starved himself till his eyes grew dim, and his skin "like a pumice stone," and whose merits, shown by these austerities, Homer himself would be unable to recount.[239]

"Theodoret [c. 393–457] relates of the much lauded Akepsismas, in Cyprus, that he spent sixty years in the same cell, without seeing or speaking to any one, and looked so wild and shaggy, that he was once actually taken for a wolf by a shepherd, who assailed him with stones, till he discovered his error, and then worshipped the hermit as a saint."[240]

The most extreme of the Eastern ascetics was St. Simeon Stylites (A.D. 390–459), who lived for thirty years on top of a pillar. Food, water, and other necessities were brought to him by his disciples who mounted ladders. "The facts would seem incredible were they not vouched for by Theodoret, who knew him [Simeon Stylites] personally."[241] In *History of European Morals*, Lecky described some of the punishments Stylites subjected himself to:

> He had bound a rope around him so that it became imbedded in his flesh, which putrefied around it. "A horrible stench, intolerable to the bystanders, exhaled from his body, and worms dropped from him whenever he moved, and they filled his bed." ... He built successively three pillars, the last being sixty feet high, and scarcely two cubits in circumference, and on this pillar, during thirty years, he remained exposed to every change of climate, ceaselessly and rapidly bending his body in prayer almost to the level of his feet. ... For a whole year, we are told, St. Simeon stood upon one leg, the other being covered with hideous ulcers, while his biographer was commissioned to stand by his side, to pick up the worms that fell from his body, and to replace them in the sores, the saint saying to the worm, "Eat what God has given you." From every quarter pilgrims of every degree thronged to do him homage. A crowd of prelates followed him to the grave. A brilliant star is said to have shone miraculously over his pillar; the general voice of mankind pronounced him to be the highest model of a Christian saint, and several other anchorites imitated or emulated his penances.[242]

THE BENEDICTINES

In the West, monasticism developed in a different form. The founder of Western monasticism is considered to be Saint Benedict of Nursia (c. A.D. 480–547) who first laid out a set of written rules on how monastic life should be conducted, the *Rule of St. Benedict*.[243] Benedict "eliminated from the idea of the monastic life the element of Oriental asceticism and extreme bodily austerity,"[244] and he established that monks should live communally in monasteries.

The chief precepts of *Benedict's Rule* for the life of a coenobite were "poverty, chastity, obedience, piety, and labor."[245] Monks were governed by an abbot, thus a monastery under the rule of an abbot was an *abbey*. Abbots had absolute executive power, but Benedict advised them to govern collegially. "Whenever anything of importance is to be done in the monastery, the abbot shall call together the whole congregation [of monks], and shall himself explain the matter in question. And, having heard the advice of the brethren, he shall think it over by himself, and shall do what he considers most advantageous."[246]

Monks were forbidden to own property. "He should have absolutely not anything, neither a book, nor tablets, nor a pen — nothing at all.... All things shall be held in common."[247] The brothers were enjoined to perform manual labor and to study approved writings on a regular schedule. "Idleness is the enemy of the soul. And therefore, at fixed times, the brothers ought to be occupied in manual labor; and again, at fixed times, in sacred reading."[248] "It was a proverb, that a laborious monk was beset by only one devil; an idle one, by a legion."[249] The requirement of reading implied that monasteries must have libraries, thus the Christian monasteries became havens that preserved ancient manuscripts.

From the sixth century A.D. onward, Western monasticism spread with "extraordinary rapidity."[250] But there was little scriptural support for the monastic lifestyle. "There is not a trace of monkish austerity and ascetic rigor in his [Jesus'] life or precepts."[251] The lives of the anchorites and coenobites demanded "entire renunciation, not only of sin, but also of property and of marriage, which are lawful in themselves, ordained by God himself, and indispensable to the continuance and welfare of the human race."[252] "The monks carried with them into their solitude their most dangerous enemy in their hearts, and there often endured much fiercer conflicts with flesh and blood, than amidst the society of men."[253]

Although the extremes to which Christian monks and ascetics subjected themselves may incite our morbid fascination, Christian monasticism was a civilizing influence in the degenerating classical world. "It was for many centuries the strongest and steadiest influence for charity and justice — the greatest civilizing power amidst periodic anarchy and general corruption. Monasteries were the natural depositories of much knowledge which otherwise would have perished."[254]

But it would be a mistake to view European monasteries of the Dark Ages as intellectual centers. What literary or intellectual activity that took place there was incidental or peripheral to the religious function of these institutions.[255] Every monastery had a library of books, but this meant a few shelves of books, not a room full of manuscripts.[256] But nevertheless the monasteries were the forerunners of the Christian Cathedral schools that spawned the great European universities in the twelfth century A.D.[257]

Attitudes Toward Philosophy

HOSTILITY TO PHILOSOPHY

Many, but not all, of the early Church Fathers were hostile to philosophy, and their writings are permeated with intolerance. Christian spirituality was conceived of as being contrary to reasoned study of the natural world. Christianity and philosophy were competitive and antithetical systems of knowledge. They could not coexist.

Irenaeus (c. A.D. 130–200) explained that it was frankly better to be ignorant than to indulge in the useless vanity of seeking knowledge. "It is therefore better and more profitable to belong to the simple and unlettered class.... One should have no knowledge whatever of any reason why a single thing in creation has been made, but should believe in God, and continue in His love.... He should search after no other knowledge except [the knowledge of] Jesus Christ the Son of God."[258]

In De Anima (On the Soul), Tertullian (c. A.D. 155–220) noted that St. Paul had been poorly received by the philosophers in Athens, and described philosophers as "patriarchs of heretics." "We should then be never required to try our strength in contests about the soul with philosophers, those patriarchs of heretics, as they may be fairly called. The apostle [Paul], so far back as his own time, foresaw, indeed, that philosophy would do violent injury to the truth. This admonition about false philosophy he was induced to offer after he had been at Athens, had become acquainted with that loquacious city, and had there had a taste of its huckstering wiseacres and talkers."[259]

Tertullian said quite plainly that philosophy must be repressed. "Whatever noxious vapors, accordingly, exhaled from philosophy, obscure the clear and wholesome atmosphere of truth, it will be for Christians to clear away, both by shattering to pieces the arguments which are drawn from the principles of things—I mean those of the philosophers—and by opposing to them the maxims of heavenly wisdom—that is, such as are revealed by the Lord; in order that both the pitfalls wherewith philosophy captivates the heathen may be removed, and the means employed by heresy to shake the faith of Christians may be repressed."[260]

In an acclamation of close-mindedness, Tertullian exclaimed that true Christians had no interest in anything but the gospel. "Indeed heresies are themselves instigated by philosophy.... We want no curious disputation after possessing Christ Jesus, no inquisition after enjoying the gospel! With our faith, we desire no further belief. For this is our palmary faith, that there is nothing which we ought to believe besides."[261]

Lactantius (A.D. 260–330) wrote a treatise titled *Of the False Wisdom of Philosophers.* He began charitably by conceding that men studied philosophy because they love truth, and this love of truth came from God.

> Nor do I now disparage the pursuit of those who wished to know the truth, because God has made the nature of man most desirous of arriving at the truth; but I assert and maintain this against them, that the effect did not follow their honest and well-directed will, because they neither knew what was true in itself, nor how, nor where, nor with what mind it is to be sought. And thus, while they desire to remedy the errors of men, they have become entangled in snares and the greatest errors. I have therefore been led to this task of refuting philosophy by the very order of the subject which I have undertaken.[262]

Lactantius conceded that philosophy had never been defined as wisdom, but as "the love of wisdom," and that philosophers have never made the pretension of being wise.[263] But he then attacked philosophers as having not even a love of wisdom, because their pursuit had been sterile.

"But I am not prepared to concede even that philosophers are devoted to the pursuit of wisdom, because by that pursuit there is no attaining to wisdom. For if the power of finding the truth were connected with this pursuit, and if this pursuit were a kind of road to wisdom, it would at length be found. But since so much time and talent have been wasted in the search for it, and it has not yet been gained, it is plain that there is no wisdom there."[264]

In Lactantius' view, philosophers were always led astray by the same device: deductive logic. "For when they have assumed anything false in the commencement of their investigations, led by the resemblance of the truth, they necessarily fall into those things which are its consequences. Thus they fall into many ridiculous things."[265]

As an example of a "ridiculous thing" entertained by the philosophers, Lactantius offered the idea that the Earth is spherical ("round like a ball").[266] He argued that the theory was nonsense. "Is there any one so senseless as to believe that there are men whose footsteps are higher than their heads? Or that the things which with us are in a recumbent position, with them hang in an inverted direction? That the crops and trees grow downwards? That the rains, and snow, and hail fall upwards to the earth?"[267]

Lactantius concluded by noting that he could prove by many arguments why the Earth cannot be spherical, but had better things to do. "But I should be able to prove by many arguments that it is impossible for the heaven to be lower than the earth, were it not that this book must now be concluded, and that some things still remain, which are more necessary for the present work."[268]

The hostility between theologians and philosophers was at least partly mutual. The neoplatonic philosopher Porphyry (c. A.D. 233–304) "wrote an extended work against the Christians,"[269] of which only fragments survive. Porphyry also implicitly endorsed the persecution of Christians, asking "how can these people be thought worthy of forbearance?"[270]

St. Athanasius (c. A.D. 295–373) contrasted the science of medicine with the miracles wrought by Jesus Christ. "Asclepius was deified among them, because he practiced medicine and found herbs for bodies that were sick; not forming them himself out of the earth, but discovering them by science drawn from nature. But what is this to what was done by the Savior, in that, instead of healing a wound, He modified a man's original nature, and restored the body whole."[271]

What is revealing about this quotation is the arbitrary opposition of medical science and religion. Both are ways of knowing and understanding the world. One might as well suppose that spirituality is fostered by study of the natural world — isn't the universe the mind of God? No, according to the Christian scriptures, God had created the world. He was outside the world, a Being infinitely greater than His creation. Knowledge of God only came through the revelation of Jesus Christ. All that remained was to wait for the end of the world and Christ's imminent return. The revelation of Christ was total, complete, and final. Therefore anything that detracted from it was evil and undesirable.

St. Hilary of Poitiers (c. 315–367) warned that the soul should not "stray and linger in some delusion of heathen philosophy."[272] It was the folly of philosophy to study the world with the hope of understanding it. The world had been made by God, and could therefore only be understood by an infinite intelligence, not our meager intellects. "Beware lest any man spoil you through philosophy and vain deceit ... steadfast faith rejects the vain subtleties of philosophic enquiry; truth refuses to be vanquished by these treacherous devices of human folly and enslaved by falsehood ... deeds of God, wrought in a manner beyond our comprehension, cannot, I repeat, be understood by our natural faculties, for the work of the Infinite and Eternal can only be grasped by an infinite intelligence."[273]

The study of nature could not be a path to spiritual enlightenment, for the universe was a creation of God, not a reflection of His nature. The cosmos was no more revealing of the mind of God than a clay pot was of the intellect of the potter. God was greater than his creation, eternal, infinite, and unknowable except by revelation. St. Basil (c. 330–379) condemned the identification of the material universe with God.

> Of what use then are geometry — the calculations of arithmetic — the study of solids and far-famed astronomy, this laborious vanity, if those who pursue them imagine that this visible world is co-eternal with the Creator of all things, with God Himself; if they attribute to this limited world, which has a material body, the same glory as to the incomprehensible and invisible nature; if they cannot conceive that a whole, of which the parts are subject to corruption and change, must of necessity end by itself submitting to the fate of its parts? But they have become "vain in their imaginations and their foolish heart was darkened. Professing themselves to be wise, they became fools."[274]

St. Basil concluded that faith is to be preferred to reason, because the philosophers all refuted each other and natural philosophy had never satisfactorily explained any natural phenomenon. "At all events let us prefer the simplicity of faith to the demonstrations of reason ... the most penetrating mind cannot attain to the knowledge of the least of the phenomena of the world, either to give a suitable explanation of it or to render due praise to the Creator, to Whom belong all glory, all honor and all power world without end. Amen."[275]

St. Ambrose (c. A.D. 339–397) condemned the most ancient and respected of the sciences, astronomy and geometry. "What shows such darkness as to discuss subjects connected with geometry and astronomy (which they [philosophers] approve of), to measure the depths of space, to shut up heaven and earth within the limits of fixed numbers, to leave aside the grounds of salvation and to seek for error? Moses, learned as he was in all the wisdom of the Egyptians, did not approve of those things, but thought that kind of wisdom both harmful and foolish."[276]

CYRIL AND HYPATIA

There were Christian scholars who advocated a more liberal approach to Greek philosophy, but during the first centuries of the Christian Era they were in the minority. The Church historian, Socrates Scholasticus (c. A.D. 380–445), defended the study of Greek literature. He had three arguments. First, he pointed out that Christ and his Apostles had never directly condemned such study. "Greek literature certainly was never recognized either by Christ or his Apostles as divinely inspired, nor on the other hand was it wholly rejected as pernicious ... wherefore by not forbidding the study of the learned works of the Greeks, they left it to the discretion of those who wished to do so."[277]

Socrates second argument was that the Scriptures were not enough by themselves, because they did not instruct in the art of reasoning which was necessary to defeat the arguments of the pagans. "The divinely inspired Scriptures undoubtedly inculcate doctrines that are both admirable in themselves, and heavenly in their character: they also eminently tend to produce piety and integrity of life in those who are guided by their precepts, pointing out a walk of faith which is highly approved of God. But they do not instruct us in the art of reasoning, by means of which we may be enabled successfully to resist those who oppose the truth."[278]

The third argument was that it was necessary to understand pagan philosophy in order to be able to defeat it.

> Adversaries are most easily foiled, when we can use their own weapons against them.... But this we cannot do, unless we possess ourselves of the weapons of our adversaries: taking care that in making this acquisition we do not adopt their sentiments, but testing them, reject the evil, but retain all that is good and true: for good wherever it is found, is a property of truth. Let it be remembered that the Apostle [Paul] not only does not forbid our being instructed in Greek learning, but that he himself seems by no means to have neglected it, inasmuch as he knows many of the sayings of the Greeks.[279]

Ultimately, more liberal voices would prevail. The Christian Church eventually embraced and subjugated Greek philosophy, especially Aristotelian logic. The way was prepared by the most influential of the Church Fathers, Augustine of Hippo (A.D. 354–430). Augustine argued that that methods of the philosophers should be enlisted in the cause of theology when it was useful to do so, and when there was no conflict with doctrine.[280]

But in the fifth century A.D., the ideas of Cyril of Alexandria (A.D. 375–444) were more in accord with the tenor of the times. Cyril "exhibits to us a man making theology and orthodoxy the instruments of his passions.... [He] furnishes a striking proof that orthodoxy and piety are two quite different things."[281] Cyril was severe and unrelenting in his persecution of heretics and unbelievers. He became Bishop of Alexandria in A.D. 412, and "exceeded Theophilus [his predecessor] in arrogance and violence."[282]

Cyril closed the churches of the Novatians, a sect he considered to be heretical, and confiscated their property. Although Jews had been a sizeable part of the Alexandrian community since the city was founded in 332 B.C., Cyril attacked the Jewish synagogues in force and drove forty thousand Jews out of the city, leaving their houses and property to be pillaged.[283] "Without any legal sentence, without any royal mandate, the patriarch, at the dawn of day, led a seditious multitude to the attack of the synagogues."[284]

Cyril's zeal offended the Roman prefect, Orestes, but he could do little to control the situation. Power in Alexandria was evenly divided between the secular and religious authority with neither party able to gain the upper hand. The Christian patriarch in Alexandria "had gradually usurped the state and authority of a civil magistrate."[285]

Tensions grew between the religious and civil authority in Alexandria. One day, the governor, Orestes, was confronted by an angry mob of five hundred monks who had "resolved to fight in behalf of Cyril."[286] Orestes "exclaimed that he was a Christian, and had been baptized ... [but the monks] gave but little heed to his protestations, and a certain one of named Ammonius threw a stone at Orestes which struck him on the head, and covered him with the blood that flowed from the wound."[287]

Orestes' fickle guards deserted him, but "the populace of Alexandria ran to the rescue of the governor, and put the rest of the monks to flight; but having secured Ammonius they delivered him up to the prefect. He immediately put him [Ammonius] publicly to the torture, which was inflicted with such severity that he died under the effects of it."[288] Securing the body of the dead monk, Cyril declared Ammonius to be a martyr of the Church.[289]

Unable to attack the civil authority directly, Cyril's followers looked around for someone to blame. They found a scapegoat in the female philosopher, Hypatia (A.D. 370–415). "It was calumniously reported among the Christian populace, that it was she who prevented Orestes from being reconciled to the bishop [Cyril]."[290]

Socrates Scholasticus described Hypatia as a "daughter of the philosopher Theon, who made such attainments in literature and science, as to far surpass all the philosophers of her own time."[291] Scholasticus' estimation of Hypatia's achievements must be interpreted with a grain of salt in light of the fact that "female philosophers were a comparative rarity in antiquity and were regarded as a marvelous phenomenon."[292]

A group of zealous Christians decided to kidnap and murder Hypatia. "Some of them therefore, hurried away by a fierce and bigoted zeal, whose ringleader was a reader named Peter, waylaid her [Hypatia] returning home, and dragging her from her carriage, they took her to the church called *Caesareum*, where they completely stripped her , and then murdered her with tiles [scraped off her flesh with sharp pieces of oyster shells]."[293]

"After tearing her [Hypatia's] body in pieces, they took her mangled limbs to a place called Cinaron and there burnt them."[294] The Christian Church responded by canonizing Cyril. For the time being, more moderate and liberal voices were left in the dust bin of history.

Demonology

PAGAN BELIEFS

When the physical world becomes unreal and irrelevant, imagination and delusions become real. Demons are "beings intermediate between the divine and man."[295] The world of the early Christians swarmed with demons of all types, mischievous beings responsible for nearly all the ills of the world. Demons were not by any means invented by Christianity — it is difficult to find any belief which is more universal amongst mankind. The superstitious conviction that the world is permeated by the presence of unseen spiritual beings is found in every civilization and tribe of humanity. A chapter of James Frazer's *The Golden Bough* is appropriately titled *The Omnipresence of Demons.*

In *Works and Days*, Hesiod (c. 700 B.C.) described the souls of the dead as benign spiritual beings that roamed through the world. "They are called pure spirits dwelling on the earth, and are kindly, delivering from harm, and guardians of mortal men; for they roam everywhere over the earth."[296]

Among the most technologically primitive and isolated of all existing cultures is that of the Australian aborigines. Yet they share with the rest of humanity an avid belief in demons. "[Amongst the aborigines] the number of supernatural beings, feared if not loved, that they acknowledge is exceedingly great; for not only are the heavens peopled with such, but the whole face of the country swarms with them; every thicket, most watering places, and all rocky places abound with evil spirits.... Every natural phenomenon is believed to be the work of demons, none of which seem of a benign nature, one and all apparently striving to do all imaginable mischief."[297]

Demons are an important part of the Hindu religion in India. "The plain fact undoubtedly is that the great majority of the inhabitants of India are [in 1885], from the cradle to the burning-ground, victims of a form of mental disease which is best expressed by the term demonphobia. They are haunted and oppressed by a perpetual dread of demons. They are firmly convinced that evil spirits of all kinds, from malignant fiends to merely mischievous imps and elves, are ever on the watch to harm, harass, and torment them, to cause plague, sickness, famine, and disaster, to impede, injure, and mar every good work."[298]

In the frozen wastelands of the North American continent, native people shared the belief. "The Eskimo are said to believe in spirits of the sea, earth and sky, the winds, the clouds and everything in nature. Every cove of the seashore, every point, every island and prominent rock has its guardian spirit. All are of the malignant type, to be propitiated only by acceptable offerings from persons who desire to visit the locality where it is supposed to reside."[299]

Civilization does not release men from superstition. "A rise in culture often results in an increase in the number of spiritual beings with whom man surrounds himself. Thus, the Koreans go far beyond the Eskimo and number their demons by thousands of billions; they fill the chimney, the shed, the living-room, the kitchen, they are on every shelf and jar; in thousands they waylay the traveler as he leaves his home, beside him, behind him, dancing in front of him, whirring over his head, crying out upon him from air, earth and water."[300]

In *Magic and Mystery in Tibet* (1932), Alexandra David-Neel (1868–1969) described how the inhabitants of this mountainous and remote realm believed that their homeland swarmed with demons of all types:

> If we were to rely on popular beliefs, we should conclude that evil spirits greatly outnumber the human population of the "Land of Snow." ... These malignant beings are said to dwell in trees, rocks, valleys, lakes, springs, and many other places. Always bent on mischief they hunt men and animals to steal their vital breath and feed upon it. ... Every traveler risks being confronted by one of them at any turning of the road.[301]

The very cradle of civilization in the Middle East was home to the most insidious sort of demons.

> Few people seem to have suffered more from the persistent assaults of demons than the ancient Babylonians and Assyrians, and the evil spirits that preyed on them were of a peculiarly cruel and malignant sort; even the gods themselves were not exempt from their attacks. ... Nothing could resist them in heaven above, nothing could withstand them on earth below. ... There was no place, however small, which they could not invade, none so large that they could not fill. And their wickedness was equal to their power.[302]

The Greeks were certainly not immune. Thales (c. 624–547 B.C.), the first natural philosopher, held that the world is "full of spirits," and that these "spirits are psychical beings."[303] In the *Symposium*, Plato expressed the sentiment that "God mingles not with man," and therefore there must exist "spirits or intermediate powers," which are "many and diverse."[304] However, it is not clear if these intermediaries are entities or spiritual principles. Plato stated, "one of them is love."[305]

Plotinus' disciple, Porphyry (c. A.D. 233–304), described demons extensively in his work *On Abstinence from Animal Food*. According to Porphyry, there were both good and bad demons. Both types were "invisible, and perfectly imperceptible by human senses."[306] However, they differed slightly in their form. "The pneumatic substance ... of good daemons, possesses symmetry, in the same manner as the bodies of the visible gods; but the spirit of malefic demons is deprived of symmetry."[307]

Good demons "are diligently employed in causing every thing to be beneficial to the subjects of their government, whether they preside over certain animals, or fruits, which are arranged under their inspective care, or over things which subsist for the sake of these, such as showers of rain, moderate winds, [and] serene weather ... they [good daemons] are also our leaders in the attainment of music, and the whole of erudition, and likewise of medicine and gymnastic."[308]

But bad demons were the ruin of the world. "Malefic demons ... are the causes of the calamities which take place about the earth, such as pestilence, sterility, earthquakes, excessive dryness, and the like ... [and they are responsible for] inflaming the minds of men with the love of riches, power, and pleasure, and filling them with the desire of vain glory, from which sedition, and war, and other things allied to these, are produced."[309]

The idea that there is a single and supreme evil deity is common to many belief systems. These include Babylonian, Egyptian, and Hindu mythology. "The opposition of good and evil is most fully carried out in Zoroastrianism. Opposed to Ormuzd, the author of all good, is Ahriman, the source of all evil."[310]

CHRISTIAN BELIEFS

The first appearance of evil in the *Bible* is in *Genesis*, where Eve is beguiled by a serpent. "The serpent was more subtle than any beast of the field ... and the serpent said unto the woman, Ye shall surely not die: For God know that in the day ye eat thereof, then your eyes shall be opened, and ye shall be as gods, knowing good and evil."[311]

"No such person as the devil of traditional theology appears in the *Old Testament*."[312]

The Scriptures of the *Old Testament* refer to Satan, an ambiguous entity who was an adversary of God. "And the Lord said unto Satan, Whence comest thou? Then Satan answered the Lord, and said, From going to and fro in the earth, and from walking up and down in it."[313]

The word *Lucifer* originally referred to the Morning Star, the planet Venus when it is visible in the morning. In *Natural History*, Pliny the Elder wrote, "Below the Sun revolves the great star called Venus ... when it precedes the day and rises in the morning, it receives the name of Lucifer."[314]

There is a passage in the *Old Testament* book of *Isaiah* that refers to the fall of Lucifer. "How art thou fallen from heaven, O Lucifer, son of the morning! how art thou cut down to the ground, which didst weaken the nations! For thou hast said in thine heart, I will ascend into heaven, I will exalt my throne above the stars of God: I will sit also upon the mount of the congregation, in the sides of the north: I will ascend above the heights of the clouds; I will be like the most High. Yet thou shalt be brought down to hell, to the sides of the pit."[315]

From the context, it seems apparent that the author of *Isaiah* used the name Lucifer poetically to refer to the "king of Babylon."[316] But in *Luke*, Jesus said that he had witnessed Satan's fall from heaven. "And he said unto them, I beheld Satan as lightning fall from heaven."[317] Thus the Lucifer referred to in *Isaiah* became identified with Satan, the adversary of God. In *Against Marcion*, Tertullian (c. A.D. 155–220) identified Satan as a fallen angel. "Before he became the devil, he stands forth the wisest of creatures.... The Lord testifies that Satan fell ... whence Satan was cast down like lightning."[318]

Although the Satan of the *Old Testament* was an ambiguous adversary, the Satan of the *New Testament* was clearly Lucifer, the fallen angel. He was the supreme evil deity, the Devil or Beelzebub, and the leader of a pack of subsidiary demons. *Matthew* records that some Pharisees accused Jesus of exorcising demons by the power of the Devil. "This fellow doth not cast out devils, but by Beelzebub the prince of devils."[319] In his reply, Jesus referred to Satan. "And if Satan cast out Satan, he is divided against himself; how shall then his kingdom stand?"[320]

In *Ephesians*, Paul the Apostle called the Devil the "prince of the power of the air,"[321] and wrote "we wrestle not against flesh and blood, but against principalities, against powers, against the rulers of the darkness of this world."[322]

Jesus repeatedly exorcised demons. "And in the synagogue there was a man, which had a spirit of an unclean devil, and cried out with a loud voice, Saying, Let us alone; what have we to do with thee, thou Jesus of Nazareth? art thou come to destroy us? I know thee who thou art; the Holy One of God. And Jesus rebuked him, saying, Hold thy peace, and come out of him. And when the devil had thrown him in the midst, he came out of him, and hurt him not."[323]

In *Mark* there is a passage (1.34) that says Jesus not only cast out demons, but forbade them to speak. The implication was that Jesus could not only could battle demons, but had dominion over them. "And at even, when the sun did set, they brought unto him all that were diseased, and them that were possessed with devils.... And he healed many that were sick of divers diseases, and cast out many devils; and suffered not the devils to speak, because they knew him."[324]

Jesus' power over demons was transferable. He gave his followers not only the power to "cast out devils," but also to speak in tongues, heal the sick, handle poisonous serpents without danger, and transmute poisons within their bodies. "And these signs shall follow them that believe; In my name shall they cast out devils; they shall speak with new tongues; They shall take up serpents; and if they drink any deadly thing, it shall not hurt them; they shall lay hands on the sick, and they shall recover."[325]

It would be generous to construe that the word "devil" used in the gospels referred to physical afflictions and mental diseases rather than spiritual beings. However it is not possible to reconcile this interpretation with a passage in *Mark* (5.8–5.13) where a multitude of demons were cast out by Jesus, only to immediately occupy a herd of pigs. The unmistakable implication is that a "devil" meant a spiritual being. "And all the devils besought him, saying, Send us into the swine, that we may enter into them. And forthwith Jesus gave them leave. And the unclean spirits went out, and entered into the swine."[326]

The Apostle Paul also cast out demons. "And it came to pass, as we went to prayer, a certain damsel possessed with a spirit of divination met us.... Paul, being grieved, turned and said to the spirit, I command thee in the name of Jesus Christ to come out of her. And he came out the same hour."[327]

But Christians could only cast out demons in the name of Jesus Christ — the authority and power were delegated. It was dangerous for anyone who was not a true believer to attempt an exorcism by invoking Jesus' name. When two Jews tried to cast out a demon in Jesus' name, the devil not only refused to obey, but responded by coming out and assaulting the would-be exorcists. "Then certain of the vagabond Jews, exorcists, took upon them to call over them which had evil spirits the name of the Lord Jesus, saying, We adjure you by Jesus whom Paul preacheth.... And the evil spirit answered and said, Jesus I know, and Paul I know; but who are ye? And the man in whom the evil spirit was leaped on them, and overcame them, and prevailed against them, so that they fled out of that house naked and wounded."[328]

The conception of Satan that developed in Christian theology over the next several hundred years was expressed in John Milton's (1608–1674) poem, *Paradise Lost* (1667).[329]

> Satan, so call him now, his former name
> Is heard no more [in] Heaven; he of the first,
> If not the first Arch-Angel, great in Power,
> In favor and pre-eminence.[330]

The Fathers of the Christian Church not only believed fervently in demons, but were almost obsessed with them. Tertullian (c. A.D. 155–220) testified to their existence. "And we affirm indeed the existence of certain spiritual essences; nor is their name unfamiliar. The philosophers acknowledge there are demons.... The poets are all acquainted with demons too; even the ignorant common people make frequent use of them in cursing. In fact, they call upon Satan, the demon-chief, in their execrations, as though from some instinctive soul-knowledge of him."[331]

According to Tertullian, demons were responsible for virtually all of the ills that beset humanity.

> Their great business is the ruin of mankind. So, from the very first, spiritual wickedness sought our destruction. They inflict ... diseases and other grievous calamities, while by violent assaults they hurry the soul into sudden and extraordinary excesses. ... As spiritual, they can do no harm; for, ... we are not cognizant of their action save by its effects, as when some inexplicable, unseen poison in the breeze blights the apples and the grain ... as though by the tainted atmosphere in some unknown way spreading abroad its pestilential exhalations. So, too ... demons and angels breathe into the soul, and rouse up its corruptions with furious passions and vile excesses; or with cruel lusts accompanied by various errors, of which the worst is that by which these deities

are commended to the favor of deceived and deluded human beings, that they may get their proper food of flesh-fumes and blood when that is offered up to idol-images.[332]

Lactantius (A.D. 260–330) also saw the universal presence of demons, wandering over the Earth, everywhere corrupting men, ruining their health, and engaging in all sorts of destructive mischief.

> These contaminated and abandoned spirits ... wander over the whole earth, and contrive a solace for their own perdition by the destruction of men. Therefore they fill every place with snares, deceits, frauds, and errors; for they cling to individuals and occupy whole houses.... Since spirits are without substance and not to be grasped, [demons] insinuate themselves into the bodies of men; and ... corrupt the health, hasten diseases, terrify their souls with dreams, harass their minds with frenzies, that by these evils they may compel men to have recourse to their aid.[333]

THE DIALOGUES OF GREGORY I

Demons were heavily commented upon by Gregory I (c. A.D. 540–604), or Gregory the Great. Bishop of Rome, it was Gregory I who built the papacy into the governing authority of the Catholic Church. He was "the last of the Latin fathers and the first of the popes."[334]

Born into a wealthy and distinguished Roman family, Gregory became prefect of Rome in A.D. 573 at the age of 33. However a year later, "he resigned his post, founded six monasteries in Sicily, and one in Rome, and ... became himself a monk."[335] Gregory "bestowed his remaining wealth upon the poor. He lived in the strictest abstinence, and undermined his health by ascetic excesses."[336]

Gregory I was "one of the best representatives of medieval Catholicism: monastic, ascetic, devout and superstitious; hierarchical, haughty, and ambitious, yet humble before God; indifferent, if not hostile, to classical and secular culture, but friendly to sacred and ecclesiastical learning; just, humane, and liberal to ostentation; full of missionary zeal in the interest of Christianity and the Roman see, which to his mind were inseparably connected."[337]

In A.D. 579 Gregory was sent by Pope Pelagius II to be ambassador to Constantinople, returning in A.D. 585 or 586 to become Abbot of St. Andrew's monastery.[338] Gregory's rule as abbot was "popular," but "characterized by great severity."[339] In A.D. 590, Rome was ravaged by a plague, and Pope Pelagius II fell victim. Gregory was elected Pope at the age of fifty. He continued to live a monastic life, dressing in the coarse robe of a common monk and eating the cheapest and simplest foods. "His mode of life was simple and ascetic in the extreme."[340] Devoted to the poor, Gregory instituted the practice of distributing a monthly allotment of food and clothing to every poor family in Rome. "It is said that he even impoverished the treasury of the Roman Church by his unlimited charities."[341] Gregory referred to himself as *servus servorum Dei*, servant of the servants of God.[342]

Gregory is known as the first pope because he asserted the supreme authority of the bishop of Rome over the entire Christian Church. "In his [Gregory's] view Rome, as the see of the Prince of the Apostles, was by divine right 'the head of all the churches.'"[343] "The primacy of the see of Rome was by him translated into a practical system as well as a theory and a creed."[344]

The authority of the bishop of Rome derived from the verse in the gospel of *Matthew*, where Jesus appointed Peter head of his church. "Thou art Peter, and upon this rock I will build my church; and the gates of hell shall not prevail against it."[345] The tradition that evolved and came to be accepted was that Peter was the first bishop of Rome, and thus his successors were the legitimate heads of the Christian Church.[346] But Gregory I was the first to assert this authority consistently and firmly. Gregory also was the first pope to assume secular and political power. "He appointed governors to cities, issued orders to generals, provided munitions of war, [and] sent his ambassadors to negotiate with the Lombard king."[347]

Demons and the Devil figure prominently in Gregory's *Dialogues* (A.D. 593).[348] Gregory's literary style reflects "an entirely practical, unspeculative, uncritical, traditional and superstitious bent of mind."[349] *Dialogues* is a description of the adventures, trials, and victories of various monks, bishops, and other Christian holy men, in their battles with the Devil. The holy men exorcise demons, work miracles, and overcome the temptations of the flesh.

In Book 1, Gregory described how a nun accidentally ingested a demon by forgetting to bless a head of lettuce before eating it.

> Upon a certain day, one of the Nuns of the same monastery, going into the garden, saw a lettuce that liked her, and forgetting to bless it before with the sign of the cross, greedily did she eat it: whereupon she was suddenly possessed with the devil, fell down to the ground, and was pitifully tormented. Word in all haste was carried to Equitius, desiring him quickly to visit the afflicted woman, and to help her with his prayers: who so soon as he came into the garden, the devil that was entered began by her tongue, as it were, to excuse himself, saying: "What have I done? What have I done? I was sitting there upon the lettuce, and she came and did eat me." But the man of God in great zeal commanded him to depart, and not to tarry any longer in the servant of almighty God, who straightways went out, not presuming to touch her.[350]

The second book of Gregory's *Dialogues* is devoted to "the life and miracles" of St. Benedict (c. A.D. 480–547), the founder of Western monasticism. Gregory described how Benedict destroyed a pagan idol and converted the local populace to Christianity. This so upset the forces of evil, that Satan himself appeared to Benedict in broad daylight. "The old enemy of mankind, not taking this in good part, did not privily or in a dream, but in open sight present himself to the eyes of that holy father, and with great outcries complained that he had offered him violence. The noise which he made, the monks did hear, but himself they could not see: but, as the venerable father told them, he appeared visibly unto him most fell and cruel, and as though, with his fiery mouth and flaming eyes, he would have torn him in pieces."[351]

On another occasion, some monks were trying without success to move a stone. After a while, they perceived that the reason the stone was unmovable was because "the devil himself did sit upon it."[352] They sent for St. Benedict. He came, blessed the stone, and the monks were able to carry the stone away, "as though it had been of no weight at all."[353]

Attitudes Toward Women

WOMEN IN ROME

Greek and Roman societies were patriarchal. In ancient Greece, women were considered to be markedly inferior to men. This belief was held not just by the vulgar, but also by men with the most incisive and brilliant minds, including Plato and Aristotle.

Patriarchy in Rome was perhaps somewhat less oppressive than in Greece. "The defense of patriarchy was not nearly so conspicuous a theme in Roman as in Greek literature."[354] But nevertheless "the wife ... [was] the property of her husband ... [and in the family] the father alone had independent authority, and so long as he lived all who were under his power—his sons, and their wives and children, and his unmarried daughters—could not acquire any property of their own."[355]

The Senate debate over the Oppian Law illustrates the role of women in society under the Roman Republic. In 195 B.C., during the Second Punic War, the Roman Senate enacted the Oppian Law, a measure that outlawed the ostentatious display of wealth by women. "No woman should possess more than half an ounce of gold, or wear a garment of various colors, or ride in a carriage drawn by horses, in a city, or any town, or any place nearer thereto than one mile [1609 meters]; except on occasion of some public religious solemnity."[356]

After the successful conclusion of the Second Punic War in 201 B.C., Rome prospered, and the Oppian Law was repealed in 195 B.C. The repeal was opposed by Cato the Censor. In his remarks in the Senate, Cato advised against increasing the rights and privileges allowed to women. "If, Romans, every individual among us had made it a rule to maintain the prerogative and authority of a husband with respect to his own wife, we should have less trouble with the whole sex."[357]

Cato was outraged that he had been accosted by women who had the audacity to confront him in public, instead of confiding their concerns privately to their husbands. "What sort of practice is this, of running out into public, besetting the streets, and addressing other women's husbands? Could not each have made the same request to her husband at home?"

Cato complained that the discipline of the ancient and venerable Roman traditions was being eroded and relaxed. "Our ancestors thought it not proper that women should perform any, even private business, without a director; but that they should be ever under the control of parents, brothers, or husbands. We, it seems, suffer them, now, to interfere in the management of state affairs, and to introduce themselves into the forum, into general assemblies, and into assemblies of election."[358]

Cato warned that granting equality to women in fact would be acquiescing to their superiority. "The moment they [women] have arrived at an equality with you, they will have become your superiors."[359]

The most derogatory descriptions of women in Roman literature are found in the satire, *The Ways of Women*, by the poet Juvenal, who wrote late in the first century A.D. and early in the second.

All women where shameless harlots that could not be trusted. "If you have the good luck to find a modest spouse, you should prostrate yourself before the Tarpeian threshold, and sacrifice a heifer with gilded horns to Juno."[360]

In any virtuous duty requiring courage, women were cowards. But if they were engaged in an act of infamy, their fortitude was boundless. "When danger comes in a right and honorable way, a woman's heart grows chill with fear; she cannot stand upon her trembling feet: but if she be doing a bold, bad thing, her courage fails not."[361]

Even if a perfect wife could be found, she would be undesirable, due to her ego and vanity. "Do you say no worthy wife is to be found among all these crowds? Well, let her be handsome, charming, rich and fertile; let her have ancient ancestors ranged about her halls; let her be more chaste than the disheveled Sabine maidens who stopped the war—a prodigy as rare upon the earth as a black swan! Yet who could endure a wife that possessed all perfections?"[362]

Any man foolish enough to be a devoted and loving husband would only be exploited by his cruel wife. "If you are honestly uxorious, and devoted to one woman, then bow your head and submit to the yoke. Never will you find a woman who spares the man who loves her; for though she be herself aflame, she delights to torment and plunder him. So the better the man, the more desirable he be as a husband, the less good will he get out of his wife."[363]

Women were disputatious. "There never was a case in court in which the quarrel was not started by a woman."[364] Men were advised that they should "give up all hope of peace so long as your mother-in-law is alive. It is she that teaches her daughter to revel in stripping and despoiling her husband ... the vile old woman finds a profit in bringing up her daughter to be vile."[365]

If a woman should accuse her husband of being unfaithful, it was only to conceal her own adultery.

> The bed that holds a wife is never free from wrangling and mutual bickerings; no sleep is to be got there! It is there that she sets upon her husband, more savage than a tigress that has lost her cubs; conscious of her own secret slips, she affects a grievance, abusing his slaves, or weeping over some imagined mistress. She has an abundant supply of tears always ready in their place, awaiting her command in which fashion they should flow. You, poor dolt, are delighted, believing them to be tears of love, and kiss them away; but what notes, what love-letters would you find if you opened the desk of your green-eyed adulterous wife![366]

It was Juvenal who originated the saying, "who will guard the guards?" "I hear all this time the advice of my old friends—keep your women at home, and put them under lock and key. Yes, but who will watch the warders? Wives are crafty and will begin with them."[367]

Poor women had to bear children. But a wealthy Roman woman could hire an abortionist. However the husband was advised by Juvenal to not resist the abortion, but assist with it. "Great is the skill, so powerful the drugs, of the abortionist, paid to murder mankind within the womb. Rejoice, poor wretch; give her the stuff to drink whatever it be, with your own hand: for were she willing to get big and trouble her womb with bouncing babes, you might find yourself the father of an Ethiopian; and some day a colored heir, whom you would rather not meet by daylight, would fill all the places in your will."[368]

The ultimate indignity for a man to bear was being forced to listen to an educated and articulate woman participate in intelligent conversations. "But most intolerable of all is the woman who as soon as she has set down to dinner commends Virgil, pardons the dying Dido, and pits the poets against each other.... She lays down definitions, and discourses on morals, like a philosopher; thirsting to be deemed both wise and eloquent."[369]

Juvenal's *Satire* has aroused the wrath of modern feminists. "[It] is probably the most horrifying of all catalogues of female vices."[370] But a satire is usually written to exaggerate a vice, and therefore ridicule it. Juvenal's tongue-in-cheek characterizations were perhaps written not to condemn women, but to poke fun at stereotypes of female behaviors.

Daughters of Eve

Christian attitudes toward women were in part influenced by the cultural norms of Rome and Greece, in which women were considered to be inferior. But the Jewish scriptures were also patriarchal. God created man first; woman was sort of an afterthought, manufactured merely to be a helper for man—a servant. "And the Lord God said, It is not good that the man should be alone; I will make him an help meet for him."[371]

Man was created "in the image of God."[372] But the first woman, Eve, was made out of rib taken out of the first man, Adam. "And the rib, which the Lord God had taken from man, made he a woman."[373] Eve "was not even created in the divine image, but only in man's; hence she is further removed from God than man is, and as a consequence more prone to folly and vice."[374]

The first thing that Eve did was to create original sin by convincing Adam to eat from the forbidden tree of the knowledge of good and evil. In the view of the Church fathers, it was the greatest crime of all time. "And when the woman saw that the tree was good for food, and that it was pleasant to the eyes, and a tree to be desired to make one wise, she took of the fruit thereof, and did eat, and gave also unto her husband with her; and he did eat."[375] "And the Lord God said unto the woman, What is this that thou hast done? And the woman said, The serpent beguiled me, and I did eat."[376]

As punishment for Eve's sin, God condemned women to suffer from pain during childbirth, and to be ruled by their husbands. "Unto the woman he said, I will greatly multiply thy sorrow and thy conception; in sorrow thou shalt bring forth children; and thy desire shall be to thy husband, and he shall rule over thee."[377]

Women were so evil they had even seduced the angels. In *Genesis 6*, it was recorded that human women had tempted the angels themselves (the "sons of God") into sin and corruption. The offspring of this illegitimate union of human woman and fallen angels was a race of giants. "There were giants in the earth in those days; and also after that, when the sons of God came in unto the daughters of men, and they bare children to them, the same became mighty men which were of old, men of renown."[378]

The author of the book *Ecclesiastes* warned, "I find more bitter than death the woman, whose heart is snares and nets, and her hands as bands: whoso pleaseth God shall escape from her; but the sinner shall be taken by her."[379] Should there be a "virtuous woman," her goodness was not deserving of recognition in itself, but only insofar as it was "a crown to her husband."[380]

The role of women in the Christian Church and society was strongly influenced by the doctrines of Paul the Apostle. Paul emphasized that women were spiritually inferior to men. "Let the woman learn in silence with all subjection. But I suffer not a woman to teach, nor to usurp authority over the man, but to be in silence. For Adam was first formed, then Eve."[381]

Women were not allowed to speak in the churches. "Let your women keep silence in the churches: for it is not permitted unto them to speak; but they are commanded to be under obedience as also saith the law. And if they will learn any thing, let them ask their husbands at home: for it is a shame for women to speak in the church."[382]

Husbands were admonished by Paul to "love your wives."[383] But women had to submit to their husband's authority. "Wives, submit yourselves unto your own husbands, as unto the Lord. For the husband is the head of the wife, even as Christ is the head of the church: and he is the saviour of the body. Therefore as the church is subject unto Christ, so let the wives be to their own husbands in every thing."[384]

In Paul's doctrine, women were considered to be subsidiary creatures that existed for the sake of men. "For the man is not of the woman: but the woman of the man. Neither was the man created for the woman; but the woman for the man."[385]

Tertullian (c. A.D. 155–220) was "the earliest and after Augustine the greatest of the ancient church writers of the West."[386] This saint had little patience with women. In his essay *On Female Dress*, he started by reminding women that they were the source of original sin. These daughters of Eve were just as guilty as the first woman. "And do you not know that you are (each) an Eve? The sentence of God on this sex of yours lives in this age: the guilt must of necessity live too. You are the devil's gateway: you are the unsealer of that (forbidden) tree: you are the first deserter of the divine law: you are she who persuaded him whom the devil was not valiant enough to attack. You destroyed so easily God's image, man. On account of your desert — that is, death — even the Son of God had to die."[387]

Although he himself was married, Tertullian compared marriage to fornication. "It is laws which seem to make the difference between marriage and fornication; through diversity of illicitness, not through the nature of the thing itself. Besides, what is the thing which takes place in all men and women to produce marriage and fornication? Commixture of the flesh, of course; the concupiscence whereof the Lord put on the same footing with fornication."[388]

Philip Schaff explained that Tertullian placed "the essence of marriage in the communion of flesh, and regard[ed] it as a mere concession, which God makes to our sensuality ... the ideal of the Christian life, with him [Tertullian], not only for the clergy, but for the laity also, is celibacy."[389]

Lactantius attributed the origin of demons in part to women. Demons were originally angels that had been sent to guard the human race. However, they were also given free will and became seduced by Satan and contaminated by having sex with human women. "God ... sent angels for the protection and improvement of the human race ... [but] while they abode among men, that most deceitful ruler of the earth [the Devil], by his very association, gradually enticed them to vices, and polluted them by intercourse with women."[390]

Women were a constant temptation for monks. Remarkable and fantastic stories constantly circulated amongst the monastic community regarding the dangers represented by women.

> Strange stories were told among the monks of revulsions of passion even in the most advanced. Of one monk especially, who had long been regarded as a pattern of asceticism, but who had suffered himself to fall into that self-complacency which was very common among the anchorites, it was told that one evening a fainting woman appeared at the door of his cell, and implored him to give her shelter, and not permit her to be devoured by the wild beasts. In an evil hour he yielded to her prayer. With all the aspect of profound reverence she won his regards, and at last ventured to lay her hand upon him. But that touch convulsed his frame. Passions long slumbering and forgotten rushed with an impetuous fury through his veins. In a paroxysm of fierce love, he sought to clasp the woman to his heart, but she vanished from his sight, and a chorus of demons, with peals of laughter, exulted over his fall.[391]

Some monks avoided temptation by a simple expedient: they stayed away from women. St. John of Lycopolis did not see a woman for 48 years.[392] Much to the annoyance of St. Arsenius, one day a woman showed up on his doorstep:

> A young Roman girl made a pilgrimage from Italy to Alexandria, to look at the face and obtain the prayers of St. Arsenius, into whose presence she forced herself. Quailing beneath his rebuff, she flung herself at his feet, imploring him with tears to grant her only request—to remember her and to pray for her. "Remember you!" cried the indignant saint, "It shall be the prayer of my life that I may forget you." The poor girl sought consolation from the Archbishop of Alexandria, who comforted her by assuring her that although she belonged to the sex by which demons commonly tempt saints, he doubted not that the hermit would pray for her soul, though he would try to forget her face.[393]

Gregory I related how St. Benedict was tempted by the memory of a desirable woman. The temptation was brought by a demon in the form of a little black bird which flitted around Benedict's head. Not one to succumb to temptation, the venerable Benedict prevailed by tearing off all his clothes and plunging naked into a briar patch.

> Upon a certain day being alone, the tempter was at hand: for a little black bird, commonly called a merle or an ousel, began to fly about his face, and that so near as the holy man, if he would, might have taken it with his hand: but after he had blessed himself with the sign of the cross, the bird flew away: and forthwith the holy man was assaulted with such a terrible temptation of the flesh, as he never felt the like in all his life. A certain woman there was which some time he had

seen, the memory of which the wicked spirit put into his mind, and by the representation of her did so mightily inflame with concupiscence the soul of God's servant, which did so increase that, almost overcome with pleasure, he was of mind to have forsaken the wilderness. But, suddenly assisted with God's grace, he came to himself; and seeing many thick briers and nettlebushes to grow hard by, off he cast his apparel, and threw himself into the midst of them, and there wallowed so long that, when he rose up, all his flesh was pitifully torn: and so by the wounds of his body, he cured the wounds of his soul, in that he turned pleasure into pain, and by the outward burning of extreme smart, quenched that fire which, being nourished before with the fuel of carnal cogitations, did inwardly burn in his soul: and by this means he overcame the sin, because he made a change of the fire. From which time forward, as himself did afterward report unto his disciples, he found all temptation of pleasure so subdued, that he never felt any such thing.[394]

According to Gregory I, St. Benedict's virtue was so great that it aroused the jealousy of a local priest name Florentius, a man "possessed with diabolical malice."[395] Florentius tried to kill Benedict, but failed. He then tried to destroy the chastity of Benedict's monks by sending naked women to dance in front of them. "And Florentius, seeing that he could not kill the body of the master, labored ... to destroy the souls of his disciples; and for that purpose he sent into the yard of the Abbey before their eyes seven naked young women, which did there take hands together, play and dance a long time before them, to the end that, by this means, they might inflame their minds to sinful lust."[396]

If Benedict had overcome temptation by mutilating his body with thorns, it was not an act without precedent in the Church. Origen (c. 185–253), who has been described as "the most distinguished and most influential of all the theologians of the ancient church, with the possible exception of Augustine,"[397] reportedly castrated himself. The source of this report is Eusebius, who wrote that Origen's inspiration was a passage in *Matthew* where Jesus said that there are those "which have made themselves eunuchs for the kingdom of heaven's sake."[398]

Origen "carried a deed into effect, which would seem, indeed, rather to proceed from a youthful understanding not yet matured.... [Origen understood the] expression 'there are eunuchs who have made themselves such for the sake of the kingdom of heaven,' in too literal and puerile a sense ... [and Origen] was led on to fulfill the words of our Savior by his deeds."[399]

Charity

GREEK AND ROMAN

One of the most significant and enduring legacies of Christianity to Western Civilization was the introduction of charity. Charity is "Christian love," or "man's love of God and his neighbor, commanded as the fulfilling of the Law."[400]

Charity can also be secondarily defined without any Christian association as "love, kindness, affection ... [or] some notion of generous or spontaneous goodness."[401] This type of charity existed before Christianity, but Christian charity was of a different type and degree from that practiced heretofore.

The personal charity of the Greeks and Romans was largely reserved for friends and neighbors. "There can, however, be no question that neither in practice nor in theory, neither in the institutions that were founded nor in the place that was assigned to it in the scale of duties, did charity in antiquity occupy a position at all comparable to that which it has obtained by Christianity.... The active, habitual, and detailed charity of private persons, which is so conspicuous a feature in all Christian societies, was scarcely known in antiquity."[402]

In *Works and Days*, Hesiod (c. 700 B.C.) said that your neighbor is the person who lives near you. You should extend the hand of friendship to your neighbor, but avoid enemies. "Call your friend to a feast; but leave your enemy alone; and especially call him who lives near you: for if any mischief happen in the place, neighbors come ungirt, but kinsmen stay to gird themselves."[403]

In its most primitive form, Hesiod's advice was an affirmation of tribalism. Your neighbor is the person who belongs to your tribe; only he is worthy of your charity. In the Greco-Roman world the poor person was not seen as being an unfortunate victim of circumstances, but as the rightful inheritor of their own laziness. "There is very little in Greek or Latin literature to suggest that the rich felt obligated to do something for the poor ... the needs of the destitute were usually not taken into account, their situation being considered the consequence of laziness."[404]

In the Roman play *Trinummus* (*Three Pieces of Money*), authored by Plautus (254–184 B.C.), one of the characters argued that giving food or drink to a beggar would merely prolong his misery. "He deserves ill of a beggar who gives him what to eat or to drink; for he both loses that which he gives and prolongs for the other a life of misery."[405]

When charitable giving did occur in Greece or Rome, it was almost always calculated to benefit the giver. To give without expectation of return was uncommon.[406] Public charities conducted by the Greeks and Romans were largely cynical manipulations instituted to gain political favor and stability.

The Greek statesman Pericles (495–429 B.C.) used public money to win popularity with the poor. "Pericles ... turned to the distribution of the public moneys; and in a short time having bought the people over, what with moneys allowed for shows and for service on juries, and what with other forms of pay and largess, he made use of them against the council of Areopagus of which he himself was no member."[407]

Having achieved power and success, Pericles maintained his popularity by employing people on public works projects. "It being his [Pericles'] desire and design that the undisciplined mechanic multitude that stayed at home should not go without their share of public salaries, and yet should not have them given them for sitting still and doing nothing, to that end he thought it fit to bring in among them, with the approbation of the people, these vast projects of buildings and designs of work."[408]

Two of the most depraved Roman Emperors, Caligula (reigned A.D. 37–41) and Nero (reigned A.D. 54–68), were also famous for manipulating public opinion with charitable gifts. Caligula once gave away 45 million sesterces, and Nero threw valuable trinkets to crowds by the thousands.[409]

In 123 B.C., the Tribune Gaius Sempronius Gracchus started subsidizing the purchase of grain. He "made the unprecedented suggestion that a monthly distribution of corn [grain] should be made to each citizen at the public expense. Thus he quickly got the leadership of the people by one political measure."[410]

The price of grain in Rome was set well below the market cost, and the subsidized grain was available not just to the poor, but to everyone. The population of Rome swelled as peasants from the countryside came into the city to take advantage of the cheap food.

The grain program was so popular that it soon exhausted the treasury and was stopped.[411] Over the next 70 years or so, the distribution of cheap grain was periodically started and discontinued again. In 58 B.C., the Tribune Clodius took the subsidy program to the logical extreme by making grain totally free for those who qualified.

To keep costs under control, in 46 B.C. Julius Caesar (100–44 B.C.) "reduced the number of those who received corn [grain] at the public cost, from three hundred and twenty, to a hundred and fifty, thousand."[412] Augustus (reigned 27 B.C.–A.D. 14) wanted to do away with the free grain distribution, but conceded to himself that it was not politically feasible. "I was much inclined to abolish for ever the practice of allowing the people corn [grain] at the public expense, because they trust so much to it, that they are too lazy to till their lands; but I did not persevere in my design, as I felt sure that the practice would some time or other be revived by some one ambitious of popular favor."[413]

Once the practice of distributing free grain had been instituted, a sizable segment of the Roman population quickly became dependent on the dole.

> The most injudicious charity, however pernicious to the classes it is intended to relieve, has commonly a beneficial and softening influence upon the donor, and through him upon society at large. But the Roman distribution of corn being merely a political device, had no humanizing influence upon the people, while, being regulated simply by indigence, and not at all by the infirmities or character of the recipient, it was a direct and overwhelming encouragement to idleness ... poor Romans readily gave up all honorable labor, all trades in the city languished, ... [and] free gifts of land were insufficient to divert the citizens to honest labor.[414]

One year, the crops failed and the supply of grain ran low. Claudius (reigned A.D. 41–54) received a first-hand lesson on the dangers of a hungry populace.

> Several prodigies occurred in that year. Birds of evil omen perched on the Capitol; houses were thrown down by frequent shocks of earthquake, and as the panic spread, all the weak were trodden down in the hurry and confusion of the crowd. Scanty crops too, and consequent famine were regarded as a token of calamity. Nor were there merely whispered complaints; while Claudius was administering justice, the populace crowded round him with a boisterous clamor and drove him to a corner of the forum, where they violently pressed on him till he broke through the furious mob with a body of soldiers. It was ascertained that Rome had provisions for no more than fifteen days.[415]

Eventually, the distribution of grain was replaced by the distribution of bread. This prompted the satirist Juvenal to note that the Roman people were now so depraved that they only cared for food and entertainment, or "bread and circuses." "The people that once bestowed commands, consulships, legions and all else, now meddles no more and longs eagerly for just two things— bread and games!"[416]

Roman circuses were games held in arenas, and included gladiatorial contests, public executions, chariot races, and various battles between men and beasts. By the reign of Constantine (A.D. 306–337), the Circus Maximus in Rome was capable of hosting 485,000 spectators if seating on adjacent hillsides was counted.[417]

It should be noted that Stoics, like Christians, also envisaged a universal human brotherhood, and therefore were an exception to general Roman ethic of conducting only selfish works. In *De Officiis* (*On Duties*), Cicero wrote "since, as the Stoics hold, all the products of the earth are destined for our use and we are born to help one another, we should here take nature for our guide and contribute to the public good by the interchange of acts of kindness, now giving, now receiving, and ever eager to employ our talents, industry and resources in strengthening the bonds of human society."[418]

But Stoics also believed in fate and predestination. If you were enslaved or poverty stricken, it was to be accepted as preordained. This gave the upper class an excuse for the maintenance of slavery, and freed them from any moral compulsion to establish social equality.

CHRISTIAN

Jesus said that the First Commandment was to "love the Lord thy God with all thy heart, and with all thy soul, and with all thy mind, and with all thy strength."[419] But Christian charity sprang from Jesus' declaration that there was a Second Commandment, "thou shalt love thy neighbor as thyself."[420]

Jesus was echoed by Paul in *Galatians*, "for all the law is fulfilled in one word, even in this; Thou shalt love thy neighbour as thyself."[421] Christian charity was also a natural outgrowth of the belief that all men were created "in the image of God,"[422] and therefore equal before God. The belief in spiritual equality helped to undermine the institution of slavery and break up the inequalities and injustices that resulted from class status. The Christian concept of the brotherhood of man was also the ethic of a global civilization. This fundamental break from tribalism enabled the evolution of human society from city-states to nations and fostered cooperation and alliances between peoples of different cultures and traditions. More than any other factor, the common religion of Christianity unified Europe.

Jesus taught that all men were brothers and neighbors, deserving of each other's respect, pity, and charity. The question was asked of Jesus, "who is my neighbor?"[423] In reply, Jesus told the parable of the Good Samaritan.[424]

A Jew was beaten by robbers and left lying on the road. Two Jews passed by, but did not stop to help him. A Samaritan then came by. The Samaritans and Jews were hereditary enemies, but the Samaritan stopped to help the beaten man. He tended to the man's wounds, took him to a nearby inn, and paid for his lodging until he recovered. After relating the story, Jesus then posed the question of what made a man a neighbor. "Which now of these three, thinkest thou, was neighbor unto him that fell among the thieves? And he said, he that showed mercy on him. Then said Jesus unto him, go, and do thou likewise."[425]

Christian charity did not spring spontaneously into being; it was a natural outgrowth of Jewish culture and religion. God had instructed Moses that farmers should not be overzealous in their harvests, but leave part of their crop in the fields for the poor to gather. "When ye reap the harvest of your land, thou shalt not wholly reap the corners of thy field, neither shalt thou gather the gleanings of thy harvest. And thou shalt not glean thy vineyard, neither shalt thou gather every grape of thy vineyard; thou shalt leave them for the poor and stranger."[426] Jesus' Second Commandment, "thou shalt love thy neighbour as thyself,"[427] is also found in the *Old Testament* book of *Leviticus*.

Pagans had largely viewed poverty as a detestable affliction to be avoided. But Jesus explicitly advocated poverty as a asset to spiritual development. "Jesus said unto him, If thou wilt be perfect, go and sell that thou hast, and give to the poor, and thou shalt have treasure in heaven: and come and follow me."[428]

Around A.D. 150, the Church established a fund in each parish to help the poor. Tertullian described the institution.

> Though we have our treasure-chest, it is not made up of purchase-money, as of a religion that has its price. On the monthly day, if he likes, each puts in a small donation; but only if it be his pleasure, and only if he be able: for there is no compulsion; all is voluntary. These gifts are, as it were, piety's deposit fund. For they are not taken thence and spent on feasts, and drinking-bouts, and eating-houses, but to support and bury poor people, to supply the wants of boys and girls destitute of means and parents, and of old persons confined now to the house; such, too, as have suffered shipwreck; and if there happen to be any in the mines, or banished to the islands, or shut up in the prisons, for nothing but their fidelity to the cause of God's Church, they become the nurslings of their confession.[429]

The Church founded hospitals, orphanages, and asylums. One of the first Christian hospitals was established c. A.D. 364 in Caesarea, the capital of Roman Palestine, by St. Basil (c. 330–379). Basil was first educated at home by his father. He then had formal instruction at Constantinople followed by four years at Athens, where he studied "rhetoric, mathematics, and philosophy."[430]

After finishing his education in A.D. 360, Basil "distributed his property to the poor"[431] and became a hermit. Basil described the beauty of his hermitage in a letter to his friend, Gregory of Nazianzus (c. 330–390). "There is a lofty mountain covered with thick woods, watered toward the north with cool and transparent streams. A plain lies beneath, enriched by the waters which are ever draining off from it; and skirted by a spontaneous profusion of trees almost thick enough to be a fence; so as even to surpass Calypso's Island, which Homer seems to have considered the most beautiful spot on the earth."[432]

In A.D. 364, Eusebius appointed Basil as a presbyter [priest].[433] In A.D. 368, a drought in Caesarea resulted in a famine. Basil organized a large-scale relief effort. "Gregory of Nazianzus gives us a picture of his illustrious friend standing in the midst of a great crowd of men and women and children, some scarcely able to breath; of servants bringing in piles of such food as is best suited to the weak state of the famishing sufferers; of Basil with his own hands distributing nourishment, and with his own voice cheering and encouraging the sufferers."[434]

When Eusebius died in A.D. 370, Basil was chosen to be his successor as Bishop of Caesarea.[435] As bishop, Basil continued to practice asceticism.

> [Basil maintained a] system of hard ascetic discipline which eventually contributed to the enfeeblement of his health and the shortening of his life. He [Basil] complains again and again in his letters of the deplorable physical condition to which he is reduced, and he died at the age of fifty.... [Basil] ate no more that was actually necessary for daily sustenance, and his fare was of the poorest. Even when he was archbishop, no flesh meat was dressed in his kitchens. His wardrobe consisted of one under- and one over-garment. By night he wore haircloth ... he [Basil] treated his body ... as an angry owner treats a runaway slave.[436]

The hospital that Basil founded in Caesarea was chiefly devoted to the treatment of lepers. "He [Basil] himself took in the sufferers, treated them as brethren, and, in spite of their revolting condition, was not afraid to kiss them."[437]

Although he may have been generous, Basil was not indiscriminate in his charity. A visitor to the hospital c. A.D. 373 wrote that Basil "said experience was needed in order to distinguish between cases of genuine need and of mere greedy begging. For whoever gives to the afflicted gives to the Lord, and from the Lord shall have his reward; but he who gives to every vagabond casts to a dog."[438]

Basil died in A.D. 379. In a funeral oration, Basil's colleague and friend, Gregory of Nazianzus, extolled the virtues of Christian charity. "A noble thing is philanthropy, and the support of the poor, and the assistance of human weakness."[439]

The ideal of Christian charity is illustrated by a story related in Sulpitius Severus' (c. 363–425) biography of St. Martin of Tours (A.D. 316–397). At the age of ten, Martin "betook himself, against the wish of his parents, to the Church, and begged that he might become a catechumen [convert before baptism]."[440]

Not yet baptized, at the age of fifteen Martin was drafted into the Roman military.[441] One night, "in the middle of winter, a winter which had shown itself more severe than ordinary, so that the extreme cold was proving fatal to many, he [Martin] happened to meet at the gate of the city of Amiens a poor man destitute of clothing."[442]

Martin was distressed at the man's nakedness, but had no means of providing aid. He had already given all of his money and possessions to the poor, and now had nothing but the clothes he wore and his military gear. Martin found a solution. "Taking, therefore, his sword with which he was girt, he divided his cloak into two equal parts, and gave one part to the poor man, while he again clothed himself with the remainder."[443]

Clothed with half a cloak, Martin became a spectacle and an object of ridicule. "The by-standers laughed, because he [Martin] was now an unsightly object, and stood out as but partly dressed."[444]

But Martin had a dream in which the poor man he had clothed was portrayed as Jesus Christ. "When Martin had resigned himself to sleep, he had a vision of Christ arrayed in that part of his cloak with which he had clothed the poor man ... he heard Jesus saying with a clear voice to the multitude of angels standing round — 'Martin, who is still but a cate-chumen, clothed me with this robe.'"[445]

The division of St. Martin's cloak illustrates the ideal of charity as held by the early Christians: every man was as deserving as Jesus Christ, no matter how dirty and mean. This was a powerful and revolutionary ethic; embraced over the centuries, it would transform Western Civilization.

CHAPTER 2

The Dark Ages
(c. A.D. 500–1000)

The Intellectual Decline of Europe

The term *Middle Ages* was first coined by the Italian humanist and historian Flavio Biondo (A.D. 1392–1463). Humanists of the Renaissance "struck upon the unfortunate opprobrious term 'middle ages' for that which stood between them and their classic ideals."[1] Although modern historians are perhaps unhappy with the concept of a Middle Age, "long use makes the term inevitable."[2]

The traditional dates that have been assigned to the beginning and end of the Middle Ages are A.D. 476 and 1453.[3] These dates reflect political events, not intellectual markers. By the fifth century A.D., the Western Roman Empire was in chaos. Rome was occupied and pillaged by Germanic tribes, first by the Visigoths (A.D. 410) and later (A.D. 455) by the Vandals. In A.D. 476, the last Emperor of the Western Roman Empire, Romulus Augustulus, was deposed, and in A.D. 1453 the Ottoman Turks captured Constantinople, effectually terminating what remained of the Roman Empire in the east.

Approximately the first half of the Middle Ages (c. A.D. 476–1000) has been called the *Dark Ages*, reflecting the near-total lack of interest in philosophy and the sciences that prevailed in Europe during this time. The term appears to have originated with Petrarch (1304–1374), an early Italian Renaissance writer.[4] Having rediscovered the classical literature of Greece and Rome during the Renaissance, Europeans came to regard the centuries that had passed between the fall of the Roman Empire and their time as a dark age.

The twentieth century saw the rise of cultural relativism in the West, and modern writers began to find the term "Dark Age" judgmental and morally repulsive. The Dark Ages was in fact, a time of continuous technological innovation throughout Europe. But in areas such as mathematics, natural philosophy, or astronomy, Europeans made few significant contributions during this time period compared to the heyday of Hellenic culture in the Mediterranean. If the term "Dark Age" is used in a proper sense, without invoking a relative moral judgment, the use is an appropriate recognition of a sparsity of original and creative work in certain areas.

If we are to swallow the proposition that the Dark Ages in Europe were not dark, it becomes very difficult to explain why, in the sixteenth century, Aristotle's works were still regarded "as the standard and basis of all philosophic enquiry,"[5] or why the standard texts in astronomy and mathematics were the *Syntaxis* of Ptolemy (c. 2nd century A.D.) and the *Elements* of Euclid (c. 3rd century B.C.).

If the Dark Ages in Europe were not dark, one is hard-pressed to explain why Galileo, at the beginning of the seventeenth century, studied and idolized the mathematical works of Archimedes, written in the third century B.C.[6] If we are to maintain that the efforts of Europeans during the Dark Ages equaled or surpassed the achievements of Hellenistic science, it becomes difficult to explain why Europeans of this time period were not capable of constructing any technological device that rivaled the Antikythera mechanism, built c. 150–100 B.C. Thus, "there is no denying that a scientific dark age had descended upon western Europe."[7]

It should be conceded that there was never any period of retrogression in northern Europe. If any area fell into a dark age, it was the Mediterranean. Northern Europe had no pedestal to fall from. In the areas occupied by present day England, France, and Germany, philosophy, science, art, and technology have been progressively developed for the last fifteen-hundred years. Greek and Roman civilization were failing, but Western Civilization was beginning.

By the time the Middle Ages began, Greek and Roman civilization had been in intellectual decline for several hundred years. As early as the first century A.D., Seneca had noted that there was little interest in philosophy and much of the old knowledge was being lost. The writings of the early Christian Fathers show that the inward turn of the European mind did not occur overnight, but had developed slowly over hundreds of years. Although there was a continuity of "technological development," the Dark Ages in Europe was marked by "political disintegration, economic depression, the debasement of religion and the collapse of literature."[8]

Natural philosophy as an intellectual movement had been deteriorating for several centuries. The Ionians, Pythagoreans, and Eleatics were preeminent from about 600 to 400 B.C., but by the time of Socrates' death in 399 B.C. the movement was spent. In later times, individuals such as Aristotle, Archimedes, Strato, and Eratosthenes made significant contributions, but natural philosophy itself was at a dead end.

The onset of a Dark Age in Europe was the inevitable culmination of history. The nearly complete absence of advancement in areas such as natural philosophy, mathematics, and astronomy, in Europe during this time was summarized succinctly in a famous quote by Alfred North Whitehead (1861–1947): "In the year A.D. 1500 Europe knew less than Archimedes who died in the year 212 B.C."[9]

Failure of Ancient Science and Natural Philosophy

INTELLECTUAL, TECHNOLOGICAL, ECONOMIC, AND MORAL SUBSTRATES

Modern science traces its origin to the natural philosophy movement started by the Ionian Greeks in the 6th century B.C. The Greeks invented naturalism, uniformity, and the principles of logic and demonstration. They developed mathematics from a set of empirical rules into an exact science. The period of time from 600 to 400 B.C. has never been equaled in its fertility of intellectual invention and discovery.

But modern science emerged in seventeenth-century England, not the classical civilizations of the Mediterranean. The Greeks never hit upon the experimental method, and they never evidenced any appreciation for technology or its synergy with science.

The most interesting and significant question in the history of science is why Greek science foundered and reached a dead end. A number of factors may have been involved, but at the present time it is not possible to give a conclusive answer.

Modern science depends for its existence upon intellectual, technological, economic, and moral substrates. Every human civilization sustains itself through ideas, technology, productivity, and morality. Ideas are the spur to innovation. Technology applied in economic activity provides the material requirements of life. Morality dictates how a civilization is ordered, and determines the rules that govern how individuals interact with each other. These factors are interrelated, overlapping, and to a certain extent, dependent upon each other.

The question is complex. The development of technology depends upon an economic system that welcomes and rewards innovation. One of the reasons the Scientific Revolution of the seventeenth century occurred in Europe is that Europeans acquired an appreciation for technology and began to understand the necessity of adopting the systematic empiricism that had always been practiced in the applied arts. Arguably, the craft tradition of the applied arts was as important as philosophy. The leaders in developing medieval technology were not philosophers, but craftsmen, merchants, and businessmen. In a word, entrepreneurs. There were profits to be derived from the new technologies. A water-powered mill required a considerable capital investment, but the investment was likely to return a significant profit. Inventive people looked for ways to improve their productivity.

The importance of cultural factors is illustrated by comparing the history of science and technology in China and Europe. The Chinese were creative. They invented innumerable technologies, but failed to economically develop them as fully as Europeans did. In China the mercantile class was suppressed by a "landowning ruling class."[10] Economic and therefore technological development were strangled by a "bureaucratic, state controlled economy."[11] It was left to Europeans to develop the promise of technologies that originated in China. The fact that Europe imported technology was not so much a weakness, as an indication that this continent hosted a "technologically progressive society"[12] that was open to the introduction of new ideas. In contrast, Chinese society was xenophobic. Convinced of their innate superiority, the Chinese were not receptive to foreign ideas.[13]

THE PROBLEM OF KNOWLEDGE

Through the invention of mathematics (as a systematic and exact science) and logic, the Greeks showed that it was possible to go beyond human opinion and find a demonstrable truth on which all men agreed. They established *method* and *demonstration*. The Greeks discovered that there were proper, methodical, and logical ways of thinking that would lead to universal truths.

But having established that a correct method could lead to demonstrable truth, Greek philosophers made little progress in establishing what that method should be. This is the "problem of knowledge," the problem of choosing the correct epistemological method for generating reliable knowledge. By "reliable knowledge," I mean knowledge that is consistent with an established criterion of truth. The only thing that may be demanded of any system of knowledge, whether it be philosophy, science, or religion, is internal consistency. It is not possible to establish the superiority or absoluteness of any single criterion of truth, because any such claim must itself by validated itself by a criterion of truth *ad infinitum*. Even geometry rests upon unprovable axioms.

Everyone agreed that geometrical reasoning led to demonstrable truths, but the methods of geometry were not capable of universal application. There was an appreciation that both observation and reason were necessary, but no consensus on the relative weight to be applied to each epistemology. On one extreme, Parmenides and the Eleatics went so far as to argue that essentially all information obtained through the senses was false and illusory. The problem with this viewpoint is that we must live in the world of the senses, not an imaginary world concocted by a philosopher or magician. In 1890, American Indians who wore "ghost skirts" thought they "would be invulnerable to bullets."[14] But they died, nonetheless.

Zeno's paradoxes were constructed to demonstrate the correctness of the Eleatic philosophy. But they demonstrated precisely the opposite. The fact that Achilles can, in fact, overtake a tortoise, does not illustrate that motion is an illusion, but that the assumption employed in the construction of the paradox was false. The paradox was based on Zeno's assumption that an infinite number of points cannot be covered in a finite time. But mathematicians were later able to demonstrate that an infinite series can have a finite sum, thus proving what was already indicated by the evidence of the senses.

This is not to say that the Eleatics made no contribution to the problem of knowledge. On the contrary, their failure demonstrated the folly of attempting to construct a system of reliable knowledge on the basis of unaided human reason.

On the other extreme, Strato emphasized a mechanistic approach to natural problems and employed the experimental method. Aristotle's position was intermediate. He conducted experiments upon occasion, and invoked observation as a conclusive argument. But he never advocated a systematic program of controlled experimentation. Experimentation and observation were incidental to his philosophy, not integral.

The philosophers would have done well to listen to the physicians. From at least the time of Hippocrates (c. 460–370 B.C.), physicians had recognized the value of empiricism. The Hippocratic school rejected supernaturalism, embraced naturalism, and believed in cause and effect. Observation was emphasized, and purely theoretical reasoning dismissed as being of little to no value. Hippocrates noted that the fact the natural philosophers all contradicted each other was evidence "of their ignorance of the whole subject."[15] He maintained that "facts are far superior to reasoning."[16]

But medicine was not philosophy or science. In classical civilization, it was regarded as a craft, like blacksmithing or winemaking.[17] Empiricism in the ancient world in the ancient world was disparaged for two reasons.

First, it was widely appreciated and conceded that information obtained through the senses was unreliable because every person saw and interpreted events and objects differently. The classic illustration of this is Diogenes Laërtius' story of the deception of Sphaerus [c. 285–210 B.C.] by Ptolemy IV. "The king [Ptolemy IV], wishing to refute him [Sphaerus], ordered some pomegranates of wax to be set before him; and when Sphaerus was deceived by them, the king shouted that he had given his assent to a false perception. But Sphaerus answered very neatly, that he had not given his assent to the fact that they were pomegranates, but to the fact that it was probable that they might be pomegranates. And that a perception which could be comprehended differed from one that was only probable."[18] Sphaerus had attempted to save himself from embarrassment, but the point had been made.

Second, the empirical data available to the Greeks and Romans consisted entirely of anecdotal information. Such data are notoriously unreliable. This was recognized in the most famous of the Hippocratic aphorisms: "the occasion [is] fleeting; experience fallacious, and judgment difficult."[19] With the notable exception of Strato, there was little to no systematic and controlled experimentation. It is not clear if Greek or Roman society would have been economically prosperous enough to support or fund such a program. Thus the necessity of an economic substrate.

DISDAIN FOR TECHNOLOGY

Technology is recognized as an indispensable aid to modern science, but there was little appreciation for technology in the ancient world. Most of the Greek philosophers and mathematicians had an intense disdain for technology and the practical arts. Xenophon quoted Socrates as stating "those arts which are called handicrafts are objectionable, and are indeed justly held in little repute in communities."[20] Plutarch related that Archimedes considered engineering to be "sordid and ignoble," and never made any written record of his mechanical works.[21] Plato criticized Archytas and Eudoxus for introducing mechanics into mathematics, thus "mechanics came to be separated from geometry, and, repudiated and neglected by philosophers."[22] In describing the practical and mechanical arts, Aristotle concluded that "the discussion of such matters is not unworthy of philosophy, but to be engaged in them practically is illiberal and irksome."[23]

In *Epistle 90, On Philosophy and the Invention of the Arts*, Seneca argued that philosophy was distinct from, and superior to, technology. The "workshop" was not a place of honor, and the practical arts were only good for making "stews and fishponds."

> Hitherto then I agree with Posidonius [c. 135–51 B.C.], but I deny that those arts which are in daily use for the necessaries of life, were the invention of philosophy; nor will I give so great an honor to the workshop. He [Posidonius] says indeed that philosophy taught men when they were scattered up and down, and lived in cottages, and in hollow rocks, and in the trunks of decayed trees, to build houses: but I can no more think that philosophy taught them to build houses upon houses, and turrets upon turrets, than that it instructed them in making stews and fishponds.[24]

From the context, it is clear that Seneca was indicating his disagreement with Posidonius. Like Seneca, Posidonius was a Stoic. But the Stoics did not agree among themselves on everything. All of Posidonius' books have been lost, but from the fragments quoted by extant authors it is evident "he [Posidonius] believed that, among early men, the philosophically wise managed everything and discovered all crafts and industry."[25] It thus seems that not all of the ancient philosophers disapproved of linking philosophy with technology.

Living himself in the most ostentatious comfort, Seneca hypocritically characterized luxury as "a revolt from nature."[26] He made the fantastic argument that men could live in harmony in nature, without the need of technology. Even if you did not have something as basic as shelter, it was not a problem. "Do not the Syrtic people live in holes dug under ground?"[27] Trivializing all human progress and technology, Seneca made the absurd claim that in former times "houses, clothing, medicine, food, and what are now thought a weighty concern, were obvious, freely given, or procured with little pains."[28]

Seneca acknowledged that there had been technological innovation during his own lifetime. But he disparaged these inventions as work fit only for "the meanest slaves."

> In our time many inventions have first been published; for instance, the windows made of fine transparent tiles [glass]; also hanging baths;[29] and pipes, of stoves, so concealed in the walls as to spread an equal heat through every part of the room; not to mention several works in marble, by which our temples, and even our houses are so finely decorated: or the huge piles of stone (pillars) which being made round and smooth form our porticos, and support such spacious buildings as will contain a multitude of people: nor need I mention the cyphers and characters

[shorthand] whereby a man can take down a whole oration, be it ever so swiftly pronounced, and with his hand keep pace with the speaker's tongue. These are, or may be, the inventions of the meanest slaves.[30]

Seneca's association of slaves with technology is a reminder that philosophers in the ancient world tended to be members of the upper class whose physical needs were provided for by slave labor. Slavery was endemic in the ancient Mediterranean. Strabo related that "the Romans, having acquired wealth after the destruction of Carthage and Corinth [146 B.C.], employed great numbers of domestic slaves."[31] The slave market at Delos [Greece] was so large that it was capable of "receiving and transporting, when sold, the same day, ten thousand slaves."[32] The proportion of slaves in Italy during Roman times has been estimated to be between 30 and 60 percent of the total population.[33] According to another estimate, at the end of the Roman Republic (27 B.C.), the total population of Italy was six million people, and one-third of these (two million) consisted of slaves.[34]

Slaves were held in contempt as a class.[35] Some relief may have been hoped for in the Stoic conception of a human brotherhood. But the Stoics also taught that individuals were to accept their fate without complaint. Thus there was little sympathy for anyone in the bondage of slavery. The contempt for slaves as a class evidently carried with it a cultural contempt for any technical art. Thus philosophers failed to appreciate the importance of technology as an adjunct to natural philosophy. They tended to lean toward the pure methods of geometrical reasoning that did not require them to get their hands dirty.

Vitruvius argued that "knowledge is the child of practice and theory."[36] Engineers have always had an appreciation for the interrelated necessity of both theory and practice, because they have had to construct machines, buildings, and infrastructure. The engineer starts with a theoretical model, but the theory is immediately and repeatedly put to the test. If the theory is found to inadequate or lacking, necessity requires that it be modified. In ancient engineering practice, "theory" may have been no more than an oral craft tradition, but nevertheless ideas concerning how things ought to be done were subjected to constant empirical testing. This was not the case for philosophy, and the ancient philosophers never acquired a significant appreciation for the importance of empiricism in science or natural philosophy.

By separating itself from technology, natural philosophy ensured that it would have no practical utility. It was widely regarded as being nothing more than idle speculation. No philosopher ever did anything to improve the life of the ordinary person. "[Greek] science did little or nothing to transform the conditions of life or to open any vista into the future."[37] Without a vital link to technology, natural philosophy was philosophy, not science.

MENDEL AND THE PRINTING PRESS

In modern science, provisional truth is established through the criterion of repeatability. A systematic program of observation or experimentation is conducted and results are compared. If nearly everyone obtains the same result, a tentative truth or consensus is agreed upon. The method works reasonably well, but it requires technological and economic substrates. There must be a community of scientists and an organizational structure supplied by one or more professional societies. These can only exist in prosperous societies. Most importantly, individual results have to be widely distributed: there has to be a printing press (or its electronic equivalent).

The importance of the printing press is illustrated by the experience of a nineteenth-century Austrian monk, Gregor Mendel (1822–1884). Mendel became a Christian monk because it "freed him at once of his struggle for existence,"[38] and enabled him to complete his education. He entered a monastery at Brünn, Austria, in 1843 at the age of 21. In 1847, he was ordained as a priest.

Mendel was an accomplished student. At the Philosophical Institute of the University of Olmütz, "he attained the highest grade in all courses except for theoretical and practical philosophy, in which he got the second-best grade."[39] But Mendel was never able to pass the state certification exam for teachers, failing in both 1850 and 1856. Mendel had a highly nervous disposition and was frequently ill. When he was assigned the duty of tending to the ill, he "was overcome with a paralyzing shyness and he himself then became dangerously ill."[40]

Mendel attended classes at the University of Vienna between 1851 and 1853. His primary studies were in physics, but he also took classes in other natural sciences, including chemistry, mathematics, zoology, and botany. In 1853, Mendel returned to the monastery at Brünn and taught natural science in the technical high school there until 1868. Evidently, he was allowed to teach even though he was never able to pass the state licensing exam.

In 1854, Mendel began to conduct breeding experiments with pea plants in the monastery garden, testing "34 varieties for constancy of their traits."[41] After two years of preliminary work was completed, Mendel chose to investigate the heritability of seven types of differences by cross-breeding pea plants. The pea plant has seven pairs of chromosomes, a fact that neither Mendel nor anyone else in the nineteenth century could have known. Seven was the largest number of differences that Mendel could have chosen to investigate and obtain meaningful results. The choice of seven was evidently based on insights obtained by Mendel through his trial experiments.

Mendel completed his study in 1863, and published his results in the *Proceedings of the Brünn Natural History Society* in 1866. It was perhaps one of the ten most important scientific papers ever published, but the manuscript was largely ignored. Up to the year 1900, there were only a handful of references to Mendel's work in the scientific literature.[42]

Five hundred copies of the journal in which Mendel's paper appeared were printed. Of these, 115 were distributed to "scientific institutes or libraries."[43] Mendel ordered 40 reprints that presumably were sent to leading scientists, including Charles Darwin. Only one person bothered to return Mendel's correspondence, Professor Nägeli of the University of Munich. And Nägeli's letter indicated he did not comprehend Mendel's work.[44] No one fully realized the significance of Mendel's findings.

Whatever his failings might have been in passing formal exams, Mendel's colleagues evidently held him in high regard. In 1868 he was elected abbot of his monastery, a position that allowed no time for scientific research. Mendel's scientific career was prematurely terminated.

In 1884, Mendel died in relative obscurity and the new abbot burned all of his papers.[45] Shortly before his death Mendel stated, "I have experienced many a bitter hour in my life. Nevertheless, I admit gratefully that the beautiful, good hours far outnumbered the others. My scientific work brought me much satisfaction and I am convinced that the entire world will recognize the results of these studies."[46]

Mendel's work lay buried in libraries for 34 years. In 1900, three other scientists independently duplicated Mendel's results. When they searched the literature, they found that the same theory of genetics had been published 34 years earlier by an unknown Austrian monk.[47]

In 1902, the journal *Nature* reported, "about two years ago the discovery was made that Gregor Mendel, sometime Abbot of Brünn, had long since, in the seclusion of his cloister, devised and carried through a very remarkable series of experiments in cross-fertilization; and had on them based a theory which bids fair, if its truth can be established, to put the whole subject of heredity on an entirely new footing."[48] In time, Mendel's theory did prove to "bid fair," and he became recognized as the founder of the science of genetics.

In the ancient world, manuscripts had to be hand-printed. It was a difficult and laborious process that restricted science to an individual activity and made it difficult to establish a criterion by which objective truths could be agreed upon. No one immediately recognized Mendel's breakthrough after widespread circulation of his results. If the reports of Mendel's results had been limited to a handful of hand-printed copies, it would have been that much more difficult.

Mendel did receive recognition, but not in his lifetime. This was only possible because his work had been widely distributed and archived. It took time, but eventually the obscure monk's scientific contributions entered the mainstream. But if Mendel had lived in the fifth century B.C., it is unlikely that anyone would have taken the time and trouble to copy and distribute the work of an unknown author, especially when no one recognized the manuscript as possessing any special value. Both Plato and Aristotle had their work preserved and recognized in part because of their political connections and class status. Many geniuses of the ancient world must have passed into oblivion, their work forever lost.

A printing press may appear to be a simple machine, but it was likely beyond the technological capabilities of the ancient Greeks and Romans. The ability to make mass copies is of no use without an abundant supply of material to print upon. Paper was invented in China in A.D. 105, but was not introduced into Europe until A.D. 1150.[49] "The chief reason for this failure to develop printing systematically lies, no doubt, in the fact that there was no abundant supply of printable material of a uniform texture and convenient form. The supply of papyrus was strictly limited, strip had to be fastened to strip, and there was no standard size of sheet. Paper had yet to come from China to release the mind of Europe. Had there been presses, they would have had to stand idle while the papyrus rolls were slowly made."[50]

Printing-press technology also depends on the metallurgical techniques necessary to produce type in mass quantities. The type first used in Europe c. 1450 "was an alloy of tin and lead," and the techniques used in its casting were likely borrowed from the manufacturer of pewter.[51] Ink was also a problem. Before the press, printing by hand was done with a water-based ink whose black color derived from lamp-black or ferric gallate. But the surface tension of water makes it difficult to apply water-based ink evenly to metal surfaces. Printing presses employing metal type used an ink based on a "linseed-oil varnish" that was likely invented by Johann Gutenberg (1398–1468).[52]

Although the technology for the development of a printing press was lacking, so was the imagination. Nowhere in any ancient manuscript is there any statement that a means of mechanical printing was possible or even desirable. There seems to have been no understanding that the widespread dissemination of knowledge would benefit humanity. Aristotle evidently gave no thought to systematically recording and distributing his knowledge. What we know of Aristotle comes from a handful of moldy manuscripts that escaped oblivion through pure serendipity. And most of these manuscripts seem to have the form of lecture notes recorded by students, rather than a careful attempt by the master to archive his thoughts.

INFLUENCE OF CHRISTIANITY

In 1925, Alfred North Whitehead (1861–1947) suggested that the long practice of Christianity and its precepts had prepared Europe for the Scientific Revolution of the seventeenth century by instilling in the Western mind the instinctive conviction that nature was a rational and ordered creation of God and therefore could be understood through systematic inquiry.

Whitehead claimed that a long preoccupation with Christianity had instilled in the Western mind the belief that nature obeyed invariant laws, and thus could be understood through systematic observation and experimentation. "There can be no living science unless there is a widespread instinctive conviction in the existence of an *Order of Things*, and, in particular, of an *Order of Nature*."[53]

Whitehead postulated that the assumption implicit in science, that effect follows cause, was a derivative of medieval theology.

> The greatest contribution of medievalism to the formation of the scientific movement ... [was] ... the inexpugnable belief that every detailed occurrence can be correlated with its antecedents in a perfectly definite manner, exemplifying general principles.... How has this conviction been so vividly implanted on the European mind?... It must come from the medieval insistence on the rationality of God.... My explanation is that the faith in the possibility of science, generated antecedently to the development of modern scientific theory, is an unconscious derivative from medieval theology.[54]

But monotheism was known well before Christianity. Many of the Greek philosophers were monotheistic. Monotheism can even be found among the Babylonian and Egyptian priesthoods as early as 1500 B.C.[55] Naturalism also depends upon the uniformity of nature, and the rational conviction of an ordered cosmos where effect invariably and predictably follows cause. Thus the qualities Whitehead attributed to medieval theology were well in place long before the Christian era.

Whitehead's thesis also suggested that philosophy was enriched by religion. But the converse was the case. The theologians were seduced by the philosophers. If there was any immediate precedent to the development of scientific methodology in Europe, it was the embracement of Aristotelian logic by theologians of the High Middle Ages. The theologians were attracted to Greek philosophy by its own innate virtue. Reason was incorporated into Church doctrines because the Scholastics found its appeal irresistible. After all, it would have been unreasonable to reject reason. Religion was enriched by philosophy, not the other way around.

If Whitehead was correct, and Christianity promoted science in Europe, then arguably Islam should have done the same in the lands of the Middle East. Both Islam and Christianity are monotheistic religions that depict an ordered cosmos governed by a personal deity. Yet the historical record is quite clear and convincing. The opposite happened. Islamic religious orthodoxy crushed science and rational philosophy out of existence.

There have been other assertions that Christianity fostered science. John Macmurray claimed "science, in its own field, is the product of Christianity, and its most adequate expression so far."[56] Citing Macmurray, Karl Popper expressed the belief that Christianity's emphasis on brotherhood facilitated the development of science. "Our Western civilization owes its rationalism, its faith in the rational unity of man and in the open society, and especially its scientific outlook, to the ancient Socratic and Christian belief in the brotherhood of all men, and in intellectual honesty and responsibility."[57]

We would like to believe this thesis. Truth is a unity, and it would be comforting to find consilience between religion and science. But the thesis that modern science was nurtured by Christianity is unconvincing, strained, and tendentious. The argument is usually offered in a form that is appealing, but generalized, vague, and without specific supporting facts.

It is true that systematic experimentation and the criterion of repeatability require cooperation. However philosophers had a spirit of cooperation before the advent of Christianity. One piece of factual evidence for this is Archimedes' correspondence with mathematicians in Alexandria.[58] The fact that the ancients had developed the concept of a "sin against philosophy"[59] implied that they had developed an ethic of disinterested cooperation toward the pursuit of objective truth.

To the extent that Christianity aided the development of science in Europe, the effect may have been indirect. Christianity provided a common creed and an ethic of brotherhood that helped to unify the diverse cultures and tribes of the continent. This aided the commercial and economic development of Europe by lessening conflicts and easing cooperation. Commercial activity itself, of course, is an incentive to cooperation. Over the ages of civilization men have gradually acquired an appreciation that it is more profitable to enlist strangers as allies in the task of production than treat them as enemies. Together, Christianity and commerce were synergistic in promoting unity, peace, and productivity in Europe.

It must also be frankly admitted that there is much truth in the traditional view that emphasizes hostility between science and religion.[60] Science and religion are competing systems of knowledge based upon different epistemological methods. Each would like to lay claim to the entire world of knowledge. It is inevitable that they should come into conflict and trespass on what each regards as their proper domain. Aristotle taught "the world is eternal,"[61] but the book of *Genesis* stated that time began when "God created the heaven and the earth."[62] When astronomers removed the Earth from the center of the universe in the seventeenth century, the moral ramifications were necessarily profound and objectionable to Christian theologians.

Cosmas Indicopleustes (c. A.D. 490–585)

In the Dark Ages (of Europe), the phenomenological world was largely understood not through observation and reasoning, but by reconciling it with divine revelation as enshrined in the Holy Scriptures. The person who exemplified this approach was "Cosmas, an Alexandrian monk, surnamed Indicopleustes (c. A.D. 490–585), after returning from a voyage to India (A.D. 535)."[63]

Cosmas was born of Greek parents in Alexandria. The young Cosmas received a rudimentary education and became a merchant who traveled extensively. Cosmas' seafaring excursions brought him to the Mediterranean Sea, the Red Sea, and the Persian Gulf. He visited Ceylon (Sri Lanka), the coastal cities of India, and Ethiopia.[64]

When his traveling days were over, Cosmas returned to his native city of Alexandria and became a Christian monk. Zealous in his religion, Cosmas took the prevailing intellectual tenor of his day to the logical extreme. His sole surviving work, *Christian Topography*, was written to show that the cosmology of the pagans was false, and the true shapes of Heaven and Earth were to be derived from the *Bible*.

In particular, Cosmas objected to the notion that the Earth was a sphere and that the planets and stars were carried on concentric, rotating crystalline-spheres. In Book 1 of

Christian Topography he explained that one cannot simultaneously be Christian and accept pagan cosmology. "[No one] can profess Christianity, while wishing at the same time to bedeck themselves with the principles, the wisdom, and the diversity of the errors of this world ... it is against such men my words are directed, for divine scripture denounces them ... they wish both to be with us and with those that are against us, thus making void their renunciation of Satan whom they renounced in baptism."[65]

Cosmas' topography was derived from an imaginative extrapolation of Biblical verses. When Moses descended from Mount Sinai he carried with him the Ten Commandments, written on stone tablets by the very finger of God. The stone tablets containing God's laws were stored in a chest, the Ark of the Covenant.

The Covenant between God and the Hebrews was the understanding that if they would obey His laws they would be His chosen people. God was specific in His instructions to Moses. "Now therefore, if ye will obey my voice indeed, and keep my covenant, then ye shall be a peculiar treasure unto me above all people: for all the earth is mine: And ye shall be unto me a kingdom of priests, and an holy nation. These are the words which thou shalt speak unto the children of Israel."[66]

The Ark was stored in the Tabernacle, a portable sanctuary that the Jews carried around with them. Cosmas maintained that God had instructed Moses to build the Tabernacle in a shape that mimicked the cosmos. In the Second Prologue of *Christian Topography*, Cosmas explained "God who created the world has ordained ... [that] the pattern of the whole world [is] the Tabernacle prepared by Moses."[67] In Book 5, he reiterated, "Then when he [Moses] had come down from the mountain he was ordered by God to make the Tabernacle, which was a representation of what he had seen in the mountain, namely an impress of the whole world."[68]

God gave Moses explicit and detailed instructions for constructing the Tabernacle. It was a rectangular tent with a vaulted top.[69] Cosmas therefore maintained that the Earth was flat, like the bottom of the Tabernacle, and was twice as long from east to west as it was from north to south. The conception of a rectangular Earth was also consistent with a passage in the book of *Isaiah* that stated God would "gather together the dispersed of Judah from the four corners of the Earth."[70] A sphere did not have corners.

In Cosmas' topography, the known lands of the Earth were surrounded by a vast ocean. In turn, this ocean was surrounded by another strip of land unknown to man, a second earth as it were. "The earth is surrounded by the ocean, and further that beyond the ocean there is another earth by which the ocean is surrounded."[71]

It was this second earth that had been the abode of man prior to the Flood, and from which Noah and his family had journeyed during the Great Flood.[72] The top of the cosmos (heaven) was vaulted or convex in its shape, but its sides extended down vertically. Where the downward extension of heaven met the sides of the second earth, the two were welded together. Cosmas explained that scriptural verses provided sufficient evidence for this architecture. "Do not the expressions about inclining it [heaven] to the earth and welding it thereto clearly show that the heaven standing as a vault has its extremities bound together with the extremities of the earth? The fact of its inclination to the earth, and its being welded with it, makes it totally inconceivable that it is a sphere."[73]

According to Cosmas, the Earth was at the bottom of the universe, not the middle or center of the universe as the pagans had maintained. "Since therefore the earth is heavier than any other body whatever, the Deity placed it as the foundation of the universe, and made it steadfast in virtue of its own inherent stability."[74]

Cosmas attacked pagan Greek cosmology by posing the question of how the Earth could hang in empty space without support. "How can this unspeakable weight of the earth be held suspended by the air and not fall down?"[75]

Equally absurd to Cosmas was the idea that the heavenly spheres containing the stars and planets were rotating in empty space, suspended from nothing. "If ... it [the heavenly realm] rolls and rotates always in the same spot without moving from place to place, then it must be upheld by supports like a turner's lathe, or an artificial globe, or on an axis like a machine or a wagon. And if so, then we must again inquire by what the supports and axles are themselves upheld, and so on *ad infinitum*."[76]

A further difficulty was apparent to Cosmas. If the heavens consisted of concentric, rotating spheres, then the axes of rotation had to pass through the center of the Earth. "And tell me, pray, how are we to suppose the axis passes through the middle of the earth, and of what material it consists."[77]

If the Earth were a sphere, then there must exist antipodal points on the other side of the Earth, directly opposite to the known lands. These supposed territories were the *Antipodes*. Cosmas pointed out that the existence of a spherical Earth necessarily implied the existence of the Antipodes, a proposition that was altogether ridiculous and indefensible. How could two men, standing on opposite sides of a spherical Earth both be upright? "But should one wish to examine more elaborately the question of the Antipodes, he would easily find them to be old wives' fables. For if two men on opposite sides placed the soles of their feet each against each, whether they chose to stand on earth, or water, or air, or fire, or any other kind of body, how could both be found standing upright? The one would assuredly be found in the natural upright position, and the other, contrary to nature, head downward. Such notions are opposed to reason, and alien to our nature and condition."[78]

The perceptive monk further noted that the existence of the Antipodes implied that rain would fall upward. "For to think that there are Antipodes compels us to think also that rain falls on them from an opposite direction to ours; and any one will, with good reason, deride these ludicrous theories, which set forth principles incongruous, ill-adjusted, and contrary to nature."[79]

For all of his denunciation of pagan cosmology, Cosmas was charitable enough to credit the Greek philosophers with the ability to accurately predict the occurrence of eclipses.

> Among the famous philosophers who flourished among the pagans, which of them, Socrates, or Pythagoras, or Plato, or Aristotle, or any other, was held worthy to foretell or announce any thing of such advantage to the world as the resurrection of the dead, and the free gift to men of the Kingdom of Heaven, which cannot be shaken? For they can announce nothing except only that, by means of calculations and secular learning, they declare when eclipses of the sun and the moon will occur, whereby, even if they predict them truly — as in fact they do — no benefit will accrue to the world, but rather the evil of pride.[80]

Cosmas apparently perceived no incongruity in the fact that a totally incorrect cosmology could be applied to make correct predictions.

In Book 4 of *Christian Topography*, Cosmas finally lost his patience with the pagan philosophers and resorted to sarcasm.

> Ye advance arguments altogether incredible ... [and] ye advance arguments which are self-contradictory and opposed to the nature of things.... How great is your knowledge! How great your wisdom! How great your intelligence! How great your inconsistency!... Let each one of you who has sound vision and the power of reasoning justly turn the earth round whatever way he pleases, and let him say whether the Antipodes can be all standing upright in the same sense of the expres-

sion. But this they will not show even should they speak unrestrained by shame. Such then is our reply to your fictitious and false theories and to the conclusions of your reasonings which are capricious, self-contradictory, inconsistent, doomed to be utterly confounded, and to be whirled round and round even more than that unstable and revolving mythical sphere of yours.[81]

Isidore of Seville (A.D. 560–636)

Isidore of Seville (A.D. 560–636) was a Spanish bishop and encyclopedist. He was born into an influential family but his parents died when he was young and he was raised by his older brother, Leander. Leander was the Bishop of Seville and the foremost churchman in Spain.[82]

Around A.D. 600, Leander died and Isidore became Bishop of Seville, the de facto leader of the Christian Church in Spain. During his tenure, he was highly regarded and successful in uniting the disparate elements of Spanish culture and suppressing the Arian heresy. Three years before his death (A.D. 633), Isidore presided at the Fourth Council of Toledo, a national meeting of all the Spanish bishops. At this council Isidore was successful in promulgating a decree that all bishops had to establish seminaries for the education of priests in secular subjects such as Greek, Hebrew, and the liberal arts.[83]

Isidore was a prolific author; his last and most important work was an encyclopedia titled *Etymologies*. It was an influential work and was widely used as a textbook in Christian educational institutions throughout the Middle Ages. "Hundreds of copies ... passed into circulation."[84] The *Etymologies* is the most important of Isidore's works in part because it summarizes and includes most of what is found in his earlier books. The subjects covered in *Etymologies* included medicine, law, theology, geography, geology, the construction of roads, agriculture, zoology, and many others. The *Etymologies* was literally a compilation of all secular knowledge possessed by Europeans during the Dark Ages. "It may be called the basic book of the entire Middle Ages."[85]

In *Etymologies*, secular knowledge was not viewed as both evil and useless. Instead of condemning philosophers as "patriarchs of heretics," Isidore praised them for their knowledge of the natural world. But he was careful to note that the minds of the philosophers had been darkened by ignorance of Christianity. "The philosophers of the world are highly praised for the measuring of time, and the tracing of the course of the stars, and the analysis of the elements. Still, they had this only from God. Flying proudly through the air like birds, and plunging into the deep sea like fishes, and walking like dumb animals, they gained knowledge of the earth, but they would not seek with all their minds to know their Maker."[86]

Ernest Brehaut (1873–1953) explained that the intellectual world in which Isidore lived was almost a perfect reverse of the modern world:

> The view held in the dark ages of the natural and supernatural and of their relative proportions in the outlook on life, was precisely the reverse of that held by intelligent men in modern times. For us the material universe has taken on the aspect of order; within its limits phenomena seem to follow definite modes of behavior, upon the evidence of which a body of scientific knowledge has been built up ... the attitude of Isidore and his time is exactly opposite to ours. To him the supernatural world was the demonstrable and ordered one. Its phenomena, or what were supposed to be such, were accepted as valid, while no importance was attached to evidence offered by the senses as to the material.... It is evident, therefore, that if we compare the dogmatic worldview of the medieval thinker with the more tentative one of the modern scientist, allowance must be made for the fact that they take hold of the universe at opposite ends. Their plans are so fundamentally different that it is hard to express the meaning of one in terms of the other.[87]

In European thought of this time, knowledge had three divisions. These were ranked from the lowest to the highest as follows: material, moral, and spiritual. Correspondingly, the three fields of study were science or natural philosophy, ethics, and theology. Science was not entirely worthless, but it was the lowest of the three because it dealt with the dross materiality of the lower world. Spirituality was to be sought directly, with faith, service, and prayer. For science, it would suffice to indiscriminately paste together scraps of knowledge from centuries-old books.[88]

Isidore's *Etymologies* was entirely derivative of Pliny the Elder's *Natural History,* as well as other Roman writers who summarized earlier knowledge. The legacy is apparent in both content and approach. *Etymologies* was a stale copy of a copy, lacking originality, insight, and perspicuity. The cosmology was primitive. Isidore's Earth was flat and his universe was small, limited in both time and space. The cosmos began with the Creation, and would end with the return of Christ.

The paucity with which *Etymologies* covered the subjects of natural philosophy and science in part also derived from the fact that Isidore knew no Greek. Many significant scientific and philosophic works were never translated into Latin. Greek continued to be the primary language of philosophy and science well into the first centuries of the Christian Era. Galen, writing in the second century A.D., wrote in Greek.[89]

In Isidore's cosmology, the Earth was located at the center of the universe, surrounded by rotating crystalline spheres that contain the stars, planets, Sun, and Moon. Although he never explicitly discussed the shape of the Earth, in a passage in his book *De Natura Rerum,* Isidore revealed his flat-earth cosmology when he stated that the frigid climate zones, found at the extremes of both north and south, were adjacent to each other. "The northern and southern circles, *being adjacent to each other,* are not inhabited, for the reason that they are situated far from the sun's course, and are rendered waste by the great rigor of the climate and the icy blasts of the winds."[90]

The discussion was accompanied by a diagram showing the earth to be round, but flat like a pancake. The flat-earth belief was further revealed when Isidore said that the inhabitants of the Antipodes were impossible. "Moreover those who are called Antipodes, because they are believed to be opposite to our feet, so that, being as it were placed beneath the earth, they tread in footsteps that are opposed to our feet. It is by no means to be believed."[91]

Isidore's chemistry was no more advanced than his cosmology. The fundamental elements were fire, air, water, and earth — the conception originated by Empedocles a thousand years earlier.[92]

In Isidore's world there was no room for intellectual inquiry, skepticism, or doubt, especially in the field of theology. He stated that we must naively accept doctrine on the basis of unquestioned faith. "We are not permitted to form any belief of our own will, or to choose a belief that someone else has accepted of his own. We have God's apostles as authorities, who did not themselves choose anything of what they should believe, but they faithfully transmitted to the nations the teaching received from Christ. As so even if an angel from heaven shall preach otherwise, let him be anathema."[93]

Isidore's world was ordered in a great *Chain of Being.* The heavens on high were occupied by angels. Descending from the heavenly realm, the air above the Earth was the home of birds and demons. Man and the animals dwelt in the lowest realm, the solid Earth.

The *Chain of Being* was a central tenet of Medieval European thought. It is "is the idea of the organic constitution of the universe as a series of links or gradations ordered in a hierarchy of creatures."[94] The origins of the *Chain of Being* lay in the writings of the Greek philosophers, and these were effortlessly absorbed into Christian theology. Plato described an abstract "Good," as the highest possible state. "The good may be said to be not only the author of knowledge to all things known, but of their being and essence."[95]

Aristotle described organic creation as ordered, from lowest to highest. In *On the Generation of Animals*, he noted "we must observe how rightly nature orders generation in regular gradation."[96] In *History of Animals*, Aristotle described a continuous variation in living things, placing plants lower on the scale and animals higher. "Nature proceeds little by little from things lifeless to animal life in such a way that it is impossible to determine the exact line of demarcation ... after lifeless things in the upward scale comes the plant, and of plants one will differ from another as to its amount of apparent vitality ... there is observed in plants a continuous scale of ascent towards the animal."[97]

The *Chain of Being* was described by the English poet Alexander Pope (1688–1744), in his *Essay on Man*.

> Vast chain of Being! which from God began,
> Natures ethereal, human, angel, man,
> Beast, bird, fish, insect, what no eye can see,
> No glass can reach; from Infinite to thee.[98]

Like Tertullian, Isidore believed that humanity was constantly besought by a flood of demons whose sole purpose was to bring about moral corruption. "They unsettle the senses, stir low passions, disorder life, cause alarms in sleep, bring diseases, fill the mind with terror, distort the limbs, control the way in which lots are cast, make a pretense at oracles with their tricks, arouse the passion of love, create the heat of cupidity, lurk in consecrated images; when invoked they appear; they tell lies that resemble the truth; they take on different forms, and sometimes appear in the likeness of angels."[99] The struggle against these intransigent enemies of humanity was constant and hard, for they were equipped with superior intelligence and were unrelenting in their persistence.

Like Pliny's *Natural History*, *Etymologies* contained curious lore and fantasies. Various types of human monstrosities existing around the world were described. "The Cynocephali are so called because they have dogs' heads and their barking betrays them as beasts rather than men. These are born in India."[100] "The Cyclopes, too, the same India gives birth to, and they are named Cyclopes because they are said to have a single eye in the midst of the forehead ... they eat nothing but the flesh of wild beasts."[101] "The Blemmyes, born in Libya, are believed to be headless trunks, having mouths and eyes in the breast; others are born without necks, with eyes in their shoulders."[102] "The Antipodes in Libya have feet turned backward and eight toes on each foot."[103]

Isidore's world was also full of mythical beasts. "The Gryphes are so called because they are winged quadrupeds.... In every part of their body they are lions, and in wings and head are like eagles, and they are fierce enemies of horses. Moreover they tear man to pieces."[104] "The dragon is the largest of all serpents and of all living things upon Earth.... And from it the elephant is not safe because of its size. For it lies in wait near the paths by which elephants usually go, and entangles the elephant's legs in its folds, and kills it by strangling."[105]

Isidore believed that the Garden of Eden was a physical site located in Asia. "Paradise is a place lying in the parts of the Orient.... In the Hebrew it is called Eden ... it is planted with every kind of wood and fruit-bearing tree, having also the tree of life; there is neither cold nor heat there, but a continual spring temperature.... Approach to this place was closed after man's sin. For it is hedged in on every side by sword-like flame, that is, girt by a wall of fire, whose burning almost reaches the heaven."[106]

From a modern viewpoint, the most inexplicable statements found in Isidore's writings were those that link totally unrelated subjects in bizarre ways. Isidore claimed that the ounce was "a lawful weight because the number of its scruples* measures [is equal to] the hours of the day and night,"[107] that the Hebrew alphabet has 22 letters because there are 22 books in the *Old Testament*, and that a man cries when he kneels, because the knees and eyes are in close proximity in the womb.[108] These statements were a reflection of the European medieval mindset. Like the Stoics, medieval Christians saw the world as an organic whole; the material world was inexorably intertwined with the moral and spiritual. Therefore, they sought ceaselessly to interpret the material world in moral terms.

---

*a "scruple" is an ancient Roman weight equal to $^1/_{24}$ of an ounce

CHAPTER 3

Islam

The Prophet Mohammed (A.D. 570–632)

THE BEDOUIN

In the 6th century A.D., Europe and the Mediterranean world had settled into intro-spection. Natural philosophy and rational inquiry were stagnant. A thousand years of Greek and Roman civilization had failed to develop the idea of a systematic scientific method or significantly improve the life of the average person. Eventually, natural philosophy would be revived in Europe. A significant factor in this revival, and in world history, would be the revelations an illiterate Arab merchant received from the angel Gabriel.

The prophet Mohammed was born in the city of Mecca in present day Saudi Arabia in the year A.D. 570. His father died before he was born, and his mother passed away when the boy was but six years of age. The young Mohammed was raised by his uncle and grand-father.[1]

Little is known about the life of the youth, but there is a tradition that the infant was sent into the desert to live with the Bedouin.[2] Nomadic shepherds, most Bedouin were illit-erate. But eloquence in speech was highly esteemed.[3] Writing c. 1815, John Lewis Burck-hardt (1784–1817) noted, "through every part of the Arabian desert, poetry is equally esteemed."[4] Desert life inculcated in the Bedouin the qualities of tenacity, strength, and individualism. "In patience, or rather endurance, both physical and moral, few Bedouins are deficient."[5]

The Bedouin lived in tents made of camel or goat hair. They subsisted by raising sheep and camel; their primary foods were dates and the milk of camels. Occasionally, their diets were supplemented with items such as grapes, almonds, sugar-cane, and watermelons raised in oases.

It was the camel that made the nomadic life of the Bedouin possible. They drank its milk, made their tents from its hair, and ate its flesh. The dung of the camel provided fuel for the Bedouin's campfires, and they applied its urine as a hair tonic.[6] Horses were a meas-ure of wealth and greatly treasured; it was said that a Bedouin would water his horse before his children.[7]

Prior to the advent of Islam, the Bedouin existed as independent tribes, with no national ruler or authority. Their culture was governed by "an unwritten code of conduct established by their ancestors, rooted in blood-kinship, based on common customs, and ... tribal honor. Their life was ruled by contracts of mutual assistance, laws of blood revenge, and bouts of tribal rivalry. It upheld the ideals of group solidarity, individual bravery, and personal equanimity."[8]

The chief activities that relieved the boredom of the Bedouin's routine were "raiding, gambling, and wine drinking."[9] Raiding was not considered to be brigandry. "The Bedouins regard the plundering of caravans or travelers as in lieu of the custom dues exacted elsewhere. The land is theirs, they argue, and trespassers on it must pay forfeit."[10] If a caravan was not available, Bedouins would conduct raids on neighboring tribes. The raids rarely resulted in serious injury or death, the conduct of the conflicts having been institutionalized by social convention into a game or sport.

In the absence of formal governmental authority, peace between the tribes was maintained by the custom of exacting payment in blood. If a member of one tribe killed a member of another tribe, justice could only be exacted by the death of a member of the offending tribe. The person killed in revenge did not have to be the murderer, it could be any member of his tribe. This convention made murder too expensive to contemplate, and exerted a powerful social pressure on tribal members to remain peaceful. Any member of a tribe who had the poor judgment to initiate hostilities exposed his entire tribe to danger. A man's entire worth, standing, and security derived from his membership in a tribe; he could not risk being expelled from it.

ARABIC RELIGION BEFORE ISLAM

"Of Arabian paganism we possess no trustworthy or complete account."[11] Before the advent of Islam in the 7th century A.D., the Arabs appear to have practiced a form of animism, "the belief that a great part if not all of the inanimate kingdom of nature as well as all animated beings, are endowed with reason, intelligence and volition identical with man."[12] The inhabitants of the Arabian peninsula worshipped "spirits and deities, the cults of stars, stones, trees, and, in some cases, idols."[13] The chief god of the Quraysh tribe in Mecca was Allah.[14]

There was no belief in an afterlife, and Bedouin culture was largely secular.[15] Among the Bedouin, "cultic practices ... were characterized by very little ritual and in turn reflected the individualism of the Bedouin and the lack of rigidity in their entire social system."[16] The Bedouin were preoccupied with fate, although fate itself was not worshipped as a deity.[17]

> The Moving Finger writes; and, having writ,
> Moves on: nor all thy Piety nor Wit
> Shall lure it back to cancel half a Line,
> Nor all thy Tears wash out a Word of it.[18]

Although he may have spent his early youth in the desert, Mohammed lived most of his life in the prosperous commercial center of Mecca where he was a member of the city's most populous tribe, the Quraysh. The youth Mohammed was employed by his uncle to conduct caravans. He must have been well-regarded by his uncle to have been entrusted with this responsibility.[19] "There seems no doubt that he [Mohammed] often accompanied Meccan caravans to the countries with which the Meccans had trade relations; such especially were Syria, and south Arabia, and perhaps Egypt and Mesopotamia."[20]

During his travels, it is likely that Mohammed would have been exposed to many different religious beliefs. There were several Jewish and Christian communities in Arabia, and dialogues and friendly disputations between Arabs, Jews, and Christians may have been common. The Arabs developed an acute sense of inferiority when comparing their religion to that practiced by the Jews and Christians. One of them explained that they lacked the written scriptures which lent authority to the religion of the Jews. "What induced us to accept Islam, apart from God's mercy and guidance, was what we used to hear the Jews say. We were polytheists worshipping idols, while they were people of the scriptures with knowledge which we did not possess."[21]

God had revealed his word to the Jews through the prophets and given them a holy book. The Christians in turn had not only the Jewish prophets of the *Old Testament*, but a genuine Messiah of their own. The Arabs had neither prophet, Messiah, nor book. "Several people in Mecca and elsewhere had arrived at the idea of monotheism,"[22] and the time was ripe for a religious revolution in Arabia.

At the age of 25 (c. A.D. 595), Mohammed married a wealthy widow, Khadija, who was fifteen years his senior. He settled down to the routine of a married life, managing Khadija's business, and fathering several children.[23] But as time passed Mohammed became more preoccupied with the spiritual life. "Behind the quiet and unobtrusive exterior of Mahomet [Mohammed], lay hid a high resolve, a singleness and unity of purpose, a strength and fixedness of will, a sublime determination, destined to achieve the marvelous work of bowing towards himself the heart of all Arabia as the heart of one man."[24]

THE KORAN

At the age of forty (c. A.D. 610), Mohammed received his first revelation from Allah. During the holy month of Ramadan, he retired to a cave on the side of Mount Hira outside of Mecca and had a fateful dream.[25] In his dream, Mohammed was confronted by the angel Gabriel, the same Being who had informed the Virgin Mary that she would bear the child Jesus.[26] Gabriel ordered Mohammed to recite a message from God, but he refused. Again, Mohammed was ordered to recite, but again he refused. Finally, the angel embraced Mohammed so tightly that he thought he would die from suffocation. Mohammed capitulated. "So I read it, and he departed from me. And I awoke from my sleep, and it was as though these words were written on my heart."[27]

The reluctant prophet tried to immediately commit suicide by walking to the top of the mountain and throwing himself off it. But he was stopped by heavenly intervention. "When I was midway on the mountain, I heard a voice from heaven saying 'O Muhammad! thou art the apostle of God and I am Gabriel.' I raised my head towards heaven to see (who was speaking), and lo, Gabriel in the form of a man with feet astride the horizon."[28]

The words that Mohammed had been ordered to recite were these:

> Recite thou, in the name of thy Lord who created; —
> Created man from CLOTS OF BLOOD: —
> Recite thou! For thy Lord is the most Beneficent,
> Who hath taught the use of the pen; —
> Hath taught man that which he knoweth not.[29]

At first, Mohammed was concerned with the source of the revelation. Was it angelic or satanic? His wife, Khadija, proposed a test. The next time that Gabriel appeared to Mohammed, his wife had him sit on her lap, facing outward. She then removed her veil and asked if Mohammed could still see Gabriel. When he answered "no," Khadija concluded the being was an angel from God, for a devil would not have turned away when she removed her veil.[30]

Over the next few years Mohammed continued to receive verses from the angel Gabriel. These messages were written down for him by family and friends, for Mohammed was illiterate. The illiteracy of the Prophet was considered to be further proof of the divine origin of his message.

The collected revelations of the Prophet became known as the *Koran*, the sacred book of Islam. "Several of Mahomet's followers, according to early tradition, could, during his [Mohammed's] lifetime, repeat with scrupulous accuracy the entire revelation."[31] After Mohammed died in A.D. 632, the contents of the *Koran* were compiled within two years.[32] There is little doubt that the *Koran* has survived over the centuries as the unaltered original intended by Mohammed. "We may upon the strongest presumption affirm that every verse in the *Coran* is the genuine and unaltered composition of Mahomet himself."[33]

There is an important difference between the Christian Bible (and Jewish *Old Testament*) and the *Koran* of Islam. Except for the words of Jesus in the *New Testament*, the Bible is considered to be the *inspired* word of God. However the *Koran* is believed by Muslims to be the *literal* word of God — Mohammed was simply the mouthpiece. Thus Muslims claim greater spiritual authenticity for the *Koran* and Islam.[34] "Muslims revere the *Koran*, and its Arabic is thought to be unsurpassed in purity and beauty."[35]

The *Koran* consists of 114 chapters or *suras* of varying length. The suras are typically arranged, not in chronological order, but in order of decreasing length with the longest sura at the beginning. A Westerner can often find little to appreciate in literal translations of the *Koran*. British historian and author Thomas Carlyle (1795–1881) had a low opinion of the *Koran*'s literary merits. "I must say, it is as toilsome reading as I ever undertook. A wearisome confused jumble, crude, incondite; endless iterations, long windedness, entanglement; most crude, incondite; — insupportable stupidity, in short! Nothing but a sense of duty could carry any European through the *Koran*."[36]

Carlyle's criticisms may have been sincere, but perhaps unfair. The *Koran* was never intended as a literary work. Muslims consider that it is impossible to properly translate the *Koran*. The *Koran* is lyric poetry that can only be appreciated when recited in the original Arabic. "Translations into other languages are viewed as violating the matchless character of the holy book."[37]

One of the *Koran*'s translators, Muhammad M. Pickthall (1875–1936) explained. "The *Qur'an* cannot be translated ... the result [of my translation] is not the Glorious *Qur'an*, that inimitable symphony, the very sounds of which move men to tears and ecstasy. It is only an attempt to present the meaning of the *Qur'an* — and peradventure something of the charm — in English. It can never take the place of the *Qur'an* in Arabic, nor is it meant to do so."[38]

CONFLICTS IN MECCA

At first, Mohammed's revelations were confined to his immediate family and friends. But after three years he began to preach publicly. Mohammed's essential message was a strict monotheism: there is only one God, Allah. He is the all-powerful Creator of the Universe, God of the Arabs, Jews, and Christians. There is both a judgment day and an afterlife, a heaven and a hell. Man's fundamental duty is to submit to the will of God; this submission became the basis of a new religion, *Islam*. Adherents to Islam were known as *Muslims*. Monotheism is expressed succinctly in Sura 112.

> Say: He is God alone:
> God the eternal!
> He begetteth not, and He is not begotten;
> And there is none like unto Him.[39]

Part of Mohammed's message was non-controversial. After all, Allah had traditionally been recognized as the head of a plethora of Arabic deities. What was not well-received was Mohammed's absolute monotheism: he demanded that his contemporaries abjure from worshipping any god but Allah. "The enemies of the new faith ... were, for the most part, simply men of the world who, proud of their social position, objected to recognizing the claims of an upstart and dreaded any sweeping change as likely to endanger the material advantages they derived from the traditional cult."[40] Mohammed was opposed by a "mercantile aristocracy,"[41] that viewed Islam as a threat to their status and income.

At first, fellow tribe members treated Mohammed with scorn and ridicule. As time passed, more people began to convert to Islam and the debate became more serious and polarizing. A delegation of influential tribe members complained to Mohammed's uncle. "We have asked you to put a stop to your nephew's activities, but you have not done so. By God, we cannot endure that our fathers should be reviled, our customs mocked, and our gods insulted."[42]

There followed an emotional scene between the Prophet and his uncle. The uncle asked his nephew to desist, but Mohammed was obstinate. He told his uncle that he would not stop. "If they brought the Sun to my right hand, and the Moon to my left, to force me from my undertaking, verily, I would not desist therefrom until the Lord made manifest my cause, or I perished in the attempt."[43] Mohammed then burst into tears and turned to depart. Seeing the depth of Mohammed's conviction, the uncle relented and promised to remain faithful to his nephew forever.[44]

The central shrine of pre–Islamic worship in Arabia was a curious cube-shaped building in Mecca named the *Kaaba*. It continues today to be viewed by Muslims as the holiest place on earth. The Kaaba is not a perfect cube; its dimensions are 40 by 35 by 50 feet [12.2 by 10.7 by 15.2 meters]. According to Muslim legend, the Kaaba was originally constructed by the first man on Earth, Adam.[45] The *Koran* (Sura 2) states that the Kaaba was rebuilt by Abraham, the Father of the Jews. "Abraham, with Ismael, raised the foundations of the House."[46]

The most holy object in the Kaaba was a black stone (perhaps a meteorite) that was said to have been given to Adam after his expulsion from the Garden of Eden. According to legend, the stone was originally white but had been turned black over the centuries by absorbing the sins of petitioners who touched it. "The black stone, according to the Mahometans, was brought down from heaven by Gabriel at the creation of the world, and was originally of a white color; but contracted the blackness that now appears on it from the guilt of these sins committed by the sons of men."[47] The stone in the Kaaba was described by John Lewis Burckhardt (1784–1817) in the early nineteenth century.

> It is an irregular oval, about seven inches in diameter, with an undulated surface, composed of about a dozen smaller stones of different sizes and shapes, well joined together with a small quantity of cement, and perfectly smoothed ... it is very difficult to determine accurately the quality of this stone, which has been worn to its present surface by the millions of touches and kisses it has received. It appeared to me like a lava, containing several small extraneous particles, of a whitish and of a yellowish substance. Its color is now of a deep reddish brown.[48]

For one month a year, Arabs who made a pilgrimage to Mecca to enter the Kaaba and touch the black stone were guaranteed safe passage throughout the land. The Meccans derived a significant economic benefit from the annual pilgrimage, and thus were jealous of preserving not only the Kaaba but also the polytheistic idols and rituals associated with it.

One day, while Mohammed was visiting the Kaaba, he overheard a group of men criticizing him. He walked up to them and made an eerie prophecy. "By him who holds my life in His hand I bring you slaughter."[49] The hearers were stunned. They remained silent, until one of them reminded Mohammed that he was not a violent man and that perhaps he should just leave peacefully.[50]

Mohammed's preaching of Islam was leading to the development of a serious schism in the Quraysh tribe. A final attempt was made to bring about a peaceful resolution. The most powerful of the clan leaders amongst the Quraysh tribe called a meeting. At the meeting, they offered to make Mohammed either the most powerful or richest man in Mecca if he would simply stop proselytizing and abandon his religious mission.[51]

However, it proved impossible to bridge the gap between the two parties. The outcome was predictable enough: there could be no compromise with the Prophet of God. Mohammed's fellow tribe members could either accept the message of God, or reject it and be subject to God's justice. One of the clan leaders replied that he would never accept Mohammed as a prophet. "I will never believe in you until you get a ladder to the sky, and mount up it until you come to it, while I am looking on, and until four angels shall come with you, testifying that you are speaking the truth, and by God, even if you did that I do not think I should believe you."[52]

Another man took a piece of bone and used it to challenge Mohammed's belief in resurrection. He asked if Mohammed believed God could bring the dead bone back to life. Then he crumbled the bone in his hand and insultingly blew the dust into the Prophet's face. Mohammed answered, "God will raise it and you, after you have become like this. Then God will send you to Hell."[53]

THE SATANIC VERSES

It was during this period of time in Mecca that the most controversial episode in the history of Mohammed and Islam occurred. Mohammed was under tremendous pressure to accept a peaceful compromise with the polytheistic members of his tribe. Accordingly, he had a revelation that it was allowed to worship not only Allah, but also three lesser female deities known as *banat al–Lab*, the Daughters of God.[54] A verse was added to the *Koran*. "These are the exalted Females, And verily their Intercession is to be hoped for."[55] The alienated members of the Quraysh were delighted. Mohammed had recognized their goddesses, and thus honored their traditions.

However, it was soon revealed to Mohammed that he had erred: the verses allowing polytheism had not come from God through the angel Gabriel, but instead had been inspired by Satan. Gabriel appeared to Mohammed and admonished him. "What is this that thou hast done? thou hast repeated before the people words that I never gave unto thee."[56]

The offending script became known as the "Satanic Verses."[57] They were expunged from the *Koran* and new verses substituted. The modified version of the *Koran* was uncompromising in its monotheism. Lesser deities were characterized as "mere names," products of human imagination. Those who worshipped them did so as a result of their own conceit and impulses. "These are mere names: ye and our fathers named them thus: God hath not sent down any warranty in their regard. A mere conceit and their own impulses do they follow."[58]

The affair of the Satanic Verses cuts right to the heart of Islam. The cornerstone of the Islamic religion is that the *Koran* is the authentic, unexpurgated word of God. If the authenticity of any one verse is questionable then the entire book falls into doubt. If Mohammed could be fooled once, there can be no assurance that he did not error repeatedly.

MIRACLES

Like Jesus, the story of Mohammed's life is adorned by miracles. These apocryphal and miraculous stories are derived from an oral tradition, and are absent in the *Koran* itself. Jesus turned water into wine,[59] walked on water,[60] raised the dead,[61] and multiplied the fish and loaves.[62]

Among the incredible stories associated with Mohammed is the story that a tree walked up to him, and then back again.[63] The presence of Mohammed as a child made camel udders swell with milk, while those of the neighbors' camels were empty.[64] And the Prophet could produce rain through prayer.[65] But the best known of the miracles are Mohammed's night trip to Jerusalem and his ascent to heaven.

One night Mohammed was raised from his sleep by the angel Gabriel. Gabriel took him by the arm and led him out the door where a winged donkey awaited them. They mounted the donkey and rode on its back, each leap of the animal traversing a distance from horizon to horizon. The winged donkey transported them to the Temple of the Jews in Jerusalem where they were met by a group of deceased prophets, including Abraham, Moses, and Jesus. Mohammed led them all in prayer. Two jugs were brought to Mohammed, one containing wine, the other milk. He chose to drink the milk, and Gabriel informed him that he had made the right decision, for "wine is forbidden to you."[66]

After the conclusion of his business in Jerusalem, Mohammed ascended that same night through the seven levels of heaven, again escorted by the angel Gabriel. Their entrance to the first level of heaven was by means of the Gate of the Watchers whose entry was guarded by the angel Isma'il. Isma'il had twelve-thousand angels under his command, and each of these in turn had twelve-thousand angels under their command. Mohammed also was introduced to the angel Malik, keeper of the gates of Hell. To satisfy Mohammed's curiosity, Malik opened the gates of hell. Mohammed said "the flames blazed high into the air until I thought that they would consume everything."[67]

As Mohammed watched, the spirits of deceased men flew through the heavenly gate where they were partitioned into good and evil by Adam. Mohammed also witnessed the fate of various categories of infidels and sinners. Usurers, "maddened by thirst," were "cast into hell."[68] Women who had cheated on their husbands and given birth to bastards were hung by their breasts.[69]

The ascension continued to the highest level, the seventh heaven. Sitting on a throne at the gate to God's mansion was Abraham, father of both the Jews and Arabs. After viewing Abraham, Mohammed said that he had never seen a man who more closely resembled himself. During Mohammed's audience with God, a duty of reciting fifty prayers a day was laid upon him and his followers. However after repeated requests for leniency, the number of prayers required daily was reduced to five.[70]

THE HEGIRA, A.D. 622

Ten years after Mohammed's first visit from the angel Gabriel (c. A.D. 619), his wife, Khadija, died. The same year, Mohammed's uncle also passed away.[71] Mohammed and Islam were at a watershed. After ten years of proselytizing, Mohammed had only found a handful of converts. No citizen of any note had been converted for the past three or four years.[72]

Mohammed realized the necessity of taking his mission to another city in Arabia. Mecca was perhaps the most unreceptive city in all of Arabia for Islam. It was the home of the Kaaba, a sacred pagan shrine, and the city's inhabitants had an economic interest in preserving paganism with its accompanying ritual of an annual pilgrimage to Mecca.

Seeking a more favorable venue, Mohammed traveled to the nearby oasis of Taif, about 75 miles (121 kilometers) southeast of Mecca. The reception there was at first cold, then hostile. After ten days, Mohammed was thrown out of town and pursued by an angry, stone-throwing mob. His legs were injured, and a companion who attempted to shield him received a serious blow to his head.[73] Eventually finding sanctuary, Mohammed prayed. "Oh Lord! I make my complaint unto Thee of the feebleness of my strength, and the poverty of my expedients; and of my insignificance before Mankind."[74]

Within two months of Khadija's death, Mohammed remarried. Shortly thereafter, he also undertook the contractual obligation of marrying a girl named Ayesha, the younger daughter of his close friend and successor, Abu Bakr. Ayesha at this time was no older than six or seven; "the real marriage with her took place not more than three years afterwards."[75]

Mohammed continued to search for a new home for himself and his followers. During the annual pilgrimage to Mecca, he was successful in negotiating with a delegation of tribal leaders from the city of Yathrib, a city later renamed Medina, the "city of the prophet." Medina was ruled by two Arab tribes at odds with each other.[76] The hostilities had erupted into open warfare a few years earlier and the tribes now co-existed in an uneasy stalemate. Both sides wanted peace but could not trust each other. In Mohammed they saw an outside arbiter that could restore the peace everyone desired.[77]

Three Jewish tribes also lived in Medina. An acquaintance with the monotheism of the Jews had prepared the Arabs in Medina for the acceptance of Islam. On his part, Mohammed believed that the Jews would welcome him. Jews were monotheists, and Judaism had a long tradition of prophecy.

Mohammed arrived in Medina on A.D. September 20, 622.[78] The migration of Mohammed and his followers, the *Hegira*, is the most important event in the history of Islam. It marks the beginning of the Islamic calendar and was the turning point in Mohammed's life. Islam now took a distinctly different turn from Christianity. According to Ibn Ishaq (c. A.D. 702–768), "the most important source for the biography of the prophet Mohammed,"[79] God now "gave permission to His apostle [Mohammed] to fight."[80] Whereas formerly Mohammed's mission was to call men to God while enduring insults and maltreatment, he was now to embark on a holy war or *jihad*.

It was at Medina that the fateful enmity between Jews and Muslims began. The relationship began with the best expectations, but both parties found the reality to be very different from their hopes. Mohammed had hoped that the Jews would be receptive to his message. The Hebrews had a long tradition of prophets and they both worshipped the same God. Mohammed went so far as to incorporate a Jewish ritual into Islam by requiring that Muslims face Jerusalem during their daily prayers. The Jews in turn had high expectations for Mohammed. They knew him by reputation to be someone who had respect for their scriptures and God.

Both the Muslims and Jews were bitterly disappointed. Mohammed considered himself to be a prophet of God, but the Jews regarded the age of the prophecy as over. "They absolutely refused to acknowledge him [Mohammed] as a prophet."[81] If anything, the Jews in Medina came to regard Mohammed as a blasphemer. It didn't help matters that Mohammed succeeded where the rabbis had failed. The Arabs in Medina had never converted to the Jewish religion, but Mohammed was remarkably successful at converting them to an Arabic monotheism.

> The Jews looked on in amazement at the people, whom they had in vain endeavored for generations to convince of the errors of polytheism and to dissuade from the abominations of idolatry, suddenly and of their own accord casting away their idols, and professing belief in the one true God. The secret lay in the adaptation of the instrument. Judaism, foreign in its growth, touched few Arab sympathies; Islam, grafted upon the faith, the superstition, the customs, the nationality of the Peninsula, gained ready access to every heart.[82]

Mohammed had little patience with the subtle theological disputations the Jewish rabbis were fond of. Illiterate, he was completely unprepared for participation in scholarly discussions of theological issues. When a group of Jews asked Mohammed "who created Allah," he became visibly angry.[83]

The hostility that developed between Mohammed and the Jews is evidenced in the *Koran*. In Sura 2.87, the Jews' rejection of Mohammed as a prophet is compared to the historical rejection of their own prophets. "Why, therefore, have ye killed the Prophets of God aforetime, if ye are Believers? And verily Moses came with evident signs; then ye took the Calf thereupon, and became transgressors."[84] The *Koran* (Sura 5.86) goes so far as to equate Jews with pagan idolaters. "Of all men thou wilt certainly find the Jews, and those who join other gods with God, to be the most intense in hatred of those who believe."[85]

No peaceful coexistence was possible between the Jews and Muslims. "Mahomet soon found that there was no possibility of compromising with them [Jews] on religious questions.... He therefore resolved on their extermination. His ruthlessness in their case ... was consistent with his principle (always faithfully observed) that no inquiry was permissible into the motives of conversion, and with his division of mankind into the two antagonistic factions: Believers and Unbelievers."[86] Ironically, the most substantive parts of Mohammed's doctrine, monotheism, prophecy, resurrection, and the existence of heaven and hell, were derived from Jewish scriptures.

JIHAD

Seven months after he arrived at Medina, Mohammed and his followers began to raid the caravans traveling to and from Mecca.[87] Their motivations were purely pecuniary. Finding that they were not able to engage in their normal economic activities, the exiled Meccans quickly became impoverished.

The first three attempts at raiding were unsuccessful. In the first two cases, the parties lacked the courage to engage, and in the third instance the Muslims failed to find the caravan they sought. Mohammed led the next three raids in person, but they also failed. The leaders of the caravans had been evading raiders for centuries and were not easily taken.[88]

Frustrated, Mohammed hit upon a desperate and risky plan. The Arabs had a holy month, Rajab, during which raiding was forbidden. "As raiding during such a season was unknown, success was practically certain."[89] Mohammed intended to break the taboo. He sent seven followers out into the desert with sealed instructions. After the two days travel, the instructions were opened. The Muslims were ordered to proceed with a caravan raid even though it was taboo. However no one who had conscientious objections was to be forced to participate. All seven Muslims decided to press forward with the raid and they captured a considerable amount of booty. During the raid, one of the caravan traders was killed. The killing was a much more serious crime than the theft of goods.[90]

The Meccans were outraged, both at the timing of the attack and the murder. Full scale warfare erupted. To convince Muslims to participate in the holy war, new verses were added to the *Koran*. "And fight for the cause of God against those who fight against you: but commit not the injustice of attacking them first: God loveth not such injustice: And kill them wherever ye shall find them, and eject them from whatever place they have ejected you; for civil discord is worse than carnage: yet attack them not at the sacred Mosque, unless they attack you therein; but if they attack you, slay them. Such is the reward of the infidels."[91]

Although historical facts appear to implicate Muslims as the aggressors, in their view the original aggression had been their forced emigration and expulsion from Mecca. The war was thus justified. A new verse in the *Koran* excused fighting during the holy month. "They will ask thee concerning war in the Sacred Month. Say: To war therein is bad, but to turn aside from the cause of God, and to have no faith in Him, and in the Sacred Temple, and to drive out its people, is worse in the sight of God."[92]

Infidels who perished were condemned to hell.

> Hell truly shall be a place of snares.
> The home of transgressors,
> To abide therein ages;
> No coolness shall they taste therein nor any drink,
> Save boiling water and running sores.[93]

But Muslims who died in battle were promised entrance into paradise. Awaiting them there were well-proportioned virgins and other delights.

> But, for the God-fearing is a blissful abode,
> Enclosed gardens and vineyards;
> And damsels with swelling breasts, their peers in age,
> And a full cup.[94]

A picture of the Paradise which is promised to the God-fearing! Therein are rivers of water, which corrupt not: rivers of milk, whose taste changeth not: and rivers of wine, delicious to those who quaff it; And rivers of honey clarified: and therein are all kinds of fruit for them from their Lord![95]

At first, the skirmishes were light. But within two years the raids had grown in to a full scale war. The first major engagement occurred at Badr in A.D. 624. Although badly outnumbered, 300 Muslims defeated 1000 men from Mecca that had been sent to protect a caravan.[96] The Muslim victory in part can be attributed to their greater willingness to fight. "The Moslems, though the aggressors, were hardened by the memory of former injuries, by the maxim that their faith severed all earthly ties without the circle of Islam, and by a fierce fanaticism for their Prophet's cause."[97]

The battle "ended in a complete victory for Mahomet."[98] The Muslims killed about seventy of the Meccans, and took an additional seventy men prisoner. Fourteen Muslims died.[99] Among those killed at Badr was Abu Jahl, one of Mohammed's foremost enemies from Mecca. Mohammed's servant, Abdallah, found Abu Jahl laying on the ground, badly wounded. The servant hurriedly sliced off the head of his master's enemy and brought it to Mohammed.[100] When the Prophet saw the great gift he exclaimed, "The head of the enemy of God! It is more acceptable to me than the choicest camel in all Arabia."[101]

The bodies of the enemy dead were cast into a hastily-dug pit. Mohammed taunted the dead. "O people of the pit, have you found that what God threatened is true? For I have found that what my Lord promised me is true."[102]

Six of the prisoners taken by the Muslims were executed. Presumably these were enemies of long standing whom Mohammed could not hope to convert to Islam. One execution in particular is infamous:

> About half-way to Medina, Ocba, another prisoner, was ordered out for execution. He ventured to expostulate, and demand why he should be treated more rigorously than the other captives. "Because of thy enmity to God and to his Prophet," replied Mahomet. "And my little girl!" cried Ocba, in the bitterness of his soul, — "who will take care of her?" — "Hell-fire!" exclaimed the heartless conqueror; and on the instant his victim was hewn to the ground. "Wretch that he was!" continued Mahomet, "and persecutor! Unbeliever in God, in his Prophet, and in his Book! I give thanks unto the Lord that hath slain thee, and comforted mine eyes thereby."[103]

The remainder of the captives were held for ransom. Mohammed's victory at Badr against three-to-one odds provided Islam with an irresistible momentum. The facts of the battle seemed to suggest that the Prophet's claim of divine intervention was justified. The few opponents who had been killed or taken captive included many of Mohammed's most influential and stubborn enemies.[104]

Back in Medina, Mohammed consolidated his power. He "ventured on a series of high-handed measures which struck terror into all his opponents. Several persons who had offended him were assassinated by his order."[105] A woman who had been an outspoken critic was murdered in her bed. As she lay sleeping with her baby at her breast, an assassin pulled the infant from her and plunged his knife through her chest so hard it protruded from her back.[106]

Apprehensive as to whether or not the killing had been justified, the next morning the murderer asked Mohammed if he had anything to worry about. "Don't worry about it," the Prophet reassured him, "two goats will not knock their heads together for it."[107]

Within a month of the victory at Badr, a Jewish tribe in Medina was besieged by the Muslims and sent into exile. Shortly thereafter, Mohammed gave Muslims permission to kill any Jew they ran into without reason. "The apostle said, 'kill any Jew that falls into your power.'"[108] One Muslim, Muheiasa, took Mohammed at his word. He killed "a Jewish merchant with whom they had social and business relations,"[109] and appropriated the dead man's wealth. When Muheiasa's older brother, Huweisa, heard of the murder, he was outraged, and began to beat his younger sibling. Muheiasa assured his brother that he would kill him also if the Prophet commanded. Impressed by his brother's earnestness, Huweisa proclaimed "verily it is a wonderful Faith," and converted to Islam on the spot.[110]

CHRISTIAN PERCEPTIONS OF ISLAM

Stories relating the violent beginnings of Islam are often not well received by Christians, whose religious model is Jesus. Jesus advised "resist not evil: but whosoever shall smite thee on thy right cheek, turn to him the other also."[111] "Muhammad was much maligned by medieval Christian writers as part of their distorted image of Islam in general, and was held to be lecherous, treacherous, and an impostor."[112] Christianity and Islam, of course, are mutually exclusive belief systems.[113]

William Muir (1819–1905), whose work I have relied upon and quoted extensively, was a Christian and a decidedly hostile source. In the third volume of his *Life of Mahomet*, Muir wrote in reference to Muslims, "The strong religious impulse, under which they always acted, untempered as it was by the divine graces and heaven-born morality of the Christian faith, hurried them into excesses of barbarous treachery."[114] William Muir was also the author of this infamous quote: "The sword of Mahomet, and the Coran, are the most fatal enemies of Civilization, Liberty, and Truth, which the world has yet known."[115]

Muir's scholarship is intelligible, because he openly expressed his bias. It is also meticulous and impressive. The first chapter of the first volume of *Life of Mahomet*, one hundred and five pages in length, is dedicated to a discussion of original sources.[116] Despite Muir's hostile opinions, I am not aware of any claims that the *Life of Mahomet* is factually inaccurate. For example, the stories of the execution of Ocba and the taunting of the dead in the pit after the battle of Badr are also found in Martin Ling's biography of Mohammed.[117] Ling was a practicing Muslim and his biography of Mohammed "won a number of prizes in the Muslim world."[118]

All historians have biases; all have perspectives. It is important to understand what an author's perspective is. But to condemn a writer for having a perspective can only be done from the viewpoint of a hostile perspective. Thus such a condemnation is self-contradictory and unintelligible as an honest standard of scholarship. I am unaware of any historian who suggests that Herodotus should not be used as a source because he wrote from a pro–Greek perspective. Bias in historiography is not a sin unless "it cannot be recognized."[119]

Neither is the bloody history of Islam unique. No faith has an unblemished history of extending charity to the enemies of God. When Christian Crusaders captured Jerusalem in A.D. 1099, they massacred virtually all the Muslims and Jews. According to ibn al–Athir (1160–1233), "for a week, the Franks continued to slaughter the Muslims ... in the Aqsa Mosque the Franks killed more than 70,000."[120] "The Jews of Jerusalem were crowded into their synagogues and burned."[121] "The slaughter was terrible; the blood of the conquered ran down the streets, until men splashed in blood as they rode."[122] Raymond of Aguilers claimed that "men rode in blood up to their knees and bridle reins."[123] This was no doubt an exaggeration, but nevertheless an indication of terrible mayhem.

The violence of the Crusades was not limited to the Middle East. In Europe, there were malicious pogroms against Jews. "Other swarms [of Crusaders], under nameless leaders, issued from Germany and France, more brutal and frantic than any that had preceded them.... They wore the symbol of the Crusade upon their shoulders, but inveighed against the folly of proceeding to the Holy Land to destroy the Turks, while they left behind them so many Jews, the still more inveterate enemies of Christ. They swore fierce vengeance against this unhappy race, and murdered all the Hebrews they could lay their hands on, first subjecting them to the most horrible mutilation."[124]

To the atrocities committed under the banner of Christianity we could add the Inquisition, the Witch Mania, and the infamous *Malleus Maleficarum* (*Hammer of the Witches*),[125] first published in A.D. 1487.

Nor are the hands of the Jews clean. God gave the Hebrews license to destroy their enemies and plunder their cities. "Thou shalt smite them, and utterly destroy them; thou shalt make no covenant with them, nor show mercy unto them."[126] "But of the cities of these people, which the Lord thy God doth give thee for an inheritance, thou shalt save alive nothing that breatheth: But thou shalt utterly destroy them; namely, the Hittites, and the Amorites, the Canaanites, and the Perizzites, the Hivites, and the Jebusites; as the LORD thy God hath commanded thee."[127]

Nevertheless, there are undeniable differences between Christianity and Islam. Christianity is focused on forgiveness, charity, and mercy, with a side dressing of apocalyptic visions, Hell, and the wrath of God. Islam is centered on justice and the destruction of unbelievers. Allah is merciful — but not to infidels. The early history of Christianity is one of persecution and martyrdom. Jesus himself submitted to crucifixion. In contrast, Islam was not born in submission and earnest entreaty, but in warfare against the enemies of God.

Consider how Jesus and Mohammed handled what was essentially the same problem. When an adulteress was brought before Jesus for judgment, the sentence dictated by Mosaic Law was death by stoning. "And the man that committeth adultery with another man's wife, even he that committeth adultery with his neighbor's wife, the adulterer and the adulteress shall surely be put to death."[128]

Jesus said, "He that is without sin among you, let him first cast a stone at her."[129] Embarrassed, the accusers dropped their rocks and walked away. Jesus told the accused woman to go home and repent.

But when a man and a woman who had committed adultery (with each other) were brought before Mohammed, he exclaimed "stone them," and the pair was executed. The Prophet explained his decision to invoke the punishment proscribed in the *Old Testament*, "I am the first to revive the order of God and His book and to practice it."[130]

Christians tend to attribute greater spiritual authenticity to Christianity because of its emphasis on mercy and forgiveness. But a careful and objective reading of the *Bible* reveals the God of the Christians to be as unrelenting as Allah in His condemnation of unbelievers. In *Luke*, Jesus described how a rich man in Hell was cruelly tortured by being burned: "I am tormented in this flame."[131] In the parable of the wheat and the tares, Jesus proclaimed that at the Last Judgment God would send out angels to gather the "children of the wicked one" and "cast them into a furnace of fire."[132]

BATTLE OF OHOD, A.D. 625

Eager to revenge their defeat at Badr, the next year (about A.D. 625) the Meccans raised a formidable army of 3,000 men to attack Mohammed and the Muslims at their home base in Medina.[133] The Muslims rode out to meet them with an army of 700 near Mt. Ohod.[134] At first, the Muslims gained the upper hand by virtue of their greater enthusiasm and religious zealotry.[135] However their position was seriously weakened when a detachment of archers abandoned their posts prematurely to plunder the enemy's camp and baggage.[136]

The Meccans immediately took advantage of the opportunity. They gathered their cavalry, swept around the Muslim's unguarded flank, and attacked them in the rear.[137] The Muslim position was thrown into disarray by the surprise attack from behind and the Meccans managed to press the attack to the Prophet himself. One of the Meccans struck Mohammed in the head with his sword, and the apostle fell to the ground stunned.[138] The attacker erroneously concluded that he had killed Mohammed. In truth the Prophet was only momentarily stunned and the bloody wound was superficial. Mohammed's followers led him to safety and the Meccans were left in sole possession of the battleground.

The Meccans now made a fatal mistake that changed the course of history. Instead of pursuing their advantage to the death of Mohammed and the occupation of Medina they declared themselves properly revenged for the defeat at Badr and turned to go home.[139]

After interpreting the victory at Badr as evidence that God was on his side, Mohammed was pressed to explain the defeat at Medina. "The success at Badr had been assumed as a proof of divine support; and, by parity of reasoning, the defeat at Ohod was subversive of the prophetic claim ... it required all the address of Mahomet to avert the dangerous imputation, sustain the credit of his cause, and reanimate his followers."[140]

Mohammed told his followers that the defeat at the battle of Ohod was God's way of testing them. Sura 3 of the *Koran* reads, "we alternate these days of successes and reverses among men, that God may know those who have believed ... and that God may test those who believe."[141]

Miraculously surviving an apparent debacle, Mohammed spent the next few years further consolidating his power. Another Jewish tribe who had lived near Medina for generations was forced into exile. "Muhammad expelled the Jewish tribes of Medina one by one, confiscating the possessions of one tribe, massacring the males of another."[142] "The Jews showed themselves wholly incapable of combining in order to resist him."[143] Caught in a desperate struggle for survival, religious plurality and toleration were luxuries Mohammed could not afford. The expulsion of one Jewish tribe was celebrated in the *Koran* (Sura 59). "He it is who caused the unbelievers among the people of the Book [Jews] to quit their homes and join those who had emigrated previously."[144]

Six or seven years after Khadija's death, Mohammed had comforted himself with five new wives but desired even more.[145] One day he visited his adopted son, Zeid, and was smitten with the man's wife, Zeinab. Zeid offered to accommodate the Prophet by divorcing Zeinab, but Mohammed told him to keep his wife and fear God.[146]

Zeid proceeded nonetheless with the divorce. Perhaps his wife was infatuated with the Prophet and the marriage ruined. Mohammed hesitated to bind the woman to him. Even though she was now divorced, it would still be a scandal for him to marry the former spouse of his own adopted son. However the union was soon sanctioned by divine revelation and the authority inscribed in the *Koran*. "And when Zaid [Zeid] had settled concerning her to divorce her, we married her to thee, that it might not be a crime in the faithful to marry the wives of their adopted sons, when they have settled the affair concerning them. And the behest of God is to be performed."[147]

However Mohammed's wives were forbidden to remarry, even after the Prophet's death. "And ye must not trouble the Apostle of God, nor marry his wives, after him, for ever. This would be a grave offence with God."[148]

Reviewing these passages of the *Koran* from the perspective of a nineteenth-century British Christian, William Muir (1819–1905) concluded that the revelations transcribed by Mohammed seemed to conveniently endorse the Prophet's own lascivious desires. "Our only matter of wonder is, that the Revelations of Mahomet continued after this to be regarded by his people as inspired communications from the Almighty, when they were so palpably formed to secure his own objects, and pander even to his evil desires."[149]

SIEGE OF MEDINA, A.D. 627

In A.D. 627, the Meccans and their allies undertook another offensive against the Muslims in Medina. They put together a formidable army of 10,000 men.[150] "This time the intention of the leaders was undoubtedly to stamp out Islam."[151] Mohammed obtained advance knowledge of the impending attack and deployed a defensive strategy heretofore unknown in Arabia.

Part of Medina was already walled in by an unbroken stretch of stone houses built adjacent to one another. To complete the defense, a deep trench was dug around the city.[152] "The apostle ... drew a trench about Medina."[153] The Meccans were baffled and frustrated by the trenchwork — they had never seen anything like it. Attempts were made to broach the defense at selected points, but the attacks were repulsed. The attackers grew discouraged; they had not anticipated a long siege. The Meccans attempted to breach the trench, "but all their endeavors were without effect. The trench was not crossed; and during the whole operation Mahomet lost only five men."[154] After fifteen days, the aggressors gave up the assault and walked away.[155]

MASSACRE OF THE JEWS

During the Siege of Medina, a nearby Jewish tribe, the Coreitza, had unwisely decided to abandon their former allegiance with Mohammed and align themselves with the attackers. When the Meccans and other allies dispersed, "the Jews who still remained in Medina [were left] to the summary vengeance of the Prophet."[156] Mohammed proceeded immediately to exact revenge for the betrayal. He marched with three thousand men and besieged the Coreitza's village.[157] After fourteen days, the Jews surrendered.[158]

The Muslims separated men from women and children, and bound the men's hands behind their backs.[159] To decide the fate of the Jews, Mohammed picked a man who had been grievously wounded during the battle of the trenches. The sentence the aggrieved warrior passed was that "the men should be killed, the property divided, and the women and children taken as captives."[160]

The Muslims proceeded to execute their Jewish captives in an efficient manner. "The Prophet ordered trenches, long and deep and narrow, to be dug in the market-place. The [Jewish] men, about seven hundred in all ... were sent for in small groups, and every group was made to sit alongside the trench that was to be his grave. Then [the Muslims] ... cut off their heads."[161] Mohammed himself picked out a particularly attractive young Jewish girl and took her as a concubine.[162] "She was a woman of great beauty and she remained the Prophet's slave."[163]

The battle of the trenches and subsequent massacre of the Jews was commemorated in the *Koran*. "And God drove back the infidels in their wrath; they won no advantage; God sufficed the faithful in the fight: for God is Strong, Mighty! And He caused those of the people of the Book [the Jews], who had aided the confederates, to come down out of their fortresses, and cast dismay into their hearts: some ye slew, others ye took prisoners."[164]

An incident that occurred shortly thereafter (c. A.D. 627–628) is the source of the *Koran*'s endorsement of amputation of the hands as a proper penalty for theft. Eight Bedouin stole some camels and cruelly murdered one of the herdsmen who tried to stop the theft. The Bedouin took the poor shepherd, cut off his hands and legs, and then pierced his tongue and eyes with thorns until he perished. Mohammed had the murderers pursued and arrested. He ordered their arms and legs to be amputated and their eyes to be gouged out. The trunks of the mutilated men were then impaled on spikes on the floor of the desert until they expired.[165]

Mohammed appears to have later concluded this method of execution was too extreme. Accordingly, he received a revelation that the only permissible means of execution were simple slayings (presumably by decapitation) or crucifixion. Gouging of the eyes was disallowed, but amputation of the hands and feet was endorsed. The revelation was recorded in the *Koran*. "As to the thief, whether man or woman, cut ye off their hands in recompense for their doings."[166] "Only, the recompense of those who war against God and his Apostle, and go about to commit disorders on the earth, shall be that they shall be slain or crucified, or have their alternate hands and feet cut off, or be banished [from] the land."[167]

CONQUEST OF MECCA

For six years the Muslims had been exiled from Mecca. For six years, Mohammed and the others had not been able to make the annual pilgrimage to Mecca, or visit the ancient shrine of the Kaaba.[168]

Mohammed resolved to force the issue. He put on the dress of a pilgrim and set forth with 1,500 followers during the holy month when warfare was forbidden. The safety of Mohammed and Muslims was provided for by the Meccan's own self-interest. Attacking the Muslims would ruin the guarantee of safe passage during pilgrimage, and the number of future pilgrims would be decreased, as would the revenues of Meccan merchants. In short, the Meccans did not want to ruin their profitable tourist trade.

The Meccans were suspicious of Mohammed's motives and suspected treachery. They refused entrance to the city, but the confrontation was turned into an opportunity to conclude a peace treaty. The terms of the treaty were that neither side was to initiate hostilities for a period of ten years, and that uncommitted individuals were free to convert to Islam or not. The Muslims were to depart from Mecca this year, but would be allowed entrance the following year.[169]

It was a complete victory for Mohammed and Islam. Six years ago, he had been a rebellious exile, now he had achieved a standing equal to the Meccan establishment. The ten years of peace was an opportunity for him gain additional converts and further increase the power and status of Islam.

Having made a temporary peace with Mecca, Mohammed turned his attention again to his old enemies, the Jews. He set forth from Medina with an army of sixteen-hundred men to attack Jewish settlements at Kheibar, about 100 miles (161 kilometers) from Medina. The Muslims met opposition at the citadel of Camuss, but defeated their foes with a loss of only nineteen men while killing ninety-three Jews.

The campaign successfully cemented Mohammed's control over every Jewish tribe north of Medina and the spoils of war were tremendous.[170] "The plunder of Kheibar was rich beyond all previous experience. Besides vast stores of dates, oil, honey, and barley, flocks of sheep and herds of camels, the spoil in treasure and jewels was very large. A fifth of the whole was as usual set apart for the use of the Prophet."[171]

In most cases Jews were left in control of their land, but a yearly tax of fifty percent of their annual production was now assessed. Later, when Muslims wanted the land for themselves, the Jewish landowners were forced into exile and their property stolen. Mohammed began a process of ethnic cleansing that continued after his death.[172]

In February of A.D. 629, Mohammed and two-thousand followers made the pilgrimage to Mecca and entered peacefully. In the Kaaba, Mohammed touched the sacred Black Stone, and then rode his camel around the shrine seven times, accompanied by his disciples. He then sacrificed sixty camels and shaved his head.

During his three days in Mecca, Mohammed also arranged for yet another marriage, bringing the total number of his wives to ten.[173] Mohammed's pilgrimage removed one of the Meccans' most substantive objections to Islam. They saw that under Islam the pilgrimage and the Kaaba would be preserved, as would the profits to be derived from them.

In December of A.D. 629, Mohammed received the excuse he needed to abrogate his peace treaty with Mecca and complete his conquest of Arabia. Two minor tribes, one allied with Mecca, the other with Mohammed, had fought. However, the tribe allied with Mecca had received assistance in the form of participation by several Meccans. Mohammed, perhaps rightfully, interpreted this to be an attack upon him and he called upon all of his alliances.

A massive army of eight to ten thousand was assembled and made camp on the hills outside Mecca. Mohammed ordered that ten-thousand campfires be lit so as to intimidate the Meccans with the sheer size of his army. The plan worked. The next day the city capitulated. When Mohammed entered the gates of Mecca there was only scattered fighting. The will of the opposition had been broken.[174]

Upon his victorious entry into Mecca, Mohammed immediately went to the Kaaba and had all images and statues of idols removed and destroyed.[175] Idols held in private homes were also destroyed. In general, Mohammed was gracious and magnanimous in his victory. A general amnesty was declared, the only exceptions being perhaps a dozen implacable foes.[176] There were some anticlimactic battles with Bedouin tribes in the days that followed, but Mohammed was now essentially in complete control of Arabia.

Mohammed's final days were blessed with an unexpected gift. One of his wives became pregnant and gave birth to a male child; it was the first offspring sired by the Prophet in twenty-five years.[177] Mohammed, now sixty-one years of age, doted on the child. But the infant fell ill. When it became apparent that the sickness was mortal, Mohammed took the boy in his arms and began to sob, uncontrollably racked by grief. His friends and followers tried to comfort him, but he could not be consoled. "This that ye see in me is but the working of pity in the heart: he that showeth no pity, unto him shall no pity be shown."[178]

In June of A.D. 632, Mohamed himself came down with a severe fever. After suffering for several days he died at the age of 63.[179] Mohammed's close friend and faithful disciple, Abu Bakr, became the first Caliph, or successor of the Prophet. The Prophet was buried at the place he passed.[180]

PILLARS OF ISLAM

Thus was born one of the world's great religions, Islam. As of 2009, Islam was the world's second largest religion. According to an estimate by the U.S. Central Intelligence Agency, 33 percent of the world's population were Christian, 21 percent Muslim, and 13 percent Hindu.[181]

The practicing Muslim has five obligatory duties, the five "pillars of the faith." The first of these is the public profession of faith, "there is no god save Allah, and Muhammad is his Prophet."[182] The second is the requirement of five daily prayers at prescribed times, starting before sunrise and ending two hours after sunset. Initially, Mohammed instructed his followers to face Jerusalem during these prayers. However in A.D. 624, Mohammed changed the direction of prayer from Jerusalem to Mecca.[183] Thus Islam acquired its own uniqueness and authority.

The third pillar of faith is the giving of alms, now institutionalized in the form of a tax. The fourth pillar of Islam is to fast during the holy month of *Ramadan*. To fast during *Ramadan* means to abstain from "eating, drinking, smoking, or sexual intercourse from dawn until sunset."[184] The fifth pillar is to make a pilgrimage to Mecca at least once during a lifetime.[185]

The fourth and fifth pillars recognized and incorporated pre-existing pagan rituals. From pre–Islamic Arabia, Islam also inherited a belief in supernatural spirits or demons called *jinn (djinn or genies)*. The *Koran* states that God "created the djinn of pure fire."[186]

Sura 72 is titled *Djinn*, and describes how "a company of djinn" exalt the *Koran* as a "marvelous discourse."[187]

In Catholicism, salvation is obtained through the sacraments of the Church, including baptism, penance, and the Eucharist. Most Protestant denominations hold the doctrine that salvation depends solely on faith in Jesus Christ. In Islam, salvation is through works, nor is salvation limited to Muslims. "Verily, they who believe (Muslims), and they who follow the Jewish religion, and the Christians, and the Sabeites—whoever of these believeth in God and the last day, and doeth that which is right, shall have their reward with their Lord."[188]

Islam is more than just a religion. Early on, Jesus began a tradition of divorcing Christianity from secular government by declaring that people should not confuse secular and spiritual obligations. "Render therefore unto Caesar the things which are Caesar's; and unto God the things that are God's."[189] Jesus also said, "My kingdom is not of this world."[190]

But Islam is not confined to spiritual matters. The *Koran* is a handbook for an entire system of government, and "Islam is ... a total way of life, and does not merely regulate the individual's private relationship with God."[191] "Scattered throughout ... [the *Koran* are] ... the archives of a theocratic government in all its departments.... The elements of a code both criminal and civil are ... introduced. Punishments for certain offences are specified, and a mass of legislation laid down for the tutelage of orphans, for marriage, divorce, sales, bargains, wills, evidence, usury and similar concerns."[192] The *Koran* "was the source of Islamic theology, morality, law, and cosmology, and thus the centerpiece of Islamic education."[193]

Second to the *Koran* in Islamic authority is *hadith*. Hadith is "the body of traditions relating to Muhammad."[194] A hadith is "a report that claims to convey a sunnah," where a *sunnah* denotes "the normative behavior of the Muslim community, putatively derived from the Prophet's teaching and conduct, and from the exemplary teaching of his immediate followers."[195] The term hadith can refer to both a "genre of literature and an individual text of this genre."[196] The validity and genuine authority of hadith is established through a scholarly process of historical and critical analysis.[197]

While "theology occupies the central place in Christianity, in Islam the central place belongs to law."[198] "Sharia, the Islamic religious law ... lays out a complete pattern of human conduct and includes every human deed within its purview ... the sharia is considered as something above human wisdom ... as an infallible and immutable doctrine of duties, it encompass the whole of Muslim religious, political, social, domestic, and private life."[199]

Personal behavior is codified in the *Koran*. Intoxicating beverages are forbidden,[200] as are gambling and the eating of pork. "Forbidden to you is ... swine's flesh."[201] Sura 2 of the *Koran* states that in both "wine and games of chance," there "is great sin."[202] "Slavery and polygamy having existed in Arabia from time immemorial ... Mahomet never thought of abolishing either the one or the other."[203] But slave-owners were admonished to treat their slaves well. "He will not enter Paradise who behaveth ill to his slaves."[204] Fornication is to be punished by scourging. "The whore and the whoremonger—scourge each of them with an hundred stripes."[205]

The *Koran* states plainly that "men are superior to women on account of the qualities with which God hath gifted the one above the other."[206] A "virtuous" woman is "obedient."[207] If she is not obedient, her husband is allowed to "remove them into beds apart, and scourge them."[208] But an "obedient" woman should not be punished.[209]

Women are commanded to dress modestly. "Believing women ... [should] throw their veils over their bosoms, and display not their ornaments."[210] If there are no children produced from a marriage, a widow inherits one-fourth of her husband's estate. But if there are children, the inheritance is reduced to one-eighth.[211]

As of the early twenty-first century, women in Islamic countries tended to have less rights and freedoms than women in Western liberal democracies. In 2005, the journal *Nature* reported that women in Pakistan "cannot marry without the written consent of a male, usually their father."[212] In rural areas of Pakistan, about 1,000 women a year [in 2005] were killed for violating their family's honor by marrying "without permission," or having "premarital sex."[213] As of 2008, in Saudi Arabia, a woman could not "travel, appear in court, marry or work without permission from a male guardian, sometimes her own son."[214] In 2009, members of the Shiite sect in Afghanistan, both male and female, "said it is their belief that men should rule over female family members."[215]

Islamic Expansion

BATTLE OF TOURS (A.D. 732)

Upon the death of Mohammed in A.D. 632, Islam should have fallen apart with the recently unified Arab tribes resuming their former status of constant bickering and internecine warfare. The fact that the Islamic movement did not crumble but instead gained strength and an irresistible momentum is a testament to the inevitability of Mohammed's message. Not only was Mohammed the right person, but he appeared at the opportune moment in world history.

The survival and evolution of Islam as a major world religion and culture also owed a debt to the foresight and vigor of Mohammed's immediate successor, Abu Bekr. Within a year of the Prophet's death, he had crushed all rebellions in Arabia. Abu Bekr also moved swiftly to preserve the Prophet's revelations by commissioning a scholar to create an official version of the *Koran*.

United under Islam, the Arab tribes could no longer fight with each other and there was an irresistible impulse for territorial expansion. Mohammed's practice of spreading Islam through military conquests was adopted as the model by his successors. There was little resistance.

To the north of the Arabian Peninsula, present day Turkey, Syria, Jordan, and part of Iraq were controlled by the Byzantine Empire. However the Byzantine suzerainty was but a mere shadow of the Roman Empire from which it had descended. To the west, Egypt was also held by the Byzantines. North and east of Arabia, eastern Iraq and all of Iran were incorporated into a Persian Empire that was little stronger than the Byzantines with whom they were constantly fighting. In Europe, the Roman Empire had broken into domains governed by French and German tribes such as the Franks, Vandals, and Visigoths.

In A.D. 634, the Arabs began making raids into Byzantine Syria and decisively defeated the Byzantine army "in several major encounters."[216] In A.D. 635, they captured the most important city in Syria, Damascus.[217] By A.D. 639, Muslims controlled all of Syria.[218]

Simultaneous with the subjugation of Syria, Arab armies were making substantial inroads against the Persians in the east and the Byzantines in Egypt. The main Persian army was defeated in A.D. 637; by the following year the Arabs were in complete control of Iraq. The conquest of Persia (Iran) was completed in A.D. 651.

In the early eighth century (A.D. 710) Muslim conquests extended as far east as Afghanistan and northwestern India. By the 16th century A.D., Islam would spread as far east as Indonesia. One of the most remarkable aspects of the Islamic expansion was its permanent nature. The territories of the globe often trade hands over the centuries as conquerors, nations, and tribes replace one another. The endurance of the Islamic conquests to the present day is a testament to the importance and power of religion in world history.

The unprecedented military successes of the Arabs represented largely a triumph of the will. War offered rewards to the impoverished desert nomads. Victory in battle was rewarded by rich spoils, and the faithful Muslim who fell in battle was rewarded by instantly being transported to Paradise. The Arabs were also superb horsemen and adept at the use of cavalry. Used to crossing the desert for several days on scant supplies, the Muslim armies could deploy themselves rapidly without being encumbered by logistical concerns.

In the west, the Muslims met stiffer resistance than in the east, in part from geographic barriers. They were frustrated from breaking into Asia Minor by the Taurus mountains in southwestern Turkey. During the seventh and eighth centuries A.D., Islamic forces launched several attacks against Constantinople, but failed to capture it.[219] Constantinople's walls had been fortified for centuries, and the Byzantines were rather more strongly motivated to defend their native city than the far-flung territories so easily captured by the Arabs.

The Muslim expansion through North Africa was slower than the rapid conquests in the east. The lands there offered less plunder and the resistance offered by the natives was stiff at times. The Egyptian city of Alexandria fell in A.D. 640. "The Greeks took to their ships, and pusillanimously deserted the beleaguered city."[220]

Further expansion in North Africa met with difficulties. Twice, the Arabs were routed from North Africa by native Berber tribes (A.D. 683 and 695). The Berbers were finally subdued in A.D. 702, and in A.D. 710, Arab armies reached the African side of the Gibraltar straights and immediately commenced raiding into Spain. By A.D. 720, the Arabs had subdued all of Spain and began advancing into France.

The Muslims were only about 133 miles (214 kilometers) from Paris when their advance into Europe was finally checked at the battle of Tours in A.D. 732.

> Exactly a century passed between the death of Mohammed and the date of the battle of Tours. During that century the followers of the Prophet had torn away half the Roman empire; and, besides their conquests over Persia, the Saracens had overrun Syria, Egypt, Africa, and Spain, in an uncheckered and apparently irresistible career of victory. Nor, at the commencement of the eighth century of our era, was the Mohammedan world divided against itself, as it subsequently became. All these vast regions obeyed the caliph; throughout them all, from the Pyrenees to the Oxus, the name of Mohammed was invoked in prayer, and the *Koran* revered as the book of the law.[221]

"The Franks stood rooted to the spot, and fought a waiting battle, till the light-horse of the Saracens had exhausted their strength in countless unsuccessful charges: then they pushed forward and routed such of the enemy as had spirit to continue the fight."[222] The Muslims were defeated decisively by the Franks, and their defeat was precipitated by the fall of the Muslim commander, Abderrahman. Europeans romanticized their victory. "The nations of the North standing firm as a wall, and impenetrable as a zone of ice, [did] utterly slay the Arabs with the edge of the sword."[223]

An Arab historian attributed the defeat of the Muslims at Tours to greed and a lack of discipline:

Abderrahman and his host attacked Tours to gain still more spoil, and they fought against it so fiercely that they stormed the city almost before the eyes of the army that came to save it; and the fury and cruelty of the Moslems toward the inhabitants of the city was like the fury and cruelty of raging tigers.... It was manifest that God's chastisement was sure to follow such excesses; and Fortune thereupon turned her back upon the Moslems ... many of the Moslems were fearful for the safety of the spoil which they had stored in their tents, and a false cry arose in their ranks that some of the enemy were plundering the camp; whereupon several squadrons of the Moslem horsemen rode off to protect their tents.... And while Abderrahman strove to check their tumult, and to lead them back to battle, the warriors of the Franks came around him, and he was pierced through with many spears, so that he died. Then all the host fled before the enemy and many died in the flight.[224]

After a few generations, the aggressive expansion of Islam ran out of steam, a victim of its own successes. The lean and hungry desert warriors gave way to generations of rich landowners who preferred the immediate luxuries of the present life to the theoretical rewards to be found in the next.

The consolidation of the Islamic Empire was facilitated by a lenient treatment of conquered peoples. They were allowed to "peacefully retain their old religions, provided only they paid ample tribute."[225] "The Arabs did not force the people they conquered to embrace their religion, laws, customs, and use their own language. They [the conquered] were to be tribute producing and the Arab ideal was to live at ease on the product of their labor."[226] The tribute or tax ceased when a person converted to Islam, so there was a mild yet persistent pressure for conversion.

Another inducement was offered captives taken in war: choose Islam or slavery. Ironically, considering the enmity between Mohammed and the Jews of Medina, Jews throughout much of the Middle East welcomed Muslim conquerors as liberators. Muslim rule was largely more accommodating and tolerant of religious diversity than the Christian rule of the Byzantine Emperors.

THE OMEYYAD AND THE ABBASID CALIPHATES

The succession of Mohammed's successors, the Caliphs, was by oligarchy. Regimes were often short-lived and the deposements could be violent. Some Caliphs were chaste, frugal, and devoted to Islam. Others were devoted patrons of the arts and sciences.

But some Caliphs were debauched hedonists, or were (like some Catholic Popes) ambitious and cruel. Abu al–Abbas, the first caliphate in the Abbasid dynasty, was descended from an uncle of Mohammed, and reigned as caliphate from A.D. 750 to his death in A.D. 754. Upon ascending to the caliphate, Abu al–Abbas began a program of extermination against the members of the previous caliphate, the Omayyads. "In Syria, the Omayyads were persecuted with the utmost rigor. Even their graves were violated, and the bodies crucified and destroyed."[227]

Abu al–Abbas "named himself *Saffah*, the blood-thirsty, and by that title he has ever since been known."[228]

His [Abu al–Abbas'] earliest care was to sweep from the face of the earth the entire Omeyyad race. Such wholesale butcheries cast into the shade anything the previous dynasty had ever been accused of. The cruelest of them was that perpetrated by the Caliph's uncle in Palestine. An amnesty was offered to the numerous branches of the family congregated there; and to confirm it they were invited, some ninety in number, to a feast. Suddenly a bard arose reciting in verse the evil deeds of the Omeyyads, and on signal given, the attendants fell on the unsuspecting guests, and put them all to death [with clubs]. A carpet was drawn over the ghastly spectacle, and the tyrant resumed his feast over the still quivering limbs of the dying.[229]

The Abbasids also excavated the grave of a deceased Omayyad caliphate and removed the body. "This they scourged with whips, hung up for a while, and then burned."[230]

"The fifth of the Abbasid caliphs," Harun al–Rashid (A.D. 766–809) was a pious man, both a "scholar and a poet."[231] "No Caliph, either before or after, displayed such energy and activity in his various progresses whether for pilgrimage, for administration, or for war. But what has chiefly made his Caliphate illustrious, is that it ushered in the era of letters. His court was the center to which, from all parts, flocked the wise and the learned, and at which rhetoric, poetry, history and law, as well as science, medicine, music, and the arts, met with a genial and princely patronage."[232] During Harun's reign as caliph, "the first paper factories were founded in Bagdad."[233] "In the ninth and tenth centuries papermaking was a flourishing business in Iran and Iraq."[234]

ARABIAN NIGHTS

The Caliph Harun was a central figure in many of the stories found in the classic of oriental literature, *Arabian Nights*, or *Thousand and One Nights*. *Arabian Nights* is a collection of folk tales whose origin has been lost in antiquity; it is the original source of stories such as *The Voyages of Sinbad the Sailor, Ali Baba and the Forty Thieves*, and *Aladdin and the Magic Lamp*. Most of these tales are probably Persian in origin; some may be Arabian or Indian. The unexpurgated version of the book is both racist and sexist.

The book "first became generally known in Europe in the early part of the 18th century through the French translation by Antoine Galland."[235] The tales contain anachronisms, implying that the text was "composed very soon after [A.D.] 1450."[236] Among the anachronisms are references to cannon and coffee. Coffee "was discovered towards the end of the 14th century [A.D.], but not generally used till 200 years later."[237]

As the *Arabian Nights* opens, a king named Shah Zaman returns home unexpectedly and finds his wife in bed with another man. "He drew his scymitar and, cutting the two into four pieces with a single blow, left them on the carpet."[238] Disconsolate, Shah Zaman retires to the palace of his brother, King Shahryar. But while his brother is on a hunting trip, Shah Zaman observes his sister-in-law engaging in a garden orgy with ten other women. Dismayed, Shah Zaman concludes "there is no woman but who cuckoldeth her husband ... no man is safe from their malice!"[239]

> Rely not on women;
> Trust not to their hearts,
> Whose joys and whose sorrows
> Are hung to their parts!
> Lying love they will swear thee
> Whence guile ne'er departs[240]

When Shah Zaman informs his brother of what he had witnessed, King Shahryar is incredulous. So he pretends to again depart on a hunting trip, but hides so that he can secretly observe and confirm his wife's infidelity.

Upon discovering that his wife is unfaithful, Shahryar executes his cheating spouse. "He also swore [to] himself by a binding oath that whatever wife he married he would abate her virginity at night and slay her [the] next morning to make sure of his honor: 'for,' said he, 'there never was nor is there one chaste woman upon the face of the earth.'"[241]

Every night for the next three years, King Shahryar married a virgin and had her decapitated the following morning. One day the King ordered his high Minister to produce another girl, but none was to be found. Unable to fulfill Shahryar's order, the Minister feared for his life. Seeing her father upset, the Minister's daughter, Scheherazade, offered to marry the King. "She [Scheherazade] had perused the works of the poets and knew them by heart; she had studied philosophy and the sciences, arts and accomplishments; and she was pleasant and polite, wise and witty, well read and well bred."[242]

The Minister argued with Scheherazade, but she was resolute. The marriage was consummated that night, but after the act the King was restless. Scheherazade offered to tell him a story, *The Trader and the Jinni*, but the tale was left unfinished. Desiring to hear the end of the story, Shahryar stayed the execution of Scheherazade until the next day.

The unfinished tales continued for one thousand and one nights, the stories told by Scheherazade constituting the *Arabian Nights*. By this time, Scheherazade had borne the King three male children. Appearing before Shahryar, she begged for a general pardon from the death sentence that had loomed over her for a thousand and one days and nights. "'O King of the age, these are thy children and I crave that thou release me from the doom of death, as a dole to these infants; for an thou kill me, they will become motherless and will find none among women to rear them as they should be reared.' When the King heard this, he wept and straining the boys to his bosom, said, 'By Allah, O Shahrazad, I pardoned thee before the coming of these children, for that I found thee chaste, pure, ingenuous, and pious!'"[243]

ECONOMIC EXPANSION

Heraclitus (c. 540–480 B.C.) said that "war is the father of all [things]."[244] The unification of diverse countries, tribes, and cultures under Islamic rule and religion promoted both mercantile and intellectual commerce.

An Empire could not be ruled from a small desert city in Arabia. By A.D. 661, the Caliph's government had moved to Damascus in Syria,[245] and in A.D. 763, the Caliphate was moved to Baghdad. A golden age of Islamic science and rational philosophy ensued from about A.D. 750 through A.D. 1100. Baghdad became the center of the intellectual world, and Arabic was the language of science.[246] Islamic civilization sprang from the grafting of Arab innovation on Persian and Greek cultures; it was funded by the material rewards of trade and conquest.

Most Islamic governments allowed commerce and trade to flourish under a policy of *laissez faire*. "Until the days of the Crusades Syria and Egypt were practically Christian lands under the rule of the Muslim Arabs, their rule mainly confined to the collection of taxes."[247]

"When the Arabs made their great conquests money became a necessity."[248] The first Islamic coin was issued in A.D. 660, and the mintage was standardized in A.D. 695. The *dinar* of gold was one of three coins. From the Chinese, the Arabs learned how to make paper and introduced the art into Europe. "In [A.D.] 751 the Arabs, who had occupied Samarkand early in the century, were attacked there by the Chinese. The invasion was repelled by the Arab governor, who in the pursuit, it is related, captured certain prisoners who were skilled in paper-making and who imparted their knowledge to their new masters. Hence began the Arabian manufacture, which rapidly spread to all parts of the Arab dominions."[249]

The economic legacy of the Islamic conquests "consists of a number of diffusions, which might have taken place anyway, but were plausibly accelerated by the Muslim conquests and their aftermath."[250] The Arabs were at least partly responsible for introducing the cultivation of some important plants to Europe. "In the ninth century [A.D.] Sicily was taken by the Saracens, and ... they at once introduced the cultivation of cotton.... In the tenth century the Muhammadans carried the self-same cotton plant across the Mediterranean to Spain, and for three centuries thereafter Barcelona had a flourishing cotton industry."[251] "The Burmese peninsula and southern China ... [are likely] the original home of the orange ... it was carried to south-western Asia by the Arabs, probably before the 9th century [A.D.]. ... it [the orange] spread ultimately, through the agency of the same race [Arabs], to Africa and Spain, and perhaps to Sicily, following everywhere the tide of Mohammedan conquest and civilization."[252] In early medieval times, the Arabs also introduced the cultivation of several other plants to southern Europe. These included rice, sugar-cane, the lemon, several vegetables, and "even some varieties of grain."[253]

In Spain, the Muslims revitalized the mining industry, and started the manufacture of paper, carpets, shawls, leather, swords, and armor. In the tenth century A.D., Cordova was "the most civilized city in Europe," and had "seventy libraries and nine hundred public baths."[254]

The system of enumeration commonly called *arabic* originated with the Hindus in India. "The nine numerals used in decimal position and using zero for an empty position were received by the Arabs from India."[255] The time of introduction into Arabia has been estimated to be A.D. 773, "when an Indian astronomer visited the court of the caliph."[256] "In Europe the complete system with the zero was derived from the Arabs in the 12th century."[257] The arabic system was recognized by Italian merchants as superior to the clumsy Roman numerals,[258] but the diffusion of arabic enumeration in Europe was "incredibly slow."[259] The most significant event in the diffusion of arabic enumeration was the publication of *Liber abaci* (*Book of Calculation*) by Fibonacci (c. A.D. 1170–1240) in A.D. 1202. This book contained "the first complete and systematic explanation of Hindu numerals by a Christian writer."[260]

Islamic Science (c. A.D. 750–1200)

THE NESTORIANS

Science and natural philosophy in Islamic civilization c. A.D. 750–1100 were derived from the works of Greek philosophers and scientists. The influence of Hellenism in Asia dated from the conquests of Alexander. When Alexander died in 323 B.C., Ptolemy I (367–283 B.C.) made Alexandria the home city of his kingdom. In Syria, Seleucus I (c. 358–281 B.C.), or Seleucus Nicator, established a dynasty of successors that lasted from 312 to 65 B.C. Between 312 and 302 B.C., Seleucus I "brought under his authority the whole eastern part of Alexander's empire."[261] By 301 B.C., he was in control of Syria, and in 300 B.C. Seleucus I founded the city of Antioch in that region.[262] Antioch "was destined to rival Alexandria in Egypt as the chief city of the nearer East, and to be the cradle of gentile Christianity ... it enjoyed a great reputation for letters and the arts."[263]

The most significant factor in the introduction of Greek science and philosophy into Islam was the work of a sect of Christian schismatics, the Nestorians.[264] As early as the 19th century, Alexander von Humboldt (1769–1859) attributed the birth of Islamic science to Nestorian translators. "The Arabs first became acquainted with Grecian literature through the Syrians, a Semitic race allied to themselves, and the Syrians, scarcely a century and a half earlier, had received the knowledge of Grecian works from the Nestorians who had been pronounced heretics."[265] Some of the early translators were pagans and Jews, but most were Nestorian Christians.[266]

Nestorius (d. c. A.D. 451) was a native Syrian who began his Christian career as a monk. Ordained a presbyter (priest), Nestorius "became celebrated ... for his asceticism, his orthodoxy and his eloquence."[267]

In December of 427, the patriarch of Constantinople died. There was a power struggle to decide his successor, with two opposing camps equal in political influence. So the Byzantine Emperor, Theodosius II (401–450), decided to appoint an outsider. He chose Nestorius of Antioch.[268]

Immediately upon assuming the role of bishop of Constantinople, Nestorius adopted a policy of absolute intolerance for heretics. He told the Emperor, "Give me, my prince, the earth purged of heretics, and I will give you heaven as recompense. Assist me in destroying heretics, and I will assist you in vanquishing the Persians."[269] Possessed of a "violent and vainglorious temperament," Nestorius "burst forth into such vehemence without being able to contain himself for even the shortest space of time; and ... showed himself a furious persecutor ... he could not rest, but seeking every means of harassing those who embraced not his own sentiments, he continually disturbed the public tranquility."[270]

The persecutor of heretics was soon himself to be declared a heretic. Nestorius brought a presbyter from Antioch with him, a man named Anastasius. One day, Anastasius delivered a sermon where he declared "let no one call Mary *Theotocos* [Mother of God]: for Mary was but a woman; and it is impossible that God should be born of a woman."[271]

According to Socrates Scholasticus (c. A.D. 380–445), "these words created a great sensation, and troubled many both of the clergy and laity; they having been heretofore taught to acknowledge Christ as God, and by no means to separate his humanity from his divinity."[272]

The controversy seemed obscure, but was important because it concerned the nature of Christ. Was Jesus Christ God or man? How could the two natures be reconciled? The reference to Jesus' mother as the "Mother of God," was "not the sense, or monstrous sense ... that the creature bore the Creator," but "was intended only to denote the indissoluble union of the divine and human natures in Christ."[273] But the Nestorian view separated the divine and human natures in Christ. "Instead of God-Man, we have here the idea of a mere God-bearing man; and the person of Jesus of Nazareth is only the instrument of the temple, in which the divine Logos dwells."[274]

What should have been a scholarly dispute for theologians became a heated political dispute, with "all parties uttering the most confused and contradictory assertions."[275] The reason is that at this time, there was a "growing veneration of Mary."[276] Therefore, the Nestorian controversy "struck into the field of devotion, which lies much nearer the people than that of speculative theology; and thus it touched the most vehement passions."[277] Nestorius was "forced into the position of one who brings technical objections against a popular term."[278]

Nestorius found himself opposed by Cyril, bishop of Alexandria, "a learned, acute, energetic, but extremely passionate, haughty, ambitious, and disputatious prelate."[279] To resolve the Nestorian controversy, emperor Theodosius II convened an Ecumenical Council of the Church at Ephesus in A.D. 431. "An uncharitable, violent, and passionate spirit ruled the transactions," and the Council was a debacle.[280]

Nestorius was in attendance, but his allies from the Eastern churches had not yet arrived. Cyril of Alexandria opened the Council before Nestorius' confederates could be in attendance. He did this in spite of the protests of the Emperor's representative. Cyril and a hundred and sixty bishops condemned Nestorius and declared him anathema.[281] Speaking for God, the Council declared "the Lord Jesus Christ, who is blasphemed by him [Nestorius], determines through this holy council that Nestorius be excluded from the episcopal office, and from all sacerdotal fellowship."

In a few days, Nestorius' allies, the eastern bishops, finally arrived. They promptly convened their own council, and declared Cyril of Alexandria to be anathema and deposed. "Now followed a succession of mutual criminations, invectives, arts of church diplomacy and politics, intrigues, and violence."[282] The emperor, Theodosius II, apparently disgusted by the proceedings, ordered both Cyril and Nestorius to be arrested.[283] Theodosius at first favored Nestorius, because Cyril had convened the initial Council against the wishes of his representative. But as time passed, it became apparent that Cyril commanded the majority position. At last, Theodosius "gave a decision in favor of the orthodox, and the council of Ephesus was dissolved."[284]

Nestorius was deposed from his position as bishop of Constantinople, and withdrew to his old monastery in Antioch. He lived there until A.D. 435, when the Emperor banished him to the city of Petra, in Arabia. Nestorius' history now becomes obscure, but it would seem that he eventually ended up in Egypt, and died there sometime after A.D. 439.[285] He "was compelled to drink to the dregs the bitter cup of persecution which he himself, in the days of his power, had forced upon the heretics."[286] Socrates Scholasticus said that Nestorius eventually recanted his heresy, but "no notice was taken of it; for his deposition was not revoked, and he was banished to the Oasis."[287]

The deposition and banishment of Nestorius was followed by a series of "stringent imperial edicts" against the Nestorians, and Nestorianism became "extinct throughout the Roman empire."[288] The Nestorians found "asylum in the kingdom of Persia."[289] In A.D. 435, one of Nestorius' pupils "settled at Nisibis [southeastern Turkey] in Persian territory ... and established a Nestorian school."[290]

The city of Edessa [southeastern Turkey] was known as "the Athens of Syria."[291] In A.D. 489, the Byzantine emperor closed the school there and "expelled its members."[292] The Nestorians fled to the east. Thus measures designed to suppress Nestorianism only promulgated its spread. The Nestorians "showed a zeal for evangelization which resulted in the establishment of their influence throughout Asia."[293]

The Nestorians "were favored by the Persian kings ... out of political opposition to Constantinople."[294] Their churches "flourished for several centuries, spread from Persia, with great missionary zeal, to India, Arabia, and even to China and Tartary."[295] "Marco Polo is witness that there were Nestorian churches all along the trade routes from Bagdad to Pekin."[296]

The Nestorian Christians were generally tolerated by the Muslims, and respected for their learning, scholarship, and intellect. "Mohammed is supposed to owe his imperfect knowledge of Christianity to a Nestorian monk ... and from him [Mohammed] the sect received many privileges, so that it obtained great consideration among the Arabians, and exerted an influence upon their culture, and thus upon the development of philosophy and science in general."[297]

THE TRANSLATORS

There was little interest in science and philosophy in Islam during the rule of the Omayyad caliphs (A.D. 661–750). The Arabic caliphs of the Omayyad dynasty were concerned primarily with political, economic, and administrative problems.[298] The "intellectual output [of the Omayyad dynasty] consisted entirely of poetry."[299]

The caliphs of the Abbasid dynasty were Persian, and had a greater interest in intellectual matters. The systematic introduction of Greek science and philosophy in Islam began with the founding of Baghdad by the caliph al–Mansur in A.D. 762.[300] Baghdad was to be "the center of the civilized world as long as the Caliphate lasted."[301] "It is certain the process of translating scientific and philosophical works did not begin in earnest until the Abbasid period, and in particular until the reign of al–Mansur."[302] There was a keen interest in Greek science at al–Mansur's court, and he invited scholars to Baghdad. In A.D. 765, al–Mansur became ill, and he sent for a Nestorian physician.[303]

Islamic civilization flowered in al–Mansur's reign. "Tradition, no longer oral, began to be embodied by the great doctors of the law in elaborate systems of jurisprudence adapted to the expanding range of Islam and the necessities of an advancing civilization. Literature, history, medicine, and especially astronomy began to be studied; and the foundations were thus laid for the development of intellectual life in subsequent reigns."[304]

In A.D. 775, al–Mansur became ill during a pilgrimage to Mecca and died.[305] He was succeeded by his son, al–Mahdi, who reigned for ten years without distinction. "His administration was upon the whole such as to promote the welfare of the nation, and usher in the brilliant era that followed; but his life was stained by many acts of tyranny and cruelty."[306]

The next caliph reigned only a year or two before dying. He was succeeded in A.D. 786 by his brother, Harun al–Rashid, "the most celebrated name among the Arabian caliphs."[307] "Harun was perhaps the ablest ruler of the Abbasside race ... his government was wise and just; as without doubt, it was grand and prosperous."[308]

Al-Rashid "took great interest in science and literature, far beyond any of his predecessors, and the Hellenistic movement in Islam matured under his auspices."[309] "His court was the center to which, from all parts, flocked the wise and the learned, and at which rhetoric, poetry, history and law, as well as science, medicine, music, and the arts, met with a genial and princely patronage."[310] During al–Rashid's reign as caliph, there was an intentional and active effort to import Greek manuscripts. Agents were sent into the Roman empire to seek and purchase scholarly books.[311] Among the first Greek works translated into Arabic were Ptolemy's *Syntaxis* and Euclid's *Elements*.[312]

The zenith of the age of translation and Greek science in Islam occurred early in the ninth century under the reign of the caliph al–Mamun, from A.D. 808 to 833. After establishing his government at Baghdad in A.D. 813, Mamun "gave himself up to science and literature. He caused works on mathematics, astronomy, medicine, and philosophy to be translated from the Greek, and founded in Bagdad a kind of academy, called the 'House of Science,' with a library and an observatory."[313] "The Greek philosophy received by the Arabs was not solely that of Plato and Aristotle, but what had been elaborated in the course of several centuries by their continuators and their commentators. Alongside Platonism and Aristotelianism there were Stoicism, Pythagorism, and, above all, the Neoplatonism of Plotinus and Proclus."[314]

The wealth and erudition of Islamic society in Baghdad during this time is illustrated by the fact that a number of private patrons competed with the caliphate in the importation of books and their translation.[315] It was not uncommon for individual Muslims to own vast libraries.

A private doctor refused the invitation of the sultan of Bochara, because the carriage of his books would have required four hundred camels. The royal library of the Fatamites consisted of one hundred thousand manuscripts, elegantly transcribed and splendidly bound, which were lent, with jealousy or avarice, to the students of Cairo. Yet this collection must appear moderate, if we can believe that the Ommiades of Spain had formed a library of six hundred thousand volumes ... and above seventy public libraries were opened in the cities of the Andalusian kingdom.[316]

By way of contrast, in Europe, Charlemagne (742–814), king of the Franks, was trying to learn to write. Charlemagne "tried to write, and used to keep tablets and blanks in bed under his pillow, that at leisure hours he might accustom his hand to form the letters; however, as he began his efforts late in life, and not at the proper time, they met with little success."[317] In the courts of Europe, "a tutor ... was rare, as was book learning for princes."[318]

The most important of the Nestorian translators was Hunayn ibn Ishaq (A.D. 808–873). Originally trained as a physician, Hunayn acquired "the best knowledge of Greek of anyone of his time."[319] Hunayn and his coworkers "were responsible for translating almost the whole Aristotelian corpus, as well as a series of Platonic and Peripatetic works."[320] Hunayn also translated nearly the entire body of Greek medical works, including books by Hippocrates, Galen, and Dioscorides.[321]

Hunayn traveled in search of manuscripts, and was in the habit of retranslating his earlier efforts to achieve perfection. His translations are noted for a "striking exactness of expression obtained without verbosity."[322] Hunayn also composed "more than a hundred original works,"[323] but most of these have been lost.

The best known and most widely read of the translated works were the books of Aristotle, the Neoplatonic works of Porphyry and Proclus, John Philoponus' (A.D. 490–570) commentaries on Aristotle, and the medical manuscripts of Galen.[324]

In addition to the efforts of the Nestorian translators, Greek science and philosophy entered Islamic culture by some other avenues. Although not as significant as the Nestorians, there were translations by scholars and monks associated with the Monophysites, another schismatic Christian sect that had been expelled from the Roman Church. The Monophysites held "the doctrine that [Jesus] Christ had but one composite nature."[325] In A.D. 451, the Council of Chalcedon decided that Jesus "Christ ... is (of) two natures, without confusion, without conversion, without severance, and without division."[326] The Monophysite doctrine was thus repudiated, and immediately afterward "bloody fights of the monks and the rabble broke out, and Monophysite factions went off in schismatic churches."[327]

The development and cultivation of science and philosophy in Baghdad was also influenced by cultural exchanges with Persians and Indians. Their influence was particularly strong in "the positive sciences, medicine, and political institutions."[328] The Arabs acquired "the bulk of the narrative literature, tales, legends, [and] novels ... in translations from the Persian ... [also] books on the science of war, the knowledge of weapons, the veterinary art, falconry, and the various methods of divination, and some books on medicine ... were likewise borrowed from the Persians."[329]

One route of diffusion was an ancient trade route between India and the Mediterranean that had been in use since the fourteenth or fifteenth century B.C. [330] But much of what the Muslims acquired from India was likely derivative from original Greek sources, especially in "mathematics and astronomy."[331] This was the opinion of the Muslim al–Biruni (A.D. 973–1048):

The Greeks ... had philosophers who ... discovered and worked out for them the elements of science ... [but] the Hindus had no men of this stamp both capable and willing to bring sciences to a classical perfection. Therefore you mostly find that even the so-called scientific theorems of the Hindus are in a state of utter confusion, devoid of any logical order, and in the last instance always mixed up with the silly notions of the crowd, e.g. immense numbers, enormous spaces of time, and all kinds of religious dogmas, which the vulgar belief does not admit of being called into question.[332]

Most Greek works had been translated into Arabic or Syriac by A.D. 900, and most of the translations that were done in Baghdad between A.D. 900 and 1000 were revisions of earlier efforts.[333] The age of translation in Asia ended in A.D. 1000. By this time, "almost the entire corpus of Greek medicine, natural philosophy, and mathematical science"[334] had been translated into Arabic. There was a final phase of translation in Islamic Spain, but the cultivation of Greek philosophy in Islam had now peaked and was on the wane.[335]

ORIGINALITY

The extent to which Islamic individuals made significant and original contributions to Greek philosophy and science is a controversial subject. Pierre Duhem (1861–1916) took the extreme view, that the Muslims made no original contributions whatsoever. "There is no Arabian science. The wise men of Mohammedanism were always the more or less faithful disciples of the Greeks, but were themselves destitute of all originality. For instance, they compiled many abridgments of Ptolemy's *Almagest*, made numerous observations, and constructed a great many astronomical tables, but added nothing essential to the theories of astronomical motion ... in physics, Arabian scholars confined themselves to commentaries on the statements of Aristotle, their attitude being at times one of absolute servility."[336]

To support his assertion of slavish devotion to Aristotle, Duhem quoted Averroes (ibn Rushd, A.D. 1126–1198) as stating Aristotle "founded and completed logic, physics, and metaphysics ... because none of those who have followed him up to our time, that is to say, for four hundred years, have been able to add anything to his writings or to detect therein an error of any importance."[337]

The Eleventh Edition (1911) of the *Encyclopædia Britannica* was similarly scornful of Islamic innovation and originality.

What is known as "Arabian" philosophy owed to Arabia little more than its name and its language. It was a system of Greek thought, expressed in a Semitic tongue, and modified by Oriental influences, called into existence amongst the Moslem people by the patronage of their more liberal princes, and kept alive by the intrepidity and zeal of a small band of thinkers, who stood suspected and disliked in the eyes of their nation.... From first to last Arabian philosophers made no claim to originality; their aim was merely to propagate the truth of Peripateticism as it had been delivered to them. It was with them that the deification of Aristotle began.[338]

The modern assessment acknowledges that some significant original contributions were made by Islamic philosophers and scientists. They "made algebra an exact science and developed it considerably and laid the foundations of analytical geometry; they were indisputably the founders of plane and spherical trigonometry ... in astronomy they made a number of valuable observations ... the Arabs kept alive the higher intellectual life and the study of science in a period when the Christian West was fighting desperately with barbarism."[339] Islamic astronomers "constructed ever more sophisticated and reliable observation instruments— sundials, armillary spheres, astrolabes, quadrants, [and] equatoria."[340]

But nevertheless, Islamic philosophy and science c. A.D. 750–1100 were derivative of work done in the Hellenistic culture of the Mediterranean region. "Muslim scientists expressed originality and innovation in the correction, extension, articulation, and application of the existing framework, rather than in the creation of a new one."[341] "Islamic philosophy is ... to be understood as that trend of Muslim thought which continues the type of Greek philosophy which the later Neoplatonists had created: a blend of Aristotelian and Platonic views as understood by philosophers in the later centuries of the Roman Empire."[342]

AL-KINDI (C. A.D. 800–866)

Al-Kindi (c. A.D. 800–866) is known as "the first Arab philosopher."[343] He was assessed by George Sarton as "the first and only great philosopher of the Arab race."[344] Al-Kindi was an exception to the rule that most of the philosophical and scientific works of this age were not generated by "genuine Arabs," but "Persians, Christians, and Jews."[345] "Several [of the learned men] were not even Muslims."[346]

Al-Kindi worked in Baghdad under the patronage of al–Mamun and two of his successors. The extent to which he engaged in translation is uncertain, as it appears his knowledge of Greek was not sufficient to allow him to function as a primary translator. Al-Kindi's translation efforts may have been limited to corrections, comments, and summaries.[347]

Al-Kindi appears to have been a prolific author, having produced as many as 242 short works that can be classified as "essays or epistles."[348] These deal with a very wide range of subjects, including "logic, metaphysics, arithmetic, spherics, music, astronomy, geometry, medicine, astrology, theology, psychology, politics, meteorology, topography, prognostics, and alchemy."[349]

Most of Al-Kindi's books have been lost. Only "fifteen philosophical works" are extant.[350] These treatises "are composed mainly of elaborately presented arguments employing numerous concepts and are thus virtually impossible to summarize faithfully."[351] On the whole, al–Kindi was a Peripatetic, but departed from Aristotle's views in those areas in which philosophy clashed with Islamic theology. Aristotle had characterized the cosmos as eternal, but al-Kindi defended the doctrine of creation *ex nihilo*. He also defended "the resurrection of the body, the possibility of miracles, [and] the validity of prophetic revelation."[352]

Like the European scholastics who followed him, al–Kindi subordinated philosophy to religion. He endorsed Aristotelean logic, but believe that philosophy must "surrender" to revelation when the two clashed.[353] "Belief in the use of astrology was widespread,"[354] and, like other men of his age, al–Kindi believed in the validity of astrology. The caliphs of the Abbasid dynasty were convinced that the heavens held "the secrets of human destiny,"[355] thus there was always a special interest in astronomy and astrology at their courts.

Amongst other subjects, al–Kindi wrote on the topic of optics, and Roger Bacon (c. A.D. 1220–1294) placed him "in the first rank after Ptolemy as a writer on optics."[356] Al-Kindi held the view that vision was accomplished by means of rays emanating from the eyes.

AL-RAZI (C. A.D. 854–925)

Al-Razi (c. A.D. 854–925), known in Medieval Europe as Rhazes, was a Persian physician who was skeptical of religion and advocated empiricism. He was "the greatest nonconformist in the whole history of Islam and undoubtedly the most celebrated medical authority in the tenth century."[357] His "fame in the West became immense and ... [his] authority remained unquestioned till the seventeenth century."[358]

Little is known of al–Razi's personal life. He was born in the town of Rayy, but practiced medicine in Baghdad. Al-Razi's medical authority must have been recognized by his contemporaries, because he was placed in charge of the hospital in Baghdad.[359] He "did not come to Baghdad until he had already a great reputation, [and] took under his care patients of all kinds without regard to their social or financial standing."[360]

Al-Razi "was the first of the Arabs to treat medicine in a comprehensive and encyclopedic manner, surpassing probably in voluminousness Galen himself, though but a small proportion of his works are extant. Rhazes is deservedly remembered as having first described small-pox and measles in an accurate manner."[361]

Al-Razi may have composed as many as 230 works.[362] His best known books are *A Treatise on the Small-pox and Measles*,[363] *The Book of Medicine Dedicated to Mansur*, and *The Comprehensive Book of Medicine*.[364] *The Book of Medicine Dedicated to Mansur* is a "short, practical textbook of medicine."[365] *The Comprehensive Book of Medicine* is a very rare and lengthy work. The original Arabic version consists of twenty-four volumes. The manuscript is unorganized and disjointed, and appears to be a compilation of al–Razi's source materials collated by his students.[366]

In terms of medical theory, al–Razi followed Galen, but he also practiced the Hippocratic tradition that emphasized the importance of objective observation.[367] No dogmatist, al–Razi authored a work titled *Doubts Concerning Galen* in which he justified his criticism of Galen. "Medicine is a philosophy, and this is not compatible with renouncement of criticism."[368] al–Razi had a progressive viewpoint that was rare for his time. He believed that the sciences "continually develop as time passes and approach more and more to perfection."[369] Thus he believed it was not only his right, but his obligation to criticize and thus improve on the work of his predecessors.

Al-Razi believed that anomalous phenomena should not necessarily be rejected out of hand, but given careful and serious consideration. In his *Book of Properties*, he pointed out that men "disbelieve all phenomena the causes of which are unknown," when "in fact they are constantly observing phenomena similar to those the truth of which they deny."[370] As an example of this, he mentioned that people will accept the fact that a magnet can attract iron, but will reject the possibility that there might exist a stone that could attract "copper or gold."[371] Everything must be "put to the test of experience."[372]

Al-Razi apparently embraced authority when he appeared to argue that one could learn more medicine from books than from practice. "A thousand physicians, for probably a thousand years, have labored on the improvement of medicine; he who reads their writings with assiduity and reflection discovers in a short life more than if he should actually run after the sick a thousand years."[373]

But it is likely al–Razi was only affirming the value of observation. Reading the works of predecessors makes a huge body of systematic observations and data available. Al-Razi also wrote that "reading does not make the physician, but a critical judgment, and the application of known truths to special cases."[374] Al-Razi's embracement of careful and meticulous observations in the Hippocratic tradition is documented by the fact that he is "the earliest [known] physician known to us who has left records of case-histories."[375] The Hippocratic writings[376] (c. 400 B.C.) contain numerous case histories, but the authorship of these writings is uncertain, and cannot definitely be attributed to Hippocrates.[377]

Al-Razi had interests beyond medicine. He wrote on "philosophy, alchemy, astronomy, grammar, theology, logic, and [in] other areas."[378] Al-Razi "believed in and practiced alchemy."[379] At this time, "both medicine and alchemy were studied for pragmatic and rational reasons."[380] A book al–Razi authored on pharmacology contained the first known mention of coffee.[381] "The first that makes mention of the property of this bean, under the name of *bunchum* in the 9th century after the birth of our savior, was Zachary Mahomet Rases, commonly called Rhasio, a very famous Arabian physician."[382]

In philosophy, al–Razi rejected Aristotle and referred to himself as a disciple of Plato.[383] al–Razi was also an atomist. He believed that the different qualities of matter resulted from atoms combining in "different proportions."[384] Al–Razi accepted the doctrine of the transmigration of the soul, and he cited this as a reason that could justify the killing of an animal. Killing a beast could speed the transmigration of its soul into a human form.[385]

There are "five eternal principles"[386] in al–Razi's metaphysics. These are "matter, space, time, the soul, and the creator." Al–Razi's creator is a *demiurge*, a lesser deity, similar to the creator mentioned in Plato's *Timaeus*. The *demiurge* is a "handicraftsman or artisan"[387] that makes the cosmos, but is not the supreme spiritual being, highest Good, or God.

Al-Razi rejected the validity of prophecy, composed "antireligious polemics," including one titled *The Tricks of the Prophets*, and concluded that "religion was definitely harmful, for fanaticism engendered hatred and religious wars."[388] "Revealed religion was to him identical with superstition."[389] These views, combined with al–Razi's rejection of Aristotle, did not sit well with orthodox Islam. In later times, al–Razi was "held in almost universal contempt as a schismatic and an infidel."[390] Moses Maimonides (A.D. 1135–1204) called him an "ignorant man," and criticized al–Razi's book *On Metaphysics* for containing "mad and foolish things."[391]

AL-FARABI (C A.D. 870–950)

Al-Farabi (c. A.D. 870–950), known in Medieval Europe as Abunaser, was a Persian philosopher who sought to harmonize Greek philosophy with Islam and apply philosophy to politics. "His logical treatises produced a permanent effect on the logic of the Latin scholars [and] he gave the tone and direction to nearly all subsequent speculations among the Arabians."[392]

Al-Farabi was born in the ancient district of Farab, in present day Kazakhstan. His father was Persian, and the boy grew up in the city of Damascus. In his youth, al–Farabi reportedly read philosophy books at night.[393] Al-Farabi initially studied logic with a Nestorian Christian, ibn Haylan. Both teacher and student relocated to Baghdad sometime between A.D. 892 and 902.[394]

A few years later (c. A.D. 902–908), al–Farabi traveled to Constantinople. He spent eight years there, "and learned the entire philosophic syllabus."[395] Between A.D. 910 and 920, al–Farabi returned to Baghdad and taught there for twenty years, acquiring a reputation "as the foremost Muslim philosopher."[396]

Al-Farabi's mastery of both Plato and Aristotle is revealed in two popular expositions he authored in Arabic as introductions to their philosophy.[397] In *Enumeration of the Sciences*, al–Farabi listed the sciences as being "linguistic, the logical, the mathematical, the physical, the metaphysical, the political, the judicial, and the theological."[398] He acknowledged that the heavens exert an influence on human events, but was skeptical concerning the validity of divination and auguries. Al-Farabi noted that the best known astrologers had no more worldly success than those with no supposed skills in reading the stars.[399]

Al-Farabi's philosophy also reflected a strong element of neoplatonism. He "was the founder of Arab Neo-Platonism."[400] Al-Farabi's book, *Opinions of the Inhabitants of the Virtuous City*, opens with a discussion of the neoplatonic process of emanation from the One.[401] In metaphysics, al–Farabi divided all things into two categories: those which must exist, and those for which existence is merely possible. A thing whose existence is necessary is a thing whose non-existence would lead to a logical contradiction. God is "a being necessary through itself."[402] Because it is possible to think or conceive of something that does not exist, that thing has an essence which is separate from its existence. Thus "essence and existence are ontologically distinct," and God is "a being in whom essence and existence are identical."[403]

Al-Farabi sought to harmonize Greek philosophy with Islamic theology, but he subordinated revelation to reason. "Prophecy ... is subordinate to philosophy and assists it."[404] The "most perfect human being" is the person who can "translate abstract metaphysics into religious symbols."[405] Like Plato, al–Farabi believed that philosophy was indispensable to politics. He wrote, "if at a given time no philosophy at all is associated with the government, the state must, after a certain interval, inevitably perish."[406] The ideal ruler is both a philosopher and prophet. If this is not possible, the state should be governed by a Peripatetic or Neoplatonic philosopher.[407]

Al-Farabi's most significant original contributions were not in the natural sciences, but in the areas of metaphysics and music. "He wrote extensively on its [music's] history, theory, and instruments."[408]

In A.D. 942, the political situation in Baghdad became unsettled, and al–Farabi traveled to Damascus, Egypt, and then back to Damascus. He died in Damascus in A.D. 950.[409]

AVICENNA (A.D. 980–1037)

Avicenna (Ibn Sina) was an "encyclopedist, philosopher, physician, mathematician, and astronomer."[410] As many as 276 manuscripts have been attributed to Avicenna,[411] but the true number of his works is likely to be closer to 100.[412]

Avicenna is best known as a doctor. He wrote a comprehensive treatise on medical practice, the *Canon*, that was a million words in length.[413] The *Canon* was regarded in Europe as the leading medical authority for six centuries, and was used as a textbook at "the universities of Louvain and Montpellier" up to the year A.D. 1650.[414] "Probably no medical work ever written has been so much studied."[415]

Avicenna "was born in the village of Kharmaithan, not far from Bukhara,"[416] in present day Uzbekistan. At that time, Bukhara was "one of the chief cities of the Moslem world, prosperous and wealthy, situated on the highways between China, India and the western countries and famous especially for its culture and learning."[417] Avicenna's father was Persian.[418]

The primary sources for Avicenna's life are a short autobiography and a brief biography by his student, al–Juzjani. Al-Juzjani's biography complements the autobiography by commencing at the point in Avicenna's life where the autobiography ends. In his autobiography, Avicenna stated that he was precocious as a child. "By the time I was ten I had mastered the *Koran* and a great deal of literature, so that I was marveled at for my aptitude."[419] Avicenna's father saw to his son's further instruction, sending him to a grocer for instruction on "Indian arithmetic," and inviting a philosopher to reside in their home and instruct his son.[420]

Whatever Avicenna's faults may have been, modesty was not one of them. He said that his teacher "marveled at me exceedingly, and warned my father that I should not engage in any other occupation but learning; whatever problem he stated to me, I showed a better mental conception of it than he."[421]

After concluding that he already knew more than his teacher, Avicenna resolved to educate himself. He studied logic, Euclid's geometry, and Ptolemy's *Almagest*. Having mastered these subjects, he then devoted himself to "natural science and metaphysics, until all the gates of knowledge were open to me."[422] From this, he next turned to medicine, and concluded "medicine is not a difficult science."[423] Avicenna began to treat patients at the age of sixteen.

The youth's study habits were intense. After acquiring a mastery of medicine at age sixteen, he informs us that he devoted the next "eighteen months ... entirely to reading."[424] He interrupted his studies by sleep when necessary, but never slept through an entire night. If Avicenna encountered a difficulty in his studies, or a problem he could not solve, he had two methods for dealing with it. He might temporarily leave his scholarly work and go to a mosque and pray. Or, he would concentrate on his problem before falling asleep at night so his mind could find the solution in a dream.[425]

Avicenna's eighteen months of study between the ages of sixteen and eighteen continued until "I had made myself master of all the sciences: I now comprehended them to the limits of human possibility."[426]

Having mastered "logic, natural sciences and mathematics," Avicenna "returned to metaphysics," but found the subject to be immensely difficult.[427] He read Aristotle's *Metaphysics* forty times, virtually memorizing the text, but still lacked an adequate comprehension of it. Visiting a bookstall one day, Avicenna happened to find a copy of a commentary on *Metaphysics* authored by al–Farabi. This book finally explained and clarified the subject for him, and al–Farabi was subsequently a significant influence on the development of Avicenna's philosophy.

At the age of eighteen, Avicenna entered the service of the Sultan of Bukhara. The Sultan came down with an illness that his own physicians could not cure, and Avicenna was consulted. Avicenna gained access to the Sultan's vast library, and continued to educate himself, reading everything he could on the subject of medicine.

When Avicenna reached the age of twenty-two, his father died, and he was obliged to travel and begin service under a series of Islamic princes and rulers.[428] His fortunes varied over the years as he fell in and out of political favor. At Hamadan [Iran], Avicenna was appointed vizier. "But the army conspired against him ... they surrounded his house, hauled him off to prison, [and] pillaged his belongings."[429] Avicenna was restored to his post when the amir suffered from "a fresh attack of illness,"[430] and required Avicenna's services as a physician.

Avicenna is infamous for having indulged himself excessively in sex and alcohol. According to his student and biographer, Avicenna "was especially strong sexually; this indeed was a prevailing passion with him, and he indulged it to such an extent that his constitution was affected."[431] The scholar and his students also liked to spend every night drinking and partying. After their studies were concluded, "the various musicians would enter; vessels were brought out for a drinking party; and so we occupied ourselves."[432]

Although the *Canon* was one of the most significant and influential works in medical literature, it was not especially original.[433] An eighteenth-century physician complained, "I could meet with little or nothing there [in Avicenna's *Canon*], but what is taken originally from Galen, or what at least occurs, with a very small variation, in Rhazes."[434]

Avicenna's medicine was derivative of Hippocrates, the Greek tradition, and the books of Galen.[435] He adopted the theory of the four humors.[436] "According to this celebrated theory, the body contains four humors—blood, phlegm, yellow bile and black bile, a right proportion and mixture of which constitute health; improper proportions or irregular distribution, disease."[437] The theory of the four humors originated with the Hippocratic writings, c. 400 B.C. In *The Nature of Man*, an ancient Greek physician wrote, "the human body contains blood, phlegm, yellow bile and black bile. These are the things that make up its constitution and cause its pains and health."[438] The idea that disease resulted from an imbalance of the body's humor's remained the dominant medical theory for nearly two thousand years.

Avicenna's *Canon* was popular in Medieval Europe because it was well-written and comprehensive. Avicenna "had the gift of popular writing and could make a subject his own and explain it briefly and succinctly to the world."[439] The *Canon* became "to the medical world, the book of books, the *Koran* of the healing art, the rule and confession of faith of all physicians throughout Persia, Syria, Arabia, and the continent of Europe, for a period of well nigh six hundred years ... [and Avicenna] was surnamed Prince of Physicians."[440] In Medieval Europe, physicians tended to view the *Canon* as "complete and sufficient," and adopted the attitude that that Avicenna's work "could not be improved."[441] George Sarton thus concluded that Avicenna's "triumph was too complete; it discouraged original investigations and sterilized intellectual life."[442]

Avicenna's philosophy was "in the main a codification of Aristotle modified by fundamental views of Neo-Platonist origin, and it tends to be a compromise with theology."[443] His metaphysics and cosmology were derivative of al–Farabi.[444] God is "a necessary being [that] has no cause."[445] "The whole world is disposed and predetermined, known and willed by God,"[446] and man is a microcosm of the universe.[447] Furthermore, "the high purpose of creation was Man, and nothing else."[448]

In metaphysics, Avicenna adopted al–Farabi's distinction of dividing things into those whose existence was necessary and those whose existence was merely possible. In his treatise, *The Healing Metaphysics*, Avicenna explained, "things which are included in existence can be divided in the mind into two [categories]. One of these is that which ... does not have its existence by necessity ... this thing is in the domain of possibility. The other of these is that which, when it is considered in itself, has its existence by necessity."[449]

Ontology is the "branch of metaphysics concerned with the nature or essence of being or existence,"[450] and Avicenna is the originator of the *Ontological Proof* for the existence of God. This proof is usually attributed to Anselm (A.D. 1033–1109), the archbishop of Canterbury. Anselm originally presented the proof in Chapter 2 of his work, *Proslogium*.

> It is one thing for an object to be in the understanding, and another to understand that the object exists. When a painter first conceives of what he will afterwards perform, he has it in his understanding, but he does not yet understand it to be, because he has not yet performed it. But after he has made the painting, he both has it in his understanding, and he understands that it exists, because he has made it. Hence, even the fool is convinced that something exists in the understanding, at least, than which nothing greater can be conceived. For, when he hears of this, he understands it. And whatever is understood, exists in the understanding. And assuredly that, than which nothing greater can be conceived, cannot exist in the understanding alone. For, suppose it exists in the understanding alone: then it can be conceived to exist in reality; which is greater. Therefore, if that, than which nothing greater can be conceived, exists in the understanding alone, the very being, than which nothing greater can be conceived, is one, than which a greater can be conceived. But obviously this is impossible Hence, there is no doubt that there exists a being, than which nothing greater can be conceived, and it exists both in the understanding and in reality.[451]

Paraphrasing, Anselm's ontological proof is that "God is that being than whom none greater can be conceived. Now, if that than which nothing greater can be conceived existed only in the intellect, it would not be the absolutely greatest, for we could add to it existence in reality. It follows, then, that the being than whom nothing greater can be conceived, i.e. God, necessarily has real existence."[452]

The weakness of the Ontological Proof is that "from a definition one may not infer the existence of the thing defined."[453] But "untenable as Anselm's argument is logically, it possesses a strong fascination, and contains a great truth. The being of God is an intuition of the mind, which can only be explained by God's objective existence."[454]

Avicenna's ontological proof was based upon his metaphysical distinction between things whose existence is necessary and those whose existence is only possible. Things that are necessarily in existence are either self-sufficient or their existence depends on another being. Avicenna argued that "only something necessary through itself exists without a cause," and that all things that exist depend upon this self-sufficient entity for their existence.[455] "Contingent beings end in a Necessary Being."[456] This ultimate, necessary, and self-sufficient being that is its own cause, "is not relative, not changeable, not multiple, not sharing in respect to the existence which is peculiar to it."[457] This unique Being is God, and all things depend on it for their existence.

Avicenna argued that intellect was primary and superior to understanding through the senses. In his "flying man,"[458] he anticipated the French philosopher René Descartes (1596–1650). Suppose a man were floating in space, cut off from all sensory perceptions. He cannot see, hear, or even feel his own limbs. Could such a man know he exists? Yes, "a man could conceive his own essence without conceiving his body,"[459] and therefore the soul is superior to the physical body. Thus the indisputable certainty was the existence of self-awareness. Descartes would later argue that "I *think*, therefore *I am*"[460] was an irrefutable truth, and use it as the foundation of a philosophic system based upon deductive logic.

In keeping with Aristotle's views, Avicenna rejected atomism and the possibility that a vacuum could exist.[461] He characterized astrology as "only a probable science."[462] Avicenna investigated alchemy, but "did not believe in the possibility of chemical transmutation."[463]

In addition to making contributions to medicine and philosophy, Avicenna studied "various physical questions— motion, contact, force, vacuum, infinity, light, heat."[464] He noted that if light had a particulate nature, its speed of propagation must be finite.[465]

According to his student, al–Juzjani, Avicenna was ordered by one of his patrons to "undertake observations of the stars."[466] In his astronomical observations, Avicenna "invented instruments the like of which had never been seen before."[467]

Avicenna also made prescient geological observations and interpretations. Some medieval Latin translations of Aristotle's *Meteorologica* contain a chapter titled *De Mineralibus* that is believed to have been authored by Avicenna.[468]

After observing that clay deposits on river banks dried and hardened in the sun, and that water dripping from the roofs of caves formed stalagmites and stalactites, Avicenna proposed that stone was formed either by "the hardening of clay," or "by the congelation of waters."[469] To explain the apparent transformation of water into stone, as well as the petrification of both plants and animals, Avicenna proposed the existence of "a powerful mineralizing and petrifying virtue which arises in certain stony spots, or emanates suddenly from the earth during earthquakes and subsidences."[470]

Avicenna recognized that the sea and land had changed place in the past, and explained "it is for this reason that in many stones, where they are broken, are found parts of aquatic animals, such as shells, etc."[471] Mountains were formed in two ways, either directly by earthquakes or indirectly by the erosion of surrounding land. "In many violent earthquakes, the wind which produces the earthquake raises a part of the ground and a height is suddenly formed."[472] However the elevation of mountains and hills could also be caused by "the excavating action of floods and winds on the matter which lies between them."[473]

In the nineteenth century, Charles Lyell (1797–1875) established the modern science of geology by invoking a rigid uniformitarianism. "All past changes on the globe had been brought about by the slow agency of existing causes."[474] He was anticipated by Avicenna, who suggested that river valleys were formed slowly over the ages by repeated floods. "This action [erosion of a valley], however, took place and was completed only in the course of many ages, so that the trace of each individual flood has not been left."[475]

Avicenna died at the relatively young age of 58. Al-Juzjani said that the cause of Avicenna's demise was "colic," abdominal pain that can be caused by a number of different diseases. Al-Juzjani also attributed his teacher's early death to overindulgence in sex and wine.[476]

AL-BIRUNI (C. A.D. 973–1050)

While Avicenna was noted primarily for his work in medicine and philosophy, his contemporary al–Biruni (c. A.D. 973–1050) was known for his contributions to the sciences. Al-Biruni was "perhaps the most prominent figure in the phalanx of those universally learned Muslim scholars who characterize the Golden Age of Islamic science."[477] George Sarton noted that "his [al–Biruni's] critical spirit, toleration, love of truth, and intellectual courage were almost without parallel in medieval times."[478] "Al-Biruni was more of a discoverer ... [while] ibn Sina [Avicenna] was essentially an organizer, an encyclopedist, [and] a philosopher."[479] Although al–Biruni was familiar with philosophy, history, and medicine, "his bent was strongly toward the study of observable phenomena."[480] His most significant contributions were in the areas of "astronomy, mathematics, geography, and history."[481]

Al-Biruni was born in the province of Khwarazm, in present day Uzbekistan, near the shoreline of the Aral Sea. Al-Biruni's family was Iranian, thus his ethnicity was likely Persian.[482] At an early age, al–Biruni studied with the mathematician and astronomer Abu Nasr Mansur, and made serious astronomical observations as early as the age of seventeen.[483]

Starting approximately in A.D. 995, al–Biruni seems to have traveled and served under the patronage of several rulers. But by A.D. 1003, he was back in his native country, and working as court astrologer for the local ruler, Abul Abbas Mamun. In addition to his scholarly responsibilities, al–Biruni seems to also have had diplomatic duties. He was sent to negotiate with tribal chiefs because he had a "tongue of silver and of gold."[484]

In A.D. 1017, Khwarazm was invaded in force by Mahmud, sultan of Ghazna in Afghanistan. Mahmud carried off al–Biruni "and other scholars to Afghanistan."[485] Although Mahmud has been assessed as "one of the greatest figures in Mohammadan history," whose "magnificent encouragement of science, art, and literature, was no less remarkable than his genius as a general and statesman,"[486] he did not have a cordial relationship with al–Biruni. Edward C. Sachau (1845–1930), translator of al–Biruni's *India*, noted that a dedication al–Biruni authored to Mahmud after the sultan's death was sparse in its praise. "The

manner in which the author [al–Biruni] mentions the dead king [Mahmud] is cold, cold in the extreme ... the words of praise bestowed upon him [Mahmud] are meager and stiff."[487]
The following apocryphal tale is told of Mahmud's mistreatment of al–Biruni.

> One day the Sultan [Mahmud], while seated in his four-doored summer-house in the Garden of a Thousand Trees in Ghazna, requested al–Biruni to forecast, by his knowledge of the stars, by which door the King would leave the building. When al–Biruni had complied with this command, and had written his answer secretly on a piece of paper which he placed under a quilt, the Sultan caused a hole to be made in one of the walls, and by this quitted the summer-house. Then he called for al–Biruni's prognostication, and found to his disgust that on it was written, "The King will go out by none of these four doors, but an opening will be made in the eastern wall by which he will leave the building." Sultan Mahmud, who had hoped to turn the laugh against al–Biruni was so angry that he ordered him [al–Biruni] to be cast down from the roof. His fall was, however, broken by a mosquito-curtain; and, on being again brought before the Sultan and asked whether he had foreseen this, he produced from his pocket a note-book in which was written, under the date, "Today I shall be cast down from a high place, but shall reach the earth in safety, and arise sound in body." Thereupon the Sultan, still more incensed, caused him [al–Biruni] to be confined in the citadel, from which he was only released after six month's imprisonment at the intercession of the prime minister.[488]

It is certain that al–Biruni accompanied Mahmud on his invasions of India. "Between [A.D.] 1001 and 1024," Mahmud conducted "raids undertaken with a view to plunder and to satisfy the righteous iconoclasm of a true Muslim ... [he] returned to Ghazna laden with costly spoils from the Hindu temples."[489] Al-Biruni noted with disgust that Mahmud's raids had "utterly ruined the prosperity of the country [India]," and as a result the "Hindu sciences have retired far away from those parts of the country conquered by us ... [and the] antagonism between them [the Hindus] and all foreigners [has] received more and more nourishment both from political and religious sources."[490]

Although Mahmud's expeditions to India appear to have been conducted primarily or solely for the purpose of gathering plunder, the raids provided al–Biruni an opportunity to become acquainted with Hindu science, culture, and society. The scholar recorded his observations and studies in *India*, a work which provides "a comprehensive survey of Indian intellectual achievements and social practices as they existed around [A.D.] 1030."[491] Because al–Biruni also systematically compared Hindu civilization with Islamic, *India* also provides invaluable information on Islamic culture of the early eleventh century A.D.

In the preface of *India*, al–Biruni stated that his goal as an historian and geographer was to compile an objective record of the facts. "This book is not a polemical one. I shall not produce the arguments of our antagonists in order to refute such of them as I believe to be in the wrong. My book is nothing but a simple historic record of facts."[492]

In Chapter 1 of *India*, al–Biruni appeared to be anything but objective when he complained of Hindu vanity and egoism. "Folly is an illness for which there is no medicine, and the Hindus believe that there is no country but theirs, no nation like theirs, no kings like theirs, no religion like theirs, no science like theirs. They are haughty, foolishly vain, self-conceited, and stolid."[493] But earlier he had confessed that all people considered themselves to be superior to foreigners. "A similar depreciation of foreigners not only prevails among us and the Hindus, but is common to all nations towards each other."[494]

Al-Biruni conceded that the Hindus had a superior arithmetic. "The Hindus use the numerical signs in arithmetic in the same way we do. I have composed a treatise showing how far, possibly, the Hindus are ahead of us in this subject."[495] He criticized the Hindus for cultural practices that differed from the Muslim norms, but then conceded that "the heathen Arabs too committed crimes and obscenities."[496]

According to al–Biruni, the foremost science in India was astronomy. "The science of astronomy is the most famous among them [the Hindus]."[497] The Hindus knew the Earth to be spherical. "According to them [the Hindus], heaven as well as the whole world is round, and the Earth has a globular shape, the northern half being dry land, the southern half being covered with water. The dimension of the Earth is larger according to them than it is according to the Greeks and modern observations."[498]

Al-Biruni noted that the Hindu "astronomers follow the theologians in everything which does not encroach upon their science,"[499] thus implying that primacy was given to science over religion in areas where the two might be in conflict.

India contains a fascinating short discussion by al–Biruni as to whether or not the Earth rotates. Al-Biruni noted that either a rotating or stationary Earth could explain the observations, and concluded that the question was difficult to resolve. "The rotation of the Earth does in no way impair the value of astronomy, as all appearances of an astronomic character can quite as well be explained according to this theory as to the other. There are, however, other reasons which make it [rotation of the Earth] impossible. This question is most difficult to solve. The most prominent of both modern and ancient astronomers have deeply studied the question of the moving of the Earth, and tried to refute it."[500]

Al-Biruni made geological observations while in India, and speculated that the country had once been an ocean basin that had been subsequently filled by sediment deposited by streams.

> If you have seen the soil of India with your own eyes ... if you consider the rounded stones found in the earth however deeply you dig, stones that are huge near the mountains and where the rivers have a violent current; stones that are of smaller size at greater distances from the mountains, and where the streams flow more slowly; stones that appear pulverized in the shape of sand where the streams begin to stagnate near their mouths and near the sea — if you consider all this, you could scarcely help thinking that India has once been a sea which by degrees has been filled up by the alluvium of the streams.[501]

Al-Biruni noted the uniformity of nature, an underlying corollary to naturalism, and the basis of all science. "Its [nature's] action is under all circumstances one and the same."[502] Al-Biruni did not consider alchemy to be a science. He characterized it as "witchcraft," defined as "making by some kind of delusion a thing appear to the sense as something different from what it is in reality."[503] And, "as that which is impossible cannot be produced, the whole affair is nothing but a gross deception. Therefore witchcraft in this sense has nothing whatever to do with science."[504]

When asked why scholars such as himself sought the patronage of princes, al–Biruni explained, "scholars are well aware of the use of money, but the rich are ignorant of the nobility of science."[505] Al-Biruni was pessimistic concerning the status and progress of the sciences in his time. "It is quite impossible that a new science or any new kind of research should arise in our days. What we have of sciences is nothing but the scanty remains of bygone better times."[506]

Al-Biruni endorsed the principle of Christian brotherhood and charity, but concluded it was impractical.

> The Christians ... [believe] to give to him who has stripped you of your coat also your shirt, to offer to him who has beaten your cheek the other cheek also, to bless your enemy and to pray for him. Upon my life, this is a noble philosophy; but the people of this world are not all philosophers. Most of them are ignorant and erring, who cannot be kept on the straight road save by

the sword and the whip. And, indeed, ever since Constantine the Victorious became a Christian, both sword and whip have ever been employed, for without them it would be impossible to rule.[507]

When he was sixty-three years old, al–Biruni made a list of his works that totaled 113.[508] But as he continued working for several more years, the total number of al–Biruni's manuscripts has been estimated to exceed 146,[509] and may be as large as 180.[510]

In addition to *India*, al–Biruni's most important works include *The Chronology of Ancient Nations*, a description and compilation of "the religious institutes of various nations and sects, founded in more ancient times, and, more or less, still practiced and adhered to by the Oriental world about A.D. 1000."[511] It is "the first work of its kind in world literature ... [and] an invaluable source of material for the history of religions and folklore."[512]

In the preface to *Chronology*, al–Biruni noted that such a history could only be compiled from historical tradition, not the methodologies of philosophy or science. "This object cannot be obtained by way of ratiocination with philosophical notions, or of inductions based upon the observations of our senses, but solely by adopting the information of those who have a written tradition."[513] In this remarkable sentence, it was revealed that al–Biruni understood philosophy to be based upon the pure exercise of reason, but the methodology of science to be empiricism and induction. He thus foreshadowed Francis Bacon's (A.D. 1561–1626) advocacy of inductive empiricism.

Al-Biruni also noted that anyone writing a history dealing with diverse peoples, cultures, and religions, should free their mind of preconceived biases. "We must clear our mind from all those accidental circumstances which deprave most men, from all causes which are liable to make people blind against the truth, e.g., inveterate custom, party-spirit, rivalry, being addicted to one's passions, the desire to gain influence, etc."[514] Al-Biruni "had a remarkably open mind, but his tolerance was not extended to the dilettante, the fool, or the bigot."[515]

Lacking quantitative means of establishing dates, al–Biruni divided the history of the world into eras. The first of these was the era of Creation. According to religious traditions, the Earth was estimated to be a few thousand years old. "The Persians and Magians ... count from the beginning of the world till Alexander 3,258 years ... [but] a section of the Persians is of [the] opinion that ... before that [human creation], already 6,000 years had elapsed."[516]

The Jews and Christians also estimated the time elapsed since Creation to have been only a few thousand years. "According to the doctrine of the Jews, the time between Adam and Alexander [356–323 B.C.] is 3,448 years, whilst, according to the Christian doctrine, it is 5,180 years."[517]

The era of Creation was followed by the era of the Deluge, defined as the era "in which everything perished at the time of Noah."[518] al–Biruni noted that the Jews estimated the time that passed between the Deluge and Alexander to be 1,792 years, but the Christian estimate was 2,938 years.[519] Although he was dealing with periods of time lasting for thousands of years, in one passage al–Biruni noted that it was theoretically possible for astronomical or stellar cycles to last for billions of years. "If you then ask the mathematicians as to the length of time, after which they [stars] would meet each other in a certain point, or before which they had met each other in that identical point, no blame attaches to him, if he speaks of billions of years."[520] But this observation is qualified by the fact that the heavenly bodies did not exist before the Creation, and therefore any such calculation must be of a theoretical nature only.

Working in the tradition apparently begun by al–Biruni, in the seventeenth century A.D. Anglican Bishop James Ussher (1581–1656) estimated the precise time of Creation to be the night preceding the 23rd of October, 4004 B.C.[521] But al–Biruni was more circumspect in his chronology, and skeptical of the ability to establish exact dates. In describing the era of Creation he stated, "everything, the knowledge of which is connected with the beginning of creation and with the history of bygone generations, is mixed up with falsifications and myths."[522] In estimating a date for the more recent Deluge, al–Biruni concluded "there is such a difference of opinions, and such a confusion, that you have no chance of deciding as to the correctness of the matter, and do not even feel inclined to investigate thoroughly its historical truth."[523]

Additional works by al–Biruni include *Astrolabe*, a book describing the use and construction of the astrolabe, and the *Tahdid*, a treatise in geography dealing with the mathematical problem of establishing coordinates.[524] In *Densities*, al–Biruni developed a technique for estimating the specific gravity of irregularly-shaped objects. Precise values are reported for various metals, stones, and liquids. The *Shadows* is concerned with all topics involving shadows, including pertinent subjects from optics and astronomy. The gnomon is discussed, and trigonometric tables are given.[525] The *Canon* is a comprehensive work on astronomy and "contains detailed numerical tables for solving all the standard problems of the medieval astronomer-astrologer."[526] The great breadth of al–Biruni's interests and works is shown by the titles of other works, including *Gems*, *Pharmacology*,[527] and *Elements of Astrology*.[528]

In A.D. 1030, the sultan Mahmud died, and it may be inferred that al–Biruni fared better in the court of his son, Masud, who ascended to the throne. Masud "was a drunkard, and lost in less than a decennium [decade] most of what his father's sword and policy had gained in thirty-three years."[529] Yet in the preface of his *Canon*, al–Biruni praised Masud profusely, and acknowledged that Masud had allowed him [al–Biruni] to "devote myself entirely to the service of science."[530]

The traditional date ascribed to al–Biruni's death is A.D. 1048.[531] However, near the beginning of the twentieth century, a previously unknown manuscript was found in which al–Biruni referred to himself as being more than eighty years old. Therefore he must have died sometime after A.D. 1050.[532]

AVERROES (IBN RUSHD, A.D. 1126–1198)

Ibn Rushd (A.D. 1126–1198), known in the West as Averroes, was a twelfth-century Islamic philosopher best known for his commentaries on Aristotle. He "was the last of the great Arabic-writing philosophers."[533] Averroes' works were a significant factor in the revival of learning in Europe. "With Aristotle there arrived Averroes."[534] Averroes was also an astronomer and physician, but his most significant contributions were made in the area of philosophy.[535]

Averroes was born in Cordova, Spain, "to an important Spanish family,"[536] with a history of serving as jurists. Initially educated in Islamic law, Averroes later studied medicine under the tutelage of Abu Ja'far. It is likely at this time that the became acquainted with the works of Aristotle and the science of astronomy.[537]

In 1153, Averroes was in Marrakesh (Morocco), where he made the acquaintance of the philosopher and astronomer, ibn Tufayl.[538] In 1169, ibn Tufayl introduced Averroes to the caliph Abu Yaqub Yusuf. The caliph asked ibn Tufayl and Averroes whether the heavens were eternal, or had been created. As the junior philosopher, Averroes initially remained quiet. But he eventually joined the conversation and impressed the caliph with his brilliance.[539]

Averroes was subsequently appointed a judge in Seville and assigned the task of writing commentaries on Aristotle's works. Reportedly, the caliph asked ibn Tufayl to author the works, but he in turn delegated the chore to Averroes, thus assuring his student's immortality.[540]

In philosophy, Averroes was thoroughly an Aristotelian. He "regarded Aristotelianism as the truth, inasmuch as truth is accessible to the human mind."[541] Averroes wrote, "The doctrine of Aristotle is the supreme truth, because his intellect was the limit of the human intellect. It is therefore rightly said that he was created and given to us by divine providence, so that we might know all that can be known."[542]

Averroes considered the demonstrations of deductive logic to be a superior epistemology, even to the evidence of the senses. If anyone observed a phenomenon that appeared to contradict Aristotle's logical proof, they must be wrong. Thus he said, "whatever Galen may have seen by anatomy, it cannot possibly contradict the conclusions of Aristotle, for the simple reason that these are universal demonstrations ... it is a character of such demonstrations that no sense perception can ever contradict them."[543]

As a student of Aristotle's, Averroes' work had two goals. First, he sought to expel Neoplatonic influences and doctrines from a corrupted Aristotelianism promulgated by Avicenna. Secondly, as a devout Muslim, Averroes attempted to reconcile Aristotelian philosophy with Islamic theology.

Averroes rejected the Neoplatonic doctrine of emanation, and held that the individual intellect does not survive death.[544] "Immortality, therefore, is general, not particular."[545] Avicenna had argued that essence or form was ontologically superior to physical existence. "Matter depends on form for its existence in the concrete and cannot exist separately from it, [but] form can."[546] Therefore, metaphysics, the study of being as being, was superior to physics, the study of things that exist. Averroes disagreed, and characterized Avicenna's metaphysics as a corruption of Aristotle's teachings. Physics was superior to metaphysics, because all of our ideas came from observation of individual things that exist. "Without the study of physics, the human mind would lack even the idea of change or movement."[547]

Averroes attempted to reconcile apparent conflicts between Islamic theology and Aristotelean philosophy. He argued that the Islamic religious law, properly understood, not only allowed the study of nature by philosophers, but obligated its pursuit. "The Law summons to reflection on beings, and the pursuit of knowledge about them,"[548] because "he who does not understand the product of art does not understand the Artisan."[549]

Averroes concluded that "demonstrative truth and scriptural truth cannot conflict."[550] "We the Muslim community know definitely that demonstrative study does not lead to [conclusions] conflicting with what Scripture has given us; for truth does not oppose truth but accords with it and bears witness to it."[551]

If there were instances in which a truth from science or natural philosophy appeared to conflict with the literal script of the *Koran*, then that verse of the *Koran* must be interpreted allegorically. The *Koran* was intended to reach all classes of men. God "has addressed each class according to the degree of their understanding,"[552] and therefore "each spirit has the right and the duty to understand and interpret the *Koran* in the most perfect way of which it is capable."[553]

In invoking allegorical interpretation of the *Koran*, Averroes in fact was on sound theological ground. The *Koran* itself stated that it was subject to interpretation, and that "none knoweth its [true] interpretation but God."[554] Symbolic interpretation was obviously necessary in some cases. Sura 20, Verse 4, stated "The God of mercy sitteth on his throne."[555] But God was an immaterial Being and did not sit as a man. Thus there had to be a theological interpretation. Averroes concluded, "whenever the conclusion of a [philosophic] demonstration is in conflict with the apparent meaning of Scripture, that apparent meaning admits of allegorical interpretation."[556] He thus gave primacy to philosophy over theology, a conclusion that was unacceptable to the religious authorities.

In astronomy, compared to philosophy, Averroes was a dilettante. However he found the Ptolemaic system of eccentrics, epicycles, and equants to be "completely unacceptable."[557] In part, this was because the system was not Aristotelean, and in part because Averroes regarded the complexities of the Ptolemaic system as being a non-physical model adopted for the purpose of calculating positions.[558]

Averroes "hesitated to offer definite solutions"[559] to astronomical problems, but favored a return to the simpler system of Aristotle based on concentric and homocentric revolving spheres. He regarded the heavenly bodies as consisting of two parts, a physical corpus and an immaterial intelligence. The associated intelligence provided each heavenly body with its movement and form. These intelligences were the "motive, efficient and final causes of the celestial bodies."[560]

The caliph Abu Yaqub Yusuf died in A.D. 1184, and Averroes continued his work under the patronage of Ya'qub al–Mansur until 1195. In that year, the faction represented by Islamic fundamentalists asserted their political power. Averroes, whose studies and writings were viewed with "deep dislike and distrust,"[561] was accused of heresy and banished to the town of Lucena located near Cordova. The caliph ordered that Averroes' books be burned, and the study of philosophy was prohibited.[562]

The caliph's action appears to have been one of short-term political necessity, perhaps to appease a religious faction in Spain, because shortly afterwards Averroes was allowed to return to Morocco and his position and honor were restored. He died shortly thereafter, in A.D. 1198 at the age of seventy-two.[563]

Decline of Islamic Science and Philosophy

THE MADRASAS (C. ELEVENTH CENTURY A.D.)

Although philosophers such as al–Kindi and Averroes tried to harmonize Greek philosophy and science with Islam, ultimately they failed. In the eleventh century A.D., Hellenistic studies in the Islamic civilization were on the wane, and by the end of the twelfth century A.D. they were essentially extinct.

The traditional areas of learning in Islam were considered to be "grammar, poetry, history, theology, and law."[564] Disciplines such as philosophy, mathematics, and astronomy were always regarded as imported productions of a foreign culture. "The foreign sciences never ceased to be viewed by the great majority of Muslims as useless, alien, and perhaps dangerous."[565] The gulf between Greek science and Islam "reappear[ed] throughout Islamic history as a kind of geological fault"[566] that could not be bridged.

In Medieval Europe, science served theology. But religious authority was never cemented through Western society in the conclusive manner that it was in Islamic civilization. After the central authority of the Catholic Church was broken by the Reformation in the sixteenth century, the practice of the sciences in Western Europe grew explosively.

But "Islam was a nomocracy,"[567] a "system of government based on a legal code,"[568] and this legal code was derived entirely from religious law. Religious and secular authority were one and the same. In Europe, law was influenced by Christianity, but not exclusively determined or controlled by religion. Religious freedom meant intellectual freedom, and the sciences were allowed to develop.

An important factor in the withering of Greek science and philosophy in Islam was the exclusion of these subjects from the institutions of higher education, the *madrasas*.[569] A *madrasas* is "an institution of higher learning where the Islamic sciences are taught."[570] In this context the phrase "Islamic sciences," most definitely excludes the rational philosophy and sciences inherited from the Greek tradition. "The madrasa was the embodiment of Islam's ideal religious science, law, and of Islam's ideal religious orientation, traditionalism."[571] "The Sunni madrasa was established essentially for the purpose of training students in the sacred law and other religious sciences; its program consisted primarily of the Quran, Hadith, exegesis, Arabic grammar and literature, law, theology and oratory."[572]

The madrasas evolved from educational courses taught in mosques, and became ascendant in the eleventh century A.D.[573] The madrasas were established "to teach the systems of *fikh*,"[574] where *fikh* is the science of Islamic religious law. Any private institution that might teach the "foreign" sciences was starved out of existence by the laws governing *waqfs*.[575] A *waqf* is a charitable endowment in Islamic law. An individual making a philanthropic gift or *waqf* had a wide latitude in determining its terms and conditions, but there was an important exception: "the terms of the waqf instrument could not in any way contravene the tenets of Islam."[576] Thus the traditionalists and religious conservatives were exclusively favored. The "foreign" sciences and rational philosophy were completely excluded from all institutions of higher education.[577]

AL-GHAZALI (A.D. 1058–1111)

One of the most important factors in the decline of Islamic philosophy and science was the work of al–Ghazali (A.D. 1058–1111). Al-Ghazali was a "jurist, theologian, philosopher, and mystic."[578] His most important works were *The Rescuer from Error*,[579] an autobiographical account of his intellectual life, and *The Incoherence of the Philosophers*,[580] a refutation of Neoplatonic Aristotelianism.

Al-Ghazali's father had been unfulfilled in his thirst for knowledge, and he bequeathed his life savings as a means of ensuring the education of his sons. Al-Ghazali studied law, which in Islam is inseparable from religion. From an early age, al–Ghazali was destined to be a scholar. He explained, "the thirst for knowledge was innate in me from an early age; it was like a second nature implanted by God, without any will on my part."[581]

During his study of jurisprudence, al–Ghazali "took copious notes, but neglected to impress on his memory what he had written."[582] While traveling, he was beset by robbers, and his notes were stolen. Frantic, al–Ghazali chased after the brigands, demanding the return of his study notes. The robbers were astonished and partially amused. "The robber chief asked him what were these notes of his. Said al–Ghazali with great simplicity, 'They are writings in that bag; I traveled for the sake of hearing them and writing them down and knowing the science in them.' Thereat the robber chief laughed consumedly and said, 'How can you profess to know the science in them when we have taken them from you and stripped you of the knowledge and there you are without any science?' But he gave them back. 'And,' says al–Ghazali, 'this man was sent by God to teach me.'"[583]

Al-Ghazali studied several more years, taking care to commit his lessons to memory. He was a student not only of Islamic law, but also applied himself to "theology, dialectic, science, philosophy, [and] logic."[584] Al-Ghazali made the acquaintance of "Nizam al–Mulk, vizier of the Saljuk sultan Malikshah."[585] Nizam al–Mulk "was the greatest man in the Empire and its real ruler ... [if he] was not the first to found Madrasas, he at least extended them largely."[586]

In A.D. 1091,[587] at the age of 33, al–Ghazali was "appointed to teach in the Madrasa at Baghdad."[588] His position was prestigious, and al–Ghazali, although relatively young, quickly acquired a reputation as a scholar and teacher. At this time, al–Ghazali intensified his studies. He later wrote, "I have interrogated the beliefs of each sect and scrutinized the mysteries of each doctrine, in order to disentangle truth from error and orthodoxy from heresy.... There is no philosopher whose system I have not fathomed, nor theologian the intricacies of whose doctrine I have not followed out."[589]

Al-Ghazali desired certain truth, not probable. "Certitude is the clear and complete knowledge of things, such knowledge as leaves no room for doubt nor possibility of error and conjecture, so that there remains no room in the mind for error to find an entrance ... forms of knowledge ... [that are not impervious] to doubt do not deserve any confidence."[590]

The young scholar began to systematically examine the epistemological basis of knowledge. He divided the possible ways of acquiring knowledge into three categories: sense perception, reason, and revelation.

At first, sense perception seemed to al–Ghazali to be the most certain way to obtain truth. But some intellectual reflection convinced him that the senses were unreliable.

> The result of a careful examination was that my confidence in them [the senses] was shaken. Our sight, for instance, perhaps the best practiced of all our senses, observes a shadow, and finding it apparently stationary pronounces it devoid of movement. Observation and experience, however, show subsequently that a shadow moves not suddenly, it is true, but gradually and imperceptibly, so that it is never really motionless. Again, the eye sees a star and believes it as large as a piece of gold, but mathematical calculations prove, on the contrary, that it is larger than the earth. These notions, and all others which the senses declare true, are subsequently contradicted and convicted of falsity in an irrefragable manner by the verdict of reason. Then I reflected in myself: "Since I can not trust to the evidence of my senses, I must rely only on intellectual notions based on fundamental principles, such as the following axioms: Ten is more than three. Affirmation and negation cannot coexist together. A thing can not both be created and also existent from eternity, living and annihilated simultaneously, at once necessary and impossible."[591]

But the recognition that reason was a superior, or more reliable, method of obtaining knowledge than perception suggested the possibility of something above human reason. If reason was superior to perception, perhaps there existed another epistemology [revelation] that was superior to reason. "Perhaps, there is above reason, another judge, who, if he appeared, would convict reason of falsehood, just as reason has confuted [perception]."[592]

Al-Ghazali considered the possibility that this third way of knowing, the one that might be superior to ratiocination, was the mystic or ecstatic communion experienced by the Sufis. It was "a state in which, absorbed into themselves and in the suspension of sense-perceptions, they have visions beyond the reach of intellect."[593]

Known variously as illumination, ecstatic communion, or intuitive knowledge, mystic communion is an experience "of a supreme, all-pervading, and indwelling power, in whom all things are one."[594] Mystic communion is the basis of revelation, prophecy, and religion. It is one of the most powerful forces in human history, and also one of the least understood.

The mystic experience was the central element in Sufism, an Islamic sect that originated in ninth century A.D. Persia "as a kind of reaction against the rigid monotheism and formalism of Islam."[595] "The word *Sufi* is generally assumed to derive from *suf* (wool) in reference to the simple clothing of the early ascetic mystics."[596] The development of Sufism in Islam may have been influenced by the tradition of mysticism in other religions, including Christianity. But mysticism found a natural home in Islam, as Mohammed himself was a mystic and the *Koran* a revelation from God.

Corresponding to the three epistemologies recognized by al–Ghazali, there were three different groups of men who professed to know the truth. These were (1) the orthodox "Scholastic theologians, who profess to follow theory and speculation, (2) the philosophers, who profess to rely upon formal logic, [and] (3) the Sufis, who call themselves the elect of God and possessors of intuition and knowledge of the truth by means of ecstasy."[597]

Al-Ghazali critically examined the claims of each group. He quickly disposed of the orthodox theologians. The basis of their beliefs was simply authority and tradition. Al-Ghazali explained, "a method of argumentation like this has little value for one who only admits self-evident truths."[598]

The claims of the philosophers had to be taken more seriously. So al–Ghazali "proceeded from the study of scholastic theology to that of philosophy."[599] He spent two years engaged in a systematic study of the different philosophic systems. To thoroughly understand philosophy, al–Ghazali felt obliged to "make a profound study of that science; [I] must equal, nay surpass, those who know most of it, so as to penetrate into secrets of it unknown to them."[600]

After studying philosophy for two years, al–Ghazali "then spent about a year meditating on these systems after having thoroughly understood them ... in this manner I acquired a complete knowledge of all their [the philosopher's] subterfuges and subtleties, of what was truth and what was illusion in them."[601]

Philosophy did not supply al–Ghazali with the certain truth that he sought. So he turned to the mystic teachings of the Sufis. But this could not be learned in the scholar's study. Mystic communion was something that had to be experienced. Al-Ghazali concluded, "I saw that in order to understand it [Sufism] thoroughly one must combine theory with practice ... it became clear to me that the last stage could not be reached by mere instruction, but only by transport, ecstasy, and the transformation of the moral being."[602]

Al-Ghazali was beset by an existential crisis that affected his physical health. He lost his appetite, energy, and will to live, for he had lost his faith in the orthodox teachings of Islam. Al-Ghazali no longer believed that Islam could be supported by the exercise of reason, and he was eaten up by his own unbearable hypocrisy as a teacher of orthodox doctrine that he considered to be unsupportable. "I perceived that I was on the edge of an abyss, and that without an immediate conversion I should be doomed to eternal fire."[603]

Al-Ghazali decided to give up his prestigious teaching position, and go live with the Sufis. But his resolve failed. "The next day I gave up my resolution."[604] He found that he was unable to "give up this fine position, this honorable post exempt from trouble and rivalry, this seat of authority safe from attack."[605]

But the storm continued to rage. Al-Ghazali was "torn asunder by the opposite forces of earthly passions and religious aspirations ... [but] my will yielded and I gave myself up to destiny. God caused an impediment to chain my tongue and prevented me from lecturing. Vainly I desired, in the interest of my pupils, to go on with my teaching, but my mouth became dumb."[606]

Al-Ghazali finally "left Bagdad, giving up all my fortune."[607] On the threshold of a brilliant career, he simply walked away. Al-Ghazali left not only his teaching job, but also a family and children. He traveled to Syria, where he devoted two years to "retirement, meditation, and devout exercises."[608]

Among the mystic Sufis al–Ghazali found the certain truth that he was seeking in the form of divine revelation. "I saw God in a dream.... He said ..." abandon thy formal rules ... I pour forth upon thee lights from the protection of My holiness, so seize them and apply thyself." Then I awoke in great joy."[609]

According to al–Ghazali, the ecstatic communion experienced by the Sufis could not be described. "They [the Sufis] come to see in the waking state angels and souls of prophets; they hear their voices and wise counsels. By means of this contemplation of heavenly forms and images they rise by degrees to heights which human language can not reach, which one can not even indicate without falling into great and inevitable errors."[610]

Divine inspiration was above human reason. It could not be described or explained, only experienced. "He who does not arrive at the intuition of these truths by means of ecstasy, knows only the name of inspiration."

Any philosopher who denied the reality of mystic communion was merely ignorant. "Beyond reason and at a higher level by a new faculty of vision is bestowed upon him, by which he perceives invisible things, the secrets of the future and other concepts as inaccessible to reason as the concepts of reason are inaccessible to mere discrimination and what is perceived by discrimination to the senses. Just as the man possessed only of discrimination rejects and denies the notions acquired by reason, so do certain rationalists reject and deny the notion of inspiration. It is a proof of their profound ignorance."[611]

Al-Ghazali had now come full circle. He could return to his former orthodox beliefs because they had been substantiated by mystic communion. "When we have ascertained the real nature of inspiration and proceed to the serious study of the *Koran* and the traditions, we shall then know certainly that Mohammed is the greatest of the prophets."[612]

The scriptural authority of the *Koran* was to be accepted. "To believe in the Prophets is to admit that there is above intelligence a sphere in which are revealed to the inner vision truths beyond the grasp of intelligence, just as things seen are not apprehended by the sense of hearing, nor things understood by that of touch."

Having direct intuition of God, al–Ghazali no longer had any need of philosophy, reason, or science. He came to realize that the source of all morality is the mystic's direct experience of a higher spiritual reality, and morality in turn is the underlying basis of all human civilization. It followed in al–Ghazali's reasoning that philosophy and science could only lead to immorality and the ultimate collapse of human civilization itself.

Al-Ghazali partitioned the "philosophic sciences" into six divisions: mathematics, logic, physics, metaphysics, politics, and moral philosophy.[613] The best of these, mathematics, was neutral, it "proves nothing for or against religion."[614] Al-Ghazali did not argue with mathematical truths. He admitted that "it rests on a foundation of proofs which, once known and understood, can not be refuted."[615]

But the study of mathematics was condemned by al–Ghazali. Mathematics tended to validate philosophy in general, and some or most mathematicians were impious. "Whoever studies this science [mathematics] admires the subtlety and clearness of its proofs. His confidence in philosophy increases, and he thinks that all its departments are capable of the same clearness and solidity of proof as mathematics."[616] So the person who studies mathematics falsely concludes that "if there was truth in religion, it would not have escaped those who have displayed so much keenness of intellect in the study of mathematics."[617]

Similarly, al–Ghazali found "nothing [intrinsically] censurable"[618] in the science of logic. But its study and cultivation were to be avoided, because "a student who is enamored of the evidential methods of logic, hearing his teachers accused of irreligion, believes that this irreligion reposes on proofs as strong as those of logic, and immediately, without attempting the study of metaphysics, shares their mistake."[619]

Al-Ghazali reserved his strongest condemnation for metaphysics. "This is the fruitful breeding-ground of the errors of philosophers."[620] He identified twenty errors made by the philosophers. Seventeen of these were merely heretical, but three were more serious. The significant "irreligious" errors were (1) denial of physical resurrection, (2) the belief that God was not aware of specific and detailed circumstances on Earth, only generalities, and (3) the belief that the cosmos was eternal, and therefore not created *ex nihilo*.[621]

In particular, al–Ghazali desired to refute the Neoplatonic metaphysics of al–Farabi and Avicenna.[622] This was the primary motivation for writing his most influential book, *The Incoherence of the Philosophers*.[623]

> In the *Tahafut* [*Incoherence of the Philosophers*] he had smitten the philosophers hip and thigh; he had turned ... their own weapons against them, and shown that with their premises and methods no certainty could be reached. In that book he goes to the extreme of intellectual skepticism, and, seven hundred years before Hume, he cuts the bond of causality with the edge of his dialectic and proclaims that we can know nothing of cause or effect, but simply that one thing follows another.... He demonstrates that they [the philosophers] cannot prove the existence of the creator, or that the creator is one; that they cannot prove that he is incorporeal, or that the world has any creator or cause at all; that they cannot prove the nature of God, or that the human soul is a spiritual essence. When he has finished there is no intellectual basis left for life.... We are thrown back on revelation, that given immediately by God to the individual soul or that given through prophets. All our real knowledge is derived from these sources.[624]

The most infamous assertion in the *Incoherence* was al–Ghazali's denial of cause and effect. He claimed that every event happened by the immediate and special will of God, not by the impersonal action of physical law.

Al-Ghazali argued that the philosophers' attempts to demonstrate causality all relied upon correlation. They observed that one thing followed another, and inferred causation. But in fact, what they had observed was simply correlation. Causation was a mere inference.

Just because we have observed cotton burning when it comes into contact with fire, does not necessarily imply that this will occur the next time the experiment is tried. The burning was caused by the will of God. "The one who enacts the burning by creating blackness in the cotton, [causing] separation in its parts, and making it cinder or ashes, is God, either through the mediation of His angels or without mediation. As for fire, which is inanimate, it has no action. For what proof is there that it is the agent? They [the philosophers] have no proof other than observing the occurrence of the burning at the [juncture of] contact with the fire ... existence 'with' a thing does not prove that it exists 'by' it."[625]

Al-Ghazali was rebutted by Averroes, who wrote a book titled *The Incoherence of the Incoherence*.[626] Systematically, point-by-point, and page by page, Averroes attempted to confute al–Ghazali's claims.

Averroes argued that al–Ghazali's denial of causation was nothing but sophistry, and that if one were to accept it, there could be no knowledge.[627] "Intelligence is nothing but the perception of things with their causes, and in this it distinguishes itself from all the other faculties of apprehension, and he who denies causes must deny the intellect ... denial of cause implies the denial of knowledge, and denial of knowledge implies that nothing in this world can be really known."[628]

But it was al–Ghazali that prevailed. By the end of the twelfth century A.D., the cultivation of the "foreign" sciences in Islamic civilization was dead. Religious orthodoxy prevailed.

In the thirteenth century A.D., the typical Muslim attitude toward philosophy was expressed by ibn Salah (A.D. 1181–1245).[629] Ibn Salah had given "up the study of logic," because it "proved to be too difficult for him."[630] He wrote a *fatwa* [legal opinion] that concluded it was not permissible to study philosophy because it was "the foundation of folly, the cause of all confusion, all errors and all heresy. The person who occupies himself with it becomes colorblind to the beauties of religious law, supported as it is by brilliant proofs. He who studies or teaches philosophy will be abandoned by God's favor, and Satan will overpower him."[631] Logic was also condemned, because "it is a means of access to philosophy."[632]

Ibn Khaldun (A.D. 1332–1406), "the greatest intellect produced by medieval Islam,"[633] proscribed the cultivation of the sciences. "The sciences (of philosophy, astrology, and alchemy) occur in civilization. They are much cultivated in the cities. The harm they (can) do to religion is great."[634]

Ibn Khaldun concluded that "the (opinion) the (philosophers) hold is wrong in all its aspects,"[635] and "we must refrain from studying these things, since such (restraint) falls under (the duty of) the Muslim not to do what does not concern him."[636] He admitted that logic had "a single fruit, namely, it sharpens the mind in the orderly presentation of proofs and arguments, so that the habit of excellent and correct arguing is obtained."[637] But the study of logic was fraught with peril. "One knows what harm it can do ... whoever studies it [logic] should do so (only) after he is saturated with the religious law and has studied the interpretation of the Qur'an and jurisprudence. No one who has no knowledge of the Muslim religious sciences should apply himself to it. Without that knowledge, he can hardly remain safe from its pernicious aspects."[638]

Thus natural philosophy and science were rejected by Islam. But the Islamic translations proved an important vehicle for the transmission of Greek science to Europe. "The Latin world was ... an empty goblet waiting to be filled with the ambrosia of Greek rationalism."[639]

CHAPTER 4

High Middle Ages in Europe
(c. A.D. 1000–1300)

Feudalism and Economic Stagnation

The repeated invasions of Italy by Germanic tribes and the fall of the Roman Empire in the west did not end the economic unity of the Mediterranean. "The aim of the invaders was not to destroy the Roman Empire but to occupy and enjoy it."[1] What stopped trading and stifled economic activity in the Mediterranean region may have been the Islamic expansion of the eighth century. "Of a regular and normal commercial activity ... no traces are to be found after the closing of the Mediterranean by the Islamic expansion."[2] But the attribution to Islamic expansion is uncertain.[3] Whatever the cause, by the ninth century, western Europe was largely an "economy of no markets."[4]

As the Roman Empire disintegrated in the West, the power, wealth and influence of the Catholic Church increased. Any land that passed into Church hands was held in perpetuity. By A.D. 700, the Church owned one-third of France. Bishops and abbots governed vast estates and ruled as feudal lords. Money was collected from the laity in the form of tithes, and priests charged fees for administering the sacraments. Funds flowed upward, from priests to bishops, from bishops to Rome.[5]

With the collapse of the central secular authority, feudalism emerged. Real estate passed into the hands of a few lords who managed vast estates. "Roman municipal institutions had given way to the rule of bishops or of feudal lords, and the people had to a large extent lost even their personal freedom."[6] "The need for protection from attack, the abuse of power by those who wielded it, and the weakness of kings combined to bring many free farmers into political and economic subjection."[7] The height of feudalism occurred at the end of the ninth century A.D., a time in Europe distinguished by virtual anarchy.

In general, there were three secular classes in feudal Europe: lords, knights, and serfs. Lords held power by ownership of one or more large estates known as manors or villas. These estates were subdivided into *fiefs*. A fief was literally income or payment granted in return for military service.[8] "The normal fief was an estate of land large enough to support by the labors of its peasants at least one armed knight and his war horse."[9] A fief was a hereditary land grant, passed from father to oldest son under the law of primogeniture. If a knight had no male heir, the land reverted to the ownership of the lord.

A knight who held a fief was required to do military service on behalf of his lord, "and forty days in the year was frequently the amount of service required. In addition to fighting for his lord in the field and mounting guard in his castles, the vassal was generally required at stated seasons to attend his lord's court, where his presence contributed to the lord's social prestige and aided him in building up something akin to political power."[10]

The third secular class consisted of serfs. "The serfs were peasants who were sold or transferred with the land which they cultivated, as if they had been so many ploughs or cows."[11] Serfs were not slaves so much as indentured servants. A lord could not break up a serf's family, or sell him into slavery. But the serf was required "to cultivate part of the estate for their master, to labor in and about his house, cut wood for his fire, cart his grain and wine and hay, [and] repair the roads and bridges on his property."[12] Everyone worked, including children.[13]

In theory, the relationship between serf and lord was one of reciprocity. In return for his labor, the lord was obligated to provide security for the serf and his family. Serfs "needed protection in a world where policemen were scarce and pirates were plentiful."[14] In the ninth and tenth centuries, Vikings regularly raided "the British Isles, the Low Countries, and France."[15] But it was a bargain made between parties of unequal power. A lord "had a natural inclination to squeeze out of his serfs all that he could get."[16]

Slavery still existed, but was not nearly as widespread as during the heyday of Roman civilization.[17] The institution of slavery was being replaced by serfdom. Christianity undermined slavery by its doctrines of charity and universal human brotherhood. Slaves were "admitted to the priesthood, and their moral value was elevated."[18] The Christian Church made the emancipation of slaves a "good work *par excellence.*"[19] On the other hand, skeptics have pointed out that the Church itself owned slaves and had no doctrine prohibiting slavery.[20] Economic and political factors also worked toward the elimination of large-scale slavery. In feudal Europe, there was no strong central government to pursue and prosecute runaway slaves. Manor lords aimed at self-sufficiency, and serfs required less supervision than slaves.[21]

The preceding characterization of feudalism is a simplification. Feudalism was "an intricate and almost hopeless tangle,"[22] and "there were different classes and varying gradations of personal subjection or freedom."[23] Nor were small freeholders extinct. In England of A.D. 1279, only sixty percent of the land was occupied by manorial estates.[24] The Domesday survey by William the Conqueror, conducted in A.D. 1086, found that the agricultural population of England consisted 70 percent of *villeins* (feudal serfs or laborers of one class or another), 9 percent of slaves, and 12 percent of freemen.

Feudal manors were almost entirely self-supporting, producing nearly everything needed to support the lords, knights, and serfs. An inventory of one of Charlemagne's (A.D. 742–814) estates contained lists of utensils, victuals, livestock, herbs, and fruit trees. Victuals included spelt, wheat, rye, barley, oats, and peas. Livestock consisted of cattle, cows, hogs, sheep, goats, geese, ducks, chickens, and peacocks. The estate produced "pears, apples, medlars, peaches, filberts, walnuts, mulberries, [and] quinces," and an assortment of herbs that included mint, parsley, celery, sage, savory, juniper, garlic, coriander, onions, cabbage, and others.[25]

Charlemagne instructed that each steward of his sixteen-hundred[26] estates "shall have in his district good workmen, namely, blacksmiths, gold-smith, silver-smith, shoe-makers, turners, carpenters, sword-makers, fishermen, foilers,[27] soap-makers, men who know how to make beer, cider, berry, and all the kinds of beverages, bakers to make pastry for our table, net-makers who know how to make nets for hunting, fishing and fowling, and the others who are too numerous to be designated."[28]

Whatever could not be produced on the estate was purchased from the occasional ped-dler. Although complete self-sufficiency was the ideal, materials such as salt, iron, parch-ment, ink, hemp (for ropes), flax, and spices, had to be imported.[29]

Agricultural production was inefficient and limited. "Clover, beets, potatoes, and many other agricultural products were unknown. Scientific farming, irrigation, and fertilizing were little known or practiced."[30] With limited crop rotation and fertilization, fields had to lay fallow every third or second year, drastically reducing the productivity of the land. "Only half or two-thirds of the arable land was under crop in any one season."[31] Agricul-tural methods "were always crude, and were often very cumbersome and wasteful ... many of the stock had to be killed before winter, as there was no proper fodder to keep them."[32] The only winter fodder that was available was hay cut from the meadows.[33] Because most of the livestock had to be slaughtered in the fall, there was never much manure available to fertilize the fields.

Agricultural commerce was limited by the simple fact that there was little to no sur-plus to trade. If there was a surplus of agricultural production one year, it went to waste, while bad weather the next year could very well lead to famine. Even if a surplus had been available, it would have been difficult to transport it any great distance. The roads were unsafe and their condition "was so bad that they seem to have been mere tracks, of serv-ice to passengers on foot or on horseback, but of little use for wagon traffic."[34] "The Roman roads were still in use, but they were too much worn and too few in number to raise the general level of transportation."[35] The general condition of the roads was so bad that in the year 1499 a man on horseback fell into a pit in the middle of a road and drowned. Bridges over streams were rare.[36]

Traveling was not only difficult, but dangerous. "Highway robbery and violence were regular and normal occurrences ... students going to college in England were encouraged to carry arms on the journey."[37]

Commerce was further hindered by the lack of national political unity and uniformity of taxation. Every feudal lord tried to take advantage of the merchants and traders that passed through his property. If the lord was not allied with bands of brigands and engag-ing in outright thievery, he imposed a toll or tax on anyone passing through his domain. "The variety of feudal tolls is almost inconceivable ... tolls were levied everywhere and on everything."[38] "In the fourteenth century there were 74 tolls on the Loire, from Roanne to Nantes; 12 on the Allier; 10 on the Sarth; 60 on the Rhone and Saone; 70 on the Garonne or on the land-routes between la Reole and Narbonne; 9 on the Seine between the Grand Pont of Paris and the Roche-Guyon. There were 13 toll-stations on the Rhine between Mainz and Cologne. In a few hours' walk around Nuremberg one passed 10 stations."[39] "The mer-chant got nothing in return"[40] for paying a toll. He "might pay a lord for a safe-conduct ... and then be robbed by the lord himself."[41]

Medieval Warm Period

Around the year A.D. 1000, the climate in Europe began to warm.[42] The best evidence for the existence of the Medieval Warm Period in Europe is found in records of changing mountain snowlines and borehole temperatures.[43] The warming was likely global in extent, and caused by a natural 1500-year solar cycle.[44] Warm weather continued until the Little Ice Age (c. 1300–1750) took hold at the beginning of the fourteenth century.[45] The surest sign of the warming climate in Europe was the settlement of Greenland by Vikings from Iceland. The Greenland settlements reached a height of prosperity in the 12th and 13th centuries when 3,000 colonists occupied 280 farms.[46] The settlements came under duress in the late 14th century due to the onset of Little Ice Age cooling; they finally perished in the 15th century.

In the Middle Ages, the economy of Europe was based almost entirely on agriculture. As the climate warmed, agricultural yields increased. Agricultural productivity was also increased by the introduction of new technologies and methods.[47] These included the heavy plow, three-field crop rotation, and the harnessing of horse power through the horse collar and iron shoe.[48] As early as the ninth century, Europeans surpassed Romans in the technologies of agriculture, metallurgy, and applied power.[49]

Marshes and swamps dried up, removing the breeding grounds of mosquitoes that spread malaria. Infant mortality fell, and the population grew. Between A.D. 700 and 1300, the population of Europe increased from 27 to 73 million.[50] From A.D. 1100 to 1300, the population of Europe increased from about 40 to 60 million.[51] In England, the population between A.D. 1086 and 1300 doubled.[52] "In every part of Europe labor was offered in superabundant quantity."[53] Large-scale reclamation projects were undertaken. Former wetlands were converted to productive farmland. Forests were cleared and planted. The Dutch began to reclaim land from the sea by constructing *polders* [dikes].[54] At the monastery of Les Dunes, in Flanders, Cistercian monks converted 25,000 acres (101.2 square kilometers) of sand and marsh desert into arable cropland.[55]

Economic and Technological Progress

The Dark Ages in Europe were giving way to the High Middle Ages. "Our modern states, literatures, laws, cities, and universities had begun by the twelfth century."[56]

There was now a surplus to trade, and commerce began to grow. Merchants emerged as a distinct class, and strove to take their place in society along with nobles and clergy. Italy led in the economic revival, and the leading commercial town was Venice. Venice's chief trading partner was Constantinople, "the greatest city of the whole Mediterranean basin."[57] By interacting with Constantinople, Venicean merchants learned commercial techniques that helped them achieve primacy. They exported wine and wheat from Italy, and brought back spices and textiles.[58] From northern Europe, Venetian traders exported "iron, lumber, and slaves"[59] to Egypt. Their profits on some of these trading expeditions may have been as high as "1000 to 1200 per cent."[60] Although great profits were possible, trading ventures were also risky. So merchants often reduced individual risk by sharing the ownership and expense of a trading mission. Both investments and rewards were divided among partners. These practices were the roots of modern joint stock corporations and insurance companies.

While merchants grew in wealth and political power, the influence of the feudal lords weakened. Merchants began to form enclaves in towns, and the cities prospered. Reading, writing, and arithmetic were essential for commercial activity. So merchants founded schools, and literacy was promoted. The vernacular, the language of commerce, thrived at the expense of Latin, the language of scholarship.[61]

The growth of commerce and trading promoted industry. To protect themselves, artisans, craftsmen, and merchants formed *guilds*. A guild is a voluntary "association formed for the mutual aid and protection of its members, or for the prosecution of some common purpose."[62] Specialized industries which had formerly been confined to manors began to expand in the towns. A town might contain "butchers, bakers, brewers, blacksmiths, gold-smiths, coppersmiths, masons, carpenters, cabinet-makers, wheelwrights, skinners or fur-riers, tanners, shoemakers, saddlers and harness makers, weavers, dyers, fullers, and tailors."[63] Guilds were granted monopolies, and in return they policed their profession, maintaining standards of quality.

The institution of trading fairs grew out of weekly farmer's markets. Buyers and sellers needed a place and time to meet. Fair sponsors sought exemptions from tolls for participants. Trading fairs were "the means by which commerce grew strong."[64] In thir-teenth-century fairs held near Paris, "one might find all the wares which formed the objects of commerce in Europe; textiles of silk, wool, and linen; minor manufactures and jewelry; drugs and spices; raw materials like salt and metals; leather, skins, and furs; foods and drinks, livestock and slaves."[65] Traders came from France, Italy, Germany, Spain, England, Flanders, and Switzerland.[66]

There was a synergistic relationship between commercial activity and technology that ultimately culminated in the Industrial Revolution of the eighteenth and nineteenth cen-turies. Technological innovation produced wealth, and wealth provided the capital for the further development of technology. Water-mills and windmills came into widespread use and the mining industry was revitalized.[67] Although the Romans and other ancient peo-ples had known how to harness water power, Europeans devised a host of technological innovations and new applications. By employing ingenious mechanisms for transferring power, they used water power to crush ores, manufacture iron, pound flax or hemp in preparation for the making of linen, turn saws and knives, and crush malt for beer, among other uses.[68]

Crusades

The Crusades were a "series of wars for delivering the Holy Land from the Mahommedans, so-called from the cross worn as a badge by the crusaders."[69] These wars were an indicator of European prosperity and expansion. For a hundred years prior to the First Crusade, Europeans had been retaking areas of Europe occupied by Muslims. In A.D. 1090, the Normans conquered Sicily, ending the reign of Islam in Italy. And the Muslims were being systematically driven out of Spain. Cordova was captured by Christians in A.D. 1236, and Seville in 1248. "The Mohammedans retained only the Kingdom of Granada, a small fraction of the peninsula."[70] In A.D. 1492, Granada was also retaken.[71]

During the ninth and tenth centuries, there was a steady stream of Christian pilgrims into Jerusalem. "The movement steadily grew. The Holy Land became to the imagination a land of wonders, filled with the divine presence of Christ. To have visited it, to have seen Jerusalem, to have bathed in the Jordan, was for a man to have about him a halo of sanc-tity."[72]

Motivated by the economic benefits to be derived from tourism, the Islamic caliphs welcomed Christian pilgrims. An immediate profit was guaranteed by the imposition of a tax on pilgrims entering Jerusalem.[73]

But in A.D. 1071, Jerusalem was captured by the Seljukian Turks, "a rougher and ruder race than the Arabs of Egypt whom they displaced."[74] The Seljuks were less tolerant of

Christian pilgrims than their predecessors. They "looked upon the [Christian] pilgrims with contempt and aversion ... they were annoyed at the immense number of pilgrims who overran the country."[75]

"Persecution of every kind awaited [the Christian pilgrims] ... they were plundered, and beaten with stripes."[76] "Western Christians could not but feel hampered and checked in their natural movement towards the fountainhead of their religion, and it was natural that they should ultimately endeavor to clear the way."[77]

The proximate cause of the First Crusade has been attributed to Peter the Hermit, a priest who may "have attempted to go on a pilgrimage to Jerusalem before A.D. 1096, and have been prevented by the Turks from reaching his destination."[78] "Enthusiastic, chivalrous, bigoted, and, if not insane, not far removed from insanity, he [Peter] was the very prototype of the time."[79] "His stature was small, his appearance contemptible; but his eye was keen and lively; and he possessed that vehemence of speech which seldom fails to impart the persuasion of the soul.... Pope Urban the Second received him as a prophet, [and] applauded his glorious design."[80] Peter preached the cause of reclaiming the Holy Land from the Muslims, "untired, inflexible, and full of devotion, communicating his own madness to his hearers, until Europe was stirred from its very depths."[81]

The First Crusade was called by Pope Urban II at the Council of Clermont [Auvergne, France] in November of 1095.[82] The Council met for seven days, and "immense crowds from all parts of France flocked into the town ... all the neighborhood presented the appearance of a vast camp."[83] The Pope delivered a speech in which he called for a Crusade to capture Jerusalem.

> From the confines of Jerusalem and from the city of Constantinople a grievous report has gone forth and has repeatedly been brought to our ears; namely, that a race from the kingdom of the Persians, an accursed race, a race wholly alienated from God ... has violently invaded the lands of those Christians and has depopulated them by pillage and fire. They have led away a part of the captives into their own country, and a part they have killed by cruel tortures. They have either destroyed the churches of God or appropriated them for the rites of their own religion.... Let the holy sepulcher of our Lord and Savior, which is possessed by the unclean nations, especially arouse you, and the holy places which are now treated with ignominy and irreverently polluted with the filth of the unclean. Oh, most valiant soldiers and descendants of invincible ancestors, do not degenerate, but recall the valor of your progenitors.[84]

In addition to religious fervor, the Pope attempted to motivate Europeans by the prospect of political expansion and economic plunder. He reminded the European lords that "this land which you inhabit, shut in on all sides by the seas and surrounded by the mountain peaks, is too narrow for your large population; nor does it abound in wealth; and it furnishes scarcely food enough for its cultivators."[85]

Pope Urban II was also employing the common device of uniting a population through opposition to a common enemy. With no strong centralized government in feudal Europe, internecine warfare was constant and costly. "As the castle suggests, war was the natural state of the feudal world."[86]

The Pope admonished the feudal lords to cease battling each other and unite in a common and holy cause.

> You murder and devour one another ... you wage war, and ... very many among you perish in intestine strife. Let hatred therefore depart from among you, let your quarrels end, let wars cease, and let all dissensions and controversies slumber. Enter upon the road to the Holy Sepulcher; wrest that land from the wicked race, and subject it to yourselves. That land which, as the Scripture says, "floweth with milk and honey" was given by God into the power of the children of

Israel. Jerusalem is the center of the earth; the land is fruitful above all others, like another paradise of delights.[87]

At the end of the Pope's impassioned speech, the crowd began to cry in unison, "It is the will of God! It is the will of God!"[88] Pope Urban II then declared that Crusaders should identify themselves by wearing the sign of the Christian cross on their breasts. "When, indeed, he shall return from his journey, having fulfilled his vow, let him place the cross on his back between his shoulders."[89]

There were a variety of different motivations for the Crusades. The population at large may have been sincerely impelled by religious fervor. "Feudalism told them they had no rights in this world, [but] religion told them they had every right in the next."[90] Cynically, Edward Gibbon observed that little motivation may have been necessary. "So familiar, and as it were natural, to man is the practice of violence that our indulgence allows the slightest provocation, the most disputable right, as a sufficient ground of national hostility."[91]

In this superstitious age, "the weak, the credulous, and the guilty ... formed more than nineteen twentieths of the population."[92] Fantastic rumors of superstitious omens, signs, and monstrosities circulated throughout Europe. "A priest ... beheld two knights, who met one another in the air and fought long, until one, who carried a great cross with which he struck the other, finally overcame his enemy ... a woman after two years gestation finally gave birth to a boy who was able to talk ... a child with a double set of limbs, another with two heads, and some lambs with two heads were also born."[93] Some people "were induced, through some sudden change of spirit or some nocturnal vision, to sell all their property and possessions,"[94] and to undertake the Crusade.

Under the Catholic *Doctrine of Merit*, the feudal lords and nobility were offered salvation in return for service in the Crusades. The *Doctrine of Merit* essentially is the proposition that salvation can be obtained through good works. "A supernatural merit can only be a salutary act, to which God in consequence of his infallible promise owes a supernatural reward, consisting ultimately in eternal life."[95]

At Clermont, Pope Urban II "proclaimed a plenary indulgence to those who should enlist under the banner of the cross: the absolution of all their sins, and a full receipt for all that might be due of canonical penance. The cold philosophy of modern times [1789] is incapable of feeling the impression that was made on a sinful and fanatic world. At the voice of their pastor, the robber, the incendiary, the homicide, arose by thousands to redeem their souls, by repeating on the infidels the same deeds which they had exercised against their Christian brethren."[96]

> The knight who joined the Crusades might thus still indulge the bellicose side of his genius—under the aegis and at the bidding of the Church; and in so doing he would also attain what the spiritual side of his nature ardently sought—a perfect salvation and remission of sins. He might butcher all day, till he waded ankle-deep in blood, and then at nightfall kneel, sobbing for very joy, at the altar of the Sepulchre—for was he not red from the winepress of the Lord? One can readily understand the popularity of the Crusades, when one reflects that they permitted men to get to the other world by fighting hard on earth, and allowed them to gain the fruits of asceticism by the ways of hedonism.[97]

"The immediate causes of the Crusades were the ill treatment of pilgrims visiting Jerusalem and the appeal of the Greek emperor, who was hard pressed by the Turks."[98] But for the Catholic Church, it was an opportunity to extend its dominion and influence. "The papacy desires a perfect and universal Church, and a perfect and universal Church must rule in the Holy Land."[99]

"Thus every motive was favorable to the Crusades. Every class of society was alike incited to join or encourage the war; kings and the clergy by policy, the nobles by turbulence and the love of dominion, and the people by religious zeal and the concentrated enthusiasm of two centuries, skillfully directed by their only instructors."[100]

By spring of A.D. 1097, a Christian army of 150,000 had assembled in Constantinople.[101] On June 18, they captured the city of Nicaea [Turkey]. From there, they besieged Antioch [Turkey], which fell on June 3, 1098.[102] After capturing Antioch, the crusaders were immediately besieged themselves by a Turkish army that had arrived too late to provide succor for the fallen city. "The crusading army was by now sadly depleted by famine, plague, and the desertion of many who had sailed away home. But the digging-up of what was supposed to be the lance that pierced the side of the crucified Christ suddenly inspired the host with renewed vigor and enthusiasm, and the Turkish force was driven off."[103]

By May of 1099, the 40,000 remaining crusaders were finally ready to march on Jerusalem. After a siege lasting a little more than a month, the city was taken on July 15, 1099. Mayhem followed. The crusaders "cut down with the sword everyone whom they found in Jerusalem, and spared no one."[104] "The streets were choked with the bodies of the slain. The Jews were burnt with their synagogues."[105] "The slaughter was terrible; the blood of the conquered ran down the streets, until men splashed in blood as they rode ... [thus] the First Crusade came to an end."[106]

Pope Urban II died two weeks later, before news of the capture of Jerusalem could reach him. Peter the Hermit returned to Europe and died in A.D. 1115.[107] The triumph of the First Crusade was short-lived. The crusaders found that winning battles was easier than "the maintenance of their rule over an alien, mixed population far more numerous than themselves, which was separated from them by the barriers of religion, language, and customs."[108]

In Europe, the excitement and religious fervor created by the Crusades led to pogroms against Jews. Fantastic stories circulated. The King of France, Philip II (A.D. 1165–1223), heard "that the Jews who dwelt in Paris were wont every year on Easter day, or during the sacred week of our Lord's Passion, to go down secretly into underground vaults and kill a Christian as a sort of sacrifice in contempt of the Christian religion."[109] Philip accordingly decided to take bold action against the Jews. "Jews throughout all France were seized in their synagogues and then bespoiled of their gold and silver and garments, as the Jews themselves had spoiled the Egyptians at their exodus from Egypt."[110]

Phillip cancelled any debt owed by a Christian to a Jew, "and kept a fifth part of the whole amount for himself."[111] This was followed in April of 1182 by the expulsion of the Jews from France. Some Jews managed to remain by agreeing to baptism and conversion to Christianity. But others, "having sold their goods ... departed with their wives and children and all their households."[112]

The First Crusade was followed by a Second (A.D. 1147–1149), a Third (A.D. 1189–1192), Fourth (A.D. 1202–1204), Fifth (A.D. 1218–1221), and Sixth (A.D. 1228–1229).[113] Christians again lost control of Jerusalem in A.D. 1244, and this led to the last major Crusade, the Seventh (A.D. 1248–1254). The Seventh Crusade ended in failure. Europeans "continued to think and talk about crusades for the next two centuries ... but no great expedition directed toward the recovery of Jerusalem actually took place."[114]

In terms of extending the sphere of Christianity, the Crusades were a failure. "They [the Crusades] ended, not in the occupation of the East by the Christian West, but in the conquest of the West by the Mahommedan East. The Crusades began with the Seljukian Turk planted at Nicaea; they ended with the Ottoman Turk entrenched by the Danube."[115]

Writing from a Christian perspective, Philip Schaff (1819–1893) concluded that the Crusades were a failure in extending Christianity's dominion and sphere of influence:

> The Crusaders sought the living among the dead. They mistook the visible for the invisible, confused the terrestrial and the celestial Jerusalem, and returned disillusioned. They learned in Jerusalem, or after ages have learned through them, that Christ is not there, that He is risen, and ascended into heaven, where He sits at the head of a spiritual kingdom.... False religions are not to be converted by violence, they can only be converted by the slow but sure process of moral persuasion. Hatred kindles hatred, and those who take the sword shall perish by the sword.[116]

To one degree or another, the Crusades affected nearly every aspect of European life. They increased the power and influence of the papacy, but simultaneously corrupted the Church by involving a spiritual authority in the promulgation of secular warfare. The Crusades "aided the development of towns by vastly increasing the volume of trade."[117] They helped familiarize Europe with "sugar and maize; lemons, apricots and melons; cotton, muslin and damask; lilac and purple; the use of powder and of glass mirrors, and also of the rosary itself — all these things came to Europe from the East and as a result of the Crusades."[118]

Cathedrals

The construction of the great Gothic cathedrals marked the apex of Christian Civilization in Europe. These "cathedrals were the greatest product of the Middle Ages."[119] In beauty, elegance, and eurythmy, they surpassed the Parthenon of the Greeks as the Parthenon surpassed the pyramids of the Egyptians. Their beauty and harmony was an external reflection of the organic unity of the medieval European perspective. The cathedrals are also a reminder that "the Church was not only rich and powerful in the Middle Ages; it dominated and directed all the manifestations of human activity."[120]

Between A.D. 1050 and 1350, 80 cathedrals and 500 large churches were built in France alone. These were accompanied by the construction of tens of thousands of smaller local churches. The piety of the population at this time is testified to by the fact that there was one church for approximately every 200 inhabitants. The total amount of stone quarried during this time period in France exceeded that excavated during the raising of the Egyptian pyramids.[121]

The term "Gothic" is something of a misnomer, as Gothic architecture has nothing to do with the Goths, a German tribe.[122] The conventional terminology "seems to have been invented in Italy during the Renaissance as a derogatory way of describing pointed medieval as distinct from classic buildings, as if they were the product of barbarians."[123]

The immediate predecessor of Gothic architecture in Europe was Romanesque. Romanesque architecture has no distinctive set of elements, rather the term is designed to encompass "that period of art which followed and partook of the nature of Roman art and yet was too far removed from it to be classed as Roman."[124]

Gothic architecture was that "which intervened between the Romanesque era and the Renaissance."[125] "Gothic is a northern art. Its steep roofs, ritual in origin, threw off northern snow; its piercing outlines tell in an atmosphere where mass and color are obscured; its pillated construction reflects the branching deciduous forests where the timber builders worked.... Gothic cathedrals are ... the outward expression of minds formed among the trees, living for generations in the knowledge of their growth, their strength, their beauty."[126]

The Gothic style grew naturally from the Romanesque. "It is a matter of dispute where the structural seed for the new synthesis was sown: whether in Lombardy, Normandy, England or the province of Paris, but there is no question as to where the seed was nurtured, grafted on the old Romanesque trunk and under its protection given a chance to come to its own efflorescence. This took place in the neighborhood of Paris between [A.D.] 1100 and 1150."[127]

The development of Gothic style was transitional, not abrupt. Before the Cathedrals could be built, there had to be progressive refinements in the arts of masonry, stone-cutting, architectural vaulting, and decorative sculpture.[128] The improvements and refinement in stone-working techniques were factors that allowed architects to dispense with the bricks used in Romanesque construction and build entirely with stone. However, the Gothic architects were not above employing "concealed iron reinforcement, brick core inside coursed ashlar [stone], and rubble infilling."[129]

The builders of the Gothic cathedrals wanted to replace the wooden roofs of Romanesque structures with stone so as "to provide a ceiling of the same texture and color as the walls below."[130] They wanted to place large expanses of window glass in the walls to let in light. And they wanted an architecture that pointed upward, one that gave a heavenly sense of elevation and illumination. "The first and outstanding characteristic of Gothic is its vertical expansion, its tendency to upwardness ... but the vertical space of Gothic is not merely high; it is also jagged, leaping, like a flame."[131] Gothic cathedrals are an embodiment of an "implacable determination to scale the skies."[132]

The Gothic cathedrals were "distinctly cruciform in plan, with transepts."[133] Each building "was conceived as a whole by a single architect and not constructed piecemeal."[134] A master mason was hired to design a Cathedral and supervise its construction. These masons had to simultaneously fulfill multiple roles. They were architects, administrators, contractors, and construction supervisors.[135] Additionally, the duties of a master mason may have required him to function as a surveyor, engineer, and be able to build both in stone and wood.[136]

These masons or architects were not educated through a course of formal instruction taught from books in a school. They learned on the job through the craft and oral tradition. Their education was "empirical and utilitarian."[137] The evolution of knowledge and technique was governed by the slow but invincible progress of trial and error.

Although they lacked the ability to draw a precise blueprint to scale, or to precisely calculate stresses and tensions, "Gothic architects were above all things mathematicians [and] geometricians."[138] The physical laws that determined their craft had been learnt by the accumulation and transmission of centuries of practical experience.

In addition to design, master masons had immense supervisory duties. Master James of St. George, a late thirteenth-century mason who built some of the "Edwardian castles of North Wales,"[139] directed "a labor force of 400 masons, 2000 minor workmen, 200 quarrymen and 30 smiths and carpenters, together with a supply organization of 100 carts, 60 wagons and 30 boats bringing stone and sea-coal to the [construction] site."[140]

The designs of the master mason were sketched on parchment in a "tracing house." These plans were used by carpenters to construct wooden molds, and the molds in turn were used as guides by stonecutters.[141]

It is in the Durham (England) Cathedral, that we find "the earliest example of the transitional style."[142] Construction began in A.D. 1093, and was completed in 1135.[143] The Durham Cathedral was the first building that contained the three key elements of Gothic construction: "the rib vault, the pointed arch, and the flying buttress."[144] Of these innovations, the stone ribs were the least impressive visually, but the most important structurally. The stone ribs were laid down first and served as a skeletal superstructure. "These ribs formed a framework not only self-supporting but able to sustain the weight of the entire vault."[145] The pointed arch achieved the visual goal of directing the eye upward and provided an ethereal sense of spirituality.

The stone walls of the Gothic cathedrals were deliberately weakened by leaving large openings for windows. By themselves, the hollowed-out walls would have been unable to support the immense weight of the stone vaults. What made Gothic construction possible was the transference of stress to flying buttresses.

A *flying buttress* is an exterior arch that supports a wall and bears stress. The concept is painfully deliberate and awkward in its intentions, unexpectedly elegant and graceful in its execution. Flying buttresses lent support to the Cathedral walls, and relieved them of much of their weight-bearing obligation. It became possible to extend cathedral walls to great heights, and the builders vied with each other to surpass previous efforts. The vault at Notre Dame in Paris reached a height of 107.6 feet (32.8 meters) in A.D. 1163. This was surpassed by the Cathedral at Amiens in A.D. 1221, which reached a height of 124.5 feet (42.3 meters).

The Medieval builders sought to go even higher, but lacked the mathematics and engineering knowledge needed to calculate the stresses and thus understand the limits of their materials and techniques. The vault at Beauvais was intended to be 157 feet (48 meters) high, but collapsed in A.D. 1284.[146]

With the external support provided by flying buttresses, the heightened walls could be opened up and filled with glass to let in light. The architects of the Gothic cathedrals were thus able to construct buildings entirely out of stone that had immense interior spaces filled with vast amounts of natural light.

> Instead of massive walls, it [the Gothic cathedral] scarcely has walls at all. Its vaulted stone roof is upheld by a network of stone ribs and flying buttresses which carry the weight to a few selected points where adequate piers and buttresses receive and support it. Instead of small apertures, the front and sides and end of the cathedral are almost continuous sheets of stained glass, separated into arched windows only by the ribs of the structural skeleton. Instead of horizontal lines, every column and arch and rib and vault and roof and buttress carries the eye upward.[147]

Cathedral windows were filled with stained glass in an array of iridescent colors. As the colored light filtered into the cavernous interior of the great Cathedrals, an ethereal sense of the heavenly realm was experienced by the faithful. The figures in the windows told stories, graphically conveying religious creeds to the illiterate. These windows "offer an encyclopedia for the use of those who cannot read."[148]

The apex of the stained-glass art was the great rosette that occupies the north window of Notre Dame. An intricate web of stone and crystal, the window has over 1300 square feet (121 square meters) of stained glass.[149] For more than seven hundred years, it has not been surpassed in beauty, skill, or splendor.

The interiors of the Cathedrals were richly decorated with large numbers of intricate stone carvings. In Notre Dame, the "whole of these doorways are covered with sculpture, much of it refined, spirited and interesting in the highest degree. You enter and find the interior surpassing even the exterior. The order of the columns and arches, and of all the details, is so noble and simple that no fault can be found with it."[150]

"The Gothic cathedral is a perfect encyclopedia of human knowledge. It contains scenes from the Scriptures and the legends of the saints; motives from the animal and vegetable kingdom; representations of the seasons of agricultural labor, of the arts and sciences and crafts, and finally moral allegories, as, for instance, ingenious personifications of the virtues and the vices."[151] "It has been calculated that Chartres Cathedral contains no less than 10,000 figures—statues and reliefs, persons and animals painted on glass."[152]

Logic and Literature

THE LATIN CLASSICS

At the beginning of the twelfth century in Europe, the majority of people were illiterate. Most of those who could read and write were monks or priests.[153] All books were hand-lettered on parchment, and the common language was Latin.[154] The intellectual centers of society were "monasteries, cathedrals, courts, towns, and universities."[155] So long as one did not contradict the doctrines of the Church, there was a relative amount of intellectual freedom, and "men were free to speculate as they would."[156] At the beginning of the twelfth century, the great European universities were yet nascent. They did not become distinct institutions until the end of the twelfth century and the first decades of the thirteenth century.

The typical library was located in a monastery or a cathedral and contained a couple hundred volumes. There were numerous copies of the *Bible* and Christian "service books," such as books containing choral verses, prayers, and monastic rules.[157] Other popular manuscripts included the works of the Church Fathers, Isidore's *Etymologies*, and manuscripts authored by Boethius (c. A.D. 480–525) and Bede (A.D. 672–735).[158] The libraries contained little to nothing on the subjects of natural philosophy, mathematics, sciences such as astronomy, or even medicine. The only works of Aristotle that were available in Europe before the twelfth century A.D. were the six books on logic that constituted the *Organon: Categories, On Interpretation, Prior Analytics, Posterior Analytics, Topics,* and *Sophistical Refutations.* Of these six books, "the advanced treatises fell into neglect,"[159] and only *Categories* and *On Interpretation* were well-known prior to the twelfth century.[160]

From the early Middle Ages, the Catholic Church was divided as to the extent to which pagan literature could or should be studied. The goal of Christian education was "to enable the future ecclesiastic to understand and expound the Canonical Scriptures, the Fathers and other ecclesiastical writings."[161] But "for the proper understanding of these sacred writings a certain amount of secular culture was considered to be necessary."[162] The *Trivium* of grammar, rhetoric, and dialectic, was established as a core curriculum by Cassiodorus (c. A.D. 485–585).[163] "It is probable that in practice boys continued to be taught grammatical Latin by reading a classical author, such as Virgil or Ovid."[164] In Medieval times, the term "grammar" meant "not merely the technical rules of grammar ... [but also] the systematic study and interpretation of the classical writers of ancient Rome."[165]

"The classics were recognized by liberal churchmen as furnishing the best means of education,"[166] but there was opposition. The Latin "classics were pagan ... [they] were pervaded by a spirit of beauty which led to aesthetic gratification, a sensual sin in the eyes of the ascetic ... [and] there was much in the classics which was considered unfit for a Christian to read."[167]

Gregory the Great's (c. A.D. 540–604) "dislike of grammar stops short of heinous crime."[168] He wrote to the Bishop of Milan, "I have been informed — I cannot repeat it without shame — that you, my brother, are teaching certain persons grammar. At this I was so grieved and felt so strong disgust that my former feelings were changed to groans and sadness; because the same mouth cannot utter the praises of Jupiter and Christ."[169]

The approach of Isidore of Seville (A.D. 560–636) was apparently inconsistent. "In his *Etymologies*, Isidore arranged and edited for Christians the pagan literature of antiquity, but in his Rule he forbade the monks to study the classics, because secular knowledge tempted the soul to pride."[170]

Odo of Cluny (c. 878–942) "had taken delight in the study of Virgil, when he was warned in a dream to abandon that perilous occupation. In his dream he saw a beautiful vase teeming with poisonous serpents; the beautiful vase (he felt assured) was the poet's verse, while the serpents were his pagan sentiments."[171] In the tenth century, the papal Curia declared "the representatives of St. Peter and his disciples will not have Plato, Virgil or Terence as their masters, or the rest of the philosophic cattle."[172]

But the "puritanical tendency could not succeed. Latin was too necessary, and the classics were too useful to be discarded."[173] Latin was the language of the Church, and the language of scholarship and learning. The classic pagan literature thus became an indispensable adjunct to the essential task of teaching literacy. A priest had to know "enough Latin to read the church services."[174] The Latin classics "were copied, read, and quoted constantly. They were used to furnish maxims and stories for sermons, for fortune-telling, and to testify to the truths of Christianity."[175]

By the twelfth century A.D., the Latin classics were widely accepted and read in Europe, including the Christian cathedral schools at Chartres and Orleans.[176] The chief Roman works that were cultivated were those by the poets Virgil (70–19 B.C.) and Ovid (43 B.C.— A.D. 18).[177]

LOGIC AND SCIENTIFIC METHOD

The European appreciation for empiricism did not begin in earnest until the thirteenth century. At the first awakening from the Dark Ages, it seemed that knowledge could be obtained through pure ratiocination. "The best intellect of this early period [late tenth century A.D.] grasped at logic not only as the most obviously needed discipline and guide, but also with imperfect consciousness that this discipline and means did not contain the goal and plenitude of substantial knowledge."[178] "About the year [A.D.] 1100 ... a belief sprang up that an intelligent apprehension of spiritual truth depended on a correct use of prescribed methods of argumentation. Dialectic was looked upon as 'the science of sciences.'"[179]

The basis of the revived interest in logic was Boethius' Latin translations of Aristotle's *Categories* and *On Interpretation*, as well as the *Isagogue*, an introduction to the *Categories* authored by Porphyry.[180] The other books of the *Organon* were virtually unknown in twelfth century Europe.

Although many writers were hostile to natural philosophy, "the theology of the Church Fathers was partly made of Greek philosophy, and was put together in modes of Greek philosophic reasoning ... in the rational process of formulating Christian dogma, Greek philosophy was the overwhelmingly important factor, because it furnished knowledge and the metaphysical concepts, and because the greater number of Christian theologians were Hellenic in spirit, and wrote Greek."[181]

In an age where knowledge was chiefly derived from authority in the form of books, logic was needed to discern between conflicting authorities. Every text required interpretation and reconciliation. Even "the *Bible* ... contained the germs of all heresies."[182]

Modern science evolved only because medieval Christian theologians embraced Greek logic. For logic is the idea that there exists a correct way of thinking and solving problems, a rational way of constructing reliable knowledge. The influence of Aristotle's logic was "persistent and pervasive."[183] Science was defined by Aristotle to be "a habit or formed faculty of demonstration"[184] that depended upon correct principles of reasoning. "It is only when the principles of our knowledge are accepted and known to us in a particular way, that we can properly be said to have scientific knowledge; for unless these principles are better known to us that the conclusions based upon them, our knowledge will be merely accidental."[185]

ANSELM OF CANTERBURY (A.D. 1033–1109)

An important indicator for the acceptance of logic by Christian theologians was Anselm of Canterbury's *Ontological Proof* (see pages 97–98). The Ontological Proof was an attempt to construct an argument for the existence of God that was based entirely on logic. Anselm was "the first of the great Schoolmen," or scholastic theologians, and "the most original thinker the Church had seen since the days of Augustine."[186] Anselm placed faith before reason, but he also sought consilience between philosophy and theology. Anselm's Ontological Proof was based on pure logic. "I began to ask myself whether there might be found a single argument which would require no other for its proof than itself alone; and alone would suffice to demonstrate that God truly exists."[187]

ADELARD OF BATH (C. A.D. 1080–1152)

Adelard of Bath was an English philosopher, scholar, and translator who traveled widely. In his book, *Questions on Natural Science*, Adelard exalted human reason over authority. "For what else can authority be called other than a halter? As brute animals are led wherever one pleases by a halter ... so the authority of written words leads not a few of you into danger, since you are enthralled and bound by brutish credulity ... reason has been given to each single individual in order to discern between true and false with reason as the prime judge."[188]

Like other men of his age, Adelard admired the works of the ancient Greeks and Romans, and considered them to be superior to those being produced in his age. "When I examine the famous writings of the ancients ... and compare their talents with the knowledge of the moderns, I judge the ancients eloquent, and call the moderns dumb."[189] However his approbation was not unconditional. "The present generation suffers from this ingrained fault, that it thinks that nothing should be accepted which is discovered by the 'moderns.'"[190]

Adelard had faith in the promise of reason as an epistemological method. "Having put on the wings of reason, let us ascend to the stars."[191] But he depreciated experience as method of gaining reliable knowledge. "Nothing is more certain than reason, nothing more deceptive than the senses! ... from the senses can arise not knowledge, but only opinion ... the senses do not only not seek out the truth: they even forcibly drive the mind away from the investigation of the truth."[192] Adelard may have derived his contempt for observation from Plato, an author he "frequently cited."[193]

PETER ABELARD (A.D. 1079–1142)

Peter Abelard was an ardent proponent of logic, and an important architect of Scholasticism, the practice of "giving a formally rational expression to the received ecclesiastical doctrine."[194] Abelard was "the last of the great monastic teachers," and the person who "inaugurated the intellectual movement out of which" the European universities were founded.[195] "In Abelard we must recognize incomparably the greatest intellect of the Middle Ages."[196] Abelard authored a short biography titled *Historia Calamitatum* (*History of Calamities*), a chronicle of his misfortunes.[197] He is also notorious for conducting a tragic, passionate, and illicit romance with a woman named Heloise.

Abelard was the eldest son of a French nobleman. From an early age, he was an extraordinarily dedicated scholar. So much so that he deserted his inheritance. "I was so enthralled by my passion for learning that, gladly leaving to my brothers the pomp of glory in arms, the right of heritage and all the honors that should have been mine as the eldest born, I fled utterly from the court of Mars that I might win learning in the bosom of Minerva."[198]

Abelard developed a love of logic. "Since I found the armory of logical reasoning more to my liking than the other forms of philosophy, I exchanged all other weapons for these, and to the prizes of victory in war I preferred the battle of minds in disputation."[199]

At this time, the standard practice of students was to travel, seeking teachers and knowledge where they could find them. In *Historia Calamitatum*, Abelard said that he journeyed "through many provinces ... debating as I went."[200] Eventually, Abelard went to Paris, because it was the place where "the art of dialectics was most flourishing."[201]

Not yet twenty years of age, Abelard studied at the cathedral school of Notre Dame with William of Champeaux (c. A.D. 1070–1121).[202] "At first, William looked upon this extraordinary stripling, who showed an acuteness and depth so far beyond his years, with pleasing admiration. But his admiration was speedily turned to concern and alarm. He found that neither his authority, nor his experience, nor his undoubted talent, could keep pace with the adroitness of a youth, who seemed bent upon displaying his dexterity by upsetting his professor. Neither grey hairs, nor position, nor prestige, had any effect on Abelard."[203]

At Notre Dame, Abelard disputed with William over the question of universals, the most important controversy in European philosophy of the Middle Ages. "The men of the middle ages had practically no other strictly philosophical problem to discuss than that of universals."[204]

Universals or *genera* were ideal forms, or abstractions. The question of universals was the same debate Plato had with Aristotle over the Doctrine of Forms. Plato had maintained that idealized forms, or universals, had a separate existence and were the only true, unchanging reality. In contrast, Aristotle acknowledged the existence of forms as abstractions, but denied that they had any reality when separated from specific physical objects (*species*).

The dispute arose primarily from a passage in Porphyry's *Isagoge*, an introduction to Aristotle's *Categories*. Porphyry had posed the question, "as to *genera* and *species*, do they actually exist or are they merely in thought; are they corporeal or incorporeal existences; are they separate from sensible things or only in and of them?"[205] As to the resolution of the question, Porphyry stated, "I refuse to answer," because "it is a very lofty business, unsuited to an elementary work."[206]

In medieval Europe, the opposing sides in this debate were known as *realists* and *nominalists*. Like Plato, William of Champeaux maintained "that the universal was a real thing;

and for that reason he was called a realist."[207] In contrast, Abelard "held that the universal was only nominally real; and on that account he was called a nominalist."[208] To a nominalist, "beauty is a conception of the mind gotten from the observation of objects which are beautiful ... individual things are first observed and the universal, or abstract conception, is derived from it."[209]

In *Historia Calamitatum*, Abelard claimed that he, the student, converted his teacher, William of Champeaux, to the nominalist position. "I compelled him by most potent reasoning first to alter his former opinion on the subject of universals, and finally to abandon it altogether."[210] William's position was that a universal or form "was a thing simultaneously present in all its individuals ... the essence of a species [or universal] was the same in all its individuals."[211] Abelard destroyed this position by pointing out that "if the whole 'thing,' i.e., the whole of the universal were 'essentially' present in each individual of the genus or species, none of it was left to be present in any other individual at the same time."[212] Abelard's argument was so cogent that it ultimately resulted in "the downfall of the philosophic theory of Realism, till then dominant in the early Middle Age."[213]

The question of universals had profound ramifications for Christian theology. Abelard triumphed in nominalism because he demonstrated that the realist position logically led to pantheism, the identification of God with the material universe. If, as Abelard argued, the whole of a universal was present in a particular thing, then the realist position implied that "the divine substance which is recognized as admitting of no form, is necessarily identical with every substance in particular and with all substance in general."[214]

Abelard was a charismatic and brilliant teacher. "Clearness, richness in imagery, and lightness of touch are said to have been the chief characteristics of his teaching ... his splendid gifts and versatility, supported by a rich voice, a charming personality, a ready and sympathetic use of human literature, and a freedom from excessive piety, gave him an immeasurable advantage over all the teachers of the day. Beside most of them, he was as a butterfly to an elephant."[215]

The pedagogic method that Abelard used was subsequently adopted as the standard method of teaching in medieval European universities. Explaining that, "in truth, constant or frequent questioning is the first key to wisdom,"[216] Abelard's method was to propose theses in the form of questions. "He then brought together under each question the conflicting opinions of various authorities, and, without stating his own view, left the student to reason for himself on the matter."[217] Examples of Abelard's theses include the statements, "that faith is based upon reason," "that God is not single," and that a lie is never permissible."[218] Abelard's method was clearly derived from Aristotle, who was in the habit of dispassionately listing the arguments both pro and con on any important philosophical issue.

"Discussion, and the free use of the faculties, chains of reasoning, startling proofs—this was Abelard's passion. Truth was indispensable for this practice; so Abelard loved truth. Error was necessary for eliciting truth; so Abelard introduced error."[219]

In addition to being a great teacher and intellect, Abelard was also exceedingly conceited. He made the unlikely claim that his colleagues were so impressed by his brilliance that one of them willingly surrendered his position, preferring to be a student of Abelard rather than a master. "My teaching won such strength and authority that even those who before had clung most vehemently to my former master, and most bitterly attacked my doctrines, now flocked to my school. The very man who had succeeded to my master's chair in the Paris school offered me his post, in order that he might put himself under my tutelage."[220]

Having surpassed his teacher in the field of logic, Abelard became restless and desired to expand his studies to the field of theology. So, as was the accepted practice of the time, he sought out the most eminent teacher in the field, "Anselm of Laon, who ... had for long years enjoyed the greatest renown."[221]

Abelard was disappointed in his new teacher. He judged him to be intellectually mediocre, and was contemptuous of Anselm's alleged insights and abilities. Anselm of Laon's "fame, in truth, was more the result of long-established custom than of the potency of his own talent or intellect. If any one came to him impelled by doubt on any subject, he went away more doubtful still.... He had a miraculous flow of words, but they were contemptible in meaning and quite void of reason. When he kindled a fire, he filled his house with smoke and illumined it not at all."[222]

Disappointed in his theology teacher, Abelard resolved to teach himself. More than four-hundred years before the Reformation, Abelard hit upon the revolutionary idea of individual study of the *Bible*. He explained, "it appeared quite extraordinary to me that educated persons should not be able to understand the sacred books simply by studying them themselves, together with the glosses thereon, and without the aid of any teacher. Most of those who were present mocked at me."[223]

Abelard followed his study by successfully lecturing on the Scriptures. His teacher became envious and resentful of Abelard's impudence. Anselm of Laon "began to persecute me for my lecturing on the Scriptures no less bitterly than my former master, William, had done for my work in philosophy."[224] But "the more obvious this rancor became, the more it redounded to my honor, and his persecution did nought save to make me more famous."[225]

In A.D. 1115, Abelard "stepped into the chair at Notre Dame, being also nominated canon."[226] It was the height of his personal success. Abelard became both famous and wealthy. "My school was notably increased in size ... and the amount of financial profit as well as glory which it brought me cannot be concealed from you, for the matter was widely talked of."[227] "Three thousand [students] are said to have paid fees to Abelard."[228]

> The years that immediately followed were the most brilliant in Abelard's career. All the world seemed about to do him homage. Scholars from all parts thronged to hear him. He lectured on philosophy and theology. He was well read in classical and widely read in sacred literature. His dialectic powers were ripe and, where arguments failed, the teacher's imagination and rhetoric came to the rescue. His books were widely read not only in the schools and convents, but in castles and guildhouses. William of Thierry said they crossed the seas and overleaped the Alps. When he visited towns, the people crowded the streets and strained their necks to catch a glimpse of him. His remarkable influence over men and women must be explained not by his intellectual depth so much as a by a certain daring and literary art and brilliance.[229]
>
> The charm of Abelard's teaching lay in its clearness and simplicity. A child could have understood him ... his powers of luminous exposition, his subtlety, his facility of expression, his erudition, his richness of allusion, his elastic *vivida vis* [living force], his boundless command of language — his *badinage* [playful and witty banter] brightening the stream of his rapid eloquence, even his literary digressions, in which he brought Horace, Virgil, Ovid, Lucan, and the poets to bear, with all the elegant taste of a scholar, upon dry matters of philosophy, then his impetuous spirit, his thirst for knowledge, and his unquenchable ambition to excel, made him stand preeminent amongst the greatest spirits of that day.[230]

Abelard's ego scaled new heights. He later wrote that at this time he had become so vain that "[I] had come to regard myself as the only philosopher remaining in the whole world."[231] But "pride goeth before destruction, and an haughty spirit before a fall."[232] Abelard was "ignorant of nothing under heaven except himself."[233] Imagining that he was immune to any misfortune, Abelard "began to loosen the rein" on his desires and appetites.[234] He confessed, "I was utterly absorbed in pride and sensuality."[235]

Abelard became infatuated with "a certain young girl named Heloise, the niece of a canon who was called Fulbert."[236] Heloise had both "youth and comeliness," but what made her irresistible to Abelard was an attainment of rare intellectual accomplishment.[237] "Of no mean beauty, she [Heloise] stood out above all by reason of her abundant knowledge of letters. Now this virtue is rare among women, and made her the most worthy of renown in the entire kingdom."[238]

Obsessed with Heloise, Abelard hit upon an artful and treacherous device for gaining access to her. "Utterly aflame with my passion for this maiden ... I persuaded the girl's uncle ... to take me into his household ... in return for the payment of a small sum."[239] The uncle was easily convinced. He could not imagine that his niece would be seduced by a supposedly chaste cleric, and he was eager to gain the income from a boarder. Abelard related, "he [Heloise's uncle] was fairly agape for my money, and at the same time believed that his niece would vastly benefit by my teaching."

Abelard was astonished at how easy it was to fool Heloise's uncle. "The man's simplicity was nothing short of astounding to me; I should not have been more smitten with wonder if he had entrusted a tender lamb to the care of a ravenous wolf."[240]

Egotistical and vain far beyond a fault, Abelard never considered the possibility that Heloise would reject him. "So distinguished was my name, and I possessed such advantages of youth and comeliness, that no matter what woman I might favor with my love, I dreaded rejection of none."[241]

Abelard's plan worked, and he began to carry on a torrid love affair with Heloise.

> We were united first in the dwelling that sheltered our love, and then in the hearts that burned with it. Under the pretext of study we spent our hours in the happiness of love, and learning held out to us the secret opportunities that our passion craved. Our speech was more of love than of the books which lay open before us; our kisses far outnumbered our reasoned words. Our hands sought less the book than each other's bosoms; love drew our eyes together far more than the lesson drew them to the pages of our text.... No degree in love's progress was left untried by our passion, and if love itself could imagine any wonder as yet unknown, we discovered it. And our inexperience of such delights made us all the more ardent in our pursuit of them, so that our thirst for one another was still unquenched.[242]

Abelard's teaching suffered. "My lecturing became utterly careless and lukewarm ... my students ... perceived ... the chaos of my mind."[243] The affair went on for several months and became common gossip — to everyone but Heloise's uncle. Finally, the uncle discovered the truth and was grief stricken.

Heloise and Abelard were separated. "The very sundering of our bodies served but to link our souls closer together; the plentitude of the love which was denied to us inflamed us more than ever."[244]

Soon after this, "Heloise found that she was pregnant."[245] Abelard secretly stole her away from her uncle's house and sent Heloise to live with his sister until the child was born. Heloise "gave birth to a son, whom she named Astrolabe."[246]

Heloise's uncle was "almost mad with grief," but feared to do bodily harm to Abelard.[247] Abelard tried to mend the difficult situation, but again his pride proved fateful. He went to the uncle and offered to marry Heloise, "provided only the thing could be kept secret, so that I might suffer no loss of reputation thereby."

The uncle accepted Abelard's offer of marriage, and promised to keep the secret of the marriage. "But her [Heloise's] uncle and those of his household, seeking solace for their disgrace, began to divulge the story of our marriage, and thereby to violate the pledge they had given me on this point. Heloise, on the contrary, denounced her own kin and swore that they were speaking the most absolute lies. Her uncle, aroused to fury thereby, visited her repeatedly with punishments. No sooner had I learned this than I sent her to a convent of nuns at Argenteuil, not far from Paris."[248]

The uncle and Heloise's relatives misinterpreted Abelard's action. "They were convinced that now I had completely played them false and had rid myself forever of Heloise by forcing her to become a nun. Violently incensed, they laid a plot against me."[249]

Heloise's uncle bribed one of Abelard's servants into revealing the location of his bedchamber. As Abelard slept, a gang of hired thugs broke into his bedroom and castrated him. "They had vengeance on me with a most cruel and most shameful punishment, such as astounded the whole world, for they cut off those parts of my body with which I had done that which was the cause of their sorrow."[250]

Abelard or his friends in turn exacted retribution. "They [the attackers] fled, but two of them were captured, and suffered the loss of their eyes and their genital organs. One of these two was the aforementioned servant, who, even while he was still in my service, had been led by his avarice to betray me."[251]

Abelard was devastated.

> I felt the disgrace more than the hurt to my body, and was more afflicted with shame than with pain ... I saw ... how justly God had punished me in that very part of my body whereby I had sinned. I perceived that there was indeed justice in my betrayal by him whom I had myself already betrayed.... How could I ever again hold up my head among men, when every finger should be pointed at me in scorn, every tongue speak my blistering shame, and when I should be a monstrous spectacle to all eyes?... God holds eunuchs in such abomination that men thus maimed are forbidden to enter a church, even as the unclean and filthy; nay, even beasts in such plight were not acceptable as sacrifices.[252]

Heloise "entered a convent ... submitting her fresh youth to the heavy and almost intolerable yoke of monastic life."[253] Abelard, now forty years old, did likewise, entering the Abbey of St. Denis as a monk.[254] Abelard was unhappy in the monastery. The monks failed to live up to his standards of conduct. The man who had betrayed a trust to seduce a young girl found the monastery to be "utterly worldly and in its life quite scandalous ... this intolerable state of things I often and vehemently denounced."[255]

After a year in the monastery, in A.D. 1120 Abelard left and reopened "his school at the Priory of Maisoncelle."[256] As always, his lectures and teachings were popular with students, and Abelard prospered. But another downfall soon followed.

In 1121, Abelard was charged with heresy for his book *Introducta ad Theologiam*.[257] A synod was convened at Soissons; Abelard was put on trial and found guilty. The assembly ordered that Abelard publicly burn *Introducta ad Theologiam*. "Without further examination or debate, did they compel me with my own hand to cast that memorable book of mine into the flames."[258]

It should be no surprise that Abelard's life was "filled with bitter opposition and persecution."[259] He believed that "reason must precede faith, and that it is not sinful to doubt."[260] Abelard advocated skepticism. "Constant and frequent questioning is the first key to wisdom ... through doubting we are led to inquire, and by inquiry we perceive the truth."[261] "He founds science, as others did more clumsily hundreds of years later, in doubt."[262]

Convicted of heresy, Abelard was sentenced to be confined in the Abbey of St. Medard. Depressed at this latest calamity, Abelard confessed "the sorrow that tortured me, the shame that overwhelmed me, the desperation that wracked my mind, all these I could then feel, but even now I can find no words to express them."[263]

Abelard was soon freed from his confinement at St. Medard. Disgusted with life, he went into the wilderness and lived as a hermit. But he immediately found himself surrounded by flocks of students. "No sooner had scholars learned of my retreat than they began to flock thither from all sides, leaving their towns and castles to dwell in the wilderness. In place of their spacious houses they built themselves huts; instead of dainty fare they lived on the herbs of the field and coarse bread; their soft beds they exchanged for heaps of straw and rushes, and their tables were piles of turf."[264]

Abelard named his wilderness retreat the *Paraclete*, meaning "helper or comforter."[265] Paraclete is also a reference to the Holy Spirit of the Christian Trinity.[266] Abelard remained at the Paraclete until offered a position as abbot at the abbey of St. Gildas in Lesser Brittany. "It proved a wretched exchange."[267] Abelard described the environment at St. Gildas as "barbarous," said the monks at the abbey had a "vile and untamable way of life," and characterized the local population in general as "uncivilized and lawless."[268]

Nevertheless, Abelard remained at St. Gildas for nearly ten years.[269] An opportunity came when Abelard's friend, the abbot of St. Denis, "got possession of the abbey of Argenteuil," where Heloise served as a nun.[270] The nuns were expelled from Argenteuil, and Abelard turned his retreat, the Paraclete, over to Heloise and her chosen associates. "The place proved itself a true Paraclete to them, making all those who dwelt round about feel pity and kindliness for the sisterhood."[271]

Abelard never found peace. In his autobiography, *Historia Calamitatum*, he wrote "I am driven hither and yon, a fugitive and a vagabond, even as the accursed Cain."[272] Abelard alleged that his enemies tried to poison him.[273] Abelard was unpopular as an abbot. He stated that, "if the monks knew beforehand that I was going anywhere on a journey, they bribed bandits to waylay me on the road and kill me."

Abelard died on A.D. April 21, 1142. Eventually his remains were united with those of Heloise, and the lovers lie together in a tomb at the cemetery of Pere-Lachaise in Paris.[274] But "the flame which Abelard's teaching had kindled was not destined to expire."[275] His students went on to found the University of Paris, which became the archetype for the modern university.

HUGH OF ST. VICTOR (A.D. 1096–1141)

In his *Didascalicon*, a "book of elementary instruction,"[276] Hugh of St. Victor embraced logic. "That logic too should be invented was essential, for no man can fitly discuss things unless he first has learned the nature of correct and true discourse ... the man who brushes aside knowledge of argumentation falls of necessity into error when he searches out the nature of things."[277]

Adumbrating the modern appreciation for technology, Hugh included the mechanical arts as a division of philosophy.[278] His *Didascalicon* listed the seven mechanical sciences as "fabric making, armament, commerce, agriculture, hunting, medicine, and theatrics."[279]

However Hugh also held the common medieval view that the arts were subservient to religion. "All the natural arts serve Divine Science, and the lower knowledge rightly ordered leads to the higher."[280] He endorsed the devices of allegory and tropology. "When ... things signify facts mystically, we have allegory; and when things mystically signify what ought to be done, we have tropology."[281]

JOHN OF SALISBURY (C. A.D. 1115–1180)

John of Salisbury, an "eager humanist"[282] and "most excellent classical scholar,"[283] wrote the *Metalogicon* to defend the *Trivium* of grammar, rhetoric, and dialectic against those critics who claimed such studies were a waste of time. "It is the first work in the Middle Ages in which the whole of Aristotle's *Organon* is turned to account."[284]

In the prologue of the *Metalogicon*, John explained "I undertake to defend logic."[285] An adversary, Cornificius, "whose name recurs as an unidentified opponent of human learning,"[286] was attacked vehemently.

"I would openly identify Cornificius and call him by his own name, I would reveal to the public his bloated gluttony, puffed-up pride, obscene mouth, rapacious greed, irresponsible conduct, loathsome habits (which nauseate all about him), foul lust, dissipated appearance, evil life, and ill repute, were it not that I am restrained by reverence for his Christian name."[287]

Although logic was not the first branch of philosophy originated by the Greeks, John gave it primacy. "Logic should be taught to those who are entering upon philosophical studies, since it serves as an interpreter of both words and meanings, and since no part of philosophy can be accurately comprehended without it."[288]

Stressing the importance of logic, John concluded "logic gives great promise. For it provides a mastery of invention and judgment, as well as supplies ability to divide, define, and prove with conviction. It is such an important part of philosophy that it serves the other parts in much the same way as the soul does the body."[289]

John acknowledged reverence for Aristotle, but added that it was the duty of those living in the present day to build on the work of the ancients. "Who is content with what Aristotle gives in *On Interpretation*? Who does not add points obtained from other sources?"[290]

On February 5, 1676, Isaac Newton wrote to Robert Hooke, "If I have seen further it is by standing on the shoulders of giants."[291] But Newton seems to have derived this metaphor from John of Salisbury, and John from Bernard of Chartres (d. circa A.D. 1130). In the *Metalogicon*, John wrote, "Bernard of Chartres used to compare us to dwarfs perched on the shoulders of giants. He pointed out that we see more and farther than our predecessors, not because we have keener vision or greater height, but because we are lifted up and borne aloft on their gigantic stature."[292] By this remark, John showed a recognition of the cumulative and progressive nature of science.

Translations

An important stimulus for the new European interest in philosophy and science was the translation of scientific books from Arabic to Latin. Although some of these books were original works by Islamic authors such as Avicenna and al-Hazen, many of the translations were of pre-existing texts by Greek scientists. The introduction of ancient Greek works in science and natural philosophy was the largest single factor in the development of science in medieval Europe.[293] "The full recovery of this ancient learning, supplemented by what the Arabs had gained from the Orient and from their own observation, constitutes the scientific renaissance of the Middle Ages."[294]

Prior to translations of works in Arabic, very little Greek work in science or philosophy was available in Europe because it had never been translated into Latin. The Romans undertook few Greek translations, because most Roman scholars read Greek.[295] Cicero (106–43 B.C.), Varro (116–27 B.C.), and Seneca (c. 4 B.C.–A.D. 65) all read Aristotle in Greek.[296] And, with the exception of Greek communities in Italy, Greek literacy was rare in Europe.[297]

The wave of translations was preceded by economic, political, and military events. European prosperity of the High Middle Ages allowed political expansion through military conquests. Christian Europeans captured Sicily in 1090 and Toledo in A.D. 1085. Sicily and southern Spain subsequently became the two most important locations for translations of Arabic works into Latin. Some translation was also done in areas of the Middle East occupied by Crusaders.[298] Translations into Latin began as early as A.D. 950, but the main period of activity was during the twelfth and thirteenth centuries.

Although there was some patronage and institutional sponsorship, most translations were undertaken through the initiative of individual scholars. In eleventh and twelfth-century Europe, there was a general appreciation among European scholars that the existing Latin literature was impoverished. Adelard of Bath (c. A.D. 1080–1152) wrote, "what French studies are ignorant of, those across the Alps will unlock; what you will not learn amongst the Latins, eloquent Greece will teach you."[299]

A motivated student might learn of the existence of a book such as Ptolemy's *Syntaxis*, but be unable to study it because there were no Latin versions. If sufficiently motivated, an ambitious person might therefore undertake the translation of the work from Arabic into Latin, even if he had to learn Arabic from scratch. Languages such as Arabic, Greek, or Hebrew were absent from the curriculum of the thirteenth-century European university. Around A.D. 1266 or 1267, Roger Bacon argued that Hebrew and Greek ought to be incorporated into university curricula. But "the first appointment of a lecturer to teach Greek literature appears to have been made in Florence in [A.D.] 1360."[300]

Translation methods varied. Some workers strove to translate word-by-word, but this method was often impractical as there might not be exact equivalents in the second language. There was also an appreciation that literal translations did not convey the original author's meaning so well as comprehending and then rephrasing the content in the new language. This philosophy of translation was expressed by Boethius (c. A.D. 480–525) when he explained, "it is not the charm of limpid speech but the unsullied truth that has to be expressed."[301]

In an age where the concepts of copyright and plagiarism were not well defined, translators could also use the venue of translation as a template for freely adding their own original additions and commentaries. But most translators of philosophical and scientific works sought to accurately render both the "substance and the sense" of the books they translated, translating *verbum ex verbo*.[302]

For some technical terms, there were no Latin equivalents. Thus Arabic manuscripts became the source of many words introduced into English. A short sampling includes *alkali, zircon, camphor, borax, elixir, talc, nadir, zenith, azure, zero, cipher, algebra, artichoke, guitar, lemon, alcohol,* and *coffee.* The star names *Aldebaran, Altair,* and *Betelgeuse* are also Arabic words.[303]

The most important geographic location for translation during the twelfth and thirteenth centuries was southern Spain, where Muslims, Jews, and Christians freely interacted. Bilingualism was common, and "in times of peace commercial and cultural relations flourished between" Muslim Spain and the Christian regions to the north.[304] The Muslim rulers had accumulated vast libraries. "The Ommiades of Spain had formed a library of six hundred thousand volumes ... and above seventy public libraries were opened in the cities of the Andalusian kingdom."[305] After A.D. 1085, the most important city for translation activity was Toledo.[306]

In Spain there was much collaboration between Jews and Christians. Many books were first translated from Arabic into Hebrew and then into Latin.[307] It is likely that Christian scholars were assisted by Spanish Jews in translating Hebrew into Latin.[308]

One of the earliest translators of scientific works from Arabic into Latin was Gerbert d'Aurillac (c. A.D. 945–1003), later Pope Sylvester II. Gerbert was interested in mathematics and astronomy, and has been described as "the most learned man of the tenth century."[309] He "wrote on the abacus and on the astrolabe,"[310] and was one of the first Europeans to work with Arabic or Hindu numerals. Attribution of Gerbert as translator of any specific manuscript is uncertain, but his work in mathematics and science was an indication that European scholars were beginning to take an interest in these subjects.[311]

Adelard of Bath (c. A.D. 1080–1152), an English scholar, was one of the first important translators. He traveled to France, Sicily, Syria, and Spain.[312] Adelard translated works in mathematics and astronomy from Arabic into Latin.[313] He was the first to translate a complete version of Euclid's *Elements* into Latin.[314]

The most important and prolific of the translators was Gerard of Cremona (c. A.D. 1114–1187). In a short biographical statement, one of Gerard's students described how his master happened to become a translator at Toledo. "For love of the *Almagest*, which he [Gerard] could not find at all among the Latins, he went to Toledo; there, seeing the abundance of books in Arabic on every subject, and regretting the poverty of the Latins in these things, he learned the Arabic language, in order to be able to translate."[315]

An incomplete list of works translated by Gerard's numbers seventy-one. The most significant books from this list include Ptolemy's *Almagest*, Euclid's *Elements*, and Avicenna's *Canon of Medicine*. Gerard also translated Aristotle's *Posterior Analytics*, *Physics*, *On the Heavens*, *On Generation and Corruption*, and *Meteorology*.[316] Although Gerard was "the greatest of all translators," it is probable that many translations attributed to him were done by others working under his supervision.[317]

The translations of Gerard of Cremona were the largest single source of Arabic science introduced into Europe.[318] Gerard translated twenty-one medical works, and about thirty books covering the exact sciences of mathematics and astronomy.[319] The influence of Gerard's translations was significant, and is revealed in "the evolution of the university curriculum during the thirteenth and fourteenth centuries."[320]

Although most translators acted upon individual initiatives without patronage, an exception was the court of Alphonso X (A.D. 1221–1284), king of Castile in central Spain from A.D. 1252 to 1284. Alphonso was a patron of scholarship who commissioned important works in law and history.[321] In the field of science, "several Jewish and Christian astronomers working under him [Alphonso] at Toledo ... prepared the celebrated Alfonsine Tables."[322] The tables were based on the Ptolemaic system and "continued in great repute for three hundred years as the best planetary tables."[323] Alphonso was a better patron of science than political ruler, for his reign was tumultuous and he "died defeated and deserted at Seville."[324]

In the thirteenth century, Sicily became a center of translation activity.[325] Since ancient times, Sicily had been "at the center of Mediterranean civilization,"[326] having been occupied by Greeks, Carthaginians, Romans, Europeans, and Muslims. Muslim invasions of Sicily began in A.D. 827. It took 138 years for the Saracens to complete the conquest of Sicily, achieving complete dominion in A.D. 965.[327] "For 263 years the Christian people of some part or other of Sicily were in subjection to Moslem masters ... [but] Christianity and the Greek tongue never died out."[328]

As European power and prosperity increased in the eleventh century, Norman invasions of Sicily began in A.D. 1060. By A.D. 1090, Sicily was completely under Norman control.[329] Norman rule was tolerant. "The Mahommedan religion was everywhere tolerated ... [and] the Norman princes protected all the races, creeds and tongues of the island, Greek, Saracen and Jew."[330]

In the midst of linguistic diversity, Sicily was a natural locus for translation. Greek, Arabic, Latin, and Hebrew were all in common use.[331] The best known of the thirteenth-century Sicilian translators was Michael Scot (fl. A.D. 1217–1235).[332] Scot was the court astrologer, companion, and scientific consultant to Emperor Frederick II (A.D. 1194–1250).[333] Frederick II was a patron of science and tolerant of Sicily's diversity. "He [Frederick] spoke all its tongues; he protected, as far as circumstances would allow, all its races."[334]

Scot translated Aristotle's works on the biology of animals: *History of Animals*, *On the Parts of Animals*, and *On the Generation of Animals*. He also translated several of Averroes' commentaries on Aristotle.[335] Roger Bacon (c. 1219–1292) criticized Scot for being ignorant of both language and science, but credited him for having an influential role in the introduction of Aristotle's natural philosophy into Europe.[336]

In addition to his translation work and astrological consulting, Scot "conducted his own experiments,"[337] in collaboration with Frederick II. This activity is evidence that as early as the thirteenth century, Europeans were going beyond logic and beginning to grasp the essential role of empiricism in constructing scientific knowledge.

Scot also authored a trilogy of original works. Part of his book *Liber particularis* is devoted to answering questions on natural science put to Scot by Frederick II. In describing the nature of the hydrologic cycle, Scot advanced the common medieval view that the circulation of water in the Earth was analogous to the circulation of blood in the human body. "Waters were created with [the] inexhaustible virtue of pouring forth so long as the world endures, and they move about in the earth like blood in the veins."[338] This view clearly reflected the influence of the ancient Doctrine of the Macrocosm and Microcosm.

Despite his recognition of the value of experiment, Scot was a man of the thirteenth century. He was "pretentious and boastful, with no clear sense of the limits of his knowledge."[339]

Aristotle and the Church, 13th Century

The most significant of the translated philosophical works being introduced to Europe were the books of Aristotle on natural philosophy. From Roman times, the only Latin manuscripts by Aristotle that had been widely read in Europe were two books of the *Organon*, *Categories* and *On Interpretation*.[340] These "had been regularly taught in the [Christian] Church's schools since the time of Charles the Great [Charlemagne, A.D. 742–814]."[341] When the four remaining books of the Organon (*Prior Analytics*, *Posterior Analytics*, *Topics*, *Sophistical Refutations*) were translated into Latin and distributed in Europe, they became known as the *New Logic*.[342]

During the course of the twelfth century, Aristotle's other works began to be translated into Latin. Working in Constantinople from Greek originals, James of Venice (fl. A.D.

1136–1148) translated the four obscure books of the *Organon*, and thus became "the first scholar of the twelfth century who brought the *New Logic* of Aristotle afresh to the attention of Latin Europe."[343] James of Venice also translated Aristotle's *Physics, On the Soul,* and *Metaphysics.*[344] James was probably the most significant individual responsible for introducing Latin translations of Aristotle's works into Europe.[345]

During the first half of the thirteenth century, Robert Grosseteste (c. 1168–1253) introduced a revised translation of the *Nicomachean Ethics.* Grosseteste also translated *De Caelo* (*On the Heavens*).[346]

William of Moerbeke (b. 1220–1235, d. before A.D. 1286) was perhaps the most productive and important translator of Greek scientific works into Latin during the thirteenth century.[347] Moerbeke wrote that he undertook translation "in spite of the hard work and tediousness which it involves, in order to provide Latin scholars with new material for study."[348] One of Moerbeke's goals was to provide Europe with a Latin version of the complete body of Aristotle's works.[349] He was the first to translate *Politics* and *Poetics* into Latin, as well as the eleventh book of *Metaphysics* and two works on the biology of animals. Moerbeke also produced the first Latin translations of *Meteorologica, De Caelo, History of Animals, On the Parts of Animals,* and *On the Generation of Animals,* made from the Greek originals.[350]

Moerbeke translated significant commentaries on Aristotle made by Philoponus (c. A.D. 490–570), Simplicius (c. A.D. 490–560), and others. Additionally, he translated several works of Archimedes.[351] Moerbeke's cumulative output totaled "almost fifty distinct translations or revisions."[352]

In addition to Aristotle's own works, the commentaries on Aristotle by Averroes (A.D. 1126–1198) were influential. Averroes attitude toward Aristotelean philosophy was close to worshipful. "The doctrine of Aristotle is the supreme truth, because his intellect was the limit of the human intellect."[353]

But Aristotle's natural philosophy was also partly heretical. The three primary heresies in Aristotle's teaching were identified by Saint Bonaventure (A.D. 1221–1274) as the claims "that the world is eternal, that there is one intellect in all men, and that it is impossible for a mortal being to attain immortality."[354]

In *Meteorologica,* Aristotle had plainly written, "there will be no end to time and the world is eternal,"[355] a plain contradiction to the account of Creation in the book of *Genesis.* The doctrine of collective intellect appeared to originate not so much with Aristotle as with Averroes, who "asserted that there was only one single intellective soul in all human bodies."[356] Therefore there could be no individual immortality or salvation.[357]

These were troubling and distinct heresies. But what made the Aristotelian philosophy more dangerous was that it offered a unified alternative to Christian theology. Whereas an occasional heretic might contradict Church dogma on one point or another, they had no complete system to offer as a replacement.

Aristotle said that it was possible to know both God and the world by the exercise of reason alone. This was an contradiction to the authority of the Christian faith which rested upon divine revelation, not only as revealed by the life and teachings of Jesus Christ, but the *Old Testament* Prophets, Saints, and Church Fathers. Simply put, the clash was between faith and reason.

At the University of Paris, "the tide of secular and scientific learning was rising."[358] Aristotle's new works and those by commentators such as Averroes began to be introduced there near the first decade of the thirteenth century. "The result of these importations was an outbreak of speculation of a much bolder character than any that had been known in the twelfth century."[359] Paris witnessed "an outburst of free-thought."[360]

"Amalric of Bena, a professor of logic and theology (1205), fearlessly taught, in his public place, that human nature could be identified with the Divinity; that the Eternal Father became incarnate in Abraham; the Eternal Son in Mary; and the Holy Ghost in us; and that all things, in reality, are one; because all things, in reality, are God."[361]

The introduction of heretical philosophical teachings was opposed by conservative theologians. A Paris synod in A.D. 1210 declared "nor shall the books of Aristotle on natural philosophy, and the commentaries [of Averroes] be read in Paris in public or in secret; and this we enjoin under pain of excommunication."[362] Additionally, "the works of one David de Dinant were condemned to the flames," and "the body of Almaric [of Bena] was ordered to be dug up and buried in unconsecrated ground, and a posthumous excommunication launched against him."[363] Ten disciples of Amalric were "burnt alive," while "others [were] condemned to prison for life."[364]

In A.D. 1215, the Papal Legate at Paris, Robert de Courçon, prescribed that "the treatises of Aristotle on logic, both the old and the new,[365] are to be read in the schools ... [but] the books of Aristotle on metaphysics or natural philosophy, or the abridgments of these works, are not to be read."

The language of this decree illustrated the Church's dilemma. Aristotle's natural philosophy was difficult to condemn wholesale, because his logic had been an integral part of the Christian curriculum for hundreds of years. Even the leader of the conservative opposition, Saint Bonaventure, had "nothing against Aristotle himself."[366] The half-hearted nature of the opposition revealed itself in the decree of Pope Gregory IX in 1231. Gregory allowed Aristotle's books on natural philosophy to be used at the University of Paris if their heretical content had been redacted. "The masters of arts ... shall not use in Paris those books on natural philosophy which for a definite reason were prohibited in the provincial council [of 1210], until they have been examined and purged from every suspicion of error."[367]

But the conservative desire to censor offensive material from Aristotle's works faced difficulties. The University of Toulouse took advantage of the restrictions imposed at Paris by circulating a flyer that read, "those who wish to scrutinize the bosom of nature to the inmost can hear the books of Aristotle which were forbidden at Paris."[368] The inference follows that the author or authors of this flyer considered the inducement significant enough to be able to lure students from Paris to Toulouse.

By the year A.D. 1255, the liberal faction had triumphed at Paris. None of Aristotle's works were excluded from the curriculum, and "nearly the whole range of the Aristotelian writings [were] prescribed [as required readings] by a statute of the Faculty of Arts as textbooks for the lectures of its Masters."[369] The required readings included *Physica*, *Metaphysica*, *De Caelo*, *Meteorologica*, and *De Animalibus*.[370] The popular saying among masters and students at Paris was, "every one is excluded and banned, who does not come clad in Aristotle's armor."[371]

By 1256, the Averroists were already attracting attention for their heresies, because in that year Pope Alexander IV asked Albertus Magnus (c. A.D. 1200–1284) to write a work exposing the errors of Averroism.[372] The heretical movement at Paris reached its height in the 1270s with the teaching of Siger of Brabant (c. A.D. 1240–1281/1284). Siger became a master of arts at Paris c. 1260–1265. He was "boisterous and pugnacious," and "the leader of the dissident minority party in the Faculty of Arts."[373] Siger was primarily an Averroist and Aristotelean philosopher, but was also influenced by Avicenna and Proclus.[374]

Perhaps even more radical than Siger was his colleague, Boethius of Dacia. Boethius taught that the exercise of philosophy should be free from any religious constraint or authority, and that the world was eternal. He denied the reality of both the Creation and the Resurrection.[375] Asserting the primacy of philosophy, Boethius wrote, "it belongs to the philosopher to determine every question which can be disputed by reason; for every question which can be disputed by rational arguments falls within some part of being. But the philosopher investigates all being — natural, mathematical, and divine. Therefore it belongs to the philosopher to determine every question which can be disputed by rational arguments."[376]

As a philosopher, Siger was inevitably led to adopt or defend doctrines such as the eternity of the world and the existence of "a single intellect for all men."[377] To save himself from the charge of heresy, Siger maintained that he had reached conclusions necessary by the methods of philosophy, but these results must be false when they contradicted the doctrines of the Church. Siger explained, "the opinion of Aristotle may not agree with truth; it is also possible that revelation has given us ... information which cannot be proved by natural reasons."[378]

This explanation was not accepted by most theologians. They wanted consilience between reason and faith. To accept that the exercise of reason and logic led invariably to conclusions that contradicted revelation would make it impossible to incorporate reason into Christian theology. "What reason demonstrates to be necessary, is necessarily true,"[379] therefore, Siger's opponents charged him with implicitly advocating a doctrine of double truth.

There is not one instance in any of Siger's writings where he explicitly stated that a proposition could simultaneously be true in philosophy but false in theology, or vice versa. On the contrary, he always maintained that philosophical conclusions that contradicted Church doctrine had to be false.[380]

Nevertheless, the conservative theologians sensed that Siger and his colleagues were being disingenuous. In 1277, they cracked down on the heretical teachings at Paris in a serious way. On January 18, 1277, Pope John XXI directed the bishop of Paris, Etienne Tempier, to "identify the errors ... being circulated at Paris and those responsible for them."[381] Tempier acted quickly, issuing a list of 219 heretical propositions on March 7. The short time taken for such a lengthy declaration implied that it had long been in preparation, the work of a determined and organized opposition. The Pope accepted Tempier's list, and backed it up with a threat of excommunication for anyone "who upheld even a single proposition."[382]

Among the condemned propositions were those that limited the power of God. It was an error to maintain "that God cannot be the cause of a new act," or "could not move the heavens with rectilinear motion," or "that the absolutely impossible cannot be done by God."[383] It was heresy to state "that the world is eternal," or to deny the possibility of miracle by insisting that "nothing happens by chance."[384]

In *De Caelo*, Aristotle had maintained that "the world must be unique. There cannot be several worlds."[385] This was not possible in Aristotelian physics, because the natural motions of the elements were directed toward the center of the universe, identified as the center of the Earth. If there existed another world, its elements would have to move toward the Earth, or the elements of the Earth would move to the center of the cosmos. This was not observed to happen. Therefore, to avoid postulating the encumbrance that elements had different properties in different locations, Aristotle was forced to conclude that "there cannot be more worlds than one."[386]

But limiting possible worlds to one was seen as heretical, because it implied that God was not omnipotent. Tempier declared that it was an error to maintain that "the first cause [God] could not make several worlds."[387]

By weakening the Aristotelian stranglehold on philosophy, Pierre Duhem (1861–1916) proposed the idea that the ecclesiastical proclamation of 1277 established the intellectual groundwork for the Scientific Revolution of the seventeenth century. "If we must assign a date for the birth of modern science, we would, without doubt, choose the year 1277 when the bishop of Paris solemnly proclaimed that several worlds could exist, and that the whole of the heavens could, without contradiction, be moved with a rectilinear motion."[388] This hypothesis is plausible, but contradicted by the fact that history records no "dramatic increase in the frequency of observation and experiment"[389] following 1277.

That the condemnation of 1277 was effective is attested to by the historical fact that both Siger of Brabant and Boethius of Dacia fled France for Italy.[390] The heretical movement at Paris lost its vigor, "partly [attributable] to the steadily vigilant authority, partly to the natural evaporation of the excitement and unsettlement which attended the first introduction of the new ideas."[391] But this was not the end of Aristotelean philosophy — far from it. Aristotle's "texts were too entrenched in the universities to be abandoned."[392] Aristotelean philosophy was absorbed into the Catholic Church through the work of Thomas Aquinas (A.D. 1225–1274), who enrolled "the whole Aristotelean Philosophy into the service of the Church."[393] The condemnation of 1277 was annulled in 1325, when the bishop of Paris declared, "we neither approve nor disapprove of these articles, but leave them for free scholastic discussion."[394]

Rise of the Universities

Monastic and Cathedral Schools

One of the most significant events of the European High Middle Ages was the founding of the universities. These institutions became the direct predecessors of modern universities in Europe and America. The European universities were not the lineal descendants of Plato's Academy, but originated as outgrowths of monastic and cathedral schools in the twelfth century A.D.[395] "The university is distinctly a medieval institution."[396]

From about A.D. 550 through 1100 in Europe, "the religious schools became the only medium whereby culture could be acquired and handed on."[397] Until the Carolingian Renaissance of the late eighth and ninth centuries, "learning was primarily a matter for the clergy."[398] Any child that might be educated in a monastery school was destined for the clergy. "The clergy were almost the only class which possessed or desired to possess even the rudiments of knowledge."[399]

In Eastern monasticism, illiteracy was common. But in the West, "the reading of Holy Scripture ... seemed essential to any full monastic life."[400] Saint Benedict of Nursia (c. A.D. 480–547), the founder of Western monasticism, in his *Rule*, established literacy and reading as indispensable obligations of a monk. "In days of Lent they [monks] shall receive separate books from the library, which they shall read entirely through in order ... moreover, on Sunday all shall engage in reading."[401]

Nevertheless, study was confined chiefly to religious materials. "If a bishop took too much trouble over the teaching of grammar he was apt to cause quite a scandal."[402] The only work on natural philosophy that had been translated into Latin was the first half of

Plato's *Timaeus*.[403] What passed for science was represented by the materials in Isidore's *Etymologies*.

The secular curriculum consisted of the seven liberal arts. These were subdivided into the *Trivium* of grammar (literature), rhetoric, and dialectic (logic), and the *Quadrivium* of geometry, arithmetic, astronomy and music. These disciplines had materialized as a core curriculum in classical times, being finalized "about the middle of the first century B.C."[404]

The disciplines of the Quadrivium received scant attention. "Arithmetic and astronomy found their way into the educational curriculum chiefly because they taught the means of finding Easter ... the real secular education of the Dark Ages was the Trivium."[405] Unlike its ultimate rejection in Islam, the study of logic found a welcome home in Christian Europe. While the study of the Latin classics, such as Virgil or Ovid, was controversial at times, "there was nothing pagan about syllogisms."[406] "Logic was the one treasure snatched from the intellectual wreckage of a by-gone civilization which he [the Christian student] was encouraged to appropriate."[407] Europeans possessed five books of Aristotle's *Organon* that had been translated by Boethius (c. A.D. 480–525).[408] Thus the revival of logic in the eleventh and twelfth centuries was the result of a long incubation.

The general method of instruction practiced in the monastic schools "was that of question and answer."[409] Students memorized rote answers to standardized questions. In the study of grammar, after learning the basic rules, pupils read "first and foremost the *Aeneid* of Virgil, and then some of Terence, Horace, Statius, Lucan, Persius, and Juvenal."[410]

The Franks were "a confederation of German tribes that alone had succeeded in establishing a permanent kingdom" in Europe.[411] The most powerful family amongst the Franks, the Carolingians, gained the throne in A.D. 751.[412] On Christmas Day of the year A.D. 800, Charlemagne (742–814), king of the Franks, was crowned "Emperor of the Romans" by the Pope.[413] The crowning of Charlemagne foreshadowed the end of the Dark Ages in Europe and the emergence of the High Middle Ages. "From that moment modern history begins."[414]

Charlemagne himself was virtually illiterate ("he also tried to write").[415] But he was astute enough to conceive that "a genuine unity of his people could be brought about only through the inner life by means of a common language, culture, and set of ideas."[416] Thus education was required.

The impetus provided to education by Charlemagne's decrees became known as the *Carolingian Renaissance* of the late eighth and ninth centuries. For the first time, not just monks, but the general public were to be educated. "A regular system of schools was planned, beginning with the village school, in charge of the parish priest for the most elementary studies, and leading up through monastic and cathedral schools to the School of the Palace."[417] Charlemagne entrusted to the Church the duty of teaching "those who by the gift of God are able to learn, according as each has capacity."[418]

With a system of elementary education in place, the best and brightest students desired more than they could obtain in a village school. As the economy of Europe prospered in the eleventh century, students multiplied. They traveled, seeking the best teachers in the cathedral schools. The most accomplished teachers, such as Peter Abelard, became both wealthy and famous.

MEDICAL SCHOOL AT SALERNO

The earliest European university was the medical school at Salerno, Italy. "The origin of the School of Salerno is veiled in impenetrable obscurity,"[419] but it seems to have been an outgrowth of a hospital run by Benedictine monks. The Benedictine hospital at Salerno was "famous as early as the first quarter of the ninth century."[420] Another significant factor was Salerno's reputation as a "health resort."[421] The presence of the Benedictines "imparted the academic atmosphere to the town, and made it possible to gather together the elements for the university which gradually came into existence around the medical school."[422]

The study and teaching of medicine at Salerno was fully revived by the eleventh century. One product of the Salerno medical school that was popular for centuries in Europe was the book, *Regimen Sanitatis Salernitanum*. The *Regimen* was composed of rhymed verses that gave prescriptions for health.[423] The prescribed regimen for long life and health recommended fresh air, moderation in diet and drink, and the avoidance of stress.

> If thou to health and vigor wouldst attain,
> Shun weighty cares—all anger deem profane,
> From heavy suppers and much wine abstain.
> Nor trivial count it, after pompous fare,
> To rise from table and to take the air.
> Shun idle, noonday slumber, nor delay
> The urgent calls of nature to obey.
> These rules if thou wilt follow to the end,
> Thy life to greater length thou mayst extend.[424]

The abbey of Monte Cassino is eighty miles (129 kilometers) from Salerno,[425] and it was there that Constantine the African (fl. 1065–1085) translated the works of Hippocrates (c. 460–370 B.C.), Hunain ibn Ishaq (A.D. 809–873), Galen (c. A.D. 129–200), and other medical writers.[426] Constantine was "the first important figure in the transmission of Greco-Arab science to the West,"[427] but he could have not have been solely responsible for the renaissance of medical scholarship at Salerno in the eleventh century. Writers at Salerno were producing medical works during the first part of the eleventh century, well before Constantine the African did his work.[428]

During the eleventh and twelfth centuries, Salerno was the premier institution for medical education in Europe. But it had no progeny. Salerno "remained without influence in the development of academic institutions."[429] "By the beginning of the fourteenth century the decline of Salerno was complete."[430]

Legal Studies at Bologna

The two earliest institutions that became archetypes for modern universities were the University of Bologna and the University of Paris. Scholars in northern Europe (e.g., France) were preoccupied with logic and theology. But in Italy the emphasis was on grammar and rhetoric. "These arts were studied as aids to the composition of legal documents."[431]

At the beginning of the eleventh century, there was a "great revival of legal studies" at Bologna.[432] The primary object of legal study was the body of Roman Law that had been condensed and archived (A.D. 528–533) by Justinian I (A.D. 483–565), Emperor of the Eastern Roman Empire.

When Justinian ascended to the throne in A.D. 528, he found the existing mass of Roman law to be highly confused. There were two primary problems. A thousand years of practice had left a body of law that was immense, and therefore simply too large to be accessible. The law also contained many contradictory provisions. Justinian therefore resolved to consolidate the great mass of existing material into a coherent and consistent form that could be a practical tool. He "made extracts from the existing law, preserving the old words, and merely cutting out repetitions, removing contradictions, retrenching superfluities, so as immensely to reduce the bulk of the whole."[433] The resulting work became known as the *Corpus Juris*.

Bologna was the natural home of legal studies, because by the year 1000, it was already known as a liberal arts school for the study of literature. In these times, there was a close connection between literature and law. "In an age wherein reading and writing were the accomplishments of the few, while all business transactions of any solemnity or importance were carried on in a dead language, it is obvious that the connection between grammar and law was indefinitely closer that it is according to modern ideas."[434]

The most prominent teacher of law at Bologna was Irnerius (c. 1050–1130). Irnerius was "the founder of the systematic study of the Roman law."[435] Irnerius' primary works were a series of glosses on the *Corpus Juris*, a *gloss* being a commentary, explanation, or interpretation of an existing scholarly work. "A new school arose called the *glossarists*, of whom Irnerius has always been rightly regarded as the founder ... he was also the first of the medievalists to treat the law in a scientific way."[436]

By the end of the eleventh century, Bologna was attracting law students from all over Europe. "From the days of Irnerius down to the close of the thirteenth century.... Bologna was generally recognized as the chief school both of the civil and the canon law."[437]

PARIS, OXFORD, AND CAMBRIDGE

In the north, universities such as Paris emerged when the cathedral schools became *Studium Generale*. "*Studium Generale* means, not a place where all subjects are studied, but a place where students from all parts are received."[438] William of Champeaux drew hundreds of students to the school at Notre Dame, and Peter Abelard attracted thousands.[439]

Both the students and teachers spontaneously formed voluntary associations, modeled after the trade guilds. "These scholars, turbulent enough themselves, and dwelling in a turbulent foreign city, needed affiliation there, and protection and support. Organization was an obvious necessity."[440] So the scholars formed *universities*, where "the word 'university' means merely a number, a plurality, an aggregate of persons ... the word used to denote the academic institution in the abstract — the Schools or the town which held them — was *Studium* rather than *Universitas*."[441]

Foreign students had to band together. Citizenship in a medieval city such as Bologna was "an hereditary possession of priceless value. The citizens of one town had, in the absence of express agreement, no civil rights in another. There was one law for the citizen; another, and a much harsher one, for the alien."[442] "To appreciate the fact that the university was in its origin nothing more than a guild of foreign students is the key to the real origin and nature of the institution."[443]

> The university, in its earliest stage of development, appears to have been simply a scholastic guild — a spontaneous combination, that is to say, of teachers or scholars, or of both combined, and formed probably on the analogy of the trades guilds, and the guilds of aliens in foreign cities, which, in the course of the thirteenth and fourteenth centuries, are to be found springing up in most of the great European centers ... and so the university, composed as it was to a great extent of students from foreign countries, was a combination formed for the protection of its members from the extortion of the townsmen and the other annoyances incident in medieval times to residence in a foreign state.[444]

The oldest universities, such as those of Paris, Bologna, and Oxford, grew up spontaneously and almost imperceptibly out of the wanderings of students and the instruction given by individual teachers in the eleventh and twelfth centuries. The informal character of this early teaching was slow to disappear, and for a long time many students took neither degrees nor examinations and attended or absented themselves from classes as they pleased. It was even longer before the universities came to possess costly permanent buildings. But gradually the teachers united into faculties, university statutes came into existence, and the students organized themselves by "nations" or in other unions.[445]

The University of Paris "was an outgrowth of the Cathedral School of Paris [Notre Dame]."[446] In the eleventh century, the School of Paris was inferior in reputation to the cathedral schools at Bec, Tours, Chartres, or Reims. But this changed. Paris became preeminent, surpassing its rivals, starting with the teaching of William of Champeaux, and then with that of his student, Peter Abelard. Abelard "first attracted students from all parts of Europe and laid the foundations of that unique prestige which the Schools of Paris retained throughout the medieval period."[447] "Paris became a city of teachers ... here then were the materials for the formation of a university."[448]

"The University [of Paris] was not made but grew."[449] By A.D. 1127, teachers at the school of Notre Dame were "too numerous to be accommodated within the cloister."[450] The masters, or professors, had organized themselves into a guild or *university* by A.D. 1175.[451] The birth of the University[452] of Paris may thus be approximately ascribed to the year A.D. 1170.

In A.D. 1200, the University obtained a "charter of privileges" from the king of France, Philip II (A.D. 1165–1223).[453] The first written statutes governing the University of Paris date from A.D. 1210.[454] "At about the same date the University acquired a definite recognition of its existence as a legal corporation."[455]

The local Church authorities struggled to maintain control over the emerging institution, but failed. "To the mind of a Canon of Paris the very existence of the University was nothing more or less than a conspiracy — an unlawful secret society formed by a certain class of inferior ecclesiastics for the purpose of resisting their canonical superiors."[456] But the Pope sided with the University, and freed it from the control of local authority.[457]

The first British university was Oxford. Unlike Paris, Oxford had no cathedral school. But Oxford's location made it a convenient meeting place for ecclesiastical councils.[458] It had facilities for accommodating travelers. Oxford thus likely became the site of a university as "an accident of its commercial importance."[459]

Hastings Rashdall (1858–1924) speculated that Oxford arose directly out of a migration from the University of Paris around A.D. 1167.[460] This theory will resonate with "the student familiar with the migratory habits of the medieval scholar and acquainted with the early history of academic constitutions."[461]

Cambridge University was founded in A.D. 1209, when some 3,000 scholars left Oxford after a dispute with townspeople.[462] Oxford's first charter of privilege was granted in 1214,[463] and in 1252 the first University statute was enacted, requiring "an Inceptor in Theology to have previously lectured as a Bachelor."[464] In other words, no one could become a Doctor in theology without first graduating as a Master of arts.

STUDENTS AND MASTERS

The universities existed in a perpetual and uneasy equilibrium between state and church. They sought the embrace of the Catholic Church so as to free themselves from the disciplines of local authorities. Conversely, they embraced secular authority whenever it would free them from following the dictates of the Church.

The usual course of study at the universities was the seven liberal arts. But the sciences received little to no attention. In the thirteenth century, faculty at the University of Paris were divided into "theology, law, and arts."[465]

Students studied for four or five years to obtain a bachelor's degree, a Master's degree required three or four additional years of postgraduate work.[466] Study of the liberal arts was considered preparation for the higher study of theology. The degree of Doctor of Theology required eight years of study, and the recipient had to be at least thirty-five years of age. "The chief subjects were Scripture and the *Sentences* of Peter Lombard."[467]

The typical student at one of the great Medieval universities of Paris, Bologna, or Oxford, was independent in spirit and from a wealthy family. This was especially true at Bologna, where "the persons who came for legal instruction were not boys getting their first education in the Arts. They were men studying a profession, and among them were many individuals of wealth and consequence."[468]

The student guild at Bologna became so powerful that it brought the professors to their knees. Bologna was "a university of students," and the students eventually succeeded "in reducing the Masters to an almost incredible servitude."[469] The power of the students came from their money and their association in guilds. If the professors or town did not meet their demands, the whole student body could simply pack up and leave, depriving both the masters and the townspeople of the income derived from their presence. "So great became the power of the student body, that it brought the professors to complete subjection, paying them their salaries, regulating the time and mode of lecturing, and compelling them to swear obedience to the Rectors. The professors protested, but they submitted."[470]

The rowdy character of the medieval universities can be inferred from a regulation at the University of Paris that forbade students from throwing stones or dung during lectures.[471]

> Paris, in early days, must have presented a spectacle of great public disorder, debauchery, and crime. The professors, in great part, were reckless adventurers—a sort of wild knight-errants, who scoured the country in search of excitement for the mind, and money for the pocket. The students were, in the main, disorderly youths, living in the very center of corruption, without control, loving a noisy, dissipated life in town. Some were destitute, quarreling with prostitutes and varlets, and filling the tribunals with their scandals and litigations.... In the evenings, and towards nightfall, the taverns in those narrow, crooked streets, would be filled with the fumes of their liquors, and the streets would echo again with their boisterous mirth.... As the drink passed round, the mirth would become more pronounced. Words would be dealt out, interspersed with knocks and blows: the tavern would become a scene of indescribable uproar and confusion ... till the mass of them would swarm out irregularly, and choke the narrow street—shouting and yelling, and brandishing their daggers, as they parted company.... Bloodshed was frequent in these brawls; death was not uncommon.[472]

Students tended to organize into groups based on nationality. The University of Paris had four *Nationes*, the French, Normans, Picards, and English.[473] Relations between the Nations were not always without friction. Jacques de Vitry (c. A.D. 1160–1240), one of the first students at the University of Paris, wrote cynical commentaries on both the students and teachers at Paris. The students, he noted, had little love of learning, and carried with them the bitter prejudices of nationality. "Very few [of the students] studied for their own edification, or that of others. They wrangled and disputed not merely about the various sects or about some discussions; but the differences between the countries also caused dissensions, hatreds and virulent animosities among them and they impudently uttered all kinds of affronts and insults against one another. They affirmed that the English were drunkards and had tails; the sons of France proud, effeminate and carefully adorned like women ... after such insults from words they often came to blows."[474]

The teachers were no better. According to de Vitry, they were all hypocrites, ignorant men whose only interest was advancing their own station in life.

> I will not speak of those logicians before whose eves flitted constantly "the lice of Egypt," that is to say, all the sophistical subtleties, so that no one could comprehend their eloquent discourses in which, as says Isaiah, "there is no wisdom." As to the doctors of theology, "seated, in Moses' seat," they were swollen with learning, but their charity was not edifying. Teaching and not practicing, they have "become as sounding brass or a tinkling cymbal," or like a canal of stone, always dry, which ought to carry water to "the bed of spices." They not only hated one another, but by their flatteries they enticed away the students of others; each one seeking his own glory, but caring not a whit about the welfare of souls ... they sought the work decidedly less than the preeminence, and they desired above all to have "the uppermost rooms at feasts and the chief seats in the synagogue, and greetings in the market."[475]

CHAPTER 5

Thomas Aquinas (1225–1274) and Scholasticism

Dominican Monk

The conflict between faith and reason that sprang from the introduction of Aristotelean natural philosophy and metaphysics into Europe was settled by Saint Thomas Aquinas (1225–1274), a man who "was destined to become the most perfect symbol of mediaevalism."[1] Aquinas enabled the Christian Church to absorb the works of Aristotle and defined the borders of Europe's intellectual world for the next several hundred years. He combined "all previous Christian thinking into one systematic and consistent and moderate whole," and is "regarded as the greatest and most authoritative of the orthodox medieval theologians."[2] "By nature and education he [Thomas] is the spirit of scholasticism incarnate."[3]

Thomas d'Aquino was born to a noble family in the city of Aquino [Rocasecca] in southern Italy, near the abbey of Monte Cassino.[4] "His mother, Theodora, was descended from the Caraccioli, a noble Norman family, and was countess of Teano in her own right."[5] Thomas had two brothers and three sisters.[6]

At the age of five, Thomas was placed by his parents as an *oblate* at the nearby abbey of Monte Cassino. An *oblate* was "a child dedicated by his or her parents to a religious house and placed there to be brought up."[7] The motivations of Thomas' family may have been pecuniary. They hoped that Thomas "would eventually join the Order [of Benedictine monks], and become master of those vast possessions which were under the dominion of its abbots."[8]

At about the age of fifteen, Thomas enrolled at the University of Naples where he studied from 1239 to 1244.[9] It was at Naples that Thomas made a decision that alienated him from his family: he decided to become a Dominican monk.

The Dominican order had been organized a few years earlier (c. A.D. 1216), and it emphasized teaching.[10] It was a reasonable choice, considering the serious scholar and theologian that Thomas would become. However the decision was viewed with alarm by Thomas' family. They had envisioned an ecclesiastical career for him, but had in mind one in which he could possess wealth and assert secular power.

The Dominicans were a mendicant order. Their "manner of life was very austere ... [entailing] midnight office, perpetual abstinence from meat, frequent disciplines, [and] prolonged fasts and silence."[11] More troubling was the fact the founder, St. Dominic, had determined "that the poverty practiced in the [Dominican] order should be not merely individual, as in the monastic orders, but corporate ... so that the order should have no possessions, except the monastic buildings and churches, no property, no fixed income, but should live on charity and begging."[12]

When Thomas' mother, Theodora, heard that he planned to become a Dominican, she was "excessively angry,"[13] and immediately departed for Naples to stop what promised to be a "death-blow to her cherished aspirations."[14]

Having some advance notice of Theodora's arrival, the Dominicans spirited Thomas off to Rome and secluded him in a Dominican monastery. Theodora "was extremely angry with the friars."[15] She followed them to Rome and demanded that they surrender her son. The Dominicans refused. Theodora responded by complaining to the Pope. She "denounced to the Pope the rapacity of the cruel friars, who, in spite of her position and all her promises, had robbed her of her boy."[16]

Evidently under political pressure to surrender Thomas, the Dominicans decided to move him again. But Theodora learned of their plans, and charged Thomas' brothers, Landulf and Reginald, with the task of capturing him. Landulf and Reginald were, at that time, "actively engaged ravaging Lombardy with a band of Frederick's [Emperor Frederick II, A.D. 1194–1250] soldiers."[17] They watched the passes through which the Dominicans might travel, and happened upon Thomas' party. "Thomas found himself, without a chance of escape, a prisoner in the hands of his brothers."[18]

Thomas was imprisoned by his own family. His mother attempted to dissuade him from joining the Dominican order. She "made use of every argument she could invent, and brought into play all the passions of her nature — her tears, her entreaties, her prayers, her fierce anger, her threats, her hatred, her love — but without effect ... Thomas was immovable."[19]

When Thomas' brothers returned from their military duties, "they found that, far from being changed himself, Thomas had converted both his sisters. They were furious."[20] The brothers conceived the device of turning Thomas from his religious calling by introducing him to the world of sensual pleasures, "a most infamous expedient."[21] The brothers hired a prostitute and "sent her secretly to his [Thomas'] cell, to tempt him to sin."[22]

The brother's plan failed. Thomas responded by chasing the woman with a burning brand he had snatched from the fireplace. The experience was followed by a prophetic dream. "No sooner had the girl been driven out, than he [Thomas] made a cross with the charred brand upon the wall, and, casting himself upon his knees before it, made a vow of chastity for life. Whilst thus praying, he fell into a calm, gentle sleep, and was ravished by a heavenly vision. He saw angels descending from the clouds, and they came and bound his loins with the girdle of continence, and armed him for life as a warrior of heaven."[23] The girdle of continence symbolized the agony of the celibate, and the intellectual strength gained by the sublimation of physical desires.

Thomas was confined by his family for approximately two years. He was finally released when the Dominicans pleaded with the Pope, and the Pope in turn appealed to Emperor Frederick II. Assisted by his sisters, Thomas escaped through a window and was escorted by the Dominicans to Naples.[24]

Thomas' mother, Theodora, remained adamant. She again appealed to the Pope. A compromise was finally proposed. Thomas would be allowed to remain a Dominican, while simultaneously being abbot of Monte Cassino, a Benedictine monastery. Thomas would thus be allowed to pursue his chosen avocation, while simultaneously having the secular and political power his family craved.

But Thomas "was inexorable."[25] He insisted on a life of poverty. Subsequently Thomas' family lost the power to contest the struggle. Thomas' brothers fell out of favor with Emperor Frederick II and were imprisoned. Shorn of power, Thomas' mother had no choice but to accept his entry into the Dominican order.[26]

Albertus Magnus (c. 1200–1280)

In A.D. 1245, Thomas went to Cologne, where he was a student of Albertus Magnus (c. A.D. 1200–1280) from 1248 to 1252.[27] Albert was the most significant writer on science and natural philosophy of the Middle Ages.[28] In his own time, he earned the appellation of "great," largely from the enormous quantity of his writings, the sum of which were "nothing short of miraculous."[29]

Albert's goal was to construct a "Latin paraphrase of all human knowledge,"[30] so that Aristotelean natural philosophy could be made "intelligible to the Latins."[31] Albert's books also reveal the influence of "Muslim and Jewish philosophy, various other sources, and even personal observation."[32] He wrote on zoology, mineralogy, mathematics, astronomy, chemistry, botany, and other subjects.

Albert was a devout theologian, but believed that God brought about natural events through natural causes. He had a "desire for concrete, specific, detailed, [and] accurate knowledge concerning everything in nature."[33] Although Albert's work was primarily based upon authority, he had some recognition for the value of observation and experiment. In discussing the proposition that a certain species of tree is able to "save doves from serpents," he concluded "this has not been sufficiently proved by certain experience."[34]

In other respects, Albert was clearly a man of the thirteenth century, and his work represented no clear break from Pliny's *Natural History* or Isidore's *Etymologies*, both compilations that in part exhibited naive credulity with little skeptical discretion or insight. Albert related that a diamond is dissolved by goat's blood, and that if an emerald ring is worn during sexual intercourse it will be cracked. Albert also claimed that he had observed a toad fracture a small emerald by gazing upon it.[35] And he believed the report of a serpent that had the head of a man.[36]

As Albert accepted Aristotelean cosmology, he believed in astrology. Being superior in creation, the heavens naturally exerted an influence on the lower terrestrial sphere. "All things which are made by nature or art are moved first by celestial virtues."[37] Albert believed that the annual flood of the Nile was either caused or influenced by the planets, especially Venus and the Moon. Comets signified "wars and the death of kings."[38] In *On Comets*, Albert concluded "the rule of Mars signifies wars and death."[39]

Albert's belief in astrology was not unusual for his age, or superstitious. Celestial influences were natural. They could not be observed directly, but then neither could the cause of gravity or magnetism. Albert believed that astrology could be reconciled with the Christian Church's doctrine of free will. The stars simply exerted a natural influence on men, one which they were free to resist or submit to, the same as any other natural factor.[40]

Reason and Revelation

At Cologne, Thomas "met his match in a teacher, whose breadth of knowledge and wide experience must have convinced him that there was something yet for him to learn."[41]

From Albert Magnus, Aquinas received an appreciation for Aristotelian philosophy, and the methods of philosophy in general. He obtained the conviction that "reason ... is the fountain of natural truth, whose chief channels are the various systems of heathen philosophy, and more especially the thoughts of Plato and the methods of Aristotle."[42]

Furthermore, philosophy, based on the exercise of human reason, is the natural complement to religion based on divine revelation. "While reason and revelation are two distinct sources of truths, the truths are not contradictory — they come from the one source of knowledge, God ... hence arises the compatibility of philosophy and theology which was the fundamental axiom of scholasticism."[43]

Albert's goals were that "Aristotle should be Christianized ... and that faith should be thrown into the form of a vast scientific organism, through the application of Christianized philosophy to the dogmata of revealed religion. Thus would the Church possess all the highest truths of Greek philosophy."[44] It was Thomas who would realize these objectives.

While Albert was superior in natural philosophy, Thomas was the better theologian. Thomas was also able to organize and write more clearly and systematically than Albert. When he first arrived in Cologne, Thomas' introverted nature was mistaken by his fellow students for stupidity. They regarded him as "a naturally dull, obtuse lad, who possessed no powers of appreciation ... Thomas was ridiculed publicly for his intellectual shortcomings, and was called, by master and pupils, the great, dumb, Sicilian ox."[45]

But eventually Albert recognized the genius of Thomas, and said "he will make such a roaring in theology that he will be heard through all the earth."[46] Thomas was eventually recognized as "one of the three master theological minds of the Western world," the other two being "Augustine and John Calvin."[47]

In 1252, Thomas went to the University of Paris where he lectured on the *Sentences* of Peter Lombard.[48] In 1256, Thomas received a master's degree in theology from Paris.[49] Between 1259 and 1268, Thomas was in Italy, where he served as a member of the papal court and taught in various Dominican houses. In 1269, Thomas returned to the University of Paris, where he remained until 1272.[50]

Summa Theologica

In Rome between the years 1265 and 1267, Thomas began work on his masterpiece *Summa Theologica*, the summation of all theological questions and knowledge.[51] The *Summa Theologica* is a seamless melding of Christian theology with Aristotelian philosophy. Thomas intended it "to be the sum of all known learning, arranged according to the best method, and subordinate to the dictates of the Church."[52]

The arrangement of the *Summa Theologica* followed the typical method of teaching at this time. A question was proposed, and the arguments on each side were listed exhaustively. The *Summa Theologica* contains 518 questions, divided into 2,652 articles. "Each article states the negative and positive sides of the proposition under discussion, the arguments for and against it, and then the author's solution."[53]

The first topic considered in *Summa Theologica* was not *The Existence of God* (it was the second), but *The Nature and Extent of Sacred Doctrine*. This subject is subdivided into ten specific questions in the form of articles. The first article or question is, "whether, besides philosophy, any further doctrine is required?"[54] After stating the arguments on each side of the question, Thomas concluded "It was necessary for the salvation of man that certain truths which exceed human reason should be made known to him by divine revelation."[55]

After establishing that revelation was necessary, Thomas next concluded that the Sacred Doctrine of the Church was a science. "Sacred doctrine is a science, because it proceeds from principles established by the light of a higher science, namely the science of God and the blessed."[56]

Thomas then came to the point. After establishing the necessity and existence of Sacred Doctrine, he accorded it a primacy that placed it above sciences based on observation and reason. "This science [Sacred Doctrine] transcends all others ... because other sciences derive their certitude from the natural light of human reason, which can err, while this derives its certitude from the light of the divine knowledge, which cannot be deceived ... this science treats chiefly of those things which by their sublimity transcend human reason, while other sciences consider only those things which are within reason's grasp."[57]

Conflicts between philosophy and religious doctrines were to be resolved simply. If a philosophical conclusion contradicted a doctrine based on revelation, it was to be condemned as false. "Whatsoever is found in other sciences contrary to any truth of this science [Sacred Doctrine], must be condemned as false."[58] Ironically, this was the same method followed by Siger of Brabant and the Paris Averroists. When their philosophical conclusions contradicted Church doctrines, they made the disclaimer that the philosophical "truth" must be false.[59]

In placing faith above reason, Thomas was following Anselm of Canterbury (A.D. 1033–1109), "the first scholastic philosopher and theologian."[60] Anselm concluded that "faith must precede knowledge."[61] In *Proslogium*, he explained, "I do not seek to understand that I may believe, but I believe in order to understand. For this also I believe, — that unless I believed, I should not understand."[62] "After the faith is held fast, the attempt must be made to demonstrate by reason the truth of what we believe. It is wrong not to do so."[63]

In Thomas' compromise, philosophy and reason were embraced, but subjugated to theology. On those questions where theology and philosophy disagreed, precedence was given to theology. Science and philosophy became handmaidens to theology.[64] This familiar formula of the Middle Ages originated with Augustine of Hippo (A.D. 354–430), the most influential of the Church Fathers.

Although many of the Church Fathers had been wholly hostile to Greek philosophy, Augustine had argued that it should be appropriated to the use of the Church when useful and not in conflict with doctrine.

> If those who are called philosophers, and especially the Platonists, have said aught that is true and in harmony with our faith, we are not only not to shrink from it, but to claim it for our own use from those who have unlawful possession of it ... [for] all branches of heathen learning have not only false and superstitious fancies ... but they contain also liberal instruction which is better adapted to the use of the truth, and some most excellent precepts of morality; and some truths in regard even to the worship of the One God ... these ... we must take and turn to a Christian use.[65]

The Church was able to thus absorb and utilize Aristotelean philosophy. But it was a compromise that carried the seeds of its own destruction. For having used reasoned argument to prove the superiority of revelation, Thomas had unwittingly acquiesced to the superiority of reason over theology. "The attempt to establish by argument the authority of faith is in reality the unconscious establishment of the authority of reason. Reason, if admitted at all, must ultimately claim the whole man."[66]

Scholasticism in Europe extended from the ninth through the beginning of the fifteenth century, but its apex was between the eleventh and fourteenth centuries.[67] Typical of Scholastic reasoning was Thomas' proof of the existence of God. Thomas argued that the existence of God can be proved in five ways. "The first ... way is the argument from motion. It is certain, and evident to our senses, that in this world some things are in motion. Now whatever is in motion is put in motion by another.... Therefore, whatever is moved must be moved by another. If that by which it is moved be itself moved, then this also must be moved by another, and that by another again. But this cannot go on to infinity.... Therefore it is necessary to arrive at a first mover which is moved by no other. And this everyone understands to be God."[68]

Thomas' first proof was straight from Aristotle. In *Metaphysics*, Aristotle had argued "there is something which moves without being moved, being eternal, substance, and actuality."[69] The argument is geometric in its logic, but rests upon unproven axioms: that perpetual motion cannot exist, or that a first motion cannot arise from a natural cause other than motion, or that the succession of motions cannot extend into infinity. One might as well try arguing that the number of integers is finite (it is not) because every number must be preceded by another.[70]

The Scholastics wanted an answer to every question. In an organic, unified, and teleological cosmos, everything had a purpose, and every question could be answered by logic and faith.

> Thomas' view, to be satisfying, had to be complete. It was knowledge united and amalgamated into a scheme of salvation. But a scheme of salvation is a chain, which can hold only in virtue of its completeness; break one link, and it snaps; leave one rivet loose, and it may also snap. A scheme of salvation must answer every problem put to it; a single unanswered problem may imperil it. The problem, for example, of God's foreknowledge and predestination — that were indeed an open link, which Thomas will by no means leave unwelded. Hence for us modern men also, whose views of the universe are so shamelessly partial, leaving so much unanswered and so much unknown, the philosophy of Thomas may be restful, and charm by its completeness.[71]

From serious theological questions, Thomas quickly advanced in the *Summa Theologica* to questions that epitomize the sterility of medieval scholasticism. From a modern perspective, reflexively conditioned to obtain knowledge from empiricism, the questions appear silly. But Thomas and his colleagues relied largely on authority.

The *Summa Theologica* contains an entire section devoted to questions concerning angels. Among the questions Thomas considered are these:

- Whether an Angel is Entirely Incorporeal?[72]
- Whether an Angel is Composed of Matter and Form?[73]
- Whether the Angels Exist in Any Great Number?[74]
- Whether the Angels Differ in Species?[75]
- Whether the Angels Are Incorruptible?[76]
- Whether Several Angels Can Be at the Same Time in the Same Place?[77]
- Whether the Movement of an Angel Is Instantaneous?[78]
- Whether There is Free Choice in the Angels?[79]
- Whether There is an Irascible and a Concupiscible Appetite in the Angels?[80]

The astute reader will note that Thomas' examination of the question how many angels can occupy the same space at the same time is essentially the same question as how many angels can dance on the head of a pin.

The most infamous question that Thomas tried to answer involved the resurrection of cannibals.[81] Medieval Christians in Europe believed in the physical resurrection of the human body. The question thus presented itself: suppose there was a cannibal who had lived his entire life by eating nothing but human flesh and this man had children. The bodies of the children would be composed entirely of the flesh of other people. "If one who partook of nothing but human flesh were to beget children, that which his child derives from him must be of the flesh of other men partaken of by his father."[82] So how could the child's body be resurrected if it was made up of other human bodies?

Scholastic Synthesis

Shortly before his death at the young age of forty-eight, Thomas had an ecstatic experience. "A marvelous rapture ... seized him, and shook his whole frame, whilst celebrating mass."[83] Thomas lost interest in writing, and "became wholly lost in contemplation."[84] He explained to his friends, "I cannot write any more ... everything that I have written appears to me as simply rubbish."[85]

In 1274, Pope Gregory X convened the Second Council of Lyons, with the objective of resolving differences between the "Latin and Greek Churches."[86] Thomas set out for Lyons in January of 1274, but fell ill before his journey could be completed. "He was carried to the Cistercian monastery of Fossa Nuova, in the diocese of Terracina."[87]

As he lay ill on his death bed, the monks asked Thomas to "expound to them"[88] on the *Song of Solomon*. It seemed an unusual request for Thomas, the author of dry, reasoned, and pedantic arguments. The *Song of Solomon* is by far the most lyrical and sensual book in the *Bible*.

> I am my beloved's, and his desire is toward me.
> Come, my beloved, let us go forth into the field; let us lodge in the villages.
> Let us get up early to the vineyards; let us see if the vine flourish, whether
>   the tender grape appear, and the pomegranates bud forth: there will I
>   give thee my loves.
> The mandrakes give a smell, and at our gates are all manner of pleasant fruits,
>   new and old, which I have laid up for thee, O my beloved.[89]

After lying ill with a fever for seven weeks, Thomas died on March 7, 1274.

Under Thomas, "the Scholastic doctrines were organized into a complete and final system."[90] He remains "the greatest and most authoritative of the orthodox medieval theologians."[91] But the Church did not immediately accept Thomas' wedding of theology and philosophy. The condemnation of 1277 included some of Thomas' teachings.

The condemnation of 1277 proved to be a short-lived reaction. Thomas Aquinas was canonized in 1323, and in 1325 the condemnation of 1277 was annulled. Part of the reason given for annulling the declaration of 1277 was that some of the condemned articles "touch the teaching of blessed Thomas."[92]

Thomas' influence grew over the centuries. He was made a doctor of the Catholic Church in 1567, and in 1879, Pope Leo XIII made the teachings of Thomas the official theology of the Roman Catholic Church.[93]

Thomas' Scholastic synthesis allowed the Christian Church to maintain jurisdiction over the entire corpus of human knowledge.

[The Church] assimilated the new learning — the revived Aristotelianism — and continued its control of the universities. In the 13th century it was supreme, and Christianity was identified with world systems of knowledge and politics. Both were deemed alike divine in origin, and to question their validity was an offence against God. Christianity thus had passed through three stages in politics as in science. At first it was persecuted by the state, then established by it, and finally dominated over it; so its teaching was at first alien to philosophy and despised by it, next was accepted by it and given form and rights through it, and finally became queen of the sciences as theology and ruled over the whole world of human knowledge.[94]

CHAPTER 6

Roger Bacon (c. 1214–1294)

Magician and Scientist

Roger Bacon was one of the first to understand and appreciate the indispensable role of empiricism in the sciences. He not only anticipated the future, but understood the deficits of his own age. Bacon's appreciation for experiment led nineteenth-century writers to eulogize him as "the first prophet of modern science."[1] "Roger Bacon's works are not only so far beyond his age in the knowledge which they contain, but so different from the temper of the times, in his assertion of the supremacy of experiment, and in his contemplation of the future progress of knowledge, that it is difficult to conceive how such a character could then exist."[2]

After his death, Bacon's abilities were so respected that he came to be regarded as a necromancer who possessed mysterious powers by which he worked miracles and outwitted the Devil. "He was by far the most learned man of his age; and his acquirements were so much above the comprehension of his contemporaries, that they could only account for them by supposing that he was indebted for them to the devil."[3]

By the end of the sixteenth century in England, Roger Bacon had been transformed into a mythical figure, the subject of a play and a book titled *The Famous Historie of Fryer Bacon, Containing the Wonderful Things That He Did in His Life: Also the Manner of His Death ... Very Pleasant and Delightfull to Be Read*. In the *Famous Historie*, Bacon was quoted as claiming that he had penetrated the mysteries of nature. "I have unlocked the secret of art and nature, and let the world see those things, that have layen hid since the death of Hermes [Mercury]."[4]

> Bacon, we hear, that long we have suspect,
> That thou art read in Magicks mysterie;
> In Piromancie to divine by flames;
> To tell by Hadromaticke, ebbs and tides;
> By Aeromancie to discover doubts,
> To plaine out questions, as Apollo did.
> I tell thee, Bacon, Oxford makes report,
> Nay, England and the court of Henrie saies,
> Thart making of a brazen head by art,
> Which shall unfold strange doubts and Aphorismes,
> And read a lecture on Philosophie;
> And, by the help of divels and ghastly fiends,
> Thou meanst, ere many yeares or daies be past,
> To compasse England with a wall of brasse.[5]

Emergence of Empiricism in the Thirteenth Century

Bacon's appreciation of empiricism was not unique, but part of an important trend that is found among other thirteenth-century writers. Although empiricism may have been foreign to theologians and philosophers, "there was much practical experimenting in Bacon's time among artisans and alchemists."[6] Many writers of the time recognized "the experimental method ... as ... a well-established method."[7]

The empiricism of thirteenth-century Europe was derivative of Greek science, but not a regurgitation. Experimentation was not unknown to the Greeks, but Europeans of the thirteenth century relied "more frequently on experience than the ancients did."[8] Pliny the Elder's (A.D. 23–79) *Natural History* was a comprehensive, albeit uncritical, synthesis of scientific knowledge in the first century A.D. But Pliny never mentioned an experimental method.[9] In contrast, Europeans of the thirteenth century had "'experiments' and 'experimenters' and entire books called experimental."[10] And scholars such as Roger Bacon "seem conscious that science is finding a new method in their day."[11]

Thirteenth-century empiricism developed gradually through a historical process that can be traced at least back to Aristotle (384–322 B.C.). Aristotle's primary epistemological method was reason, but in *Metaphysics* he noted that science depended on experience. "Science and art come to men through experience ... and men of experience succeed even better than those who have theory without experience."[12] The role of empiricism was also mentioned in *Posterior Analytics*. "From experience ... originate[s] the skill of the craftsman and the knowledge of the man of science."[13]

Aristotle's books on natural philosophy also mentioned empirical methods. In *De Caelo* (*On the Heavens*), Aristotle claimed that "the principles of sensible things are sensible," and therefore "practical knowledge culminates in the work produced, natural philosophy in the facts as presented consistently and indubitably to sense-perception."[14] By noting that observations must be "consistent and indubitable," Aristotle recognized the danger of anecdotal data, and adumbrated the modern method of systematic and controlled experimentation.

Aristotle himself performed experiments. In *Meteorologica* (*Meteorology*), Aristotle observed that he knew "by experiment"[15] that seawater became fresh after undergoing evaporation and distillation. In *De Generatione Animalium* (*On the Generation of Animals*), Aristotle established that observational facts must take precedence over theory. "Credit must be given rather to observation than to theories, and to theories only if what they affirm agrees with the observed facts."[16]

Unlike metaphysics, observation of the natural world through the senses entailed no theological difficulties. The door had been opened by Paul the Apostle (c. A.D. 0–60) in *Romans*, where he wrote that God could be known through the study of nature. "For the invisible things of him from the creation of the world are clearly seen, being understood by the things that are made, even his eternal power and Godhead; so that they are without excuse."[17]

The physician Galen (c. A.D. 129–200) was likely a significant influence toward the recognition of empiricism.[18] His works were widely read in medieval Europe, and he "exerted a great influence ... medieval writers cite him [Galen] as an authority for the recognition of experience and reason as criteria of truth."[19] It was difficult to conduct systematic observations or experiments in medicine, for ethical reasons and the impossibility of controlling circumstances between individual patients. But Galen understood and advocated the experimental method.[20] He wrote that "in believing what has been well found there are two criteria for all men, reason and experience."[21]

Some of the Islamic writers endorsed empiricism. The physician al–Razi (c. A.D. 854–925), known in Medieval Europe as Rhazes, concluded that no report was reliable until it was "put to the test of experience."[22] In a remarkable sentence that adumbrated Francis Bacon (A.D. 1561–1626), al–Biruni (c. A.D. 973–1050) described "inductions based upon the observations of our senses"[23] as an epistemological method different from that employed in philosophy, and one that unfortunately could not be employed in historical studies. But not all of the Islamic philosophers endorsed empiricism. No one was more widely read or influential in Europe than ibn Rushd (Averroes, A.D. 1126–1198). And ibn Rushd claimed that deductive proofs, or *demonstrations*, were invariably superior to the evidence of the senses. Any observation that apparently contradicted a logical proof had to be flawed.[24]

To the extent that Adelard of Bath's (c. 1080–1152) writing may be taken as representative of twelfth-century attitudes, an appreciation for empiricism in Europe was largely lacking before the thirteenth century. Adelard emphasized that there is "nothing more deceptive than the senses!"[25] He went so far as to state that "the senses ... [were] worthy of hatred and a curse."[26]

A significant factor in the development of empiricism in thirteenth-century Europe may have been the 1277 condemnation of 219 heretical articles being taught at the University of Paris. The Paris condemnation made it dangerous to engage in metaphysical speculation and reasoning. Empiricism became the logical alternative for philosophers to pursue. "From the moment this line of attack was adopted and the metaphysical competence of philosophy challenged through a criticism of knowledge, it was inevitable that the outcome would be a philosophical empiricism."[27]

Among the thirteenth-century champions of empiricism was the Emperor Frederick II (A.D. 1194–1250). Frederick had "a love of luxury and beauty, an intellect refined, subtle, [and] philosophical."[28] He was "a sensualist, yet also a warrior and a politician; a profound lawgiver and an impassioned poet."[29] In an age obsessed with the problem of universals, Frederick had an "intense curiosity about the particulars of nature."[30] "Profoundly rationalistic, he [Frederick] applied the test of reason and experience to affairs of state as well as to matters of science."[31]

Frederick maintained a scholarly court in Sicily, where Michael Scot (fl. A.D. 1217–1235) was employed as astrologer and scientific consultant. Relentless in his pursuit of knowledge, Frederick posed a series of questions for Michael Scot. "Explain to us the foundations of the earth, that is, to say how it is established over the abyss and how the abyss stands beneath the earth, and whether there is anything else than air and water which supports the earth."[32]

Frederick also was in the habit of interrogating Islamic philosophers on profound subjects such as "the eternity of matter and the immortality of the soul."[33] Typical of his questions was one that demanded proof for Aristotle's doctrine of eternity. "Aristotle the sage in all his writings declares clearly the existence of the world from all eternity. If he demonstrates this, what are his arguments, and if not, what is the nature of his reasoning on this matter?"[34]

Frederick was deeply interested in both animals and hunting, especially falconry. He wrote a treatise on falconry that contains detailed "personal observations of the habits of birds,"[35] and conducted experiments to test various propositions. "On hearing that ostrich eggs were hatched by the sun in Egypt, he [Frederick] had eggs and experts brought to Apulia that he might test the matter for himself. The fable that barnacle geese were hatched from barnacles he exploded by sending north for such barnacles, concluding that the story arose from ignorance of the actual nesting-places of the geese.... Nests, eggs, and birds were repeatedly brought to him for observation and note, and the minute accuracy of his descriptions attests the fidelity with which his observations were made."[36]

Frederick respected Aristotle, but was not afraid to deviate from the Philosopher's teachings or criticize Aristotelian philosophy in instances where it contradicted his own experience. Frederick wrote that he "followed the prince of philosophers where required, but not in all things, for we have learned by experience that at several points he deviates from the truth."[37] Frederick noted that especially in the sport of falconry, his own experience exceeded Aristotle, because the Philosopher "rarely or never had experience of falconry."[38]

Exemplary of Frederick's scientific and empirical outlook are apocryphal stories concerning morbid experiments he conducted. Frederick reportedly "shut up [a man] in a wine cask to prove that the soul died with the body."[39] More gruesome is the tale that he had two men "disemboweled in order to show the respective effects of sleep and exercise on digestion."[40] And it is said that Frederick "caused [children] to be brought up in silence in order to settle the question 'whether they would speak Hebrew, which was the first language, or Greek or Latin or Arabic or at least the language of their parents; but he [Frederick] labored in vain, for the children all died.'"[41]

Albertus Magnus (c. A.D. 1200–1280), who was certainly one of the most prolific thirteenth-century writers on scientific subjects, "both recognizes experience as a criterion of truth, and frequently states the results of his personal observations."[42] Albert wrote that "every hypothesis which is confirmed by the senses is better than that which contradicts sense."[43] This is quite a contrast with Adelard of Bath's twelfth-century disparagement of empiricism. Adelard claimed that "the senses ... forcibly drive the mind away from the investigation of the truth."[44]

The influence of Aristotle on the development of empiricism in clearly revealed in *Summa Theologia*, where Albert's student, Thomas Aquinas (1225–1274), noted "the Philosopher [Aristotle] says that the beginning of our knowledge is from the senses."[45]

Amongst other thirteenth-century writers, Arnald of Villanova (c. 1240–1311) was a physician who tried to "develop a coherent, systematic science of medicine."[46] Arnald argued that "the properties of things cannot be discovered by reason but only by experiment or revelation."[47]

Oxford and Robert Grosseteste

Roger Bacon was born c. A.D. 1214 or 1220.[48] In 1267, Bacon wrote that "I have labored much at sciences and languages, and it is now forty years since I first learnt the alphabet: I have always been studious, and except for two of those forty years I have always been in studio."[49] Some scholars have interpreted this phrase to imply that Bacon was born c. 1214, while others have estimated his birthdate as c. 1220.

Bacon's family was apparently wealthy, but later fell on hard times and became impoverished.[50] Few of the significant dates in Bacon's life are known with any certainty because he left no autobiography. Our knowledge of the important events in Bacon's life must be patched together and inferred piecemeal from his writings.

Bacon attended Oxford University, perhaps starting at an age as young as 13 or 14 years of age. At Oxford more attention was given to the sciences than at Paris.[51] Bacon was instructed in the *Quadrivium* of arithmetic, geometry, music, and astronomy. Among the writers that impressed him were the Romans, Seneca and Cicero.[52]

At Oxford, it is likely that Bacon's interests in mathematics, languages, and experimental science — especially optics — were aroused by Robert Grosseteste (c. A.D. 1168–1253). "Grosseteste fills so important a position in Bacon's early life that it is impossible to pass him by."[53]

Robert Grosseteste, Bishop of Lincoln, was "the first lecturer to the Franciscans at Oxford."[54] Grosseteste was also an empiricist who used observation to falsify or verify theories.[55] Grosseteste "wrote various mathematical treatises," and "did more than any one else to give a strong impulse to the study of astronomy and of mathematics in the thirteenth century."[56]

Grosseteste "appears to have been the first to set out a systematic and coherent theory of experimental investigation and rational explanation by which the Greek geometrical method was turned into modern experimental science."[57] He based his method upon, or was strongly influenced by, Aristotle's *Posterior Analytics*. Grosseteste acknowledged that Aristotle "shows us how from sensibles are acquired memories and from memories empirical knowledge and from empirical knowledge a universal which is a principle of science, and with this discovery of principles begins the work of demonstration."[58]

Grosseteste utilized falsification for discriminating between alternative theories. He thus implicitly recognized the necessity of adopting multiple working hypotheses. Grosseteste's falsification was developed from the logical tool of *reductio ad impossibile* or *reductio ad absurdum*, a method by which a premise is demonstrated to be false because it irresistibly leads to a result universally acknowledged to be impossible or absurd.[59]

In *Analytica Priora* (*Prior Analytics*), Aristotle had recognized that it was possible to prove certain syllogisms by "reducing them *ad impossibile*."[60] *Reductio ad absurdum* was also a common method in Euclid's *Elements*.[61] At the University of Oxford, in the thirteenth century, Greek logic was evolving into the methodology of modern experimental science.

Again following Aristotle,[62] Grosseteste recognized the uniformity of nature. "Things of the same nature are productive of the same operations according to their nature."[63] Writing before William of Ockham (c. A.D. 1280–1349) was born, Grosseteste endorsed the principle of parsimony, explaining "that is better and more valuable which requires fewer, other circumstances being equal."[64] Parsimony, or the principle of economy in the formulation of hypotheses, had also been recognized by Aristotle and others.[65] The Ptolemaic System was notorious for its complexity, but even Claudius Ptolemy endorsed simplicity by noting that hypotheses that were simpler were "more reasonable."[66]

Roger Bacon was a critical person, not given to praising people simply because of their eminence. Bacon declared that Aquinas' *Summa Theologia* was "full of errors, and displayed ignorance of physics, of metaphysics, and even of logic."[67] But Bacon acknowledged his debt to Grosseteste. When speaking of Grosseteste, "the language used [by Bacon is] that of a grateful pupil speaking of a revered master."[68] Bacon "thoroughly grasped," and "elaborately developed Grosseteste's attitude to nature and theory of science."[69]

Bacon said "one man alone had really known the sciences, namely, Robert, Bishop of Lincoln ... the Lord Robert alone, on account of his long life and the wonderful methods which he employed, excelled all men in his knowledge of the sciences."[70] It was Grosseteste who made Bacon aware that "the power of mathematics is capable of unfolding the causes of all things, and of giving a sufficient explanation of human and divine phenomena."[71]

Bacon testified that Grosseteste conducted his own experiments, and was no slave to Aristotelean philosophy. "The lord Robert neglected altogether the books of Aristotle and their methods, and by his own experiments, and with the aid of other authors, and by means of other sciences, employed himself in the scientific questions which Aristotle had treated."[72]

Paris, Magnets, and Occult Forces

Bacon received a Master of Arts degree from either Oxford or Paris before 1239.[73] It is likely that he began higher studies in theology at Oxford.[74] By 1240, Bacon was in Paris, "the most international of cities."[75] Bacon earned a doctorate in theology from the University of Paris around or before 1247.[76] He "acquired fame by his lectures at Oxford and Paris ... [and] wrote many elementary treatises for students."[77]

In Paris, Bacon was influenced by Peter Peregrinus, or Peter of Maricourt (fl. c. 1269). Peter was the author of *Epistola de magnete* (*Letter on the Magnet*, A.D. 1269), a book describing the properties of magnets.[78] Peter was also an advocate of the experimental method. His book on the magnet showed that experimental science was flourishing outside Oxford, although perhaps not at the University of Paris.

The magnet, or lodestone, had been known since at least the time of the ancient Greeks. It was mentioned by the Epicurean Roman poet, Titus Lucretius Carus (c. 99–55 B.C.), in *De Rerum Natura* (*On the Nature of Things*). "The stone which the Greeks call a *magnet*, from the country that produces it ... has the virtue to attract iron."[79] In *Natural History*, Pliny described magnets as possessing "an influence at once mysterious and unseen."[80] "The moment the metal [iron] comes near it [the magnet], it springs towards the magnet, and, as it clasps it, is held fast in the magnet's embraces."[81]

But while the ancient Greeks and Romans were aware of, and described the magnet's properties, Europeans of the thirteenth century were conducting systematic experiments with magnets and seeking ways to apply its properties advantageously in technological applications.

The first ten chapters of Peter's *Letter on the Magnet* were devoted to discussing the "general properties of the lodestone."[82] Peter described "how to discover the poles of a lodestone and how to tell which is north and which south."[83] He discovered the law that opposite magnetic poles attract, while the same poles in different magnets repel each other.[84] Peter noted that it was "really true" that opposite magnet poles would attract each other more strongly than a single pole would attract a piece of iron, and that this was "shown by experiment."[85]

Peter described a crude magnetic compass. "When an elongated piece of iron has touched a lodestone and is then fastened to a light block of wood or to a straw and made [to] float on water, one end will turn to the star which has been called the sailor's star because it is near the pole; the truth is, however, that it does not point to the star but to the pole itself."[86]

After "having fully examined all the properties of the lodestone and the phenomena connected therewith,"[87] in the first ten chapters of *Letter on the Magnet*, Peter devoted the last three chapters to technological applications. He described the construction of two types of magnetic compasses, and then presented a short plan for making a perpetual motion machine powered by magnets. The construction of a perpetual motion machine was an object of fascination in thirteenth-century Europe. This is shown by Peter's comment, "I have seen many persons vainly busy themselves and even becoming exhausted with much labor in their endeavors to invent such a wheel."[88]

Although the preoccupation with perpetual motion may seem chimerical from a modern perspective, it was likely a motivation for the development of mechanical devices and the harnessing of natural power to industrial applications in thirteenth-century Europe. By the thirteenth century, Europeans were utilizing water power for crushing ores, forging iron, operating saws, powering grindstones, manufacturing paper, and processing wool in fulling mills.[89] In places where water power was not available, Europeans turned to the wind. In the later part of the twelfth century, windmills originated in Europe, and they became commonplace during the thirteenth.[90]

Neither was perpetual motion obviously impossible. The world itself seemed to operate on an endless and perpetual flow of energy from the Sun, and through the endless natural movements of water and wind. The concept of a perpetual motion machine apparently originated in India during the twelfth century and diffused to Europe. Hindus viewed the universe as both eternal and cyclic. If the cosmos itself were a perpetual motion machine, there was no logical impediment to constructing an analogous microcosm.[91]

Roger Bacon described Peter of Maricourt as a "perfect mathematician," and apparently regarded Peter as "an idealistic and indefatigable scientist."[92] According to Bacon, Peter also experimented with the construction of burning mirrors.[93] "For the last three years he [Peter] has been working at the production of a mirror that shall produce combustion at a fixed distance."[94] Bacon was enthralled with Peter's adoption of the experimental method:

> One man I know, and one only, who can be praised for his achievements in this science [experimental research]. Of discourses and battles of words he takes no heed: he follows the works of wisdom, and in these finds rest. What others strive to see dimly and blindly, like bats in twilight, he gazes at in the full light of day, because he is a master of experiment. Through experiment he gains knowledge of natural things, medical, chemical, indeed of everything in the heavens or earth. He is ashamed that any things should be known to laymen, old women, soldiers, [or] ploughmen, of which he is ignorant. Therefore he has looked closely into the doings of those who work in metals and minerals of all kinds; he knows everything relating to the art of war, the making of weapons, and the chase; he has looked closely into agriculture, mensuration, and farming work; he has even taken note of the remedies, lot-casting, and charms used by old women and wizards and magicians, and of the deceptions and devices of conjurers, so that nothing which deserves inquiry should escape him, and that he may be able to expose the falsehoods of magicians. If philosophy is to be carried to its perfection and is to be handled with utility and certainty, his aid is indispensable.[95]

The existence of magnetism itself must have been a powerful spur to experimentation and empiricism. The magnet produced action at a distance by means of some unseen, or occult force. Magnetism was a phenomenon that could not possibly have been anticipated through the pure exercise of human reason. It could only be experienced, not predicted or understood through metaphysical or logical reasoning.

Contemplating the inexplicable but indisputable existence of magnetism, Bacon and his colleagues must have been forced to conclude that the only way to investigate the hidden forces of nature was by the experimental method. Bacon explained, "if the experiment on iron were not known, it would be viewed as a great miracle. And surely in respect to the action of the magnet on iron there are phenomena unknown to those who use the magnet which show in a wonderful way the dissolutions of nature."[96] In Bacon's view, "there are innumerable things that have strange virtues, whose potencies we are ignorant of solely from our neglect of experiment."[97] Bacon may have been influenced by Galen, who believed that herbal drugs obtained their efficacy from occult virtues.[98]

The experimental science of Peter Peregrinus and Roger Bacon was a complete break from Scholasticism. At the University of Paris, professors taught that truth was to found from the authorities of Holy Scripture and Aristotle, augmented and interpreted by reason. Imagine the absurdity, a man who claimed that more could be learned by talking to old women and ploughmen than studying Aristotle. Surely, this was a joke. But to Bacon, it was no laughing matter. Dissatisfied with the methods of his day, "Bacon was thirsting for reality in a barren land infested with metaphysical mirage."[99]

> [Bacon] was not slow to perceive that the men who taught this philosophy [Scholasticism] were, for the most part, wholly destitute of positive knowledge. They knew no language but Latin. Beyond the shreds of arithmetic, mensuration, and astronomy taught in the manuals of the Quadrivium, they were ignorant of mathematics. Of the possibility of applying mathematical knowledge to the facts of nature they had formed no conception whatever. Their philosophy was a tangle of barren controversies reducible, for the most part, to verbal disputes. It bore no relation to the facts of real life.[100]

Enamored with experimental science, around 1247 Roger Bacon returned to Oxford and began a frenzy of study.[101] He bought instruments, performed experiments, and questioned everyone he could find. Neither did Bacon abandon the fields of theology and philosophy. He concluded that Aristotle could only be appreciated in the original Greek, and that the Scriptures were best studied in the original Hebrew. Accordingly, he learned Greek and hired Jews to teach him how to read Hebrew.

At the same time, Bacon sought ceaselessly to transmit his methods to the young. Twenty years later, he described his intellectual fervor. "I sought the friendship of all wise men among the Latins; and I caused young men to be trained in languages, in geometrical figures, in numbers, in the construction of tables, in the use of instruments, and in many other necessary things.... During this time I spent more than two thousand pounds* in those things and in the purchase of books and instruments."[102]

Sometime between 1245 and 1257, Bacon became a Franciscan monk, placing himself under the control of conservative elements in the Christian Church.[103] In 1256, Saint Bonaventure (A.D. 1221–1274) became the General of the Franciscans. Bonaventure was skeptical of philosophy and had little regard for reason in theology. "Reason can discover some of the moral truths which form the groundwork of the Christian system, but others it can only receive and apprehend through divine illumination. In order to obtain this illumination the soul must employ the proper means, which are prayer, the exercise of the virtues, whereby it is rendered fit to accept the divine light, and meditation which may rise even to ecstatic union with God."[104] Although he died in 1274, it was Bonaventure who initiated and was largely responsible for the condemnation of Averroism at the University of Paris in 1277.[105]

In A.D. 1257, Bonaventura ordered that Roger Bacon should leave Oxford and come to Paris where he could be closely supervised.[106] At Paris, Bacon was forbidden from writing anything for publication. No manuscript could be distributed to anyone outside the Fran-

---

*According to J. H. Bridges (*The Life & Work of Roger Bacon*, 1914, p. 17) these were likely French pounds, equivalent to 600–700 English pounds Sterling. It is difficult to equate to modern currencies, but certainly a small fortune.

ciscan order. But Bacon's precise status between 1257 and 1266 is unclear. Some historians have claimed that he was not "imprisoned or banished at this time,"[107] but withdrew from activate participation in scholarly work due to poor health.

The Franciscan crackdown may have been motivated by Bacon's "audacity in speculation, by [his] experiments looked upon as magical, or by [Bacon's] frank exposure of the ignorance of professorial magnates."[108] A proximate cause may have been Roger Bacon's endorsement of astrology. Astrology was considered by some theologians to be heretical, because they thought it contradicted the Christian doctrine of free will. Among the articles condemned at Paris in 1277 was the proposition that human "will is subject to the power of the celestial bodies."[109]

Bonaventure was of the opinion that any intellectual pursuit that was not immediately relevant to theology was potentially dangerous. He condemned astrology as "repugnant to both faith and reason."[110] But Bacon was enthusiastic in his endorsement of the science. He believed that events on Earth were either controlled or strongly influenced by the movements and positions of the planets and stars.[111] "In all things that are brought forth on earth, whether for good or evil, the sun and the heavens are the moving cause."[112]

Bacon argued that the historical record revealed the influence of the stars. "One can examine history at past periods, and study the effects of the heavens from the beginning of the world, as in the case of floods, earthquakes, pestilences, famines, comets, prodigies, and other things without number ... and he will find that there are constellations corresponding in an appropriate way to the effects in each case."[113]

Bacon's view on the matter was hardly superstitious. He cited the obvious influence of the sun on the seasons and the moon on the tides of the sea. "All things produced on the earth grow more about the summer solstice, when the sun is at its apsis [the point at which a celestial body is either closest to, or farthest from, the Earth], and gain more vigor in one day than at other times in a week. And when the moon is at the apsides of her circles, as at new moon and at full moon, her actions are more vigorous, as is obvious in the tides of the sea."[114]

But from these observations, Bacon seamlessly passed on to unsupportable inferences regarding the other planets. "Jupiter and Venus are benevolent and fortunate planets, Saturn and Mars malevolent and unfortunate ones. Mercury ... is in a middle position, because he is good with the good, and evil with the evil, since he is of a changeable nature. Of the benevolent and fortunate planets ... Jupiter is the better and that greater good fortune is owed to him, and less to Venus."[115]

Bacon's belief in astrology was almost universal in his time. "When the earth was regarded as the center of a spherical and limited universe, it was impossible not to believe that the motions of the heavenly were followed by corresponding changes in terrestrial bodies."[116] Any objections were theological, not scientific. "The influence of the stars over human life was a belief almost universally held by all instructed men from the thirteenth to the sixteenth century."[117] Bacon's views on magic and astrology were "not novelties," and were shared by Albertus Magnus.[118]

In advocating astrology, Bacon had to confront the Church's condemnation of the practice. Astrology was considered heretical largely because astrological determinism was seen as being contradictory to the doctrine of free will. Bacon dealt with this by insisting that the celestial bodies only exerted influences, they did not absolutely predetermine all events on Earth. "What is true is that the influences of the stars implant certain tendencies to good or evil action, always at the same time leaving free scope to human will ... that climate [for example] affects character is obvious to everyone."[119] Bacon's view was shared by Thomas Aquinas, who wrote that the human will "can evidently be influenced by heavenly bodies ... but there is no direct action of heavenly bodies upon the will."[120]

As all men are, Bacon was instilled with most of the prejudices and beliefs of his age. He was not a modern scientist, but a man of the thirteenth century. Because Bacon believed that nature was full of occult forces and hidden mysteries, he tended to be unduly credulous. "The man without experience must not seek a reason in order that he may first understand, for he will never have this reason except after experiment."[121]

Bacon argued that a person unacquainted with the phenomenon of magnetism would never believe in its existence unless told of it by others who had experience. He concluded that we "must believe those who have made the experiment."[122] By this reasoning, Bacon was led to accept apocryphal stories of the elongation of human life. He believed that there were men "who prolonged their life for centuries," including "Artephius, who ... lived a thousand and twenty-five years."[123]

Roger Bacon's naive credulity even led him to outright silliness, reminiscent of Pliny's *Natural History* and Isidore's *Etymologies*. He claimed that there lived men who saddled and rode dragons. "It is certain that wise men of Aethiopia have come to Italy, Spain, France, England, and those lands of the Christians in which there are good flying dragons, and by the secret art they possess lure the dragons from their caverns. They have saddles and bridles in readiness, and they ride on these dragons and drive them in the air at high speed."[124]

Opus Majus

In 1257, Bacon was confined by the Franciscans at Paris. He may have been free to write, but was not allowed to circulate his manuscripts to anyone outside the Franciscan order. This restriction "nearly drove him to despair."[125]

Bacon's luck changed when Pope Clement IV (c. A.D. 1195–1268) assumed the papacy in 1265. A few years earlier, when the new Pope had been a Cardinal, Bacon had approached him through an intermediary with the suggestion of reforming the Church's educational institutions. Bacon wanted to introduce the study of languages and experimental science, reforms that were hundreds of years ahead of the time.[126]

Unfortunately, Bacon's message to the new Pope had been garbled. The Pope was given to believe that Bacon had written a treatise that he wished him to read. However Bacon had written nothing. In 1266, Bacon received a confidential letter from the new Pope, "bidding him send a fair copy of the works ... previously mentioned, secretly and without delay, notwithstanding any constitution of the Franciscan Order to the contrary."[127] It is possible that the Pope had asked Bacon for confidentiality because he knew that Bacon's views on subjects such as astrology were controversial. Was the condemnation of Bacon's views justified? The Pope may have wanted to read them and judge for himself before linking his name with Bacon.[128]

It was simultaneously the worst and best of opportunities. Bacon wrote, "I feel myself elevated above my ordinary strength; I conceive a new fervor of spirit. I ought to be more than grateful since your Beatitude [the Pope] has asked me for that which I have most ardently desired to communicate, which I have worked at with immense toil and brought into light after manifold expenses."[129]

But Bacon faced immense difficulties. Not only did the work requested by the Pope not exist, it had to be constructed without Bacon's immediate supervisors finding out what he was doing. Bacon complained of "weak health, want of money, lack of assistants, the obstacles thrown in his way by his superiors, [and] the impossibility of finding competent and trustworthy copyists."[130]

The lack of money was a special problem. Bacon needed to purchase ink, paper, and pens. He had to hire copyists. Bacon wrote to his brother in England requesting funds, but the civil war there had gone against his family and they were penniless. There was no money to send, and no reply to Bacon's request. The secretive nature of the project added to Bacon's difficulties. He tried to find a wealthy patron to fund the work, but when they asked him what the money was for, he couldn't answer.

Somehow, Bacon succeeded in obtaining the funds needed for the drafting of a manuscript. In eighteen months, Bacon produced his most significant work, the *Opus Majus*. As afterthoughts, or perhaps revisions and supplements, the *Opus Majus* was succeeded by the *Opus Minus* and the *Opus Tertium*, both significantly shorter than the *Opus Majus*.

There is much in the *Opus Majus* that is typical of Bacon's time. For example, Bacon has the chief view of his age, that theology is the queen of the sciences, and that all other branches of knowledge must be subordinated to her. "There is one wisdom that is perfect and ... this is contained in the Scriptures. From the roots of this wisdom all truth has sprung. I say, therefore, that one science is the mistress of the others, namely, theology."[131] Of course, because the *Opus Majus* was addressed to the Pope, Bacon could hardly have entertained any other view.

The *Opus Majus* also contains much material that is visionary. The work itself is divided into seven sections:

- Causes of Error
- Philosophy
- Study of Tongues
- Mathematics
- Optical Science
- Experimental Science
- Moral Philosophy

The beginning is breathtaking. Bacon listed four causes of error, or false knowledge.[132]

- faulty and unworthy authority
- custom
- popular opinion
- the conceit of knowledge

Authority as a fountain of ignorance had to be qualified so as not to question the authority of the Church. Of the four causes of the error, the worst by far was the conceit of knowledge. It was, in fact, the source of the other three. "This is an extraordinary wild beast, devouring and destroying all reason, namely, the desire to appear wise, by which every man is influenced. For however little and worthless our knowledge we nevertheless extol it."[133]

Bacon showed that he understood a key precept of science, the provisional nature of all knowledge. "Since the truths relating to God and his creatures are infinite, and in each there are innumerable gradations, of necessity few facts are known by any one, and for this reason no one should boast of the many things he knows.... It is impossible ... for man to attain perfect knowledge in this life, and it is exceedingly difficult for him to attain imperfect truth and he is very prone and disposed toward whatever is false and empty."[134]

In 1623, Galileo would open the door to the future by insisting that mathematics was essential to natural philosophy. "Philosophy is written ... in the mathematical language, and the symbols are triangles, circles, and other geometrical figures."[135]

But 355 years earlier, Bacon had said much the same thing. In the section of the *Opus Majus* titled *Mathematics*, Bacon stated that mathematics was indispensable to science. "The gate and key [to the sciences] is mathematics."[136] "He who knows not mathematics cannot know any other sciences; what is more, cannot discover his own ignorance or find its proper remedies."[137]

In this age, the accepted means of discerning truth in philosophy was by the use of logic through rhetoric and dialectic. This would remain the standard practice in European universities for another three hundred years. But Bacon said, "the sciences cannot be known by logical and sophistical arguments, as is ordinarily the case, but by mathematical demonstrations ... without mathematics they [the sciences] cannot be understood or set forth, taught, or learned."[138]

Bacon also employed mathematics in his own scientific work in optics. His "treatises [on perspective] contain an abundance of serious geometrical arguments, supported by a multitude of geometrical diagrams."[139]

Under mathematics, Bacon grouped the sciences of geography, astronomy, and astrology. In discussing the size of the world, Bacon cited Aristotle and Seneca as stating that India could be reached by voyaging westward across the Atlantic Ocean. "Aristotle says that the sea is small between the end of Spain on the west and the beginning of India on the east. Seneca in the fifth book on *Natural History* says that this sea is navigable in a very few days if the wind is favorable."[140]

Bacon's assertion may have influenced Christopher Columbus's discovery of America. Columbus relied upon the book *Imago Mundi* (*Image of the World*), by Pierre d'Ailly (A.D. 1351–1420), which gave a value of 20,400 miles (32,831 kilometers) for the Earth's circumference, a figure eighteen percent lower than the correct circumference of 40,030 kilometers.[141] And Pierre d'Ailly evidently relied upon the *Opus Majus*.[142]

The real gem of *Opus Majus* was in the sixth section, *Experimental Science*. Here, for the first time, was an advocacy of experiment, not as incidental, but as essential to the sciences. Bacon argued, "without experiment it is impossible to know anything thoroughly. There are two ways of acquiring knowledge, one through reason, the other by experiment. Argument reaches a conclusion and compels us to admit it, but it neither makes us certain nor so annihilates doubt that the mind rests calm in the intuition of truth, unless it finds this certitude by way of experience."[143]

Since at least the fifth century B.C., philosophers had argued that information obtained through the senses was unreliable. Therefore, the experimental method had to be unreliable. But Bacon supported his thesis with a compelling example. "Even if a man that has never seen fire, proves by good reasoning that fire burns, and devours and destroys things, nevertheless the mind of one hearing his arguments would never be convinced, nor would he avoid fire until he puts his hand or some combustible thing into it in order to prove by experiment what the argument taught. But after the fact of combustion is experienced, the mind is satisfied and lies calm in the certainty of the truth. Hence argument is not enough, but experience is.... It is necessary, then, to prove everything by experience."[144]

Bacon's argument for the necessity of experience was an echo of a nearly identical statement by Galen (c. A.D. 129–200). Galen believed that experience had to be combined with reason. But he also stressed the necessity for empiricism. "How is it that we know that fire is hot? ... and how do we learn that ice is cold except from the senses?"[145] Bacon must have read Galen, because he referred to Galen three times in the *Majus Opus*.[146] In one section of the *Opus Majus*, Bacon quoted Galen to support his belief that the Moon affected human health.[147] Thus the philosophers were finally acquiring an appreciation for empiricism from the physicians.

Bacon went so far as to state that experimental science "directs other sciences as its handmaids."[148] But he never presented a plan for a generalized scientific method based upon experimentation, a systematic methodology to be applied in each science. Instead, he grouped "experimental science" as a separate discipline. Neither was Bacon's empiricism the meticulous, double-blind study of the modern scientist. Under the category of empirical knowledge, Bacon was ready to accept hearsay "or lore allegedly acquired by empirical means."[149]

Bacon's knowledge of experimental science was more than just theoretical. After absorbing "the full corpus of translated Greek and Arabic works"[150] on optics, he conducted experiments himself. Bacon experimented "with visual phenomena such as pinhole images and the measurement of the visual field ... [and he] correctly calculated the maximum degree of elevation for the rainbow."[151] He employed mirrors, crystals, and pinholes in his investigations of optical phenomena.[152]

Roger Bacon also experimented with gunpowder. In the *Opus Majus*, he described the ignition of a small amount of this substance. "From the force of the salt called saltpeter so horrible a sound is produced at the bursting of so small a thing, namely, a small piece of parchment, that we perceive it exceeds the roar of sharp thunder, and the flash exceeds the greatest brilliancy of the lightning accompanying the thunder."[153]

Although he conducted experiments with gunpowder, Roger Bacon did not invent or discover the substance. The means by which gunpowder was introduced into Europe are obscure, but it almost certainly originated in China.[154] Military uses of gunpowder in China appear to date from approximately A.D. 1000. "Around the year 1000 the Chinese had flame throwing devices. By 1132 they were using long bamboo tubes filled with explosive powder, and by 1259 bullets were inserted in these tubes and ejected by touching off the powder."[155] In Europe, iron cannon were "in use by 1325," and "were becoming almost commonplace" by the middle of the fourteenth century.[156]

Europeans of the thirteenth century were also developing an appreciation for technology that was lacking amongst the ancient Greeks and Romans. In *Epistola de Secretis Operibus*, Roger Bacon foresaw the possibility of constructing mechanically-powered ships, automobiles, and airplanes. "Machines for navigating are possible without rowers, so that great ships suited to river or ocean, guided by one man, may be borne with greater speed than if they were full of men. Likewise cars may be made so that without a draught animal they may be moved *cum impetu inaestimabili* [rapidly], as we deem the scythed chariots to have been from which antiquity fought. And flying machines are possible, so that a man may sit in the middle turning some device by which artificial wings may beat the air in the manner of a flying bird."[157]

The roots of the industrial revolution of the eighteenth and nineteenth centuries were already present in thirteenth-century Europe. The Dark Ages had ended, and Europeans were harnessing new sources of power and developing technologies unknown to the ancient Greeks and Romans. The universe was seen as a reservoir of energy that could be tapped and adapted to human uses.[158]

Compendium Studii Philosophiae

There is no record of how the Pope received Bacon's communications. He may have interceded on Bacon's behalf, because in 1268 Bacon was released from supervision at Paris and returned to Oxford.[159] It looked as if the wheel of fortune was finally turning in a favorable direction.

But at this moment in history, fate intervened. Pope Clement IV died in November of 1268. It was the last chance that Bacon had for his reforms and ideas to be accepted. Embittered, Bacon vented his wrath in *Compendium Studii Philosophiae,* published in A.D. 1271. The vigor of his invective was astonishing.

Bacon attacked the Papacy:

> There has never been so great ignorance and such deep error.... For more sins reign in these days than in any past age; and sin is incompatible with wisdom. Let us look upon all conditions in the world, and consider them diligently; everywhere we shall find boundless corruption, and first of all in the Head. For the Court of Rome, which once was ruled by God's wisdom, and should always be so ruled, is now debased.... The Holy See is torn by the deceit and fraud of unjust men. Justice perisheth, all peace is broken, infinite scandals are aroused. This beareth its fruit in utterly perverse manners; pride reigneth, covetousness burneth, envy gnaweth upon all, the whole [Papal] Court is defamed of lechery, and gluttony is lord of all.[160]

Next, Bacon attacked bishops, cardinals, and lawyers. "Let us see the prelates; how they run after money, neglect the cure of souls, promote their own nephews, and other carnal friends, and crafty lawyers who ruin all by their counsels."[161]

Then he proceeded to denounce priests and monks. "Let us consider the religious Orders: I exclude none from what I say. See how far they are fallen.... The whole clergy is intent upon pride, lechery, and avarice."[162]

After condemning the entire Church, Bacon proceeded to damn the laity. No part of humanity was free from his vituperative wrath. "Princes and barons and knights oppress and rob each other, and trouble their subjects with infinite wars.... Men care not what is done nor how, whether by right or wrong, if only each may have his own will; meanwhile they are slaves to gluttony and lechery and the wickedness of other sins.... Of merchants and craftsmen there is no question, since fraud and deceit and guile reign beyond all measure in all their words and deeds."[163]

Bacon singled out scholastic professors in the universities and proclaimed them to be icons of ignorance. "Certain men have arisen in the universities who have created themselves masters and doctors in theology and philosophy, though they themselves have never learned anything of any account ... infinite error reigneth among them."[164]

Aristotle was next on his list. "If I had power over the books of Aristotle, I would burn them all; for to study therein is but lost time, and a source of error and a multiplication of ignorance beyond all human power to describe."[165]

Bacon clarified that his objection was not to Aristotle, but to corrupt translations of Aristotle's original works. "The labors of Aristotle are the foundation of all wisdom, therefore no man may tell how much the Latins waste now because they have accepted evil translations of the Philosopher.... Whosoever will glory in Aristotle's science, he must needs learn it in its own native tongue."[166]

For his refusal to suffer fools, Bacon has been treated harshly by historians. George Sarton concluded Bacon's influence was limited by his disagreeable disposition. "Unfortunately he was of a quarrelsome disposition ... and too temperamental to exert much influence upon his contemporaries; his immoderate criticism of the other leaders was bound to antagonize their followers instead of conciliating them."[167]

Sarton's criticism was accurate, but missed the point. A man of quiet disposition, one predisposed to accept the status quo, could never have innovated. It is sometimes necessary to resort to a frontal attack. After dismissing Bacon as flawed by temperament, Sarton then characterized Bacon as "a true harbinger of modern civilization."[168] All significant advances are made by unreasonable men, because reasonable men are satisfied with things the way they are. The elaboration of human knowledge is simultaneously a destructive and constructive process. Only the belligerent and uncompromising can bring about constructive change.

In 1274, the General of the Franciscan order, Bonaventure, died. Unfortunately for Bacon, Bonaventure's successor, Jerome de Ascoli (1227–1292), was as conservative as his predecessor. "He was a pious, peace-loving monk with no ambition save for the church, the crusades and the extirpation of heresy."[169]

Matters came to a head in 1277. The conservative theologians had endured enough. The Bishop of Paris formally condemned 219 heresies.[170] The list of offenses even included some of the teachings of Thomas Aquinas. Roger Bacon was charged with maintaining "certain suspicious novelties."[171] Bacon's crimes may have included his views on "astrology, alchemy, prophecy, prediction of the future,"[172] as well as the strong criticisms he made of his colleagues in *Compendium Studii Philosophiae* (1271).

Scholars differ as to whether or not Bacon was imprisoned. According to the Eleventh Edition of the *Encyclopædia Britannica*, Bacon "was thrown into prison for fourteen years."[173] But Crowley (1950) concluded, "it is scarcely credible that this offense would have been punished by imprisonment."[174] Because Bacon "returned from Paris to Oxford around 1280," it is most likely that he was not punished by imprisonment.[175]

Bacon's final work, *Compendium Studii Theologiae*, was published in 1292. He died about the same year, passing from life into legend. Perhaps the most astonishing aspect of Bacon's legacy is the fact that many historians still regard his contributions to humanity as less deserving than those of Thomas Aquinas. "Aquinas, as a student of man and of society, and as the constructive thinker who gave coherency to the vast fabric of Catholic discipline, achieved results which, judged at the distance of six centuries, Bacon neither equaled nor approached."[176] This judgment defies history. Bacon opened the door to the future, while Aquinas preserved the past.

CHAPTER 7

Technological Innovation During the Middle Ages

Unwritten History

The Dark Ages in Europe may have seen little new in the way of philosophy, litera-ture, and theoretical science, but in terms of technology there was " a steady and uninter-rupted advance over the Roman Empire."[1] During the Middle Ages, Europeans were developing new technologies that would culminate in the Industrial Revolution of the late eighteenth and early nineteenth century. "The medieval period was one of the greatest peri-ods of technical advance in history ... this was the age that produced a number of the basic inventions on which the whole secular fabric of our civilization ... rests."[2]

Most history is unwritten. The view of history we obtain from written documents is distorted because it is heavily weighted toward literary and philosophical topics. Before the eighteenth century, knowledge of the arts and crafts was mostly transmitted orally, through apprenticeship and occupational training. The first systematic exposition of the technological arts in literary form appeared in the French *Encyclopédie*, published between 1751 and 1765.

There is a synergy between technology and science. Science depends upon technology to increase the range and accuracy of observational data, and technology can be improved through the systematic knowledge obtained through scientific methods. But the synergis-tic nature of the relationship between science and technology was not appreciated until the modern age.

The diffusion of technology was related to, and affected by, commerce. Commercial interactions offered opportunities for spreading knowledge. Many important technologi-cal innovations were not invented in Europe, but imported and developed. The manufac-ture of paper and gunpowder originated in China. The padded horse collar and the stirrup were probably introduced into Europe from the East. The precise means by which techno-logical knowledge was transmitted is often obscure, but we know that West and East have engaged in trading for thousands of years. Europeans imported silk from China, and there must have been opportunities for traders and merchants to observe and report on new tech-nologies. The relationship between technology and commerce was also synergistic. New technologies made the production of commodities more efficient and resulted in greater surpluses to trade. Increased commercial activity in turn offered more opportunities for the transfer and diffusion of technology.

Agriculture

THE HEAVY PLOW

From the sixth through the ninth centuries A.D., Europeans invented, developed, and adopted new agricultural technologies that dramatically increased their agricultural productivity. As agriculture was the dominant, if not the overwhelming, element of the economy at this time, the agricultural revolution was a significant factor in the economic prosperity of the High Middle Ages.

One of the most important of the new agricultural methods was the adoption of a heavy wheeled plow. The plow itself likely originated in prehistoric times as a pointed stick or hoe used to scratch a furrow in the ground in which seeds were planted. Plows pulled by teams of oxen were in use in Egypt during the third millennium B.C.[3] Plows must have been used in Sumeria in the fourth millennium B.C., because a plow is depicted on a seal that was recovered from a grave in the city of Ur.[4]

In the light, sandy soils of the Mediterranean region, farmers utilized a "scratch" plow that consisted of little more than a stick attached to frame pulled by oxen. But the soils of northern Europe were more difficult to plow. They were clay-rich, and tended to be wetter and heavier.[5]

The Romans were aware of the existence of wheeled plows. In *Natural History*, Pliny the Elder described a type of wheeled plow that had been recently invented in Gaul. "There has been invented, at a comparatively recent period, in that part of Gaul known as Rhaetia, a plow with the addition of two small wheels."[6]

But it is likely that the heavy wheeled-plow adopted in Europe was not imported, but developed there to enable the exploitation of the heavy, clay-rich soils that were difficult to turn over with the common "scratch" plow used in the Mediterranean.[7] The Slavs had heavy plows as early as the sixth century, and heavy plows were used in Germany during the seventh century.[8]

The heavy wheeled-plow developed in northern Europe had three parts: the coulter, plowshare, and mouldboard. The *coulter* was a vertically-mounted knife blade. Set in front of the other components, the coulter cut a furrow in the soil. The *plowshare* was a horizontal blade. The plowshare followed the coulter, and sliced through the ground horizontally. After being cut both vertically and horizontally, the sod was ready to be overturned by the third component, the *mouldboard*. The blade of the plowshare was often mounted on the front of the mouldboard.[9]

The heavy plow broke up the soil so efficiently that cross-plowing was not necessary. Thus time was saved, and more land could be plowed. Soil clods were broken up by harrows pulled by horses in a direction at right angles to plowed furrows. The harrow was a "wooden framework in which iron pegs or tines are set."[10] The Romans had harrows, but mainly used them for pulling weeds.[11] Europeans used harrows "for leveling ridges left by the plough ... covering in seeds after sowing, tearing up and gathering weeds, ... [and] pulverizing the top soil and so conserving moisture."[12]

With no need to cross-plow, uninterrupted plowing favored the development of long, narrow strips of land. The heavy plow made it possible to farm on fertile land that was difficult to develop with the Mediterranean "scratch" plow, and thus opened up new areas for agricultural production and made it profitable to clear forests for conversion to arable land. All of these factors meant increased food production, wealth, and prosperity. In turn, increased food production fostered the fundamental processes of civilization: the growth of cities and specialized occupations.[13]

The adoption of the heavy plow also required greater cooperation, and thus promoted the manorial system of communal labor. The heavy plow was an expensive and specialized piece of machinery, and was usually pulled by a team of four oxen. It was more efficient to share this resource than for every serf to own their own plow and undertake the expense and responsibility for maintaining a team of draft animals.

HARNESSING HORSES

The Greek and Romans used horses for pulling, but did not know how to harness them efficiently. The Romans used a throat-and-girth harness in which a strap was placed across the animal's neck. As soon as the horse began to pull, he choked himself. Thus the pulling power of the horse was considerably reduced.[14]

The improved method of harnessing horses that began to be adopted in Europe during the ninth century was a padded collar. The origin of the padded horse collar is obscure, but it may have been introduced into Europe from China. The padded collar rests upon a horse's shoulder, and enables them to exert full power without choking themselves.[15]

The difference in traction force that can be obtained from the two harnessing methods is dramatic. It has been demonstrated by experiment that a team of horses equipped with collars can pull four to five times as much weight as horses harnessed across the throat.[16]

Horses had advantages over oxen as plow animals. Both horses and oxen are approximately equal in their pulling power, but horses are capable of moving fifty percent faster. The horse can also work an hour or two longer per day compared to the ox.[17]

Nevertheless, Europeans were slow to replace oxen as draft animals, especially in England. Horse-drawn plows did not become common until after the twelfth century.[18] Horses required oats, and some people argued that oxen were cheaper to maintain.[19]

A second factor that allowed horse power to be used in northern Europe was the nailed iron horse shoe. The Romans rode horses, but the nature of the relatively dry soils and terrain in the Mediterranean did not make it necessary to shoe their horses. Under wet conditions, the hoof of a horse softens and becomes easily worn or damaged. The iron horse shoe appears to have originated in Siberia in the ninth or tenth century.[20] By the eleventh century, the horseshoe in Europe had become a common necessity.[21]

The widespread utilization of horses also fostered commerce and the growth of towns. With fast-moving horses harnessed efficiently, it was possible to transport goods up to 35 kilometers in one day if a sufficiently good road was available.[22] There was now a way to dispose of an agricultural surplus and create wealth that could be used for investments in technology and infrastructure. Increased transportation speeds meant that farmers did not have to live so close to the fields they tilled. Thus the amount of land available for crop production increased.[23]

THREE-FIELD CROP ROTATION

The third significant factor in the Medieval agricultural revolution was the introduction of three-field crop rotation.

The Romans recognized the value of crop rotation, but practiced two-field crop rotation. Under this system, half the land was allowed to lay fallow while the other half was planted with a winter grain. Livestock pastured on the fallow land enriched it with manure.

There is some fragmentary evidence that the concept of planting both fall and spring crops originated in Britain. According to Diodorus Siculus (fl. 1st century B.C.), Hecataeus of Miletus (c. 550–476 B.C.) reported that Britons in the sixth century B.C. planted and harvested two crops annually. "Hecateus and some others say, that there is an island in the ocean over against Gaul ... [where] the soil is very rich, and very fruitful; and the climate is temperate, insomuch as there are two crops in the year."[24]

The inauguration of the three-field system dates from the eighth century. Land was divided into three sections. On the first part, a crop of winter grain (wheat or rye) was planted for food. The second section was planted with a spring crop of oats, barley, or a legume such as peas, lentils, or beans. The third part was left fallow. The next year, the use was rotated such that each section of land went through a complete rotation in three years.[25]

Compared to the ancient two-field system, the three-field system had some advantages. Because the land was in production two-thirds of the time, instead of only half, production was increased. The systematic use of legumes added nitrogen to the soil and increased the yield of the grain crop the following season. The cultivation and consumption of legumes such as beans added valuable protein to Medieval European diets.[26]

The Romans were aware that legumes enriched the soil. In *De Agricultura*, Cato the Censor (234–149 B.C.) noted "lupines, field beans and vetch manure corn [grain] land."[27] But there is no evidence that the Romans ever systematically cultivated legumes for the purpose of fertilizing their farm soils.

Under the three-field system, the work of plowing was more evenly divided throughout the year. More efficient use of time and less fallow time increased total productivity by a full fifty percent.[28] And the harvesting of two crops annually instead of one was insurance against crop failure and famine.[29] Synergy came into play. With increased productivity, less land had to be planted for food, and oats could be sown for horses. Horses in turn allowed faster plowing, and enabled transportation of agricultural surpluses to towns.

It has been estimated that the Medieval agricultural revolution dramatically increased yields of the most important food crop, grain. In the eleventh century, the average yield was 2.5 seeds for every seed planted. By the thirteenth century, this had increased to 4.0. Because 1 seed of grain had to be returned to the land for planting, this meant that the yield for human consumption increased from 1.5 to 3.0. The doubling of food output must have been a large factor in the population surge of the High Middle Ages.[30] More efficient farming techniques would not be developed until the agricultural revolution of the eighteenth century introduced four-crop rotation.

Power

The water mill evolved as an application of machine power to the primitive grain mill, the rotary *quern*. The quern consists of two stones in moving contact. When grains were caught between them, they were ground into flour. The rotary quern was known in Greece in the third century B.C., but may have been developed earlier.[31]

There were three types of water mills: horizontal, undershot, and overshot. The water mill most commonly found in Roman times was the horizontal mill. In the horizontal mill, water was typically diverted from a stream and channeled against mill blades attached to a vertical shaft. The shaft could then be used to produce flour by turning a rotary quern.[32] The horizontal mill dates from c. 200 B.C.[33]

The undershot mill generated more power than the horizontal. In the undershot mill, a vertical wheel is inserted directly into a stream of flowing water. The wheel is turned by the force of the water impacting blades on the bottom of the wheel (thus "undershot"). The wheel is geared so that the rotation of the wheel can be converted into the horizontal rotary motion needed to mill grain.[34] The undershot mill was described by Vitruvius (c. 30 B.C.). "Wheels ... are also constructed in rivers. Round their faces floatboards are fixed, which, on being struck by the current of the river, make the wheel turn."[35]

At some point it was discovered that more power could be extracted from the water wheel by letting water run over the top of it (thus "overshot"). Impetus was provided by the release of potential energy as the wheel turned and the water descended. This type of design was known in the fourth or fifth century A.D., but Roman examples are sparse.[36]

The evolution of mechanical progress was toward greater power. The hand- or animal-powered quern mill produced about 0.5 horsepower. A horizontal water-mill produced "slightly more" power.[37] The undershot mill made about 3 horsepower available, but the overshot mill typically produced 40 to 60 horsepower.[38]

Water power was known to the Romans. Strabo (c. 64 B.C.–A.D. 24) mentioned "at Cabeira was the palace of Mithridates [and] the water-mill."[39] The undershot wheel was described by Vitruvius (c. 30 B.C.). Near Arles, France, the Romans constructed an impressive flour mill that was powered by "two sets of eight overshot wheels."[40] This mill was capable of producing 240 to 320 kilograms of flour per hour.[41]

But except for some notable and isolated exceptions, the Romans made few applications of water power. The only use to which water power was used was milling grain. A single, dubious exception is found in a manuscript dating to A.D. 369 that mentions water-powered marble saws.[42]

Compared to northwest Europe, the Mediterranean littoral region offered fewer sites that provided a constant and abundant supply of running water. In contrast, the northwest sections of Europe had an abundance of mountain streams that ran year-round.[43] Slavery may have also been a factor. With an abundant supply of manual labor, the Romans had little incentive to develop artificial or mechanical power sources. Suetonius related that the Emperor Vespasian (reigned A.D. 69–79) rejected technology because it would have led to unemployment. "Some one offering to convey some immense columns into the Capitol at a small expense by a mechanical contrivance, he [Vespasian] rewarded him very handsomely for his invention, but would not accept his service, saying, 'suffer me to find maintenance for the poor people.'"[44]

As early as A.D. 370, an unknown Latin author noted the "mechanical inventiveness" of the "barbarian peoples."[45] By the tenth century, Europeans had begun a wholesale conversion of their civilization from human and animal-power to water power. The water-mill came to be viewed not just as a grain mill, but as a generalized source of power that could be adopted for many uses. As noted by Lynn White (1907–1987), "a new attitude ... was to alter the whole pattern of human life."[46]

By the eleventh century, the number of water-powered grain mills in Europe had increased enormously. The Domesday book of A.D. 1086, a written record of the survey of England ordered by William the Conqueror (A.D. 1027/1028–1087), lists 5,624 water mills. A century earlier, there had been fewer than 100 such mills in England.[47] The number of water mills in France also grew rapidly. From the eleventh to the thirteenth century, the number of water mills in the department [administrative division] of Aube in northeast

France increased from 14 to more than 200.[48] Mill construction was fostered by the fact that a mill usually was a profitable investment.[49]

In the eleventh century, water power was adopted for fulling (cleaning) wool and processing hemp fibers.[50] Northern Europe contained more iron resources than the Mediterranean region, and Europeans developed new power technologies to manufacture iron.[51] As early as the eleventh century, Europeans utilized water power in the manufacture of iron to power bellows and drive forge hammers.[52] Water-powered hammers used for forging iron could have a mass as great as 1,600 kilograms, and water-powered bellows produced air blasts powerful enough to raise furnace temperatures as high as 1,500 degrees Celsius.[53]

Monks were technological pioneers in finding new uses and applications for water power. The Cistercians, in particular, pioneered and utilized the most advanced technologies and created an economic empire in Europe.[54] Cistercians were the leading iron producers in the Champagne region of France from the middle of the thirteenth century through the seventeenth century.[55]

As early as the beginning of the tenth century, a Benedictine abbey in Switzerland applied water power to process beer mash.[56] By the thirteenth century, water power was also being utilized in sawmills, tanning mills, to turn wood lathes and grinding stones, and to manufacture paper.[57]

The utilization of water power in these many forms required that Europeans develop methods for transferring and redirecting power, crucial technologies for the Industrial Revolution of the late eighteenth century. Most important of these was the crank. The *crank* is a device that allows rotary motion to converted into reciprocal motion, or vice versa. The crank probably originated in late antiquity as a perpendicular stick handle attached to a hand-operated rotary quern. By moving the handle back and forth, the reciprocal motion of the person operating the quern was converted into rotary motion.[58]

For an industrial or technological civilization, the importance of the crank is second only to that of the wheel itself. It is of crucial importance to any technology or industry that relies upon an artificial power technology. Yet the crank was largely unknown to the Greeks and Romans. Without the crank, "machine civilization is inconceivable."[59] By the late Middle Ages, Europeans had developed a crank and connecting-rod technology that enabled them to efficiently transfer and utilize water and wind power for diverse applications and ends.[60]

Because water power was only available where streams were located, other sources of power were developed. Tidal power was exploited in Ireland as early as the seventh century. The Domesday book of 1086 notes the presence of a tidal mill near Dover. Tidal power was also utilized in Venice c. A.D. 1050 or earlier, and in Brittany and the Bay of Biscay.[61] In the thirteenth century, there were three tidal mills in Devon and Cornwall. But the exploitation of tidal power was limited by location, exposure to storms, and the fact that tidal mills could only draw power for the few hours when the tide was flowing in the appropriate direction. The time of high tide also varied daily.[62]

Wind mills were used in Persia in the tenth century for pumping irrigation water and grinding grain. But the European windmill has a different design, and appears to be of independent origin.[63] The first windmill in Europe dates from A.D. 1085. Over the next hundred years, the technology spread rapidly over the plains of northern Europe.[64] Windmills provided power in the cold of winter when water mills were shut down by frozen streams.

The Mechanical Clock

The earliest timekeepers were sundials and water clocks. The simple water clock, the *clepsydra*, measured time by water running out of a hole situated near the bottom of a vessel. The oldest known example of this simple device dates to 1380 B.C.[65] But the water clock was almost certainly in use much earlier.[66]

As the clepsydra empties, the rate of flow diminishes. The water level in the clepsydra does not fall at a uniform rate, and the device is therefore inherently inaccurate. Attempts were made to compensate for this by tapering the sides of the vessels, but it nevertheless proved impossible for this type of mechanism to be an accurate timekeeper.[67]

The accuracy of the water clock was improved by the invention of the constant-flow clepsydra. The constant-flow clepsydra consisted of two or more vessels. Water from the first vessel, the outflow, flowed into the second, the inflow. Time was marked by the rise of water in the inflow vessel. The flow rate from the outflow was kept constant by means of maintaining a constant water level through an overflow outlet. In other words, the outflow vessel was constantly filled by a flow of water from some source, the excess of which escaped through an overflow outlet. The inflow vessel commonly contained a float. A pointer attached to the float measured the passage of time by its proximity to a graduated scale.[68]

The constant-flow clepsydra may have been invented by Ctesibius (fl. 270 B.C.) in Alexandria.[69] Ctesibius' inventions were described by Vitruvius (c. 30 B.C.), who noted that Ctesibius began the construction of his water clocks "by making an orifice in a piece of gold, or by perforating a gem, because these substances are not worn by the action of water, and do not collect dirt so as to get stopped up."[70]

The water clock was certainly in use in Rome by the second century B.C. or earlier. In *De Natura Deorum* (*Of the Nature of the Gods*), Cicero (106–43 B.C.) wrote, "when you see a [sun]dial or water-clock, you believe the hours are showed by art, and not by chance."[71] The clepsydra was accurate enough to be useful in many situations. In legislative conventions and meetings it could be used to measure the time allotted to each speaker. If the speaker were interrupted for any reason, the passage of his time could be stopped simply by plugging the hole in the clepsydra. The clock would then be restarted when the legislator resumed his speech.[72]

Toward the end of the eleventh century, water clocks reached a high degree of sophistication. A Chinese manuscript dating from A.D. 1090 described an enormous water-driven "astronomical clock-tower."[73] The mechanism was 35 feet [10.7 meters] high and apparently constructed to provide constant and regulated motive power for a monumental *armillary sphere*, a mechanical model of the celestial sphere. This device was evidently one of the first attempts to provide a clock drive for an instrument used in astronomical observations.[74] Monumental water clocks were also constructed by Muslims and Europeans. There are references in extant literature to ten or twelve such clocks built before the year 1250.[75]

The mechanical clock was invented in Europe near the end of the thirteenth century or the beginning of the fourteenth century. A manuscript authored by Robertus Anglicus in A.D. 1271 discussed the attempts of the makers of *horologia* [clocks] to make accurate instruments. Anglicus concluded, "they cannot quite complete their task which if they could, it would be a really accurate horologium [clock]."[76] From the context, it is clear that the reference to horologia referred to mechanical time-keeping devices, not water clocks.

The first mechanical clocks were powered by falling weights. The problem that had to be solved was how to release the potential energy of the weight in a graduated and uniform manner. Falling weights accelerate, so their motion has be checked and the conversion of potential to kinetic energy regulated so that it occurs at a constant rate. The ingenious solution that was found was the *verge escapement*. The verge escapement has been called "one of the fundamental inventions in the history of technology,"[77] and "the greatest single human invention since the appearance of the wheel."[78]

The verge escapement regulated the motion of a crown wheel powered by a falling weight. The mechanism of the verge escapement is more easily depicted than described verbally, but a key feature was that it allowed the pace of a clock to be adjusted or regulated by moving weights attached to the ends of the escapement.[79]

With astronomical observations serving as a benchmark, regulated mechanical clocks were reasonably accurate. In an age where plumbing was exceptional, they were more convenient than water clocks, especially for installation in large buildings. Instead of filling a reservoir with water, a mechanical clock could be "wound" simply by raising the weight that drove the mechanism.

The first mechanical clocks were large, and their mechanisms were constructed by blacksmiths. The smiths had some experience with the construction of large geared wheels, as these were used in water mills for transferring power.[80] There are no surviving examples of clocks from the fourteenth century, but it is probable that these devices had an accuracy of about plus or minus fifteen minutes per day.[81] The first large mechanical clocks were commonly installed in the towers of churches or cathedrals.[82] By the year 1370, about thirty such clocks had been built and installed in Europe.[83]

Prior to the widespread use of mechanical clocks, the practice had been to divide night and day into twelve hours, regardless of the season. This remained the practice at the city of Nuremberg until the early seventeenth century.[84] Thus the length of the hours varied with the seasons. In the northern hemisphere, a winter night-hour was longer than a winter day-hour. But by the year 1500, nearly every town in Europe had a central tower clock.[85] With mechanical clocks providing precision timekeeping, it became feasible to adopt an hour of uniform length and standard time keeping. Such a practice facilitated the development of a technological civilization dependent on coordinating complex administrative and commercial interactions.[86]

Europeans continued to perfect the mechanical clock for hundreds of years. Between 1348 and 1362, Giovanni de' Dondi constructed a complex mechanical clock that accurately reproduced the motions of the Sun, Moon, and five planets.[87] The Strasbourg clock of 1354 introduced *automata*, mechanically powered representations of living things. The Strasbourg clock was 38 feet [11.6 meters] high, and featured a mechanized cock that "opened its beak, stretched out its tongue, crowed, flapped its wings, and spread its feathers."[88] By the year 1500, it was possible to make portable clocks, including watches, by replacing the weight drive with a coiled spring. The driving force of the unwinding spring was regulated by two new inventions, the *fusee* and the *stackfreed*.[89]

Although the mechanical clock had arguably evolved into a precision instrument by the end of the sixteenth century,[90] it was dramatically improved by the use of the pendulum to regulate time. The fact that the pendulum had a constant period was first noticed by Galileo in 1581. But the application to mechanical clocks was pioneered by Christiaan Huygens (1629–1695).[91] Huygens "invented the pendulum clock" in 1656.[92]

The implications of the mechanical clock went beyond timekeeping. The invention of this device demonstrated that Europeans of the fourteenth century had definitely advanced beyond the ancient artisans who crafted the Antikythera mechanism in the second century B.C. The techniques developed in clockwork for regulating and transferring power were essential for the complex machinery of the Industrial Revolution and the technological civilization that was developing in Europe.

Military and Economic Technology

THE STIRRUP

The *stirrup* is a contrivance suspended from a saddle that supports the foot of the rider and stabilizes him in his mount. Although the device seems trivial, its invention may have had profound consequences for military strategy and political and social organization in Europe. Lynn White proposed that adoption of the stirrup may have been the primary stimulus for the development of feudalism in Medieval Europe.[93]

It is surprising that the invention of the stirrup was delayed for many centuries after people began riding horses. There was an obvious need to stabilize a rider, especially one weighted down with armor who needed a steady platform from which to deploy his weapons. The precarious instability of an armed horseman is illustrated by the demise of Cambyses, king of Persia. According to Herodotus, Cambyses accidentally killed himself in 522 B.C. while attempting to hurriedly mount his horse. "He [Cambyses] sprang hastily upon his steed ... as he made his spring, the button of his sword-sheath fell off, and the bared point entered his thigh."[94] The wound proved fatal.

For a long time, it was well known that a well-trained and equipped cavalry was more important than vast numbers of infantry. After the Carthaginians defeated the Romans at the Battle of Cannae in 216 B.C., Polybius noted "[It is] a lesson to posterity that in actual war it is better to have half the number of infantry, and the superiority in cavalry, than to engage your enemy with an equality in both."[95]

But the stirrup was unknown to the Greeks and Romans.[96] Xenophon (c. 431–355 B.C.) advised riders to stabilize themselves by grabbing onto a horse's mane. "As the horse is leaping over a ditch, or stretching up an ascent, it is well for the rider to take hold of the mane."[97]

The stirrup appears to have originated as a simple loop that was initially used only as an aid in mounting a horse. The earliest representation is found on a vase from India from the fourth century B.C.[98] Stirrups are also depicted on Indian sculptures from the second century B.C.[99]

Between the second and fourth centuries A.D., the Romans may have developed handgrips attached to the front of their saddles.[100] Apparently, these devices were meant to support the rider, and speak to the absence of the stirrup, rather than a stage in its development. The stirrup proper, a metal framework designed to stabilize a rider, appears to have been developed in China. The earliest example extant is a "gilded bronze stirrup" recovered from a grave dated to the early or middle of the fourth century A.D.[101] During the fourth century A.D., the technology of the stirrup diffused from China into Korea and Japan.[102]

In Europe, the first stirrups were used in Hungary. Cast-iron examples recovered from graves have been dated to the sixth century A.D.[103] A book on military tactics, *Of Strategems*, describes the stirrup as a standard piece of equipment in late sixth-century Constantinople.[104] This work has been ascribed the Byzantine Emperor, Mauricius Flavius Tiberius

(c. A.D. 539–602), but is likely "a contemporary work of unknown authorship."[105] It is also possible that *Of Stratagems* was not written during the late sixth century, but the early eighth century.[106]

By the eighth century, Vikings in northwestern Europe were using stirrups.[107] The technology was quickly adopted in France. In the late seventh century, the Franks relied primarily upon infantry. But by the eighth century, cavalry had become the most important component of the Frankish military forces.[108]

The stirrup effectively welded the rider to the horse. With a more stable platform, the cavalryman became a more effective archer, and could wield his sword with greater effect. The stirrup also made it possible to deploy the long, heavy lance. The weight of the blow was no longer struck by the human arm, but by the combined impetus of the horse and its rider. This introduced what Lynn White characterized as "mounted shock combat."[109]

The increase in offensive weaponry and effectiveness initiated a corresponding upscale of defensive technology. Horse riders adopted the characteristic full body armor associated with knights. Most common armor was not in the form of plates, but chain mail.[110] Thus the familiar armored knight of the Middle Ages came into existence as a logical consequence of the lowly stirrup.

After the fall of the Roman Empire in the West, the mining and production of metals decreased. But with the advent of the heavy plow and the use of iron armor, there was an increased demand for iron. Accordingly, iron mining and fabrication increased, assisted by the use of water power to drive bellows and forge hammers. The blacksmith became the most valued craftsman of the Middle Ages.[111]

Lynn White (1907–1987) proposed that the stirrup played a critical role in the development of feudalism in Europe. After defeating the Muslims at the Battle of Tours in A.D. 732, Charles Martel (c. A.D. 688–741), a leader of the Franks, decided that effective military strategy required an increased number of cavalry.

Because the recently-introduced stirrup favored, or even required, heavily armored and highly trained professional soldiers, Martel decided to create a network of fiefdoms managed by knights at his disposal. Worthy individuals would be awarded estates. In return, they would be obligated to provide military service when called upon. Accordingly, Martel seized land wholesale from the Christian Church and parceled it out to those who swore allegiance to him. White concluded that "a sudden and urgent demand for cavalry led the early Carolingians to reorganize their realm along feudal lines to enable it to support mounted fighters in much greater numbers than ever before."[112]

White's thesis of attributing the rise of feudalism to the introduction of the stirrup is interesting, but controversial. On the contrary, it has been noted that the military campaigns of both Charles Martel and Charlemagne (A.D. 742–814) consisted largely of "sieges and raids," not the "shock combat" envisioned by White.[113] Many other factors likely contributed to development of feudalism. There was a long cultural tradition, both in the Roman Empire, and among the peoples of northern Europe, of allegiance to a strong male leader.[114]

Another reason for the emergence of the feudal system in Europe was that it provided an effective means of defense against external threats. A key element in feudalism was a centralized and fortified stronghold, a manor or a castle. It was a place where local inhabitants could retreat in times of external threats. During the ninth and tenth centuries, Western Europe suffered repeated and destructive incursions from Viking and Magyar raiders. The invaders looted, burned, and pillaged. In response, "the new military class of feudalism opposed a solid wall."[115]

TREBUCHETS AND FIREARMS

The Romans had catapults for throwing arrows or stones, but these were powered by torsion. Hair or sinews were twisted to provide the power to throw a projectile.[116] Vitruvius described the construction of catapults for throwing arrows and *ballistae* for hurling stones.[117] These were powered by "twisted hair, generally women's, or [strings] of sinew."

Feudal castles in Europe were initially constructed of wood and earth. But in the eleventh and twelfth centuries, these were replaced by the familiar and formidable stone castle.[118] The increased effectiveness of the stone fortifications may have precipitated the development of the trebuchet.

The *trebuchet* was a machine for throwing heavy stones that originated in China sometime between the fifth and third century B.C.[119] The trebuchet first appeared in Europe around the year A.D. 1100.[120] The trebuchet consisted of a heavy timber beam hinged on a timber frame. A sling containing a projectile was attached to the long end of the beam. The range and effectiveness of the trebuchet were increased by constructing a trough on the base of the machine in which the projectile began its movement. The trough enabled the sling to be longer and increased its mechanical advantage.

The shorter end of the trebuchet beam was attached to a counter-weight, an empty wooden box that was weighted by filling it with dirt or stones. The weighted end of the trebuchet was held aloft. When it was released, the downward motion propelled the sling end to swing upward and throw its missile.[121]

A trebuchet described by Villard de Honnecourt (c. A.D. 1230) was counter-weighted by "a hopper full of earth which is two large toises [3.9 meters] long and nine feet [2.6 meters] across and twelve feet [3.9 meters] parfront."[122] If the counter-weight bucket had a volume of 39.5 cubic meters, as Honnecourt attested, then the total mass of the counter-weight would have been approximately 59,000 kilograms, or 59 metric tons.[123] It is possible that there existed trebuchets large enough to handle projectiles with masses in the range of 900 to 1,360 kilograms.[124]

Modern experiments have found that a trebuchet with a counterweight mass of 10 tons is capable of propelling a stone with a mass of 100 to 150 kilograms a distance of 150 meters. In comparison, Roman catapults were much weaker. A Roman catapult could throw a projectile with a mass of 20–30 kilograms a distance of 225 meters.[125]

Trebuchets could also be filled with incendiary materials, or infected corpses. In the 1332 siege of the castle of Schwanau, sixty men were killed, and their dismembered body parts flung into the castle by means of trebuchets.[126] Typically, medieval siege warfare involved the deployment of a handful of trebuches. In 1296, the English army of Edward I (1239–1307) used three trebuchets to attack the abbey of Holyrood near Edinburgh. In 1304, the same forces employed thirteen trebuchets in the siege of Stirling.[127]

With the invention of gunpowder and cannon, trebuchets became obsolete, falling into disuse by the end of the fourteenth century.[128] The last known use of a trebuchet in warfare was by the Spanish conquistador Hernan Cortes (1485–1547). Assaulting Mexico City in 1521, Cortes's forces resorted to the improvised construction of a trebuchet when their gunpowder ran low. However, the machine malfunctioned and self-destructed on the first firing.[129]

Gunpowder originated in China, but firearms were a European invention.[130] They may have evolved from the Byzantine practice of propelling a substance known as Greek Fire from copper tubes.[131]

Incendiary warfare was practiced by the Greeks as early as the fifth century B.C. According to Thucydides, at the siege of Plataea in 429 B.C., the Spartans cast "in lighted brands with brimstone and pitch, [and] set them all on fire."[132] *Greek Fire* was "the name applied to inflammable and destructive compositions used in warfare during the Middle Ages and particularly by the Byzantine Greeks at the sieges of Constantinople."[133] The exact composition of Greek Fire is unknown, but it may have been composed of "such materials as sulphur and naphtha with quicklime."[134] Greek Fire was first used in A.D. 673 to defend Constantinople against an Islamic maritime attack.[135]

Cannon date from the first part of the fourteenth century in Europe, and were common by 1350. The primary use of these weapons was in siege warfare. Trebuchets and catapults quickly became obsolete. Even the strongest fortifications were now vulnerable. The protection offered by a stone castle was eviscerated.[136]

The first handguns came into use as early as the fourteenth century. "These were simply small cannon, provided with a stock of wood, and fired by the application of a match to the touch-hole."[137] Personal firearms did not become effective weapons until the sixteenth century.[138] Swords and pikes remained important military weapons through the sixteenth and seventeenth centuries.[139] During the course of the sixteenth century, the bow was displaced by the firearm as the standard military firearm. In the fourteenth and fifteenth centuries, the bow was still equal or superior to the primitive firearms then available in its rate of fire, accuracy, and range.[140]

"The hand gun came into practical use in 1446 and was of very rude construction."[141] The first firearms ignited by means of a touch hole. Personal firearms evolved into efficient military weapons with the invention of the matchlock late in the fifteenth century. The matchlock brought the means of ignition into contact with the gunpowder in the barrel by means of a lever or trigger mechanism. The wheel-lock, an improved matchlock design, was invented in 1517, and made the handgun an effective weapon.[142] Muskets were introduced by the Spanish in 1540, and soon became the standard military weapon throughout Europe. The flintlock was devised in 1635, and replaced matchlock mechanisms, becoming the standard ignition mechanism in the later part of the seventeenth century.[143]

The use of cannon in particular helped break up feudalism, as it made central fortifications obsolete. The possession of personal firearms gave individuals more political power, and was an engine for social and political change. The firearm was also the first internal combustion engine, and demonstrated the enormous potential power that lay in confined and controlled combustion.[144]

NAVIGATION

Improvements in the technologies of maritime navigation during the Middle Ages increased the efficiency of commerce and made possible the European Age of Exploration that began in the fifteenth century. Prior to the later Middle Ages, long voyages were impossible. Hull construction was relatively weak, and susceptible to damage during storms. Navigators lacked charts, compasses, and other navigational instruments. Sails and rigging were inadequate for long voyages. And voyages, even close to the coastline, were usually not attempted during winter months.[145]

From ancient times, ships had been steered by quarter-rudders mounted on the sides, but toward the sterns of ships. With ship size increasing in the High Middle Ages, there was a need for an improved rudder. The mechanism that was developed was the *stern-post rudder*, a steering device attached to the stern of a ship. Stern-post rudders first appeared in northern Europe during the thirteenth century.[146]

The *lateen* was a triangular-shaped sail that became common in the Mediterranean region by the year A.D. 800. The lateen made it easier to sail close to or against a headwind. "Motion directly towards the wind cannot be maintained, but by sailing obliquely towards it first to one side and then to the other progress is made in advance."[147] With the lateen sail, ships became more maneuverable. In northern Europe, the first ships were powered by paddling or rowing. The earliest surviving archeological specimen of ship incorporating sails is a Viking vessel dating from the ninth century.[148]

The magnetic compass likely originated in China during the late eleventh or early twelfth century.[149] It was found that an iron needle stroked with a lodestone acquired a magnetization. Floating on the surface of water, or stuck in a floating cork, the magnetized needle aligned itself with the Earth's magnetic field. Around A.D. 1180, Alexander Neckam (1157–1218) described a "pivoted needle."[150] In the thirteenth century Peter Peregrinus, or Peter of Maricourt (fl. c. 1269), described how to construct a compass encased in brass and divided into 360 degrees. "Bring either the north or the south pole of a lodestone near the cover so that the needle may be attracted and receive its virtue from the lodestone."[151]

Conclusion

The classical civilizations of Greece and Rome made significant contributions to what would eventually become known as Western Civilization. In philosophy, physics, chemistry, medicine, and mathematics, Greek knowledge was ascendant for nearly two thousand years. There is little evidence of Roman originality in philosophy or science, but the Romans were great engineers and had a genius for law and civil administration.

Human beings tend to construct and maintain social organizations that meet their needs. Where classical civilization ultimately failed was in its inability to politically unite diverse peoples under a common creed. The Greeks had intelligence and courage, but couldn't get along with each other or unify their city-states under a common government. The singular example of destructive Greek enmity was the Peloponnesian War. The Romans were more successful at maintaining peace, but the *Pax Romana* was imposed by brute force, not the thoughtful and spontaneous cooperation of people with diverse interests.

Before the advent of civilization conflict between tribes of foragers was incessant. When people adopted agriculture, animal husbandry, and began to live in cities, they became more peaceful and necessarily cooperative. For the past ten thousand years, the long term global trend has been for human beings to form larger social groups. Tribes came together in cities, cities united to form nations, and nations forged alliances and empires. Gradually, people came to the realization that it is more profitable to engage others as allies in the task of economic production, rather than regard them as enemies to be destroyed.

Christianity in Europe, or something like it, was perhaps inevitable because it supplied a missing moral substrate. The Christian concept of universal brotherhood is the ethic of a global-scale civilization in which diverse peoples cooperate productively. Christian charity introduced the revolutionary idea that the only tribe is the human tribe. Similarly, Islam united diverse tribes and groups under a common creed. Thus the advent of these great religions fostered the cooperation and unity necessary for the progress of, civilization, science, and commerce. Science and philosophy remain activities that take place in civilizations forged by religions.

As early as the first century A.D., the European mind was turning inward. Science and the natural world received little attention. The supernatural world was considered to be the demonstrative and ordered one, and theology, morality, and ethics became the most important fields of study. Medieval Europe was a comfortable place for men. Man was understood to have been created in God's image, and the Earth had been provided for his use. The physical location of the Earth at the center of universe demonstrated a correspondence and harmony between the physical, moral, and spiritual worlds. The Great Chain of Being provided everyone with an understanding of their place and role in life. The construction of Gothic Cathedrals in the twelfth and thirteenth centuries symbolized the apex of Christian civilization in Europe.

After the collapse of the Roman Empire in the West, philosophy and science stagnated in Europe. But much important work continued to be done in the crafts and applied arts. During the Middle Ages, Europeans developed improved agricultural techniques. They harnessed horses, introduced three-field crop rotation, and began to utilize water power on a scale never envisaged by the Romans or Greeks. As early as the ninth or tenth century, the technological achievements of Europeans surpassed those of the ancient Mediterranean civilizations. Europeans invented machines such as the mechanical clock, and devised ingenious mechanisms for transferring, controlling, and directing mechanical power.

A new attitude also emerged. Europeans needed technology, because their economies were not based on large-scale human slavery. Medieval Europeans thus gained an appreciation and respect for the practical arts that the Greek and Roman philosophers had disdained.

What we know as modern science began in the twelfth and thirteenth centuries when Christian theologians fused Aristotelian logic with empiricism. Islamic theologians rejected rational philosophy, but the even the most conservative and doctrinaire of the Christians found the appeal of logic to be irresistible. Both reason and revelation were ways of knowing God. Truth was a unity. It was inconceivable that the God known from human reason could be any different from the God revealed by revelation.

In the High Middle Ages, Europeans also gained an appreciation for empiricism. The existence of magnetism demonstrated unequivocally that nature contained hidden forces and attributes that could never be anticipated or explained through rational thought alone. Experimental philosophy began in the thirteenth century when Christian theologians in Europe began to apply Aristotelian logic to empirical methods.

Although the reflexive modern tendency is to equate science with technology, their historical development was not so much synergistic, as parallel. It was only gradually that people came to have an appreciation that science ought to be directed towards discovering reliable information that might have technological applications. Thus a natural philosophy concerned with speculation about final causes eventually came to be replaced by an experimental science that studied efficient causation.

Chapter Notes

Chapter 1

1. Crossan, J. D., 1991, *The Historical Jesus*. Harper, San Francisco, p. 427.
2. Ibid., p. 430.
3. *Encyclopædia Britannica*, Eleventh Edition, 1911, Jesus Christ, vol. 15. Encyclopædia Britannica Company, New York, p. 353.
4. Crossan, J. D., 1991, *The Historical Jesus*. Harper, San Francisco, p. 430–431.
5. *Encyclopædia Britannica*, Eleventh Edition, 1911, Jesus Christ, vol. 15. Encyclopædia Britannica Company, New York, p. 353.
6. Crossan, J. D., 1991, *The Historical Jesus*. Harper, San Francisco, p. xxx.
7. Bible, King James Version, John 20:31.
8. Josephus, F., 1987, *The Antiquities of the Jews*, Book 18, Chapter 3, Paragraph 3, in *The Works of Josephus*, translated by William Whiston (1667–1752). Hendrickson Publishers, Peabody, Massachusetts, p. 480.
9. Tacitus, 1942, *Annals*, Book 15, Paragraph 44 *The Complete Works of Tacitus*, translated by Alfred John Church (1824–1912) and William Jackson Brodribb (1829–1905). Modern Library, New York, p. 380–381.
10. Pliny the Consul, 1809, *The Letters of Pliny the Consul*, Book 10, Letter 97, translated by William Melmoth, vol. 2. E. Larkin, Boston, p. 258.
11. Ibid., p. 259.
12. Ibid., p. 256.
13. Ibid., p. 257.
14. Ibid., Book 10, Letter 98, p. 259.
15. Ibid.
16. Ibid., p. 261.
17. Ibid.
18. Bible, King James Version, Luke 1: 26–1:35; Matthew 1:18.
19. Macculloch, J. A., 1902, *Comparative Theology*. Methuen & Co., London, p. 138.
20. Ibid., p. 138–139.
21. Bible, King James Version, Luke 2:4–2:7.
22. Ibid., Matthew 2:1–2:2.
23. Ibid., Matthew 2:16.
24. Ibid., Matthew 2:13.
25. Ibid., Matthew 2:19–2:23.
26. Crossan, J. D., 1991, *The Historical Jesus*. Harper, San Francisco, p. 19.
27. Bible, King James Version, Matthew 13:55–13:56.
28. *Encyclopædia Britannica*, Eleventh Edition, 1910, Christianity, vol. 6. Encyclopædia Britannica Company, New York, p. 281.
29. Bible, King James Version, Luke 2:46–2:47.
30. Ibid., Mark 1:6.
31. Ibid., Luke 3:7–3:9.
32. Ibid., Mark 6:18.
33. Ibid., Matthew 14:9–14:12.
34. Ibid., Matthew 3:13.
35. Ibid. Matthew 4:1–4:4.
36. Ibid., Matthew 4:8–4:10.
37. Ibid., Luke 4:24.
38. Ibid., Matthew 5:39.
39. Ibid., Matthew 5:5.
40. Ibid., Mark 11:15.
41. Ibid., Matthew 26:52.
42. Ibid., Luke 22:36.
43. Ibid., Matthew 5:9.
44. Ibid., Matthew 10:34.
45. Ibid., Matthew 16:16.
46. Ibid., Matthew 19:17.
47. Ibid., Luke 6:37.
48. Ibid., Matthew 10:14–10:15.
49. Ibid., Genesis 19:24–19:25.
50. Ibid., Matthew 5:3–5:10.
51. Ibid., John 14–6.
52. Ibid., Mark 9:43.
53. Ibid., Matthew 10:28.
54. Ibid., Luke 16:22–16:24.
55. Ibid., Mark 13:14.
56. Ibid., Mark 13:22.
57. Ibid.
58. Ibid., Mark 13:25–13:27.
59. Ibid., Mark 13:32.
60. Ibid., Matthew 13:24–30, 13:36–13:43.
61. Ibid., Matthew 13:37–13:42.
62. Josephus, F., 1987, *The Antiquities of the Jews*, Book 13, Chapter 5, Paragraph 9 in, *The Works of Josephus*, translated by William Whiston (1667–1752). Hendrickson Publishers, Peabody, Massachusetts, p. 346.
63. *Encyclopædia Britannica*, Eleventh Edition, 1911, Pharisees, vol. 21. Encyclopædia Britannica Company, New York, p. 347.
64. Ibid.
65. Bible, King James Version, Mark 2:16.
66. *Encyclopædia Britannica*, Eleventh Edition, 1911, Jesus Christ, vol. 15. Encyclopædia Britannica Company, New York, p. 349.
67. Bible, King James Version, Mark 2:23.
68. *Encyclopædia Britannica*, Eleventh Edition, 1911, Jesus Christ, vol. 15. Encyclopædia Britannica Company, New York, p. 349.
69. Bible, King James Version, Exodus 20:9–20:10.
70. Ibid., Matthew 22:15–22:21.
71. Ibid., John 8:3–8:11.
72. Ibid., John 8:4.
73. Ibid., Leviticus, 20:10.
74. Ibid., John 8:3–8:7.
75. Ibid., Matthew 23:33.
76. Ibid.
77. Ibid., Matthew 23:15.
78. Ibid., Matthew 23:24.
79. Ibid., Matthew 23:27–23:28.
80. *Encyclopædia Britannica*, Eleventh Edition, 1911, Jesus Christ, vol. 15. Encyclopædia Britannica Company, New York, p. 347.
81. Bible, King James Version, Matthew 26:14–26:16.
82. Ibid., Mark 14:18–14:25.
83. Ibid., Mark 14:22.

84. Ibid., Mark 14:44.
85. Ibid., Mark 14:46.
86. Ibid., Mark 14:50.
87. Ibid., Mark 14:53.
88. Ibid., Mark 14:61.
89. Ibid., Mark 14:62.
90. Ibid., Daniel 7:13–7:14.
91. *Encyclopædia Britannica*, Eleventh Edition, 1911, Jesus Christ, vol. 15. Encyclopædia Britannica Company, New York, p. 352.
92. *Catholic Encyclopedia*, 1911, Pilate, Pontius, vol. 12. Encyclopedia Press, New York p. 84.
93. Ibid.
94. Bible, King James Version, Matthew 27:17.
95. Ibid., Matthew 27:20.
96. Ibid., Matthew 27:22.
97. Ibid., Matthew 27:23.
98. Ibid., Matthew 27:24.
99. Ibid., Mark 15:16–15:20.
100. Ibid., Mark 15:15.
101. *Encyclopædia Britannica*, Eleventh Edition, 1911, Cross, vol. 7. Encyclopædia Britannica Company, New York, p. 506.
102. Ibid.
103. Bible, King James Version, Mark 15:21.
104. Ibid., Mark 15:24.
105. Ibid., Mark 15:30.
106. Ibid., Mark 15:32.
107. Ibid., Mark 15:44.
108. Ibid., Mark 15:43–15:45.
109. Ibid., Mark 15:46.
110. Ibid., Matthew 27:64.
111. Ibid., Mark 16:4.
112. Ibid., Mark 16:5.
113. Ibid., Matthew 28:3.
114. Ibid., Mark 16:6.
115. Ibid., Mark 16:9.
116. Ibid., John 20:19–20:20.
117. Ibid., John 20:25.
118. Ibid., John 20:28.
119. Ibid., John 20:29.
120. *Encyclopædia Britannica*, 1972, Jesus Christ, vol. 12. William Benton, Chicago, p. 1021.
121. Doane, T. W., 1884, *Bible Myths and Their Parallels in Other Religions*, Third Edition. J. W. Bouton, New York, p. 215–232.
122. *Encyclopædia Britannica*, 1972, Adonis vol. 1. William Benton, Chicago, p. 164–165.
123. Frazer, J. G., 1900, *The Golden Bough*, Second Edition, vol. 2. Macmillan, New York, p. 116.
124. Ibid., p. 115, 118.
125. Josephus, F., 1987, *The Wars of the Jews*, Book 5, Chapter 11, Paragraph 1, in *The Works of Josephus*, translated by William Whiston (1667–1752). Hendrickson Publishers, Peabody, Massachusetts, p. 720.
126. Josephus, F., 1987, *The Life of Flavius Josephus*, Paragraph 75, in *The Works of Josephus*, translated by William Whiston (1667–1752). Hendrickson Publishers, Peabody, Massachusetts, p. 25.
127. Bible, King James Version, Matthew 26:35, 26:74.
128. Butterfield, H., 1973, Christianity in History, in *Dictionary of the History of Ideas*, vol. 1, edited by Philip P. Wiener. Charles Scribner's Sons, New York, p. 412.
129. Bible, King James Version, Exodus 20:3.
130. *Encyclopædia Britannica*, Eleventh Edition, 1911, Christianity. Encyclopædia Britannica Company, New York, p. 281.
131. Montague, F. C. (editor), 1903, *Critical and Historical Essays Contributed to the Edinburgh Review by Lord Macaulay* (Essay on Lord Bacon, July, 1837). G. P. Putnam's Sons, New York, p. 198–199.
132. Sarton, G., 1927, *Introduction to the History of Science*, vol. 1. Carnegie Institution, Washington, DC, p. 10.
133. Phillips, W. D., 1985, *Slavery from Roman Times to the Early Transatlantic Trade*. University of Minnesota Press, Minneapolis, p. 19–21.

134. Bible, King James Version, Matthew 22:37–22:39.
135. *Encyclopædia Britannica*, Eleventh Edition, 1910, Christianity. Encyclopædia Britannica Company, New York, page 282.
136. Bible, King James Version, John 21:25.
137. Bornkamm, G., 1971, *Paul*, translated by D. M. G. Stalker. Harper & Row, New York, p. 4–5.
138. Bible, King James Version, Acts 6:8.
139. Ibid., Acts 6:11.
140. Ibid., Acts 7:52.
141. Ibid., Acts 7:56.
142. Ibid., Acts 7:59.
143. Ibid., Acts 8:1.
144. Ibid., Acts 8:3.
145. Ibid., Acts 9:1–9:2.
146. Ibid., Acts 9:3–9:5, 9:8–9:9.
147. Ibid., 1 Corinthians 15:8.
148. Ibid., Acts 9:18, 9:20.
149. *Encyclopædia Britannica*, Eleventh Edition, 1911, Paul, the Apostle, vol. 20. Encyclopædia Britannica Company, New York, page 941.
150. Bible, King James Version, Galatians 2:16.
151. *The Living Bible Paraphrased*, 1971, Galatians 2:19. Tyndale House Publishers, Wheaton, Illinois, p. 942.
152. *Encyclopædia Britannica*, Eleventh Edition, 1911, Paul, The Apostle, vol. 20. Encyclopædia Britannica Company, New York, p. 941.
153. *Encyclopædia Britannica*, Eleventh Edition, 1911, Church History, vol. 6. Encyclopædia Britannica Company, New York, p. 331.
154. Bible, King James Version, Romans 5:12.
155. Ibid., Romans 5:18.
156. *The Living Bible Paraphrased*, 1971, Romans 8:23. Tyndale House Publishers, Wheaton, Illinois, p. 904.
157. *Encyclopædia Britannica*, Eleventh Edition, 1911, Paul, The Apostle, vol. 20. Encyclopædia Britannica Company, New York, p. 939.
158. Ibid.
159. *Encyclopædia Britannica*, Eleventh Edition, 1910, Christianity, vol. 6. Encyclopædia Britannica Company, New York, p. 284.
160. *The Living Bible Paraphrased*, 1971, 2 Corinthians 12:3–12:4. Tyndale House Publishers, Wheaton, Illinois, p. 939.
161. Bible, King James Version, 1 Corinthians 1:19–1:20.
162. Ibid., Collosians 2:8–2:10.
163. Ibid., Galatians 1:17.
164. Ibid., Galatians 1:11–1:12.
165. Ibid., Galatians 1:18.
166. Ibid., 2 Corinthians 11:24–11:27.
167. Ibid., Genesis 17:9–17:10.
168. Ibid., Romans 2:28–2:29.
169. Ibid., Acts 15:28–15:29.
170. Ibid., Acts 21:27–21:28.
171. Ibid., Acts 22:25.
172. Ibid., Acts 23:6–23:9.
173. Ibid., Acts 23:24.
174. Ibid., Acts 24:26–24:27.
175. Ibid., Acts 25:9.
176. Ibid., Acts 25:11.
177. Ibid., Acts 26:24.
178. Ibid., Acts 26:31–26:32.
179. Ibid. Acts 28:30–28:31.
180. *Encyclopædia Britannica*, Eleventh Edition, 1911, Paul, The Apostle, vol. 20. Encyclopædia Britannica Company, New York, p. 952.
181. Frazer, J. G., 1919, *The Golden Bough*, Third Edition, vol. 2. Macmillan, London, p. 119.
182. Frazer, J. G., 1920, *The Golden Bough*, vol. 9, The Scapegoat. Macmillan, London, p. 328.
183. Frazer, J. G., 1920, *The Golden Bough*, vol. 9, The Scapegoat. Macmillan, London, p. 421.
184. Cyprian, 1844, *The Epistles of S. Cyprian*, Epistle 73, Paragraphs 18, 21. John Henry Parker, Oxford. p. 255, 257.

185. Schaff, P., 1884, *History of the Christian Church*, vol. 2, *Ante-Nicene Christianity A.D. 100–325*. Charles Schribner's Sons, New York, p. 124.

186. Burkhart, R. L. R., 1942, The Rise of the Christian Priesthood. *The Journal of Religion*, vol. 22, no. 2, p. 198.

187. Schaff, P., 1884, *History of the Christian Church*, vol. 2, *Ante-Nicene Christianity A.D. 100–325*. Charles Schribner's Sons, p. 128.

188. Ibid.

189. Ibid., p. 41.

190. Ibid., p. 43.

191. Ibid., p. 44.

192. Ibid., p. 48.

193. Ibid., p. 43.

194. Ibid., p. 54.

195. Antoninus, Marcus Aurelius, 1875, *The Thoughts of the Emperor M. Aurelius Antoninus*, Book 11, Paragraph 3, translated by George Long, Second Edition. George Bell & Sons, London, p. 186.

196. Gibbon, E., 1909, *The History of the Decline and Fall of the Roman Empire*, Chapter 16, edited by J. B. Bury, vol. 2. Methuen & Co., London, p. 112.

197. Schaff, P., 1884, *History of the Christian Church*, vol. 2, *Ante-Nicene Christianity A.D. 100–325*. Charles Schribner's Sons, New York, p. 60.

198. Ibid., p. 63.

199. Gibbon, E., 1909, *The History of the Decline and Fall of the Roman Empire*, Chapter 16, edited by J. B. Bury, vol. 2. Methuen & Co., London, p. 124.

200. Schaff, P., 1884, *History of the Christian Church*, vol. 2, *Ante-Nicene Christianity A.D. 100–325*. Charles Schribner's Sons, New York, p. 71.

201. Gibbon, E., 1909, *The History of the Decline and Fall of the Roman Empire*, Chapter 16, edited by J. B. Bury, vol. 2. Methuen & Co., London, p. 128.

202. Ibid.

203. Ibid., p. 130–131.

204. Lecky, W. E. H., 1897, *History of European Morals*, Third Edition, Revised, vol. 1. D. Appleton, New York, p. 463.

205. Eusebius, 1851, *Ecclesiastical History*, Book 8, Chapter 6, translated by C. F. Cruse. Henry G. Bohn, London, p. 306.

206. Ibid., Book 8, Chapter 10, p. 313.

207. Ibid., Book 8, Chapter 12, p. 317.

208. Ibid.

209. *Encyclopædia Britannica*, Eleventh Edition, 1910, Constantine I, vol. 6. Encyclopædia Britannica Company, New York, p. 989.

210. Mommsen, T., 1996, *A History of Rome Under the Emperors*. Routledge, London, p. 441.

211. Eusebius, 1845, *The Life of the Blessed Emperor Constantine*, Book 1, Chapter 27, in *The Greek Ecclesiastical Historians of the First Six Centuries of the Christian Era*, vol. 1. Samuel Bagster and Sons, London, p. 25.

212. Ibid., Book 1, Chapter 28, p. 26–27.

213. Ibid., Book 1, Chapter 29, p. 27.

214. Schaff, P., 1884, *History of the Christian Church*, vol. 3, *Nicene and Post-Nicene Christianity A.D. 311–600*. Charles Schribner's Sons, New York, p. 20–21.

215. Wells, H. G., 1921, *The Outline of History*, Third Edition. Macmillan, New York, p. 519.

216. Schaff, P., 1884, *History of the Christian Church*, vol. 2, *Ante-Nicene Christianity A.D. 100–325*. Charles Schribner's Sons, New York, p. 72.

217. Eusebius, 1845, *The Life of the Blessed Emperor Constantine*, Book 4, Chapter 62, in *The Greek Ecclesiastical Historians of the First Six Centuries of the Christian Era*, vol. 1. Samuel Bagster and Sons, London, p. 225.

218. *Encyclopædia Britannica*, Eleventh Edition, 1910, Constantine I, vol. 6. Encyclopædia Britannica Company, New York, p. 989.

219. Schaff, P., 1884, *History of the Christian Church*, vol. 3, *Nicene and Post-Nicene Christianity A.D. 311–600*. Charles Schribner's Sons, New York, p. 620.

220. Ibid., p. 621.

221. *Encyclopædia Britannica*, Eleventh Edition, 1910, Christianity, vol. 6. Encyclopædia Britannica Company, New York, p. 284.

222. Schaff, P., 1884, *History of the Christian Church*, vol. 3, *Nicene and Post-Nicene Christianity A.D. 311–600*. Charles Schribner's Sons, New York, p. 623.

223. *Encyclopædia Britannica*, Ninth Edition, 1890, Creeds, vol. 6. Henry G. Allen, New York, p. 560.

224. *Encyclopædia Britannica*, Eleventh Edition, 1910, Christianity, vol. 6. Encyclopædia Britannica Company, New York, p. 284.

225. Ibid.

226. *Encyclopædia Britannica*, Eleventh Edition, 1911, Church History, vol. 6. Encyclopædia Britannica Company, New York, p. 332.

227. Schaff, P., 1884, *History of the Christian Church*, vol. 3, *Nicene and Post-Nicene Christianity A.D. 311–600*. Charles Schribner's Sons, New York, p. 63–64.

228. Lecky, W. E. H., 1897, *History of European Morals*, Third Edition, Revised, vol. 1. D. Appleton, New York, p. 335.

229. Eusebius, 1851, *Ecclesiastical History*, Book 1, Chapter 2, translated by C. F. Cruse. Henry G. Bohn, London, p. 6–7.

230. Tertullian, 1869, Ad Martyras, Paragraph 2, in *Ante-Nicene Christian Library*, edited by Rev. Alexander Roberts and James Donaldson, vol. 11, *The Writings of Tertullian*, vol. 1. T. & T. Clark, Edinburgh, p. 2.

231. Tertullian, 1869, *Apologeticus*, Paragraph 45, in *Ante-Nicene Christian Library*, edited by Rev. Alexander Roberts and James Donaldson, vol. 11, *The Writings of Tertullian*, vol. 1. T. & T. Clark, Edinburgh, p. 127.

232. Ibid.

233. Hippolytus, 1868, *The Refutation of All Heresies*, Book X, Chapter 30, in *Ante-Nicene Christian Library*, edited by Rev. Alexander Roberts and James Donaldson, vol. 7, *Hippolytus, Bishop of Rome*, vol. 1. T. & T. Clark, Edinburgh, p. 401.

234. Ibid., p. 401–402.

235. Gregory Nazianzen, 1894, *Orations*, Oration 2, Paragraph 7, in *A Select Library of Nicene and Post-Nicene Fathers of the Christian Church*, edited by Philip Schaff and Henry Wace, vol. 7. The Christian Literature Company, New York, p. 206.

236. *Encyclopædia Britannica*, Eleventh Edition, 1911, Monasticism, vol. 18. Encyclopædia Britannica Company, New York, p. 687.

237. Schaff, P., 1884, *History of the Christian Church*, vol. 2, *Ante-Nicene Christianity A.D. 100–325*. Charles Schribner's Sons, New York, p. 390.

238. Schaff, P., 1884, *History of the Christian Church*, vol. 3, *Nicene and Post-Nicene Christianity A.D. 311–600*. Charles Schribner's Sons, New York, p. 156.

239. Lecky, W. E. H., 1897, *History of European Morals*, Third Edition, Revised, vol. 2. D. Appleton, New York, p. 107–108.

240. Schaff, P., 1884, *History of the Christian Church*, vol. 3, *Nicene and Post-Nicene Christianity A.D. 311–600*. Charles Schribner's Sons, New York, p. 167.

241. *Encyclopædia Britannica*, Eleventh Edition, 1911, Simeon Stylites, St., vol. 25. Encyclopædia Britannica Company, New York, p. 122.

242. Lecky, W. E. H., 1897, *History of European Morals*, Third Edition, Revised, vol. 2. D. Appleton, New York, p. 111–112.

243. Ogg, F. A. (editor), 1908, *A Source Book of Mediaeval History*. American Book Company, New York, p. 84.

244. *Encyclopædia Britannica*, Eleventh Edition, 1911, Monasticism, vol. 18. Encyclopædia Britannica Company, New York, p. 688.

245. Ogg, F. A. (editor), 1908, *A Source Book of Mediaeval History*. American Book Company, New York, p. 84.

246. Ibid., p. 86–87.

247. Ibid., p. 87.

248. Ibid., p. 88.

249. Schaff, P., 1884, *History of the Christian Church*, vol. 3, *Nicene and Post-Nicene Christianity A.D. 311–600*. Charles Schribner's Sons, New York, p. 160.

250. Ibid., p. 168.

251. Ibid., p, 162.
252. Ibid., p. 159.
253. Ibid., p. 170.
254. Sarton, G., 1927, *Introduction to the History of Science*, vol. 1. Carnegie Institution, Washington, DC, p. 347.
255. Haskins, C. H., 1957, *The Renaissance of the 12th Century* (first published in 1927 by Harvard University Press, Cambridge, Massachusetts). Meridian Books, New York, p. 33.
256. Ibid., p. 71.
257. Ibid., p. 368–396.
258. Irenaeus, 1903, *Against Heresies*, Book 1, Chapter 26, Paragraph 1, in *The Ante-Nicene Fathers, vol. 1, The Apostilic Fathers with Justin Martyr and Irenaeus*, edited by Alexander Roberts and James Donaldson. Charles Scribner's Sons, New York, p. 347.
259. Tertullian, 1870, *De Anima (On the Soul)*, Chapter 3, in *Anti-Nicene Christian Library*, vol. 15, *The Writings of Tertullian*, vol. 2, edited by Alexander Roberts and James Donaldson. T. & T. Clark, Edinburgh, p. 416–417.
260. Ibid., p. 417.
261. Tertullian, 1870, *On Prescription Against Heretics*, Chapter 7, in *Anti-Nicene Christian Library*, edited by Alexander Roberts and James Donaldson, vol. 15, *The Writings of Tertullian*, vol. 2. T. & T. Clark, Edinburgh, p. 9–10.
262. Lactantius, 1871, *The Divine Institutes*, Book 3, *Of the False Wisdom of the Philosophers*, Chapter 1, in *Ante-Nicene Christian Library*, vol. 21, *The Works of Lactantius*, vol. 1, edited by Alexander Roberts and James Donaldson. T. & T. Clark, Edinburgh, p. 139.
263. Ibid., Chapter 2, p. 141.
264. Ibid.
265. Ibid., Chapter 24, p. 196.
266. Ibid., p. 196–197.
267. Ibid., p. 196.
268. Ibid., p. 197.
269. Schaff, P., 1884, *History of the Christian Church*, Revised Edition, *Ante-Nicene Christianity*, A.D. 100–325. T. & T. Clark, Edinburgh, p. 101.
270. Digeser, E. D., 1998, Lactantius, Porphyry, and the Debate Over Religious Toleration. *Journal of Roman Studies*, vol. 88, p. 129.
271. St. Athanasius, 1892, *On the Incarnation of the Word*, Chapter 49, in *A Select Library of Nicene and Post-Nicene Fathers, Second Series*, vol. 4, *St. Athanasius, Select Works and Letters*, edited by Philip Schaff and Henry Wace. The Christian Literature Society, New York, p. 63.
272. St. Hilary, 1902, *On the Trinity*, Book I, Paragraph 13, in *A Select Library of Nicene and Post-Nicene Fathers, Second Series*, vol. 9, edited by Philip Schaff and Henry Wace. Charles Scribner's Sons, New York, p. 43.
273. Ibid., p. 43–44.
274. St. Basil, 1895, *The Hexaemeron*, Homily 1, Paragraph 3, in *A Select Library of Nicene and Post-Nicene Fathers of the Christian Church*, vol. 8, *St. Basil. Letters and Select Works*, edited by Philip Schaff and Henry Wace. The Christian Literature Company, New York, p. 53–54.
275. Ibid., Homily 1, Paragraphs 10, 11, p. 57–58.
276. St. Ambrose, 1896, *Duties of the Clergy*, Book I, Chapter 26, Paragraphs 122–123, in *A Select Library of Nicene and Post-Nicene Fathers of the Christian Church, Second Series*, vol. 10, *St. Ambrose Select Works and Letters*, edited by Philip Schaff and Henry Wace. The Christian Literature Company, New York, p. 21.
277. Socrates Scholasticus, 1890, *Ecclesiastical History*, Book 3, Chapter 16, in *A Select Library of Nicene and Post-Nicene Fathers, Second Series*, vol. 2, edited by Philip Schaff and Henry Wace. The Christian Literature Company, New York, p. 87.
278. Ibid.
279. Ibid., p. 87–88.
280. St. Augustine, 1887, *On Christian Doctrine*, Book 2, Chapter 40, Paragraph 60, translated by J. F. Shaw, in *A Select Library of Nicene and Post-Nicene Fathers*, vol. 2, *St. Augustine's City of God and Christian Doctrine*, edited by Philip Schaff. Charles Scribner's Sons, New York, p. 554.

281. Schaff, P., 1884, *History of the Christian Church*, vol. 3, *Nicene and Post-Nicene Christianity* A.D. 311–600. Charles Schribner's Sons, New York, p. 942, 944.
282. Ibid., p. 942.
283. Ibid., p. 942–943.
284. Gibbon, E., 1911, *The History of the Decline and Fall of the Roman Empire*, Chapter 47, edited by J. B. Bury, vol. 5. Methuen & Co., London, p. 116.
285. Ibid., p. 115.
286. Socrates Scholasticus, 1890, *Ecclesiastical History*, Book 7, Chapter 14, in *A Select Library of Nicene and Post-Nicene Fathers, Second Series*, vol. 2, edited by Philip Schaff and Henry Wace. The Christian Literature Company, New York, p. 160.
287. Ibid.
288. Ibid.
289. Ibid.
290. Ibid., Book 7, Chapter 15, p. 160.
291. Ibid.
292. Rist, J. M., 1965, Hypatia. *Phoenix*, no. 3., vol. 19, p. 220.
293. Socrates Scholasticus, 1890, *Ecclesiastical History*, Book 7, Chapter 15, in *A Select Library of Nicene and Post-Nicene Fathers, Second Series*, vol. 2, edited by Philip Schaff and Henry Wace. The Christian Literature Company, New York, p. 160.
294. Ibid.
295. Trimpi, H. P., 1973, Demonology, in *Dictionary of the History of Ideas*, vol. 1, edited by Philip P. Wiener. Charles Scribner's Sons, New York, p. 667.
296. Hesiod, 1920, Works and Days (lines 122–124), in *Hesiod, the Homeric Hymns and Homerica*, with an English translation by Hugh G. Evelyn-White. London, William Heinemann, p. 11.
297. Oldfield, A., 1865, On the Aborigines of Australia. *Transactions of the Ethnological Society of London, New Series*, vol. 3, p. 228.
298. Williams, M., 1885, *Religious Thought and Life in India*. John Murray, London, p. 210–211.
299. *Encyclopædia Britannica*, Eleventh Edition, 1910, Demonology, vol. 8. Encyclopædia Britannica Company, New York, p. 5.
300. Ibid.
301. David-Neel, A., 1932, *Magic and Mystery in Tibet*, First Edition. Claude Kendall, New York, p. 141.
302. Frazer, J. G., 1913, *The Golden Bough*, Third Edition, vol. 6, The Scapegoat. Macmillan, London, p. 102.
303. Fairbanks, A. 1898, *The First Philosophers of Greece*. Kegan Paul, Trench, Trübner & Co., Ltd., London, p. 6.
304. Plato, 1937, Symposium, in *The Dialogues of Plato*, translated into English by Benjamin Jowett (1817–1893), vol. 1. Random House, New York, p. 328 (203).
305. Ibid.
306. Porphyry, 1823, *On Abstinence from Animal Food*, Book 2, Chapter 39, in *Select Works of Porphyry*, translated by Thomas Taylor. Thomas Rodd, London, p. 76.
307. Ibid.
308. Ibid., Book 2, Chapter 38, p. 75.
309. Ibid., Book 2, Chapter 40, p. 77.
310. *Encyclopædia Britannica*, Eleventh Edition, 1910, Devil, vol. 8. Encyclopædia Britannica Company, New York, p. 121.
311. Bible, King James Version, Genesis 3:1, 3:4–3:5.
312. Caldwell, W., 1913, The Doctrine of Satan. I. In the Old Testament. *The Biblical World*, no. 1, vol. 41, p. 29.
313. Bible, King James Version, Job 1:7.
314. Pliny the Elder, 1855, *The Natural History of Pliny*, translated by John Bostock and H. T. Riley, Book 2, Chapter 6, vol. 1. Henry G. Bohn, London, p. 29.
315. Bible, King James Version, Isaiah 14:12–14:15.
316. Ibid., Isaiah 14:4.
317. Bible, King James Version, Luke 10:18.
318. Tertullian, 1868, *Against Marcion*, Book 2, Chapter 10, in *Ante-Nicene Christian Library*, vol. 7, *Tertullianus Against Marcion*, edited by Alexander Roberts and James Donaldson. T. & T. Clark, Edinburgh, p. 80–81.
319. Bible, King James Version, Matthew 12:24.
320. Ibid., Matthew 12:26.

321. Ibid., Ephesians 2:2.

322. Ibid., Ephesians 6:12.

323. Ibid., Luke 4:33–4:35.

324. Ibid., Mark 1:32, 1:34.

325. Ibid, Mark 16:17–16:18.

326. Ibid., Mark 5:12–5:13.

327. Ibid., Acts 16:16, 16:18.

328. Ibid., Acts 19:13, 19:15–19:16.

329. Milton, J., 1667, *Paradise Lost. A Poem Written in Ten Books*. Peter Parker, London.

330. Ibid., Book 5, Lines 655–658.

331. Tertullian, 1903, Apology, Chapter 22, in *The Ante-Nicene Christian Fathers*, vol. 3, *Latin Christianity. Its Founder, Tertullian*, edited by Alexander Roberts and James Donaldson. Charles Scribner's Sons, New York, p. 36.

332. Ibid.

333. Lactantius, 1871, *The Divine Institutes*, Book 2, Chapter 15, in *Ante-Nicene Christian Library*, vol. 21, *The Works of Lactantius*, vol. 1, edited by Alexander Roberts and James Donaldson. T. & T. Clark, Edinburgh, p. 128.

334. Schaff, P., 1885, *History of the Christian Church*, vol. 4, Medieval Christianity A.D. 590–1073. Charles Schribner's Sons, New York, p. 212.

335. *Encyclopædia Britannica*, Eleventh Edition, 1910, Gregory (Popes), vol. 12. Encyclopædia Britannica Company, New York, p. 566.

336. Schaff, P., 1885, *History of the Christian Church*, vol. 4, Medieval Christianity A.D. 590–1073. Charles Schribner's Sons, New York, p. 213.

337. Ibid., p. 212.

338. Ibid., p. 213.

339. *Encyclopædia Britannica*, Eleventh Edition, 1910, Gregory (Popes), vol. 12. Encyclopædia Britannica Company, New York, p. 566.

340. Ibid., p. 567.

341. Ibid.

342. Greenwood, T., 1858, *A Political History of the Greek Latin Patriarchate*, Books III. IV. & V.. C. J. Stewart, London, p. 207.

343. *Encyclopædia Britannica*, Eleventh Edition, 1910, Gregory (Popes), vol. 12. Encyclopædia Britannica Company, New York, p. 567.

344. Hutton, W. H., 1913, Gregory the Great, in *The Cambridge Medieval History*, edited by H. H. Gwatkin and J. P. Whitney, vol. 2. Macmillan, New York, p. 261.

345. Bible, King James Version, Matthew 16:18.

346. *Encyclopædia Britannica*, Eleventh Edition, 1911, Pope, vol. 22. Encyclopædia Britannica Company, New York, p. 81.

347. *Encyclopædia Britannica*, Eleventh Edition, 1910, Gregory (Popes), vol. 12. Encyclopædia Britannica Company, New York, p. 567.

348. Schaff, P., 1885, *History of the Christian Church*, vol. 4, Medieval Christianity A.D. 590–1073. Charles Schribner's Sons, New York, p. 228.

349. Ibid., p. 226.

350. Gregory I, 1911, *The Dialogues of St. Gregory*, Book I, Chapter 4. Philip Lee Warner, London, p. 17–18.

351. Ibid., Book 2, Chapter 8, p. 68.

352. Ibid., Book 2, Chapter 9, p. 69.

353. Ibid.

354. Rogers, K. M., 1966, *The Troublesome Helpmate*. University of Washington Press, Seattle, p. 37.

355. *Encyclopædia Britannica*, Eleventh Edition, 1910, Charity and Charities, vol. 5. Encyclopædia Britannica Company, New York, p. 865.

356. Livius, T., 1850, *The History of Rome*, Books Twenty-Seven to Thirty-Six, Book 34, Chapter 1, translated by Cyrus Edmonds. Henry G. Bohn, London, p. 1490.

357. Ibid., Book 34, Chapter 2, p. 1491.

358. Ibid.

359. Ibid., Book 34, Chapter 3, p. 1491.

360. Juvenal, 1918, Satire 6, *The Ways of Women*, Lines 50–52, in *Juvenal and Perseus*, translated by G. G. Ramsay. William Heinemann, London, p. 87.

361. Ibid., Lines 92–96, p. 91.

362. Ibid., Lines 161–168, p. 97.

363. Ibid., Lines 207–213, p. 100–101.

364. Ibid., Lines 242–243, p. 103.

365. Ibid., Lines 232–241, p. 102–103.

366. Ibid., Lines 268–280, p. 105.

367. Ibid., Lines 246–349, p. 111.

368. Ibid., Lines 593–601, p. 133.

369. Ibid., Lines 434–447, p. 119.

370. Rogers, K. M., 1966, *The Troublesome Helpmate*. University of Washington Press, Seattle, p. 38.

371. Bible, King James Version, Genesis 2:18.

372. Ibid., Genesis 1:27.

373. Ibid. Genesis 2:22.

374. Rogers, K. M., 1966, *The Troublesome Helpmate*. University of Washington Press, Seattle, p. 4.

375. Bible, King James Version, Genesis 3:6.

376. Ibid., Genesis 3:13.

377. Ibid., Genesis 3:16.

378. Ibid., Genesis 6:4.

379. Ibid., Ecclesiastes 7:26.

380. Ibid., Proverbs 12:4.

381. Ibid., 1 Timothy 2:11–2:13.

382. Ibid., 1 Corinthians 14:34–14:35.

383. Ibid., Ephesians 5:25.

384. Ibid., Ephesians 5:22–5:24.

385. Ibid., 1 Corinthians 11:8–11:9.

386. *Encyclopædia Britannica*, Eleventh Edition, 1911, Tertullian, vol. 26. Encyclopædia Britannica Company, New York, p. 661.

387. Tertullian, 1869, *On Female Dress*, Book I, Chapter 1, in *Ante-Nicene Christian Library*, edited by Rev. Alexander Roberts and James Donaldson, vol. 11, *The Writings of Tertullian*, vol. 1. T. & T. Clark, Edinburgh, p. 304–305.

388. Tertullian, 1870, *On Exhortation to Chastity*, Chapter 9, in *Ante-Nicene Christian Library*, edited by Rev. Alexander Roberts and James Donaldson, vol. 18, *The Writings of Tertullian*, vol. 3. T. & T. Clark, Edinburgh, p. 14.

389. Schaff, P., 1859, *History of the Christian Church*, A.D. 1–311. Charles Scribner, New York, p. 333–334.

390. Lactantius, 1871, *The Divine Institutes*, Book 2, Chapter 15, in *Ante-Nicene Christian Library*, vol. 21, *The Works of Lactantius*, vol. 1, edited by Alexander Roberts and James Donaldson. T. & T. Clark, Edinburgh, p. 126–127.

391. Lecky, W. E. H., 1897, *History of European Morals*, Third Edition, Revised, vol. 2. D. Appleton, New York, p. 118–119.

392. Ibid., p. 120.

393. Ibid., p. 121.

394. Gregory I, 1911, *The Dialogues of St. Gregory*, Book 2, Chapter 2. Philip Lee Warner, London, p. 55.

395. Ibid., Book 2, Chapter 8, p. 65.

396. Ibid., p. 66.

397. *Encyclopædia Britannica*, Eleventh Edition, 1911, Origen, vol. 20. Encyclopædia Britannica Company, New York, p. 270.

398. Bible, King James Version, Matthew 19:12.

399. Eusebius, 1851, *Ecclesiastical History*, Book 6, Chapter 8, translated by C. F. Cruse. Henry G. Bohn, London, p. 212.

400. *Oxford English Dictionary*, 1989, Second Edition, Online Version.

401. Ibid.

402. Lecky, W. E. H., 1897, *History of European Morals*, Third Edition, Revised, vol. 2. D. Appleton, New York, p. 78–79.

403. Hesiod, 1920, *Works and Days* (lines 342–345), in *Hesiod, the Homeric Hymns and Homerica*, with an English translation by Hugh G. Evelyn-White. London, William Heinemann, p. 29.

404. Hamel, G., 1990, *Poverty and Charity in Roman Palestine, First Three Centuries C.E.*. University of California Press, Berkeley, p. 219.

405. Plautus, 1852, *Trinummus (Three Pieces of Money)*, Act 2, Scene 2, in *The Comedies of Plautus*, vol. 1, translated by Henry Thomas Riley. Henry G. Bohn, London, p. 18–19.

406. Hands, A. R., 1968, *Charities and Social Aid in Greece and Rome.* Cornell University Press, Ithaca, New York, p. 26–28.

407. Plutarch, 1952, Pericles, in *The Lives of the Noble Grecians and Romans*, translated by John Dryden (1631–1700), *Great Books of the Western World*, vol. 14. William Benton, Chicago, p. 125.

408. Ibid., p. 127.

409. Ierley, M., 1984, *Charity for All. Welfare and Society, Ancient Times to the Present.* Praeger, New York, p. 12.

410. Appian, 1913, *The Civil Wars*, Book 1, Chapter 3, Paragraph 21, translated by Horace White, in *Appian's Roman History*, vol. 3. William Heinemann, London, p. 43.

411. Ierley, M., 1984, *Charity for All. Welfare and Society, Ancient Times to the Present.* Praeger, New York, p. 7–8.

412. Suetonius, C. T., 1906, *The Lives of the Twelve Caesars*, Julius Caesar, Paragraph 41. George Bell & Sons, London, p. 28.

413. Ibid., Augustus, Paragraph 42, p. 105.

414. Lecky, W. E. H., 1897, *History of European Morals*, Third Edition, Revised, vol. 2. D. Appleton, New York, p. 75.

415. Tacitus, 1942, *Annals*, Book 12, Paragraph 43, in *The Complete Works of Tacitus*, translated by Alfred John Church (1824–1912) and William Jackson Brodribb (1829–1905). Modern Library, New York, p. 270.

416. Juvenal, 1918, Satire 10, *The Vanity of Human Wishes*, Lines 76–80, in *Juvenal and Perseus*, translated by G. G. Ramsay. William Heinemann, London, p. 199.

417. Ierley, M., 1984, *Charity for All. Welfare and Society, Ancient Times to the Present.* Praeger, New York, p. 11.

418. Cicero, 1899, *De Officiis (On Duties)*, Book 1, Chapter 7, translated by George B. Gardiner. Methuen & Co., London, p. 11.

419. Bible, King James Version, Mark 12:30.

420. Ibid., Mark 12:31.

421. Ibid., Galatians 5:14.

422. Ibid., Genesis 1:27.

423. Ibid., Luke 10:29.

424. Ibid., Luke 10:30–10:37.

425. Ibid., Luke 10:36–10:37.

426. Ibid., Leviticus 19:9–19:10.

427. Ibid., Leviticus 19:18.

428. Ibid., Matthew 19:21.

429. Tertullian, 1869, *Apology*, Paragraph 39, in *Ante-Nicene Christian Library*, edited by Rev. Alexander Roberts and James Donaldson, vol. 11, *The Writings of Tertullian*, vol. 1. T. & T. Clark, Edinburgh, p. 119.

430. Schaff, P., 1884, *History of the Christian Church*, vol. 3, *Nicene and Post-Nicene Christianity* A.D. *311–600.* Charles Scribner's Sons, New York, p. 894.

431. Ibid., p. 899.

432. St. Basil, 1895, Letter 14, in *A Select Library of Nicene and Post-Nicene Fathers of the Christian Church, Second Series*, edited by Philip Schaff and Henry Wace, vol. 8, *St. Basil, Letters and Select Works.* The Christian Literature Company, New York, p. 124.

433. Anonymous, 1895, *Prolegomena, Sketch of the Life and Works of Saint Basil*, Chapter 5, The Presbyterate, in *A Select Library of Nicene and Post-Nicene Fathers of the Christian Church, Second Series*, edited by Philip Schaff and Henry Wace, vol. 8, *St. Basil, Letters and Select Works.* The Christian Literature Company, New York, p. xix.

434. Ibid., p. xxi.

435. Ibid., p. xxi–xxii.

436. Ibid., Chapter 3, Life at Caesarea; Baptism; and Adoption of Monastic Life, p. xvii–xviii.

437. Schaff, P., 1884, *History of the Christian Church*, vol. 3, *Nicene and Post-Nicene Christianity* A.D. *311–600.* Charles Scribner's Sons, New York, p. 902.

438. St. Basil, 1895, Letter 150, Paragraph 3, in *A Select Library of Nicene and Post-Nicene Fathers of the Christian Church, Second Series*, edited by Philip Schaff and Henry Wace, vol. 8, *St. Basil, Letters and Select Works.* The Christian Literature Company, New York, p. 208.

439. Gregroy Nazianzen, 1894, Oration 43, The Panegyric on S. Basil, Paragraph 63, in *A Select Library of Nicene and Post-Nicene Fathers of the Christian Church, Second Series*, edited by Philip Schaff and Henry Wace, vol. 7, *St. Cyril of Jerusalem, S. Gregory Nazianzen.* The Christian Literaure Company, New York, p. 416.

440. Sulpitius Severus, 1894, *Life of St. Martin*, Chapter 2, in *A Select Library of Nicene and Post-Nicene Fathers of the Christian Church, Second Series*, edited by Philip Schaff and Henry Wace, vol. 11. The Christian Literature Company, New York, p. 4.

441. Ibid., p. 5.

442. Ibid., Chapter 3, p. 5.

443. Ibid.

444. Ibid.

445. Ibid.

Chapter 2.

1. *Encyclopædia Britannica*, Eleventh Edition, 1911, Middle Ages, vol. 18. Encyclopædia Britannica Company, New York, p. 412.

2. Ibid., p. 409.

3. Ibid.

4. Mommsen, T. E., 1942, Petrarch's Conception of the 'Dark Ages.' *Speculum*, no. 2, vol. 17, p. 226–242.

5. Barnard, H. C., 1922, *The French Tradition in Education.* Cambridge University Press, p. 18.

6. Drake, S., 1978, *Galileo at Work, His Scientific Biography* (first published by the University of Chicago Press in 1978). Dover, New York, p. 377.

7. Grant, E., 1977, *Physical Science in the Middle Ages.* Cambridge University Press, Cambridge, p. 12.

8. White, L., 1940, Technology and Invention in the Middle Ages. *Speculum*, no. 2, vol. 15, p. 149.

9. Whitehead, A. N., 1967, *Science and the Modern World* (first published in 1925 by Macmillan, New York). Free Press, New York, p. 6.

10. Ta-k'un, W., 1952, An Interpretation of Chinese Economic History. *Past and Present*, no. 1, vol. 1, p. 9.

11. Ibid.

12. Cardwell, D. S. L., 1972, *Turning Points in Western Technology.* Science History Publications, New York, p. 5.

13. Landes, D. S., 1969, *The Unbound Prometheus.* Cambridge University Press, Cambridge, p. 28.

14. Mooney, J., 1896, The Ghost-Dance Religion and the Sioux Outbreak of 1890, in *Fourteenth Annual Report of the Bureau of Ethnology*, Part 2. U. S. Government Printing Office, Washington, p. 831.

15. Hippocrates, 1846, On the Nature of Man, in *The Writings of Hippocrates and Galen*, translated by John Redman Coxe. Lindsay and Blakiston, Philadelphia, p. 148.

16. Hippocrates, 1846, On the Art of Medicine, in *The Writings of Hippocrates and Galen*, translated by John Redman Coxe. Lindsay and Blakiston, Philadelphia, p. 54.

17. Nutton, V., 2004, *Ancient Medicine.* Routledge, London, p. 87, 152–153.

18. Diogenes Laërtius, 1905, *The Lives and Opinions of Eminent Philosophers*, Book 7, translated by C. D. Yonge. George Bell & Sons, London, p. 326.

19. Hippocrates, 1886, *The Genuine Works of Hippocrates*, vol. 2, translated by Francis Adams. William Wood and Company, New York, p. 192.

20. Xenophon, 1898, *Oeconomicus*, Chapter 4, Paragraphs 2 and 3, in *Xenophon's Minor Works*, translated by J. S. Watson. George Bell & Sons, London, p. 86.

21. Plutarch, 1952, Marcellus, in *The Lives of the Noble Grecians and Romans*, translated by John Dryden (1631–1700), *Great Books of the Western World*, vol. 14. William Benton, Chicago, p. 253.

22. Ibid., p. 252.

23. Aristotle, 1885, *The Politics of Aristotle*, vol. 1, Book 1, Chapter 11, translated by Benjamin Jowett (1817–1893). Oxford at the Clarendon Press, London, p. 20 (1258b).

24. Seneca, Lucius Annaeus, 1786, *The Epistles of Lucius Annaeus Seneca*, Epistle 90, vol. 2. W. Woodfall, London, p. 117.

25. Warmington, E. H., 2008, Posidonius, in *Complete Dictionary of Scientific Biography*, edited by Charles Gillispie, vol. 11. Cengage Learning, New York, p. 103.

26. Seneca, Lucius Annaeus, 1786, *The Epistles of Lucius Annaeus Seneca*, Epistle 90, vol. 2. W. Woodfall, London, p. 120.

27. Ibid., p. 119.

28. Ibid., p. 120.

29. Evidently these "hanging baths" were "heated tanks of some sort." Fagan, G. G., 1999, *Bathing in Public in the Roman World*. University of Michigan Press, Ann Arbor, p. 98.

30. Seneca, Lucius Annaeus, 1786, *The Epistles of Lucius Annaeus Seneca*, Epistle 90, vol. 2. W. Woodfall, London, p. 122.

31. Strabo, 1856, *The Geography of Strabo*, Book 14, Chapter 5, Paragraph 2, vol. 3, translated by H. C. Hamilton and W. Falconer. Henry G. Bohn, London, p. 51.

32. Ibid.

33. Yavetz, Z., 1988, *Slaves and Slavery in Ancient Rome*. Transaction Books, New Brunswick, New Jersey, p. 11.

34. Phillips, W. D., 1985, *Slavery from Roman Times to the Early Transatlantic Trade*. University of Minnesota Press, Minneapolis, p. 18.

35. *Encyclopædia Britannica*, Eleventh Edition, 1911, Slavery, vol. 25. Encyclopædia Britannica Company, New York, p. 218.

36. Vitruvius, 1960, *The Ten Books on Architecture*, Book 1, Chapter 1, Paragraph 1, translated by Morris Hicky Morgan (first published by Harvard University Press in 1914). Dover, New York, p. 5.

37. Bury, J. B., 1955, *The Idea of Progress* (first published in 1920 by MacMillan, London). Dover, New York, p. 7.

38. Weiling, F., 1991, Historical Study. Johann Gregor Mendel, 1822–1884. *American Journal of Medical Genetics*, vol. 40, p. 4.

39. Ibid., p. 3.

40. Ibid., p. 5.

41. *Encyclopædia Britannica Online*, 2009, Mendel, Gregor, retrieved March 16.

42. Weiling, F., 1991, Historical Study. Johann Gregor Mendel, 1822–1884. *American Journal of Medical Genetics*, vol. 40, p. 10–11.

43. Ibid., p. 10.

44. Henig, R. M., 2000, *The Monk in the Garden*. Houghton Mifflin, New York, p. 152.

45. Ibid., p. 171.

46. Weiling, F., 1991, Historical Study. Johann Gregor Mendel, 1822–1884. *American Journal of Medical Genetics*, vol. 40, p. 21–23.

47. Henig, R. M., 2000, *The Monk in the Garden*. Houghton Mifflin, New York, p. 179–198.

48. F. A. D., 1902, Mendel's Theory of Heredity. *Nature*, no. 1719, vol. 66, p. 573.

49. Singer, C., 1956, Epilogue. East and West in Retrospect, in *A History of Technology*, vol. 2, edited by Charles Singer. Oxford University Press, London, p. 771.

50. Wells, H. G., 1921, *The Outline of History*, Third Edition. Macmillan, New York, p. 347.

51. Clapham, M., 1957, Printing, in *A History of Technology*, Chapter 15, vol. 3, edited by Charles Singer. Oxford University Press, London, p. 386.

52. Ibid., p. 381.

53. Whitehead, A. N., 1967, *Science and the Modern World* (first published in 1925 by Macmillan, New York). Free Press, New York, p. 3–4.

54. Ibid., p. 12–13.

55. Whittaker, T., 1911, *Priests, Philosophers and Prophets*. Adam and Charles Black, London, p. 11.

56. Macmurray, J., 1939, *The Clue to History*. Harper & Brothers, New York, p. 86.

57. Popper, K., 1966, *The Open Society and Its Enemies*, Fifth Edition, vol. 2. Princeton University Press, Princeton, New Jersey, p. 243–244.

58. Archimedes, 2002, *The Works of Archimedes*, edited by T. L. Heath, first published as *The Works of Archimedes* (1897,

Cambridge Univ. Press) and *The Method of Archimedes* (1912, Cambridge Univ. Press). Dover, Mineola, New York, p. 151.

59. Aelianus, Claudius, 1665, *Claudius Aelianus his Various History*, Book 3, Chapter 36, translated by Thomas Stanley. Thomas Dring, London, p. 92.

60. White, A. D., 1909, *A History of the Warfare of Science with Theology in Christendom*, vol. 1 and 2. D. Appleton, New York.

61. Aristotle, 1923, *Meteorologica* (*Meteorology*), Book 1, Chapter 9, translated by E. W. Webster. Oxford at the Clarendon Press, London, p. 353a.

62. Bible, King James Version, Genesis 1:1.

63. *Encyclopædia Britannica*, Eleventh Edition, 1911, Map, vol. 17. Encyclopædia Britannica Company, New York, p. 638.

64. McCrindle, J. W., 1897, Introduction, *Christian Topography*. Hakluyt Society, London, p. iv–viii.

65. Cosmas Indicopleustes, 1897, *Christian Topography*, translated by J. W. McCrindle. Hakluyt Society, London, p. 9–10.

66. Bible, King James Version, Exodus 19:5–19:6.

67. Cosmas Indicopleustes, 1897, *Christian Topography*, translated by J. W. McCrindle. Hakluyt Society, London, p. 5.

68. Ibid., p. 145.

69. Bible, Exodus 26.

70. Bible, King James Version, Isaiah 11:12.

71. Cosmas Indicopleustes, 1897, *Christian Topography*, translated by J. W. McCrindle. Hakluyt Society, London, p. 43–44.

72. Bible, Genesis 6–8.

73. Cosmas Indicopleustes, 1897, *Christian Topography*, translated by J. W. McCrindle. Hakluyt Society, London, p. 30.

74. Ibid., p. 28.

75. Ibid., p. 16.

76. Ibid, p. 15.

77. Ibid.

78. Ibid., p. 17.

79. Ibid.

80. Ibid., p. 121.

81. Ibid., p. 136–137.

82. Schaff, P., 1885, *History of the Christian Church*, vol. 4, *Medieval Christianity* A.D. *590–1073*. Charles Scribner's Sons, New York, p. 662.

83. *Catholic Encyclopedia*, 1910, Isidore of Seville, vol. 8. Encyclopedia Press, New York, p. 186.

84. Haskins, C. H., 1957, *The Renaissance of the 12th Century* (first published in 1927 by Harvard University Press, Cambridge, Massachusetts). Meridian Books, New York, p. 304.

85. Curtius, E. R., 1990, *European Literature and the Latin Middle Ages*, translated from German by Willard R. Trask. Princeton University Press, Princeton, New Jersey, p. 496.

86. Brehaut, E., 1912, *An Encyclopedist of the Dark Ages, Isidore of Seville*, Studies in History, Economics, and Law, vol. 48, no. 1. Columbia University, New York, p. 78.

87. Ibid., p. 67–68.

88. Ibid., p. 77.

89. Haskins, C. H., 1957, *The Renaissance of the 12th Century* (first published in 1927 by Harvard University Press, Cambridge, Massachusetts). Meridian Books, New York, p. 279.

90. Brehaut, E., 1912, *An Encyclopedist of the Dark Ages, Isidore of Seville*, Studies in History, Economics, and Law, vol. 48, no. 1. Columbia University, New York, p. 51.

91. Ibid., p. 212.

92. Ibid., p. 55.

93. Ibid., p. 70.

94. Formigari, L., 1973, Chain of Being, in *Dictionary of the History of Ideas*, vol. 1, edited by Philip P. Wiener. Charles Scribner's Sons, New York, p. 325.

95. Plato, 1937, *The Republic*, Book 6, in *The Dialogues of Plato*, translated into English by Benjamin Jowett (1817–1893), vol. 1. Random House, New York, p. 770 (509).

96. Aristotle, 1912, *De Generatione Animalium* (*On the Generation of Animals*), Book 2, Chapter 1, translated by Arthur

Platt, in *The Works of Aristotle Translated into English*, vol. 5, edited by J. A. Smith and W. D. Ross. Oxford University Press, London, p. 733b.

97. Aristotle, 1910, *Historia Animalium (History of Animals)*, Book 8, Chapter 1, translated by D'Arcy Wentworth Thompson, in *The Works of Aristotle Translated into English*, vol. 4, edited by J. A. Smith and W. D. Ross. Oxford University Press, London, p. 588b.

98. Pope, A., 1907, Essay on Man, Lines 237–240, in *The Poetical Works of Alexander Pope*, edited by Adolphus Wiliam Ward. Macmillan, London, p. 199.

99. Brehaut, E., 1912, *An Encyclopedist of the Dark Ages, Isidore of Seville*, Studies in History, Economics, and Law, vol. 48, no. 1. Columbia University, New York, p. 72.

100. Ibid., p. 219.

101. Ibid., p. 219–220.

102. Ibid., p. 220.

103. Ibid.

104. Ibid., p. 225.

105. Ibid., p. 227–228.

106. Ibid., p. 244–245.

107. Ibid., p. 63.

108. Ibid., p. 63–64.

Chapter 3.

1. Watt, W. M., 1987, Muhammad, in *Dictionary of the Middle Ages*, vol. 8, edited by Joseph R. Strayer. Charles Scribner's Sons, New York, p. 522.

2. Lings, M., 1983, Muhammad, *His Life Based on the Earliest Sources*. Inner Traditions, Rochester, Vermont, p. 23.

3. Ibid.

4. Burckhardt, J. L., 1831, *Notes on the Bedouins and Wahabys*, vol. 1. Henry Colburn and Richard Bentley, London, p. 251.

5. *Encyclopædia Britannica*, Eleventh Edition, 1910, Bedouins, vol. 3. Encyclopædia Britannica Company, New York, p. 624.

6. Hitti, P. K., 1968, *The Arabs. a Short History* (first published in 1948 by Macmillan, London). St. Martin's Press, New York, p. 12.

7. Ibid., p. 13.

8. Böwering, G., 1985, Islam, Religion, in *Dictionary of the Middle Ages*, vol. 6, edited by Joseph R. Strayer. Charles Scribner's Sons, New York, p. 575.

9. Ibid.

10. *Encyclopædia Britannica*, Eleventh Edition, 1910, Bedouins, vol. 3. Encyclopædia Britannica Company, New York, p. 623.

11. *Encyclopædia Britannica*, Eleventh Edition, 1911, Mahomet, vol. 17. Encyclopædia Britannica Company, New York, p. 401.

12. Zwemer, S. M., 1920, *The Influence of Animism on Islam*. Macmillan, New York, p. 3.

13. Böwering, G., 1985, Islam, Religion, in *Dictionary of the Middle Ages*, vol. 6, edited by Joseph R. Strayer. Charles Scribner's Sons, New York, p. 575.

14. Margoliouth, D. S., 1905, *Mohammed and the Rise of Islam*, Third Edition, G. P. Putnam's Sons, New York, p. 19.

15. Rahman, F., 2005, Islam. An Overview, in *Encyclopedia of Religion*, Second Edition, edited by Lindsay Jones, vol. 7. Macmillan Reference, Detroit, p. 4561.

16. Henninger, J., 1981, Pre–Islamic Bedouin Religion, in *Studies on Islam*, translated and edited by Merlin L. Swartz. Oxford University Press, New York, p. 15.

17. Rahman, F., 2005, Islam. an Overview, in *Encyclopedia of Religion*, Second Edition, edited by Lindsay Jones, vol. 7. Macmillan Reference, Detroit, p. 4561.

18. Omar Khayyam, 1896, *Rubaiyat of Omar Khayyam*, Twenty-Sixth American Edition, Poem 71, translated by Edward Fitzgerald. Houghton, Mifflin and Company, Boston, p. 54.

19. Watt, W. M., 1987, Muhammad, in *Dictionary of the Middle Ages*, vol. 8, edited by Joseph R. Strayer. Charles Scribner's Sons, New York, p. 522.

20. *Encyclopædia Britannica*, Eleventh Edition, 1911, Mahomet, vol. 17. Encyclopædia Britannica Company, New York, p. 400.

21. Ibn Ishaq (died c. 768), 1967, *The Life of Muhammad* (first published in 1955 by Oxford University Press, London), translated by Alfred Guillaume (1888–1965). Ameena Saiyid, Oxford University Press, Karachi, Pakistan, p. 93.

22. Rahman, F., 2005, Islam. An Overview, in *Encyclopedia of Religion*, Second Edition, edited by Lindsay Jones, vol. 7. Macmillan Reference, Detroit, p. 4561.

23. Watt, W. M., 1987, Muhammad, in *Dictionary of the Middle Ages*, vol. 8, edited by Joseph R. Strayer. Charles Scribner's Sons, New York, p. 522.

24. Muir, W., 1861, *The Life of Mahomet*, vol. 2. Smith, Elder and Co., London, p. 31.

25. Böwering, G., 1985, Islam, Religion, in *Dictionary of the Middle Ages*, vol. 6, edited by Joseph R. Strayer. Charles Scribner's Sons, New York, p. 576.

26. Bible, Luke 1:26–1:38.

27. Ibn Ishaq (died c. 768), 1967, *The Life of Muhammad* (first published in 1955 by Oxford University Press, London), translated by Alfred Guillaume (1888–1965). Ameena Saiyid, Oxford University Press, Karachi, Pakistan, p. 106.

28. Ibid.

29. Koran, 1861, Sura 96, verses 1–5, translated by John Medows Rodwell (1808–1900). Williams and Norgate, London, p. 1–2.

30. Ibn Ishaq (died c. 768), 1967, *The Life of Muhammad* (first published in 1955 by Oxford University Press, London), translated by Alfred Guillaume (1888–1965). Ameena Saiyid, Oxford University Press, Karachi, Pakistan, p. 107.

31. Muir, W., 1858, *The Life of Mahomet*, vol. 1. Smith, Elder and Co., London, p. v.

32. Ibid., p. xxi.

33. Ibid., p. xxvii.

34. Böwering, G., 1985, Islam, Religion, in *Dictionary of the Middle Ages*, vol. 6, edited by Joseph R. Strayer. Charles Scribner's Sons, New York, p. 578.

35. Ibid.

36. Carlyle, T., 1840, *On Heroes, Hero-Worship and the Heroic in History*. Frederick A. Stokes, New York, p. 72.

37. Böwering, G., 1985, Islam, Religion, in *Dictionary of the Middle Ages*, vol. 6, edited by Joseph R. Strayer. Charles Scribner's Sons, New York, p. 578.

38. Pickthall, M. M., 1977, *The Meaning of the Glorious Qur'an, Text and Explanatory Translation*. Muslim World League, U.N. Office, New York, p. iii.

39. Koran, 1861, Sura 112, translated by John Medows Rodwell (1808–1900). Williams and Norgate, London, p. 13.

40. Bevan, A. A., 1913, Mahomet and Islam, Chapter 10 of *Cambridge Medieval History*, vol. 2, *The Rise of the Saracens and the Foundation of the Western Empire*, edited by H. M. Gwatkin and J. P. Whitney. Macmillan, New York, p. 310.

41. Rahman, F., 2005, Islam. An Overview, in *Encyclopedia of Religion*, Second Edition, edited by Lindsay Jones, vol. 7. Macmillan Reference, Detroit, p. 4561.

42. Ibn Ishaq (died c. 768), 1967, *The Life of Muhammad* (first published in 1955 by Oxford University Press, London), translated by Alfred Guillaume (1888–1965). Ameena Saiyid, Oxford University Press, Karachi, Pakistan, p. 119.

43. Muir, W., 1861, *The Life of Mahomet*, vol. 2. Smith, Elder & Co., London, p. 163.

44. Ibn Ishaq (died c. 768), 1967, *The Life of Muhammad* (first published in 1955 by Oxford University Press, London), translated by Alfred Guillaume (1888–1965). Ameena Saiyid, Oxford University Press, Karachi, Pakistan, p. 119.

45. *Encyclopædia Britannica*, 1972, Ka'ba, vol. 13. William Benton, Chicago, p. 178.

46. Koran, 1861, Sura 2, Verse 121, translated by John Medows Rodwell (1808–1900). Williams and Norgate, London, p. 446.

47. *Encyclopædia Britannica*, Sixth Edition, 1823, Caaba, vol. 5. Archibald Constable, Edinburgh, p. 36.

48. Burckhardt, J. L., 1829, *Travels in Arabia*, vol. 1. Henry Colburn, London, p. 249–250.

49. Ibn Ishaq (died c. 768), 1967, *The Life of Muhammad* (first published in 1955 by Oxford University Press, London), translated by Alfred Guillaume (1888–1965). Ameena Saiyid, Oxford University Press, Karachi, Pakistan, p. 131.

50. Ibid.

51. Ibid., p. 133–134.

52. Ibid., p. 135.

53. Ibid., p. 165.

54. Armstrong, K., 1994, *A History of God*. Alfred A. Knopf, New York, p. 148.

55. Muir, W., 1861, *The Life of Mahomet*, vol. 2. Smith, Elder & Co. London, p. 150.

56. Ibid., p. 151.

57. Ibid., p. 152.

58. Koran, 1861, Sura 53, Verse 23, translated by John Medows Rodwell (1808–1900). Williams and Norgate, London, p. 66.

59. Bible, John 2:1–2:11.

60. Bible, Matthew 14:22–14:33.

61. Bible, John 11:38–11:44.

62. Bible, Matthew 14:15–14:21.

63. Ibn Ishaq (died c. 768), 1967, *The Life of Muhammad* (first published in 1955 by Oxford University Press, London), translated by Alfred Guillaume (1888–1965). Ameena Saiyid, Oxford University Press, Karachi, Pakistan, p. xxiii.

64. Ibid., p. 71.

65. Muir, W., 1858, *The Life of Mahomet*, vol. 1. Smith, Elder & Co. London, p. lxxxv.

66. Ibn Ishaq (died c. 768), 1967, *The Life of Muhammad* (first published in 1955 by Oxford University Press, London), translated by Alfred Guillaume (1888–1965). Ameena Saiyid, Oxford University Press, Karachi, Pakistan, p. 182.

67. Ibid., p. 185.

68. Ibid., p. 186.

69. Ibid.

70. Ibid., p. 186–187.

71. Watt, W. M., 1987, Muhammad, in *Dictionary of the Middle Ages*, vol. 8, edited by Joseph R. Strayer. Charles Scribner's Sons, New York, p. 523.

72. Muir, W., 1861, *The Life of Mahomet*, vol. 2. Smith, Elder & Co., London, p. 193–198.

73. Ibid., p. 200.

74. Ibid., p. 202–203.

75. Ibid., p. 208.

76. Bevan, A. A., 1913, Mahomet and Islam, Chapter 10 of *Cambridge Medieval History*, vol. 2, *The Rise of the Saracens and the Foundation of the Western Empire*, edited by H. M. Gwatkin and J. P. Whitney. Macmillan, New York, p. 312.

77. Böwering, G., 1985, Islam, Religion, in *Dictionary of the Middle Ages*, vol. 6, edited by Joseph R. Strayer. Charles Scribner's Sons, New York, p. 576–577.

78. *Encyclopædia Britannica*, Eleventh Edition, 1911, Mahomet, vol. 17. Encyclopædia Britannica Company, New York, p. 404.

79. *Encyclopædia Britannica*, 1972, Ibn Ishaq, vol. 11. William Benton, Chicago, p. 1020.

80. Ibn Ishaq (died c. 768), 1967, *The Life of Muhammad* (first published in 1955 by Oxford University Press, London), translated by Alfred Guillaume (1888–1965). Ameena Saiyid, Oxford University Press, Karachi, Pakistan, p. 212.

81. Bevan, A. A., 1913, Mahomet and Islam, Chapter 10 of *Cambridge Medieval History*, vol. 2, *The Rise of the Saracens and the Foundation of the Western Empire*, edited by H. M. Gwatkin and J. P. Whitney. Macmillan, New York, p. 314.

82. Muir, W., 1861, *The Life of Mahomet*, vol. 2. Smith, Elder & Co., London, p. 217.

83. Ibn Ishaq (died c. 768), 1967, *The Life of Muhammad* (first published in 1955 by Oxford University Press, London), translated by Alfred Guillaume (1888–1965). Ameena Saiyid, Oxford University Press, Karachi, Pakistan, p. 270.

84. Muir, W., 1861, *The Life of Mahomet*, vol. 3. Smith, Elder & Co., London, p. 291.

85. Koran, 1861, Sura 5, Verse 6, translated by John Medows Rodwell (1808–1900). Williams and Norgate, London, p. 645.

86. *Encyclopædia Britannica*, Eleventh Edition, 1911, Mahomet, vol. 17. Encyclopædia Britannica Company, New York, p. 404.

87. Muir, W., 1861, *The Life of Mahomet*, vol. 3. Smith, Elder & Co., London, p. 64.

88. Ibid., p. 64–69.

89. *Encyclopædia Britannica*, Eleventh Edition, 1911, Mahomet, vol. 17. Encyclopædia Britannica Company, New York, p. 405.

90. Muir, W., 1861, *The Life of Mahomet*, vol. 3. Smith, Elder & Co., London, p. 70–73.

91. Koran, 1861, Sura 2, Verses 186–187, translated by John Medows Rodwell (1808–1900). Williams and Norgate, London, p. 456.

92. Ibid., Sura 2, Verse 214, p. 460.

93. Ibid., Sura 78, Verses 21–25, p. 42.

94. Ibid., Sura 78, Verses 31–34, p. 42.

95. Ibid., Sura 96, Verses 16–17, p. 491.

96. *Encyclopædia Britannica*, Eleventh Edition, 1911, Mahomet, vol. 17. Encyclopædia Britannica Company, New York, p. 405.

97. Muir, W., 1861, *The Life of Mahomet*, vol. 3. Smith, Elder & Co., London, p. 94.

98. *Encyclopædia Britannica*, Eleventh Edition, 1911, Mahomet, vol. 17. Encyclopædia Britannica Company, New York, p. 405.

99. Bevan, A. A., 1913, Mahomet and Islam, Chapter 10 of *Cambridge Medieval History*, vol. 2, *The Rise of the Saracens and the Foundation of the Western Empire*, edited by H. M. Gwatkin and J. P. Whitney. Macmillan, New York, p. 317.

100. Ibn Ishaq (died c. 768), 1967, *The Life of Muhammad* (first published in 1955 by Oxford University Press, London), translated by Alfred Guillaume (1888–1965). Ameena Saiyid, Oxford University Press, Karachi, Pakistan, p. 304.

101. Muir, W., 1858, *The Life of Mahomet and History of Islam, to the Era of the Hegira*, vol. 3. Smith, Elder & Co., London, p. 108.

102. Ibn Ishaq (died c. 768), 1967, *The Life of Muhammad* (first published in 1955 by Oxford University Press, London), translated by Alfred Guillaume (1888–1965). Ameena Saiyid, Oxford University Press, Karachi, Pakistan, p. 305.

103. Muir, W., 1861, *The Life of Mahomet*, vol. 3. Smith, Elder & Co., London, p. 116–117. Also. Ibn Ishaq (died c. 768), 1967, *The Life of Muhammad* (first published in 1955 by Oxford University Press, London), translated by Alfred Guillaume (1888–1965). Ameena Saiyid, Oxford University Press, Karachi, Pakistan, p. 308.

104. Muir, W., 1861, *The Life of Mahomet*, vol. 3. Smith, Elder & Co., London, p. 126.

105. Bevan, A. A., 1913, Mahomet and Islam, Chapter 10 of *Cambridge Medieval History*, vol. 2, *The Rise of the Saracens and the Foundation of the Western Empire*, edited by H. M. Gwatkin and J. P. Whitney. Macmillan, New York, p. 318.

106. Muir, W., 1861, *The Life of Mahomet*, vol. 3. Smith, Elder & Co., London, p. 131.

107. Ibid., p. 131–132.

108. Ibn Ishaq (died c. 768), 1967, *The Life of Muhammad* (first published in 1955 by Oxford University Press, London), translated by Alfred Guillaume (1888–1965). Ameena Saiyid, Oxford University Press, Karachi, Pakistan, p. 369.

109. Ibid.

110. Muir, W., 1861, *The Life of Mahomet*, vol. 3. Smith, Elder & Co., London, p. 148–149.

111. Bible, King James Version, Matthew 5:39.

112. Watt, W. M., 1987, Muhammad, in *Dictionary of the Middle Ages*, vol. 8, edited by Joseph R. Strayer. Charles Scribner's Sons, New York, p. 525.

113. Except that Islam does not limit salvation to Muslims. Jews and Christians are also saved if they believe in God and the Last Judgment, and do good works. Koran, 1861, Sura 2, Verse 59, translated by John Medows Rodwell (1808–1900). Williams and Norgate, London, p. 436–437. Nevertheless, it is difficult to simultaneously be a Christian and Muslim.

114. Muir, W., 1861, *The Life of Mahomet*, vol. 3. Smith, Elder & Co., London, p. 147.

115. Muir, W., 1861, *The Life of Mahomet*, vol. 4. Smith, Elder & Co., London, p. 322.

116. Muir, W., 1858, *The Life of Mahomet*, vol. 1. Smith, Elder & Co., London, p. i–cv.

117. Lings, M., 1983, Muhammad, *His Life Based on the Earliest Sources*. Inner Traditions, Rochester, Vermont, p. 151–152.

118. Anonymous, 2005, Martin Lings—Obituary. *Times* (London), May 25, p. 59.

119. Butterfield, H., 1965, *The Whig Interpretation of History* (first published in 1931 by G. Bell and Sons, London). W. W. Norton & Company, New York, p. 105.

120. al-Athir, Ibn, 2006, *The Chronicle of Ibn al-Althir for The Crusading Period*, part 1, translated by D. S. Richards, vol. 13 of *Crusade Texts in Translation*. Ashgate, Burlington, Vermont, p. 21.

121. Bowman, S., 2003, Twelfth-Century Jewish Responses to Crusade and Jihad, in *Crusaders, Condottieri, and Cannon. Medieval Warfare in Societies Around the Mediterranean*, edited by Donald J. Kagay and L. J. Andrew Villaion. Brill, Leiden, p. 421.

122. *Encyclopædia Britannica*, Eleventh Edition, 1910, Crusades, vol. 7. Encyclopædia Britannica Company, New York, p. 529.

123. Krey, A. C., 1921, *The First Crusade, the Accounts of Eye-Witnesses and Participants*. Princeton University Press, Princeton, p. 261.

124. Mackay, C., 1841, *Memoirs of Extraordinary Popular Delusions*, vol. 2. Richard Bentley, London, p. 35–36.

125. Institoris, H., and Sprenger, J., 1928, *Malleus Maleficarum*, translated by Montague Summers (1880–1948). J. Rodker, London.

126. Bible, King James Version, Deuteronomy 7:2.

127. Ibid., Deuteronomy 20:16–20:17.

128. Ibid., Leviticus 20:10.

129. Ibid., John 8:7.

130. Ibn Ishaq (died c. 768), 1967, *The Life of Muhammad* (first published in 1955 by Oxford University Press, London), translated by Alfred Guillaume (1888–1965). Ameena Saiyid, Oxford University Press, Karachi, Pakistan, p. 267.

131. Bible, King James Version, Luke 16:24.

132. Ibid., Matthew 13:38–13:42.

133. Muir, W., 1861, *The Life of Mahomet*, vol. 3. Smith, Elder & Co., London, p. 155.

134. Ibid., p. 165.

135. Ibid., p. 169.

136. Ibid., p. 170.

137. Ibid.

138. Ibid., p. 172–173.

139. Ibid., p. 173.

140. Ibid., p. 189.

141. Koran, 1861, Sura 3, Verses 134–135, translated by John Medows Rodwell (1808–1900). Williams and Norgate, London, p. 512.

142. Böwering, G., 1985, Islam, Religion, in *Dictionary of the Middle Ages*, vol. 6, edited by Joseph R. Strayer. Charles Scribner's Sons, New York, p. 577.

143. Bevan, A. A., 1913, Mahomet and Islam, Chapter 10 of *Cambridge Medieval History*, vol. 2, *The Rise of the Saracens and the Foundation of the Western Empire*, edited by H. M. Gwatkin and J. P. Whitney. Macmillan, New York, p. 319.

144. Koran, 1861, Sura 59, Verse 2, translated by John Medows Rodwell (1808–1900). Williams and Norgate, London, p. 557.

145. Muir, W., 1861, *The Life of Mahomet*, vol. 3. Smith, Elder & Co., London, p. 227.

146. Ibid., p. 228.

147. Koran, 1861, Sura 33, Verse 37, translated by John Medows Rodwell (1808–1900). Williams and Norgate, London, p. 566–567.

148. Ibid., Sura 33, Verse 53, p. 569.

149. Muir, W., 1861, *The Life of Mahomet*, vol. 3. Smith, Elder & Co., London, p. 231.

150. Ibid., p. 255–256.

151. *Encyclopædia Britannica*, Eleventh Edition, 1911, Ma-homet, vol. 17. Encyclopædia Britannica Company, New York, p. 406.

152. Muir, W., 1861, *The Life of Mahomet*, vol. 3. Smith, Elder & Co., London, p. 257.

153. Ibn Ishaq (died c. 768), 1967, *The Life of Muhammad* (first published in 1955 by Oxford University Press, London), translated by Alfred Guillaume (1888–1965). Ameena Saiyid, Oxford University Press, Karachi, Pakistan, p. 450.

154. Muir, W., 1861, *The Life of Mahomet*, vol. 3. Smith, Elder & Co., London, p. 263.

155. Ibid., p. 267–268.

156. *Encyclopædia Britannica*, Eleventh Edition, 1911, Ma-homet, vol. 17. Encyclopædia Britannica Company, New York, p. 406.

157. Muir, W., 1861, *The Life of Mahomet*, vol. 3. Smith, Elder & Co., London, p. 270.

158. Ibid., p. 272.

159. Lings, M., 1983, Muhammad, *His Life Based on the Earliest Sources*. Inner Traditions, Rochester, Vermont, p. 231.

160. Ibn Ishaq (died c. 768), 1967, *The Life of Muhammad* (first published in 1955 by Oxford University Press, London), translated by Alfred Guillaume (1888–1965). Ameena Saiyid, Oxford University Press, Karachi, Pakistan, p. 464.

161. Lings, M., 1983, Muhammad, *His Life Based on the Earliest Sources*. Inner Traditions, Rochester, Vermont, p. 232.

162. Muir, W., 1861, *The Life of Mahomet*, vol. 3. Smith, Elder & Co., London, p. 272.

163. Lings, M., 1983, Muhammad, *His Life Based on the Earliest Sources*. Inner Traditions, Rochester, Vermont, p. 233.

164. Koran, 1861, Sura 33, Verses 25–26, translated by John Medows Rodwell (1808–1900). Williams and Norgate, London, p. 564.

165. Muir, W., 1861, *The Life of Mahomet*, vol. 4. Smith, Elder & Co., London, p. 18–19.

166. Koran, 1861, Sura 5, Verse 42, translated by John Medows Rodwell (1808–1900). Williams and Norgate, London, p. 638.

167. Ibid., Sura 5, Verse 37, p. 637–638.

168. Muir, W., 1861, *The Life of Mahomet*, vol. 4. Smith, Elder & Co., London, p. 22.

169. Ibid., p. 25–35.

170. Ibid., p. 73.

171. Ibid., p. 73–74.

172. Ibid., p. 75.

173. Ibid., p. 89.

174. Ibid., p. 109–127.

175. Ibid., p. 127–129.

176. Ibid., p. 130.

177. Ibid., p. 158–159.

178. Ibid., p. 165.

179. Watt, W. M., 1987, Muhammad, in *Dictionary of the Middle Ages*, vol. 8, edited by Joseph R. Strayer. Charles Scribner's Sons, New York, p. 525.

180. Muir, W., 1861, *The Life of Mahomet*, vol. 4. Smith, Elder & Co., London, p. 293.

181. CIA Factbook, "World," www.cia.gov, accessed April 8, 2009.

182. Böwering, G., 1985, Islam, Religion, in *Dictionary of the Middle Ages*, vol. 6, edited by Joseph R. Strayer. Charles Scribner's Sons, New York, p. 582.

183. Muir, W., 1861, *The Life of Mahomet*, vol. 3. Smith, Elder & Co., London, p. 43–44.

184. Rahman, F., 2005, Islam. an Overview, in *Encyclopedia of Religion*, Second Edition, edited by Lindsay Jones, vol. 7. Macmillan Reference, Detroit, p. 4565.

185. Ibid.

186. Koran, 1861, Sura 48, Verse 14, translated by John Medows Rodwell (1808–1900). Williams and Norgate, London, p. 71.

187. Ibid., Sura 72, p. 157–159.

188. Ibid., Sura 2:59, p. 436–437.

189. Bible, King James Version, Matthew 22:21.

190. Ibid., John 18:36.

191. Rahman, F., 2005, Islam. An Overview, in *Encyclope-*

dia of Religion, Second Edition, edited by Lindsay Jones, vol. 7. Macmillan Reference, Detroit, p. 4561.

192. Muir, W., 1861, *The Life of Mahomet*, vol. 3. Smith, Elder & Co., London, p. 295–296.

193. Lindberg, D. C., 1992, *The Beginnings of Western Science*. University of Chicago Press, Chicago, p. 166.

194. *Oxford English Dictionary*, 1989, Second Edition, On-line Version.

195. Rahman, F., 2005, Islam. an Overview, in *Encyclopedia of Religion*, Second Edition, edited by Lindsay Jones, vol. 7. Macmillan Reference, Detroit, p. 4565.

196. Motzki, H., 2004, Hadith, in *Encyclopedia of Islam and the Muslim World*, vol. 1, edited by Richard C. Martin. Macmillan Reference, New York, p. 285.

197. Rahman, F., 2005, Islam. an Overview, in *Encyclopedia of Religion*, Second Edition, edited by Lindsay Jones, vol. 7. Macmillan Reference, Detroit, p. 4565.

198. Ibid., p. 4566.

199. Böwering, G., 1985, Islam, Religion, in *Dictionary of the Middle Ages*, vol. 6, edited by Joseph R. Strayer. Charles Scribner's Sons, New York, p. 580–581.

200. Ibn Ishaq (died c. 768), 1967, *The Life of Muhammad* (first published in 1955 by Oxford University Press, London), translated by Alfred Guillaume (1888–1965). Ameena Saiyid, Oxford University Press, Karachi, Pakistan, p. 182.

201. Koran, 1861, Sura 16, Verse 16, translated by John Medows Rodwell (1808–1900). Williams and Norgate, London, p. 251.

202. Ibid., Sura 2, Verse 16, p. 461.

203. Bevan, A. A., 1913, Mahomet and Islam, Chapter 10 of *Cambridge Medieval History*, vol. 2, *The Rise of the Saracens and the Foundation of the Western Empire*, edited by H. M. Gwatkin and J. P. Whitney. Macmillan, New York, p. 315.

204. al-Suhrawardy, A. A, 1999, *The Sayings of Muhammad*, no. 390. Citadel Press, Secaucus, New Jersey, p. 111.

205. Koran, 1861, Sura 24, Verse 2, translated by John Medows Rodwell (1808–1900). Williams and Norgate, London, p. 573.

206. Ibid., Sura 4, Verse 8, p. 534.

207. Ibid.

208. Ibid.

209. Ibid.

210. Ibid., Sura 24, Verse 31, p. 577.

211. Ibid., Sura 4, Verse 14, p. 530–531.

212. Masood, E., 2005, Women at Work. *Nature*, vol. 433, p. 453.

213. Ibid.

214. Ambah, F. S., 2008, Saudi Women See a Brighter Road on Rights. *Washington Post*, January 31, p. A-15.

215. Constable, P., 2009, Afghan Law on Women Brings Societal Conflict onto World Stage. *Washington Post*, April 5, p. A-13.

216. Donner, F. M., 1985, Islam, Conquests of, in *Dictionary of the Middle Ages*, vol. 6, edited by Joseph R. Strayer. Charles Scribner's Sons, New York, p. 568.

217. Muir, W., 1892, *The Caliphate, Its Rise, Decline, and Fall*, Second Edition. Religious Tract Society, London, p. 101.

218. Goldston, R., 1979, *The Sword of the Prophet*. Dial Press, New York, p. 52.

219. Donner, F. M., 1985, Islam, Conquests of, in *Dictionary of the Middle Ages*, vol. 6, edited by Joseph R. Strayer. Charles Scribner's Sons, New York, p. 572.

220. Muir, W., 1892, *The Caliphate, Its Rise, Decline, and Fall*, Second Edition. Religious Tract Society, London, p. 169.

221. Creasy, E. S., 1908, *The Fifteen Decisive Battles of the World from Marathon to Waterloo*, Everyman's Library Edition. E. P. Dutton, New York, p. 163–164.

222. Oman, C. W. C., 1885, *The Art of War in the Middle Ages*, A.D. *378–1515*. B. H. Blackwell, London, p. 18.

223. Creasy, E. S., 1908, *The Fifteen Decisive Battles of the World from Marathon to Waterloo*, Everyman's Library Edition. E. P. Dutton, New York, p. 167.

224. Ibid., p. 168–169.

225. Becker, C. H., 1913, The Expansion of the Saracens, Chapter 11 of *Cambridge Medieval History*, vol. 2, *The Rise of the Saracens and the Foundation of the Western Empire*, edited by H. M. Gwatkin and J. P. Whitney. Macmillan, New York, p. 330.

226. O'Leary, D. L., 1948, *How Greek Science Passed to the Arabs*. Routledge and Kegan Paul, London, p. 135.

227. *Encyclopædia Britannica*, Eleventh Edition, 1910, Caliphate, vol. 5. Cambridge University Press, Cambridge, p. 40.

228. Muir, W., 1892, *The Caliphate, Its Rise, Decline, and Fall*, Second Edition. Religious Tract Society, London, p. 428.

229. Ibid., p. 435.

230. Ibid., p. 436.

231. *Encyclopædia Britannica*, Eleventh Edition, 1910, Harun al-Rashid, vol. 13. Encyclopædia Britannica Company, New York, p. 37.

232. Muir, W., 1892, *The Caliphate, Its Rise, Decline, and Fall*, Second Edition. Religious Tract Society, London, p. 482–483.

233. *Encyclopædia Britannica*, Eleventh Edition, 1910, Caliphate, vol. 5. Cambridge University Press, Cambridge, p. 45.

234. Sabra, A. I., 1988, Science, Islamic, in *Dictionary of the Middle Ages*, vol. 11, edited by Joseph R. Strayer. Charles Scribner's Sons, New York, p. 84.

235. *Encyclopædia Britannica*, Eleventh Edition, 1910, Thousand and One Nights, vol. 26. Encyclopædia Britannica Company, New York, p. 883.

236. Ibid., p. 884.

237. Ibid., p. 885.

238. Burton, R. F. (translator), 1894, *The Book of the Thousand Nights and a Night*, vol. 1. H. S. Nichols & Co., London, p. 4.

239. Ibid., p. 6.

240. Ibid., p. 11.

241. Ibid., p. 12–13.

242. Ibid., p. 13.

243. Ibid., vol. 8, p. 51.

244. Bakewell, C. M., 1907, *Source Book in Ancient Philosophy*. Charles Scribner's Sons, New York, p. 31.

245. Goldston, R., 1979, *The Sword of the Prophet*. Dial Press, New York, p. 59.

246. Sarton, G., 1927, *Introduction to the History of Science*, vol. 1. Carnegie Institution, Washington, DC, p. 17.

247. O'Leary, D. L., 1948, *How Greek Science Passed to the Arabs*. Routledge and Kegan Paul, London, p. 136.

248. *Encyclopædia Britannica*, Eleventh Edition, 1911, Numismatics, vol. 19. Cambridge University Press, Cambridge, p. 904.

249. *Encyclopædia Britannica*, Eleventh Edition, 1911, Paper, vol. 20. Encyclopædia Britannica Company, New York, p. 725.

250. Cook, M. A., 1974, Economic Developments, in *The Legacy of Islam*, Second Edition, edited by Joseph Schacht and C. E. Bosworth. Oxford at the Clarendon Press, London, p. 238.

251. Watt, G., 1907, *The Wild and Cultivated Cotton Plants of the World*. Longmans, Green, and Co., London, p. 15.

252. *Encyclopædia Britannica*, Eleventh Edition, 1911, Orange, vol. 20. Encyclopædia Britannica Company, New York, p. 148–149.

253. Cook, M. A., 1974, Economic Developments, in *The Legacy of Islam*, Second Edition, edited by Joseph Schacht and C. E. Bosworth. Oxford at the Clarendon Press, London, p. 211.

254. Heaton, H., 1936, *Economic History of Europe*. Harper & Brothers, New York, p. 85.

255. Kunitzsch, P., 2003, The Transmission of Hindu-Arabic Numerals Reconsidered, in *The Enterprise of Science in Islam, New Perspectives*, edited by Jan P. Hogendijk and Abdelhamid I. Sabra. MIT Press, Cambridge, Massachusetts, p. 1.

256. Smith, D. E., and Karpinski, L. C., 1911, *The Hindu-Arabic Numerals*. Ginn and Company, Boston and London, p. 92.

257. *Encyclopædia Britannica*, Eleventh Edition, 1911, Numeral, vol. 19. Cambridge University Press, Cambridge, p. 867.

258. Crombie, A. C., 1995, *The History of Science, from Augustine to Galileo*, Second Edition. Dover, New York, p. 66.

259. Sarton, G., 1931, *Introduction to the History of Science*, vol. 2, part 1. Carnegie Institution of Washington, Washington, DC, p. 4.

260. Ibid.

261. *Encyclopædia Britannica*, Eleventh Edition, 1911, Seleucid Dynasty, vol. 24. Encyclopædia Britannica Company, New York, p. 603.

262. *Encyclopædia Britannica*, Eleventh Edition, 1910, Antioch, vol. 2. Encyclopædia Britannica Company, New York, p. 130.

263. Ibid., p. 130–131.

264. O'Leary, D. L., 1948, *How Greek Science Passed to the Arabs*. Routledge and Kegan Paul, London, p. 61.

265. von Humboldt, A., 1848, *Kosmos, a General Survey of the Physical Phenomena of the Universe*, vol. 2. Hippolyte Bailliere, London, p. 244.

266. Sabra, A. I., 1988, Science, Islamic, in *Dictionary of the Middle Ages*, vol. 11, edited by Joseph R. Strayer. Charles Scribner's Sons, New York, p. 81, 83.

267. *Encyclopædia Britannica*, Eleventh Edition, 1911, Nestorius, vol. 19. Cambridge University Press, Cambridge, p. 409.

268. Socrates Scholasticus, 1890, *Ecclesiastical History*, Book 7, Chapter 29, in *A Select Library of Nicene and Post-Nicene Fathers, Second Series*, vol. 2, edited by Philip Schaff and Henry Wace. The Christian Literature Company, New York, p. 169.

269. Ibid.

270. Ibid.

271. Ibid., Book 7, Chapter 32, p. 170.

272. Ibid.

273. Schaff, P., 1884, *History of the Christian Church*, vol. 3, *Nicene and Post-Nicene Christianity* A.D. *311–600*. Charles Schribner's Sons, New York, p. 716–717.

274. Ibid., p. 719.

275. Socrates Scholasticus, 1890, *Ecclesiastical History*, Book 7, Chapter 32, in *A Select Library of Nicene and Post-Nicene Fathers, Second Series*, vol. 2, edited by Philip Schaff and Henry Wace. The Christian Literature Company, New York, p. 171.

276. Schaff, P., 1884, *History of the Christian Church*, vol. 3, *Nicene and Post-Nicene Christianity* A.D. *311–600*. Charles Schribner's Sons, New York, p. 718.

277. Ibid.

278. *Encyclopædia Britannica*, Eleventh Edition, 1911, Nestorius, vol. 19. Cambridge University Press, Cambridge, p. 411.

279. Schaff, P., 1884, *History of the Christian Church*, vol. 3, *Nicene and Post-Nicene Christianity* A.D. *311–600*. Charles Schribner's Sons, New York, p. 721.

280. Ibid., p. 722.

281. Ibid., p. 724.

282. Ibid., p. 725.

283. *Encyclopædia Britannica*, Eleventh Edition, 1911, Nestorius, vol. 19. Cambridge University Press, Cambridge, p. 410.

284. Ibid.

285. Ibid., p. 411.

286. Schaff, P., 1884, *History of the Christian Church*, vol. 3, *Nicene and Post-Nicene Christianity* A.D. *311–600*. Charles Schribner's Sons, New York, p. 728.

287. Socrates Scholasticus, 1890, *Ecclesiastical History*, Book 7, Chapter 34, in *A Select Library of Nicene and Post-Nicene Fathers, Second Series*, vol. 2, edited by Philip Schaff and Henry Wace. The Christian Literature Company, New York, p. 172.

288. *Encyclopædia Britannica*, Eleventh Edition, 1911, Nestorius, vol. 19. Cambridge University Press, Cambridge, p. 411.

289. Schaff, P., 1884, *History of the Christian Church*, vol. 3, *Nicene and Post-Nicene Christianity* A.D. *311–600*. Charles Schribner's Sons, New York, p. 731.

290. *Encyclopædia Britannica*, Eleventh Edition, 1911, Nestorians, vol. 19. Cambridge University Press, Cambridge, p. 407.

291. Ibid.

292. Ibid.

293. Ibid., p. 408.

294. Schaff, P., 1884, *History of the Christian Church*, vol. 3, *Nicene and Post-Nicene Christianity* A.D. *311–600*. Charles Schribner's Sons, New York, p. 731.

295. Ibid.

296. *Encyclopædia Britannica*, Eleventh Edition, 1911, Nestorius, vol. 19. Cambridge University Press, Cambridge, p. 409.

297. Schaff, P., 1884, *History of the Christian Church*, vol. 3, *Nicene and Post-Nicene Christianity* A.D. *311–600*. Charles Schribner's Sons, New York, p. 731.

298. Fakhry, M., 1970, *A History of Islamic Philosophy*. Columbia University Press, New York, p. 5.

299. O'Leary, D. L., 1948, *How Greek Science Passed to the Arabs*. Routledge and Kegan Paul, London, p. 146.

300. Fakhry, M., 1970, *A History of Islamic Philosophy*. Columbia University Press, New York, p. 15.

301. *Encyclopædia Britannica*, Eleventh Edition, 1910, Caliphate, vol. 5. Cambridge University Press, Cambridge, p. 42.

302. Fakhry, M., 1970, *A History of Islamic Philosophy*. Columbia University Press, New York, p. 18.

303. O'Leary, D. L., 1948, *How Greek Science Passed to the Arabs*. Routledge and Kegan Paul, London, p. 149–150.

304. Muir, W., 1892, *The Caliphate, Its Rise, Decline, and Fall*, Second Edition. Religious Tract Society, London, p. 462–463.

305. *Encyclopædia Britannica*, Eleventh Edition, 1910, Caliphate, vol. 5. Cambridge University Press, Cambridge, p. 43.

306. Muir, W., 1892, *The Caliphate, Its Rise, Decline, and Fall*, Second Edition. Religious Tract Society, London, p. 469.

307. *Encyclopædia Britannica*, Eleventh Edition, 1910, Caliphate, vol. 5. Cambridge University Press, Cambridge, p. 44.

308. Muir, W., 1892, *The Caliphate, Its Rise, Decline, and Fall*, Second Edition. Religious Tract Society, London, p. 473.

309. O'Leary, D. L., 1948, *How Greek Science Passed to the Arabs*. Routledge and Kegan Paul, London, p. 151.

310. Muir, W., 1892, *The Caliphate, Its Rise, Decline, and Fall*, Second Edition. Religious Tract Society, London, p. p. 482–483.

311. O'Leary, D. L., 1948, *How Greek Science Passed to the Arabs*. Routledge and Kegan Paul, London, p. 151.

312. Ibid., p. 152–153.

313. *Encyclopædia Britannica*, Eleventh Edition, 1910, Caliphate, vol. 5. Cambridge University Press, Cambridge, p. 47.

314. Anawati, G. C., 1974, Philosophy, Theology, and Mysticism, in *The Legacy of Islam*, Second Edition, edited by Joseph Schacht and C. E. Bosworth. Oxford at the Clarendon Press, London, p. 353.

315. Fakhry, M., 1970, *A History of Islamic Philosophy*. Columbia University Press, New York, p. 22.

316. Gibbon, E., 1909, *The History of the Decline and Fall of the Roman Empire*, Chapter 52, edited by J. B. Bury, vol. 6. Methuen & Co., London, p. 30.

317. Ogg, F. A., 1908, *A Source Book of Medieval History*. American Book Company, New York, p. 113.

318. Haskins, C. H., 1957, *The Renaissance of the 12th Century* (first published in 1927 by Harvard University Press, Cambridge, Massachusetts). Meridian Books, New York, p. 55.

319. Anawati, G. C., 2008, Hunayn Ibn Ishaq Al-Ibadi, Abu Zayd, in *Complete Dictionary of Scientific Biography*, edited by Charles Gillispie, vol. 15. Cengage Learning, New York, p. 230.

320. Fakhry, M., 1970, *A History of Islamic Philosophy*. Columbia University Press, New York, p. 26.

321. Anawati, G. C., 2008, Hunayn Ibn Ishaq Al-Ibadi, Abu Zayd, in *Complete Dictionary of Scientific Biography*, edited by Charles Gillispie, vol. 15. Cengage Learning, New York, p. 230.

322. bid., p. 231.

323. O'Leary, D. L., 1948, *How Greek Science Passed to the Arabs*. Routledge and Kegan Paul, London, p. 169.

324. Walzer, R., 1967, Early Islamic Philosophy, in *The*

Cambridge History of Later Greek and Early Medieval Philosophy, edited by A. H. Armstrong. Cambridge at the University Press, Cambridge, p. 649–650.

325. *Encyclopædia Britannica*, Eleventh Edition, 1911, Monophysites, vol. 18. Encyclopædia Britannica Company, New York, p. 732.

326. Schaff, P., 1884, *History of the Christian Church*, vol. 3, *Nicene and Post-Nicene Christianity* A.D. *311–600*. Charles Schribner's Sons, New York, p. 745–746.

327. Ibid., p. 764–765.

328. Fakhry, M., 1970, *A History of Islamic Philosophy*. Columbia University Press, New York, p. 45.

329. Sachau, E. C., 2003, Preface, in *Alberuni's India* (first published in 1888 by K. Paul, Trench, Trübner & Co., London). Low Price Publications, Dehli, India, p. xxix.

330. O'Leary, D. L., 1948, *How Greek Science Passed to the Arabs*. Routledge and Kegan Paul, London, p. 96.

331. Ibid., p. 106.

332. Sachau, E. C. (translator and editor), 2003, *Alberuni's India* (first published in 1888 by K. Paul, Trench, Trübner & Co., London). Low Price Publications, Dehli, India, p. 24–25.

333. Grant, E., 2007, *A History of Natural Philosophy*. Cambridge University Press, Cambridge, p. 67.

334. Lindberg, D. C., 1992, *The Beginnings of Western Science*. University of Chicago Press, Chicago, p. 170.

335. O'Leary, D. L., 1948, *How Greek Science Passed to the Arabs*. Routledge and Kegan Paul, London, p. 170.

336. Duhem, P., 1913, *The Catholic Encyclopedia*, Physics, vol. 12. The Encyclopedia Press, New York, p. 48.

337. Ibid.

338. *Encyclopædia Britannica*, Eleventh Edition, 1910, Arabian Philosophy, vol. 2. Encyclopædia Britannica Company, New York, p. 276–277.

339. de Vaux, C, 1931, Astronomy and Mathematics, in *The Legacy of Islam*, First Edition, edited by T. Arnold, and A. Guillaume, Oxford University Press, London, p. 376.

340. Sabra, A. I., 1988, Science, Islamic, in *Dictionary of the Middle Ages*, vol. 11, edited by Joseph R. Strayer. Charles Schribner's Sons, New York, p. 86.

341. Lindberg, D. C., 1992, *The Beginnings of Western Science*. University of Chicago Press, Chicago, p. 176.

342. Walzer, R., 1967, Early Islamic Philosophy, in *The Cambridge History of Later Greek and Early Medieval Philosophy*, edited by A. H. Armstrong. Cambridge at the University Press, Cambridge, p. 648.

343. Fakhry, M., 1970, *A History of Islamic Philosophy*. Columbia University Press, New York, p. 82.

344. Sarton, G., 1927, *Introduction to the History of Science*, vol. 1. Carnegie Institution of Washington, Washington, DC, p. 559.

345. Plessner, M., 1974, Science, The Natural Sciences and Medicine, in *The Legacy of Islam*, Second Edition, edited by Joseph Schacht and C. E. Bosworth. Oxford at the Clarendon Press, London, p. 427.

346. de Vaux, C, 1931, Astronomy and Mathematics, in *The Legacy of Islam* (First Edition), edited by T. Arnold, and A. Guillaume, Oxford University Press, London, p. 377.

347. Jolivet, J., and Rashed, R., 2008, Al-Kindi, Abu Yusuf Ya'qub Ibn Ishaq Al-Sabbah, in *Complete Dictionary of Scientific Biography*, edited by Charles Gillispie, vol. 7. Cengage Learning, New York, p. 261.

348. Fakhry, M., 1970, *A History of Islamic Philosophy*. Columbia University Press, New York, p. 84.

349. Ibid.

350. Jolivet, J., and Rashed, R., 2008, Al-Kindi, Abu Yusuf Ya'qub Ibn Ishaq Al-Sabbah, in *Complete Dictionary of Scientific Biography*, edited by Charles Gillispie, vol. 7. Cengage Learning, New York, p. 261.

351. Ibid., p. 262.

352. Fakhry, M., 1970, *A History of Islamic Philosophy*. Columbia University Press, New York, p. 85.

353. Ibid., p. 109.

354. Sabra, A. I., 1988, Science, Islamic, in *Dictionary of the Middle Ages*, vol. 11, edited by Joseph R. Strayer. Charles Schribner's Sons, New York, p. 83.

355. Fakhry, M., 1970, *A History of Islamic Philosophy*. Columbia University Press, New York, p. 20.

356. *Encyclopædia Britannica*, Eleventh Edition, 1911, Kindi, vol. 15. Encyclopædia Britannica Company, New York, p. 802.

357. Fakhry, M., 1970, *A History of Islamic Philosophy*. Columbia University Press, New York, p. 115.

358. Plessner, M., 1974, Science, The Natural Sciences and Medicine, in *The Legacy of Islam*, Second Edition, edited by Joseph Schacht and C. E. Bosworth. Oxford at the Clarendon Press, London, p. 434.

359. Fakhry, M., 1970, *A History of Islamic Philosophy*. Columbia University Press, New York, p. 115.

360. Meyerhof, M., 1935, Thirty-Three Clinical Observations by Rhazes. *Isis*, no. 2, vol. 23, p. 355.

361. *Encyclopædia Britannica*, Eleventh Edition, 1911, Medicine, vol. 18. Encyclopædia Britannica Company, New York, p. 45.

362. Meyerhof, M., 1935, Thirty-Three Clinical Observations by Rhazes. *Isis*, no. 2, vol. 23, p. 323.

363. al-Razi, 1848, *A Treatise on the Small-Pox and Measles*, translated by William Alexander Greenhill. Sydenham Society, London.

364. Meyerhof, M., 1935, Thirty-Three Clinical Observations by Rhazes. *Isis*, no. 2, vol. 23, p. 324.

365. Ibid.

366. Ibid., p. 329.

367. Ibid, p. 326.

368. Pines, S., 2008, Al-Razi, Abu Bakr Muhammad Ibn Zakariyya, in *Complete Dictionary of Scientific Biography*, edited by Charles Gillispie, vol. 11. Cengage Learning, New York, p. 323.

369. Pines, S., 1963, What Was Original in Arabic Science? in, *Scientific Change, Historical Studies in the Intellectual, Social and Technical Conditions for Scientific Discovery and Technical Invention, from Antiquity to Present*, edited by A. C. Crombie. Heinemann, London, p. 196.

370. Ibid., p. 195.

371. Ibid.

372. Ibid.

373. Baas, J. H., 1889, *Outlines of the History of Medicine and the Medical Profession*, translated by H. E. Handerson. J. H. Vail & Co., New York, p. 221.

374. Ibid.

375. Pines, S., 1963, What Was Original in Arabic Science? in, *Scientific Change, Historical Studies in the Intellectual, Social and Technical Conditions for Scientific Discovery and Technical Invention, from Antiquity to Present*, edited by A. C. Crombie. Heinemann, London, p. 194.

376. Hippocrates, 1950, *The Medical Works of Hippocrates*, translated by John Chadwick and W. N. Mann. Charles C. Thomas, Springfield, Illinois.

377. Lloyd, G. E. R., 1970, *Early Greek Science. Thales to Aristotle*. W. W. Norton, New York, p. 50.

378. Fakhry, M., 1970, *A History of Islamic Philosophy*. Columbia University Press, New York, p. 116.

379. Pines, S., 1963, What Was Original in Arabic Science? in, *Scientific Change, Historical Studies in the Intellectual, Social and Technical Conditions for Scientific Discovery and Technical Invention, from Antiquity to Present*, edited by A. C. Crombie. Heinemann, London, p. 194.

380. Plessner, M., 1974, Science, The Natural Sciences and Medicine, in *The Legacy of Islam*, Second Edition, edited by Joseph Schacht and C. E. Bosworth. Oxford at the Clarendon Press, London, p. 429.

381. Wright, C. A., 2004, Food. Coffee, in *Encyclopedia of the Modern Middle East and North Africa*, edited by Philip Mattar, vol. 2. Macmillan Reference, New York, p. 837.

382. Dufour, P. S., 1685, *The Manner of Making Coffee, Tea, and Chocolate*. William Crook, London, p. 3.

383. Pines, S., 2008, Al-Razi, Abu Bakr Muhammad Ibn Zakariyya, in *Complete Dictionary of Scientific Biography*, edited by Charles Gillispie, vol. 11. Cengage Learning, New York, p. 324.

384. Pines, S., 1963, What Was Original in Arabic Science? in, *Scientific Change, Historical Studies in the Intellectual, Social and Technical Conditions for Scientific Discovery and Tech-

nical Invention, from Antiquity to Present, edited by A. C. Crombie. Heinemann, London, p. 194.

385. Pines, S., 2008, Al-Razi, Abu Bakr Muhammad Ibn Zakariyya, in *Complete Dictionary of Scientific Biography*, edited by Charles Gillispie, vol. 11. Cengage Learning, New York, p. 325.

386. Fakhry, M., 1970, *A History of Islamic Philosophy*. Columbia University Press, New York, p. 121.

387. *Encyclopædia Britannica*, Eleventh Edition, 1910, Demiurge, vol. 8. Encyclopædia Britannica Company, New York, p. 1.

388. Pines, S., 2008, Al-Razi, Abu Bakr Muhammad Ibn Zakariyya, in *Complete Dictionary of Scientific Biography*, edited by Charles Gillispie, vol. 11. Cengage Learning, New York, p. 323.

389. Walzer, R., 1967, Early Islamic Philosophy, in *The Cambridge History of Later Greek and Early Medieval Philosophy*, edited by A. H. Armstrong. Cambridge at the University Press, Cambridge, p. 651.

390. Fakhry, M., 1970, *A History of Islamic Philosophy*. Columbia University Press, New York, p. 124.

391. Maimonides, M., 1956, *Guide for the Perplexed*, Book 3, Chapter 12, translated by M. Friedlander (Second Revised Edition, first published in 1904 by Routledge & Kegan Paul). Dover, New York, p. 267–268.

392. *Encyclopædia Britannica*, Eleventh Edition, 1910, Arabian Philosophy, vol. 2. Encyclopædia Britannica Company, New York, p. 278.

393. Fakhry, M., 1970, *A History of Islamic Philosophy*. Columbia University Press, New York, p. 125–126.

394. Wright, O., 2008, Al-Farabi, Abu Nasr Muhammad Ibn Muhammad Ibn Tarkhan Ibn Awzalagh, in *Complete Dictionary of Scientific Biography*, edited by Charles Gillispie, vol. 4. Cengage Learning, New York, p. 523.

395. Ibid., p. 523–524.

396. Ibid., p. 524.

397. Fakhry, M., 1970, *A History of Islamic Philosophy*. Columbia University Press, New York, p. 128.

398. Ibid., p. 131.

399. Ibid., p. 132–133.

400. Ibid., p. 147.

401. Ibid., p. 136.

402. Hyman, A., and Walsh, J. J., 1967, *Philosophy in the Middle Ages*. Harper & Row, New York, p. 211–212.

403. Ibid., p. 212.

404. Walzer, R., 1967, Early Islamic Philosophy, in *The Cambridge History of Later Greek and Early Medieval Philosophy*, edited by A. H. Armstrong. Cambridge at the University Press, Cambridge, p. 663.

405. Ibid., p. 664.

406. Ibid., p. 654.

407. Ibid., p. 660.

408. Wright, O., 2008, Al-Farabi, Abu Nasr Muhammad Ibn Muhammad Ibn Tarkhan Ibn Awzalagh, in *Complete Dictionary of Scientific Biography*, edited by Charles Gillispie, vol. 4. Cengage Learning, New York, p. 525.

409. Ibid., p. 524.

410. Sarton, G., 1927, *Introduction to the History of Science*, vol. 1. Carnegie Institution, Washington, DC, p. 709.

411. Fakhry, M., 1970, *A History of Islamic Philosophy*. Columbia University Press, New York, p. 150.

412. Hyman, A., and Walsh, J. J., 1967, *Philosophy in the Middle Ages*. Harper & Row, New York, p. 237.

413. Sarton, G., 1927, *Introduction to the History of Science*, vol. 1. Carnegie Institution, Washington, DC, p. 710.

414. *Encyclopædia Britannica*, Eleventh Edition, 1910, Avicenna, vol. 3. Encyclopædia Britannica Company, New York, p. 63.

415. Meyerhof, M., 1931, Science and Medicine, in *The Legacy of Islam* (First Edition), edited by T. Arnold, and A. Guillaume, Oxford University Press, London, p. 330.

416. Fakhry, M., 1970, *A History of Islamic Philosophy*. Columbia University Press, New York, p. 148.

417. Dawson, J. B., 1928, Avicenna. the Prince of Physicians. *The Medical Journal of Australia*, vol. 2, p. 751.

418. *Encyclopædia Britannica*, Eleventh Edition, 1910, Avicenna, vol. 3. Encyclopædia Britannica Company, New York, p. 62.

419. Avicenna, 1951, *Autobiography*, translated by Arthur J. Arberry, in *Avicenna on Theology*. John Murray, London, p. 9.

420. Ibid., p. 9–10.

421. Ibid., p. 10.

422. Ibid., p. 10.

423. Ibid.

424. Ibid., p. 11.

425. Ibid.

426. Ibid.

427. Ibid., p. 12.

428. *Encyclopædia Britannica*, Eleventh Edition, 1910, Avicenna, vol. 3. Encyclopædia Britannica Company, New York, p. 62.

429. al-Juzjani, 1951, Biography of Avicenna, translated by Arthur J. Arberry, in *Avicenna on Theology*. John Murray, London, p. 16.

430. *Encyclopædia Britannica*, Eleventh Edition, 1910, Avicenna, vol. 3. Encyclopædia Britannica Company, New York, p. 62.

431. al-Juzjani, 1951, Biography of Avicenna, translated by Arthur J. Arberry, in *Avicenna on Theology*. John Murray, London, p. 22.

432. Ibid., p. 17.

433. Baas, J. H., 1889, *Outlines of the History of Medicine and the Medical Profession*, translated by H. E. Handerson. J. H. Vail & Co., New York, p. 229.

434. Freind, J., 1727, *The History of Physick; From the Time of Galen, to the Beginning of the Sixteenth Century*, Second Edition, Corrected. J. Walthoe, London, p. 73.

435. Sarton, G., 1927, *Introduction to the History of Science*, vol. 1. Carnegie Institution, Washington, DC, p. 710.

436. Iskandar, A. Z., 2008, Ibn Sina (Medicine), in *Complete Dictionary of Scientific Biography*, edited by Charles Gillispie, vol. 15. Cengage Learning, New York, p. 498.

437. *Encyclopædia Britannica*, Eleventh Edition, 1911, Medicine, vol. 18. Encyclopædia Britannica Company, New York, p. 42.

438. Hippocrates, 1950, The Nature of Man, Paragraph 4, translated by J. Chadwick, and W. N. Mann, in *The Medical Works of Hippocrates*. Charles C. Thomas, Springfield, Illinois, p. 204.

439. Guillaume, A., 1931, Philosophy and Theology, in *The Legacy of Islam*, First Edition, edited by T. Arnold, and A. Guillaume, Oxford University Press, London, p. 257.

440. Fisher, G. J., 1883, Abu Ali El-Hosein Ibn-Abdallah Ibn Sina, Commonly Called Avicenna. *Annals of Anatomy and Surgery*, vol. 7, p. 23–24.

441. Iskandar, A. Z., 2008, Ibn Sina (Medicine), in *Complete Dictionary of Scientific Biography*, edited by Charles Gillispie, vol. 15. Cengage Learning, New York, p. 498.

442. Sarton, G., 1927, *Introduction to the History of Science*, vol. 1. Carnegie Institution, Washington, DC, p. 711.

443. *Encyclopædia Britannica*, Eleventh Edition, 1910, Arabian Philosophy, vol. 2. Encyclopædia Britannica Company, New York, p. 278.

444. Fakhry, M., 1970, *A History of Islamic Philosophy*. Columbia University Press, New York, p. 152.

445. Avicenna, 1951, On the Nature of God, translated by Arthur J. Arberry, in *Avicenna on Theology*. John Murray, London, p. 26.

446. Avicenna, 1951, Predestination, translated by Arthur J. Arberry, in *Avicenna on Theology*. John Murray, London, p. 38.

447. Avicenna, 1951, On Prayer, translated by Arthur J. Arberry, in *Avicenna on Theology*. John Murray, London, p. 50.

448. Ibid.

449. Hyman, A., and Walsh, J. J., 1967, *Philosophy in the Middle Ages*. Harper & Row, New York, p. 240.

450. *Oxford English Dictionary*, Draft Revision Sept. 2008, Online Version.

451. St. Anselm, 1903, *Proslogium; Monologium; an Appendix in Behalf of the Fool by Gaunilon; and Cur Deus Homo,*

translated by Sidney Norton Deane. Open Court, Chicago, p. 7–8.

452. *Encyclopædia Britannica*, Eleventh Edition, 1910, Anselm, vol. 2. Encyclopædia Britannica Company, New York, p. 82.

453. Taylor, H. O., 1914, *The Mediaeval Mind*, Second Edition, vol. 1. Macmillan, London, p. 279.

454. Schaff, P., and Schaff, D. S., 1907, *History of the Christian Church*, vol. 5, part 1, *The Middle Ages, from Gregory VII, 1049, to Boniface VIII, 1294*. Charles Schribner's Sons, New York, p. 604.

455. Hyman, A., and Walsh, J. J., 1967, *Philosophy in the Middle Ages*. Harper & Row, New York, p. 234.

456. Avicenna, 1951, On the Nature of God, translated by Arthur J. Arberry, in *Avicenna on Theology*. John Murray, London, p. 25.

457. Hyman, A., and Walsh, J. J., 1967, *Philosophy in the Middle Ages*. Harper & Row, New York, p. 241.

458. Ibid., p. 233–234.

459. Gilson, E., 1955, *History of Christian Philosophy in the Middle Ages*. Random House, New York, p. 198.

460. Descartes, R., 1649, *A Discourse of a Method for the Well Guiding of Reason, and the Discovery of Truth in the Sciences*. Thomas Newcombe, London, p. 53.

461. Anawati, G. C., 2008, Ibn Sina (Philosophy and Science), in *Complete Dictionary of Scientific Biography*, edited by Charles Gillispie, vol. 15. Cengage Learning, New York, p. 495–496.

462. Ibid., p. 497.

463. Sarton, G., 1927, *Introduction to the History of Science*, vol. 1. Carnegie Institution, Washington, DC, p. 710.

464. Ibid.

465. Ibid.

466. al-Juzjani, 1951, Biography of Avicenna, translated by Arthur J. Arberry, in *Avicenna on Theology*. John Murray, London, p. 19.

467. Ibid., p. 22.

468. Adams, F. D., 1954, *The Birth and Development of the Geological Sciences* (first published in 1938 by William & Wilkins, Baltimore). Dover, New York, p. 18.

469. Ibid., p. 333.

470. Ibid., p. 334.

471. Ibid.

472. Ibid.

473. Ibid.

474. Lyell, C., 1892, *Principles of Geology*, Eleventh Edition, vol. 1. D. Appleton, New York, p. 75.

475. Adams, F. D., 1954, *The Birth and Development of the Geological Sciences* (first published in 1938 by William & Wilkins, Baltimore). Dover, New York, p. 334.

476. al-Juzjani, 1951, Biography of Avicenna, translated by Arthur J. Arberry, in *Avicenna on Theology*. John Murray, London, p. 23.

477. Meyerhof, M., 1931, Science and Medicine, in *The Legacy of Islam*, First Edition, edited by T. Arnold, and A. Guillaume, Oxford University Press, London, p. 332.

478. Sarton, G., 1927, *Introduction to the History of Science*, vol. 1. Carnegie Institution, Washington, DC, p. 707.

479. Ibid., p. 693.

480. Kennedy, E. S., 2008, Al-Biruni, in *Complete Dictionary of Scientific Biography*, edited by Charles Gillispie, vol. 2. Cengage Learning, New York, p. 151.

481. Ibid., p. 148.

482. Boilot, D. J., 2009, al-Biruni, in *Encyclopedia of Islam*, Second Edition, edited by P. Bearman et al.. Brill Online, accessed April 10, 2009.

483. Kennedy, E. S., 2008, Al-Biruni, in *Complete Dictionary of Scientific Biography*, edited by Charles Gillispie, vol. 2. Cengage Learning, New York, p. 148.

484. Ibid., p. 149.

485. Sachau, C. E., 1879, Preface, in *The Chronology of Ancient Nations*. William H. Allen, London, p. viii.

486. Lane-Poole, S., 1894, *The Mohammadan Dynasties*. Archibald Constable, Westminster (London), p. 286, 288.

487. Sachau, E. C., 2003, Preface, in *Alberuni's India* (first published in 1888 by K. Paul, Trench, Trübner & Co., London). Low Price Publications, Dehli, India, p. xi.

488. Browne, E. G., 1906, *A Literary History of Persia*. Charles Schribner's Sons, New York, p. 97–98.

489. Lane-Poole, S., 1894, *The Mohammadan Dynasties*. Archibald Constable, Westminster (London), p. 287.

490. al-Biruni, 2003, *Alberuni's India*, Chapter 1 (first published in 1888 by K. Paul, Trench, Trübner & Co., London). Low Price Publications, Dehli, India, p. 22.

491. Saliba, G., 1983, Biruni, in *Dictionary of the Middle Ages*, vol. 2, edited by Joseph R. Strayer. Charles Schribner's Sons, New York, p. 249.

492. al-Biruni, 2003, *Alberuni's India*, Preface (first published in 1888 by K. Paul, Trench, Trübner & Co., London). Low Price Publications, Dehli, India, p. 7.

493. Ibid, Chapter 1, p. 22.

494. Ibid, Chapter 1, p. 20.

495. Ibid., Chapter 16, p. 177.

496. Ibid., Chapter 16, p. 185.

497. Ibid., Chapter 14, p. 152.

498. Ibid., Chapter 26, p. 265.

499. Ibid.

500. Ibid., Chapter 26, p. 277.

501. Ibid., Chapter 18, p. 198.

502. Ibid., Chapter 47, p. 400.

503. Ibid., Chapter 17, p. 187.

504. Ibid.

505. Ibid., p. 188.

506. Ibid., Chapter 14, p. 152.

507. Ibid., Chapter 71, p. 161 (pagination follows original edition in two volumes).

508. Kennedy, E. S., 2008, Al-Biruni, in *Complete Dictionary of Scientific Biography*, edited by Charles Gillispie, vol. 2. Cengage Learning, New York, p. 151.

509. Saliba, G., 1983, Biruni, in *Dictionary of the Middle Ages*, vol. 2, edited by Joseph R. Strayer. Charles Schribner's Sons, New York, p. 249.

510. Boilot, D. J., 2009, al-Biruni, in *Encyclopedia of Islam*, Second Edition, edited by P. Bearman et al.. Brill Online, accessed April 10, 2009.

511. Sachau, C. E., 1879, Preface, in *The Chronology of Ancient Nations*. William H. Allen, London, p. ix.

512. Plessner, M., 1974, Science, The Natural Sciences and Medicine, in *The Legacy of Islam*, Second Edition, edited by Joseph Schacht and C. E. Bosworth. Oxford at the Clarendon Press, London, p. 437.

513. al-Biruni, 1879, *The Chronology of Ancient Nations*, Preface, translated by C. Edward Sachau. William H. Allen, London, p. 3.

514. Ibid.

515. Kennedy, E. S., 2008, Al-Biruni, in *Complete Dictionary of Scientific Biography*, edited by Charles Gillispie, vol. 2. Cengage Learning, New York, p. 156.

516. al-Biruni, 1879, *The Chronology of Ancient Nations*, Chapter 3 translated by C. Edward Sachau. William H. Allen, London, p. 17.

517. Ibid., p. 18.

518. Ibid., p. 27.

519. Ibid.

520. Ibid., p. 30.

521. Ussher, J., 1658, *The Annals of the World Deduced from the Origin of Time*. E. Tyler, London, p. 1.

522. al-Biruni, 1879, *The Chronology of Ancient Nations*, Chapter 3, translated by C. Edward Sachau. William H. Allen, London, p. 16.

523. Ibid., p. 27.

524. Kennedy, E. S., 2008, Al-Biruni, in *Complete Dictionary of Scientific Biography*, edited by Charles Gillispie, vol. 2. Cengage Learning, New York, p. 152–153.

525. Ibid., p. 153.

526. Ibid., p. 154.

527. Ibid., p. 155.

528. Saliba, G., 1983, Biruni, in *Dictionary of the Middle Ages*, vol. 2, edited by Joseph R. Strayer. Charles Schribner's Sons, New York, p. 250.

529. Sachau, C. E., 1879, Preface, in *The Chronology of Ancient Nations*. William H. Allen, London, p. xii.

530. Ibid., p. xiv.

531. Sarton, G., 1927, *Introduction to the History of Science*, vol. 1. Carnegie Institution, Washington, DC, p. 707.

532. Boilot, D. J., 2009, al-Biruni, in *Encyclopedia of Islam*, Second Edition, edited by P. Bearman et al.. Brill Online, accessed April 10, 2009.

533. Sarton, G., 1931, *Introduction to the History of Science*, vol. 2, part 1. Carnegie Institution of Washington, Washington, DC, p. 358.

534. Haskins, C. H., 1957, *The Renaissance of the 12th Century* (first published in 1927 by Harvard University Press, Cambridge, Massachusetts). Meridian Books, New York, p. 346.

535. Arnaldez, R., 2008, Ibn Rushd, in *Complete Dictionary of Scientific Biography*, edited by Charles Gillispie, vol. 12. Cengage Learning, New York, p. 1–9.

536. Arnaldez, R., 2009, Ibn Rushd, in, *Encyclopedia of Islam*, Second Edition, edited by P. Bearman et al.. Brill Online, accessed April 14, 2009.

537. Arnaldez, R., 2008, Ibn Rushd, in *Complete Dictionary of Scientific Biography*, edited by Charles Gillispie, vol. 12. Cengage Learning, New York, p. 1.

538. Ibid., p. 2.

539. Ibid.

540. Ibid.

541. Ibid., p. 5.

542. Gilson, E., 1955, *History of Christian Philosophy in the Middle Ages*. Random House, New York, p. 220.

543. Ibid., p. 642.

544. Ibid., p. 225.

545. Hyman, A., and Walsh, J. J., 1967, *Philosophy in the Middle Ages*. Harper & Row, New York, p. 285.

546. Fakhry, M., 1970, *A History of Islamic Philosophy*. Columbia University Press, New York, p. 169.

547. Arnaldez, R., 2008, Ibn Rushd, in *Complete Dictionary of Scientific Biography*, edited by Charles Gillispie, vol. 12. Cengage Learning, New York, p. 6.

548. Hyman, A., and Walsh, J. J., 1967, *Philosophy in the Middle Ages*. Harper & Row, New York, p. 288.

549. Ibid., p. 290.

550. Ibid., p. 292.

551. Averroes, 1961, *On the Harmony of Religion and Philosophy*, Chapter 2, Lines 3–5, translated by George F. Hourani, E. J. W. Gibb Memorial Series, New Series 21. Luzac & Co. for the Trustees of the E. J. W. Gibb Memorial, London, p. 50.

552. Fakhry, M., 1970, *A History of Islamic Philosophy*. Columbia University Press, New York, p. 312.

553. Gilson, E., 1955, *History of Christian Philosophy in the Middle Ages*. Random House, New York, p. 218.

554. Koran, 1861, Sura 3, Verse 5, translated by John Medows Rodwell (1808–1900). Williams and Norgate, London, p. 495.

555. Ibid., Sura 20, Verse 4, p. 97.

556. Hyman, A., and Walsh, J. J., 1967, *Philosophy in the Middle Ages*. Harper & Row, New York, p. 292.

557. Arnaldez, R., 2008, Ibn Rushd, in *Complete Dictionary of Scientific Biography*, edited by Charles Gillispie, vol. 12. Cengage Learning, New York, p. 4.

558. Ibid.

559. Ibid., p. 3.

560. Gilson, E., 1955, *History of Christian Philosophy in the Middle Ages*. Random House, New York, p. 223.

561. *Encyclopædia Britannica*, Eleventh Edition, 1910, Averroes, vol. 3. Encyclopædia Britannica Company, New York, p. 58.

562. Fakhry, M., 1970, *A History of Islamic Philosophy*. Columbia University Press, New York, p. 303.

563. Ibid., p. 304.

564. Lindberg, D. C., 1992, *The Beginnings of Western Science*. University of Chicago Press, Chicago, p. 173.

565. Ibid.

566. Fakhry, M., 1970, *A History of Islamic Philosophy*. Columbia University Press, New York, p. 6.

567. Grant, E., 2007, *A History of Natural Philosophy*. Cambridge University Press, Cambridge, p. 69.

568. *Oxford English Dictionary*, Draft Revision Sept. 2008, Online Version.

569. Grant, E., 2007, *A History of Natural Philosophy*. Cambridge University Press, Cambridge, p. 90–92.

570. Pedersen, J., et al., Madrasa, in *Encyclopedia of Islam*, Second Edition, edited by P. Bearman et al.. Brill Online, accessed April 16, 2009.

571. Makdisi, G., 1981, *The Rise of Colleges, Institutions of Learning in Islam and the West*. Edinburgh University Press, Edinburgh, p. xiii.

572. Nasr, S. H., 1992, *Science and Civilization in Islam* (first published in 1968 by Harvard University Press, Cambridge, Massachusetts). Barnes & Noble, New York, p. 72.

573. Makdisi, G., 1981, *The Rise of Colleges, Institutions of Learning in Islam and the West*. Edinburgh University Press, Edinburgh, p. 28.

574. Pedersen, J., et al., Madrasa, in *Encyclopedia of Islam*, Second Edition, edited by P. Bearman et al.. Brill Online, accessed April 16, 2009.

575. Grant, E., 2007, *A History of Natural Philosophy*. Cambridge University Press, Cambridge, p. 90–91.

576. Makdisi, G., 1981, *The Rise of Colleges, Institutions of Learning in Islam and the West*. Edinburgh University Press, Edinburgh, p. 36.

577. Ibid., p. 77–78.

578. Fakhry, M., 1970, *A History of Islamic Philosophy*. Columbia University Press, New York, p. 244.

579. al-Ghazali, 1917, *The Rescuer from Error*, in *The Sacred Books and Early Literature of the East, vol. 6, Medieval Arabic, Moorish, and Turkish*, edited by Charles F. Horne. Parke, Austin, and Lipscomb, New York, p. 102–133.

580. al-Ghazali, 1997, *The Incoherence of the Philosophers*, translated by Michael E. Marmura. Brigham Young Press, Provo, Utah.

581. al-Ghazali, 1917, *The Rescuer from Error*, in *The Sacred Books and Early Literature of the East*, vol. 6, Medieval Arabic, Moorish, and Turkish, edited by Charles F. Horne. Parke, Austin, and Lipscomb, New York, p. 103.

582. MacDonald, D. B., 1899, The Life of al-Ghazali, with Especial Reference to His Religious Experiences and Opinions. *Journal of the American Oriental Society*, vol. 20, p. 76.

583. Ibid.

584. Ibid., p. 77.

585. Fakhry, M., 1970, *A History of Islamic Philosophy*. Columbia University Press, New York, p. 244.

586. MacDonald, D. B., 1899, The Life of al-Ghazali, with Especial Reference to His Religious Experiences and Opinions. *Journal of the American Oriental Society*, vol. 20, p. 78–79.

587. Fakhry, M., 1970, *A History of Islamic Philosophy*. Columbia University Press, New York, p. 244.

588. MacDonald, D. B., 1899, The Life of al-Ghazali, with Especial Reference to His Religious Experiences and Opinions. *Journal of the American Oriental Society*, vol. 20, p. 79.

589. al-Ghazali, 1917, *The Rescuer from Error*, in *The Sacred Books and Early Literature of the East, vol. 6, Medieval Arabic, Moorish, and Turkish*, edited by Charles F. Horne. Parke, Austin, and Lipscomb, New York, p. 103.

590. Ibid., p. 104.

591. Ibid., p. 105.

592. Ibid.

593. Ibid., p. 106.

594. *Encyclopædia Britannica*, Eleventh Edition, 1911, Mysticism, vol. 19. Cambridge University Press, Cambridge, p. 123.

595. Ibid.

596. al-Faruqi, M. J., 2004, Sufism and the Sufi Orders, in *Encyclopedia of the Modern Middle East and North Africa*, 2nd Edition, edited by Philip Mattar, vol. 4. Macmillan Reference, New York, p. 2111.

597. al-Ghazali, 1917, *The Rescuer from Error*, in *The Sacred Books and Early Literature of the East, vol. 6, Medieval Arabic, Moorish, and Turkish*, edited by Charles F. Horne. Parke, Austin, and Lipscomb, New York, p. 107–108.

598. Ibid., p. 109.

599. Ibid.

600. Ibid., p. 109–110.

601. Ibid., p. 110.

602. Ibid., p. 121.

603. Ibid., p. 122.

604. Ibid.

605. Ibid., p. 123.

606. Ibid.

607. Ibid., p. 124.

608. Ibid.

609. MacDonald, D. B., 1899, The Life of al-Ghazali, with Especial Reference to His Religious Experiences and Opinions. *Journal of the American Oriental Society*, v. 20, p. 89–90.

610. al-Ghazali, 1917, *The Rescuer from Error*, in *The Sacred Books and Early Literature of the East, vol. 6, Medieval Arabic, Moorish, and Turkish*, edited by Charles F. Horne. Parke, Austin, and Lipscomb, New York, p. 125.

611. Ibid., p. 127–128.

612. Ibid., p. 129.

613. Ibid., p. 112.

614. Ibid.

615. Ibid.

616. Ibid.

617. Ibid., p. 113.

618. Ibid., p. 114.

619. Ibid., p. 115.

620. Ibid.

621. Ibid., p. 116.

622. Fakhry, M., 1970, *A History of Islamic Philosophy*. Columbia University Press, New York, p. 250.

623. al-Ghazali, 1997, *The Incoherence of the Philosophers*, translated by Michael E. Marmura. Brigham Young Press, Provo, Utah.

624. MacDonald, D. B., 1899, The Life of al-Ghazali, with Especial Reference to His Religious Experiences and Opinions. *Journal of the American Oriental Society*, v. 20, p. 103.

625. al-Ghazali, 1997, *The Incoherence of the Philosophers*, translated by Michael E. Marmura. Brigham Young Press, Provo, Utah, p. 171.

626. Averroes, 1954, *Averroes' Tahafut al-Tahafut* (*The Incoherence of the Incoherence*), translated by Simon Van Den Berg, vol. 1 and 2. University of Cambridge Press for the Gibb Memorial Trust, Cambridge.

627. Ibid., p. 318–319.

628. Ibid., p. 319.

629. Goldziher, I., 1981, The Attitude of Orthodox Islam Toward the "Ancient Sciences," in, *Studies on Islam*, translated and edited by Merlin L. Swartz. Oxford University Press, New York, p. 206.

630. Ibid., p. 205.

631. Ibid.

632. Ibid.

633. Grant, E., 2007, *A History of Natural Philosophy*. Cambridge University Press, Cambridge, p. 89.

634. Ibn Khaldun, 1958, *The Muqaddimah, an Introduction to History*, Chapter 6, Section 30, translated by Franz Rosenthal, vol. 3, Bollingen Series 43. Princeton University Press, Princeton, New Jersey, p. 246.

635. Ibid., p. 250.

636. Ibid., p. 251.

637. Ibid., p. 257.

638. Ibid., p. 257–258.

639. Stock, B., 1978, Science, Technology, and Economic Progress in the Early Middle Ages, in *Science in the Middle Ages*, edited by David C. Lindberg. University of Chicago Press, Chicago, p. 39.

Chapter 4.

1. Pirenne, H., 1948, *Medieval Cities, Their Origins and the Revival of Trade*, translated by Frank D. Halsey. Princeton University Press, Princeton, p. 8.

2. Ibid., p. 35.

3. Heaton, H., 1936, *Economic History of Europe*. Harper & Brothers, New York, p. 85–86.

4. Pirenne, H., 1948, *Medieval Cities, Their Origins and the Revival of Trade*, translated by Frank D. Halsey. Princeton University Press, Princeton, p. 46.

5. Heaton, H., 1936, *Economic History of Europe*. Harper & Brothers, New York, p. 88–89.

6. Thorndike, L., 1917, *The History of Medieval Europe*. Houghton Mifflin Company, Boston, p. 327.

7. Heaton, H., 1936, *Economic History of Europe*. Harper & Brothers, New York, p. 76.

8. Reynolds, R. L., 1961, *Europe Emerges*. University of Wisconsin Press, Madison, p. 164.

9. Thorndike, L., 1917, *The History of Medieval Europe*. Houghton Mifflin Company, Boston, p. 243.

10. Ibid., p. 242.

11. Ibid., p,. 233.

12. Ibid., p. 234.

13. Heaton, H., 1936, *Economic History of Europe*. Harper & Brothers, New York, p. 108.

14. Thorndike, L., 1917, *The History of Medieval Europe*. Houghton Mifflin Company, Boston, p. 238.

15. Heaton, H., 1936, *Economic History of Europe*. Harper & Brothers, New York, p. 79.

16. Thorndike, L., 1917, *The History of Medieval Europe*. Houghton Mifflin Company, Boston, p. 235.

17. Gies, F., and Gies, J., 1994, *Cathedral, Forge, and Waterwheel*. HarperCollins, New York, p. 44.

18. Boissonnade, P., 2002, *Life and Work in Medieval Europe* (first published in 1927 by A. A. Knopf, New York). Dover, New York, p. 94.

19. Ibid., p. 95.

20. Phillips, W. D., 1985, *Slavery from Roman Times to the Early Transatlantic Trade*. University of Minnesota Press, Minneapolis, p. 51.

21. Ibid., p. 55.

22. Thorndike, L., 1917, *The History of Medieval Europe*. Houghton Mifflin Company, Boston, p. 253.

23. Ibid., p. 237.

24. Heaton, H., 1936, *Economic History of Europe*. Harper & Brothers, New York, p. 91.

25. Ogg, F. A. (editor), 1908, *A Source Book of Mediaeval History*. American Book Company, New York, p. 129.

26. Heaton, H., 1936, *Economic History of Europe*. Harper & Brothers, New York, p. 93.

27. evidently, a "foiler" was "one who foils," where "foil" means "to spread over with a thin sheet of metal or other substance," *Oxford English Dictionary*, 1989, Second Edition, Online Version.

28. Ogg, F. A. (editor), 1908, *A Source Book of Mediaeval History*. American Book Company, New York, p. 127.

29. Heaton, H., 1936, *Economic History of Europe*. Harper & Brothers, New York, p. 113.

30. Thorndike, L., 1917, *The History of Medieval Europe*. Houghton Mifflin Company, Boston, p. 236.

31. Heaton, H., 1936, *Economic History of Europe*. Harper & Brothers, New York, p. 72.

32. Day, C., 1922, *A History of Commerce*. Longmans, Green, and Co., New York, p. 35.

33. Heaton, H., 1936, *Economic History of Europe*. Harper & Brothers, New York, p. 106–107.

34. Day, C., 1922, *A History of Commerce*. Longmans, Green, and Co., New York, p. 33.

35. Ibid., p. 54.

36. Ibid., p. 55.

37. Ibid., p. 56.

38. Ibid., p. 57.

39. Ibid., p. 58.

40. Ibid., p. 59.

41. Ibid.

42. Folland, C. K., Karl, T. R., and Vinnikov, K. Y. A., 1990, Observed Climate Variations and Change, in *Climate Change, The IPCC Scientific Assessment*, edited by J. T. Houghton, G. J. Jenkins, and J. J. Ephraums. Cambridge University Press, Cambridge, p. 202.

43. Broecker, W. S., 2001, Was the Medieval Warm Period Global? *Science*, no. 5508, vol. 291, p. 1497–1499.

44. Bond, G., et al., 2001, Persistent Solar Influence on North Atlantic Climate During the Holocene. *Science*, no. 5549, vol. 294, p. 2130–2136.

45. Lamb, H. H., 1982, *Climate, History and the Modern World*. Methuen, London, p. 162–177.

46. *Encyclopædia Britannica*, 1972, Greenland, vol. 10. William Benton, Chicago, p. 898.

47. Stock, B., 1978, Science, Technology, and Economic Progress in the Early Middle Ages, in *Science in the Middle Ages*, edited by David C. Lindberg. University of Chicago Press, Chicago, p. 27.

48. White, L., 1962, *Medieval Technology and Social Change*. Oxford at the Clarendon Press, Oxford, p. 39–76.

49. Gies, F., and Gies, J., 1994, *Cathedral, Forge, and Waterwheel*. HarperCollins, New York, p. 80.

50. Gimpel, J., 1976, *The Medieval Machine*. Holt, Rinehart and Winston, New York, p. 57.

51. Moore, T. G., 1995, *Global Warming. A Boon to Humans and Other Animals*. Hoover Institution Essays in Public Policy No. 61. Stanford University, Stanford, California.

52. Hinde, A., 2003, *England's Population, a History Since the Domesday Survey*. Hodder Arnold, London, p. 25.

53. Pirenne, H., 1948, *Medieval Cities, Their Origins and the Revival of Trade*, translated by Frank D. Halsey. Princeton University Press, Princeton, p. 80.

54. Ibid., p. 81.

55. Gimpel, J., 1976, *The Medieval Machine*. Holt, Rinehart and Winston, New York, p. 47.

56. Thorndike, L., 1914, Roger Bacon and Experimental Method in the Middle Ages. *The Philosophical Review*, no. 3, vol. 23, p. 276.

57. Pirenne, H., 1948, *Medieval Cities, Their Origins and the Revival of Trade*, translated by Frank D. Halsey. Princeton University Press, Princeton, p. 84.

58. Ibid., p. 85.

59. Heaton, H., 1936, *Economic History of Europe*. Harper & Brothers, New York, p. 87.

60. Ibid., p. 88.

61. Pirenne, H., 1948, *Medieval Cities, Their Origins and the Revival of Trade*, translated by Frank D. Halsey. Princeton University Press, Princeton, p. 230–233.

62. *Oxford English Dictionary*, 1989, Second Edition, Online Version.

63. Day, C., 1922, *A History of Commerce*. Longmans, Green, and Co., New York, p. 49.

64. Ibid., p. 64.

65. Ibid., p. 67.

66. Ibid.

67. Derry, T. K., and Williams, T. I., 1993, *A Short History of Technology, From the Earliest Times to A.D. 1900* (first published in 1960 by Oxford University Press). Dover, New York, p. 33.

68. Gimpel, J., 1976, *The Medieval Machine*. Holt, Rinehart and Winston, New York, p. 1–23.

69. *Encyclopædia Britannica*, Eleventh Edition, 1910, Crusades, vol. 7. Cambridge University Press, New York, p. 524.

70. Thorndike, L., 1917, *The History of Medieval Europe*. Houghton Mifflin Company, Boston, p. 304.

71. *Encyclopædia Britannica*, Eleventh Edition, 1911, Spain, vol. 25. Cambridge University Press, New York, p. 550.

72. Schaff, P., 1907, *History of the Christian Church*, Third Edition, vol. 5, part 1, *The Middle Ages, from Gregory VII, 1049, to Boniface VIII, 1294*. Charles Scribner's Sons, New York, p. 222.

73. Mackay, C., 1841, *Memoirs of Extraordinary Popular Delusions*, vol. 2. Richard Bentley, London, p. 4.

74. *Encyclopædia Britannica*, Eleventh Edition, 1910, Crusades, vol. 7. Cambridge University Press, New York, p. 525.

75. Mackay, C., 1841, *Memoirs of Extraordinary Popular Delusions*, vol. 2. Richard Bentley, London, p. 7.

76. Ibid.

77. *Encyclopædia Britannica*, Eleventh Edition, 1910, Crusades, vol. 7. Cambridge University Press, New York, p. 525.

78. *Encyclopædia Britannica*, Eleventh Edition, 1911, Peter the Hermit, vol. 21. Encyclopædia Britannica Company, New York, p. 294.

79. Mackay, C., 1841, *Memoirs of Extraordinary Popular Delusions*, vol. 2. Richard Bentley, London, p. 8.

80. Gibbon, E., 1912, *The History of the Decline and Fall of the Roman Empire*, Chapter 58, edited by J. B. Bury, vol. 6. Methuen & Co., London, p. 269–270.

81. Mackay, C., 1841, *Memoirs of Extraordinary Popular Delusions*, vol. 2. Richard Bentley, London, p. 13.

82. *Encyclopædia Britannica*, Eleventh Edition, 1910, Crusades, vol. 7. Cambridge University Press, New York, p. 526.

83. Mackay, C., 1841, *Memoirs of Extraordinary Popular Delusions*, vol. 2. Richard Bentley, London, p. 15.

84. Robinson, J. H., 1904, *Readings in European History*, vol. 1. Ginn and Company, Boston, p. 313.

85. Ibid., p. 314.

86. Thorndike, L., 1917, *The History of Medieval Europe*. Houghton Mifflin Company, Boston, p. 249.

87. Robinson, J. H., 1904, *Readings in European History*, vol. 1. Ginn and Company, Boston, p. 314.

88. Ibid., p. 315.

89. Ibid., p. 316.

90. Mackay, C., 1841, *Memoirs of Extraordinary Popular Delusions*, vol. 2. Richard Bentley, London, p. 9.

91. Gibbon, E., 1912, *The History of the Decline and Fall of the Roman Empire*, Chapter 58, edited by J. B. Bury, vol. 6. Methuen & Co., London, p. 276.

92. Mackay, C., 1841, *Memoirs of Extraordinary Popular Delusions*, vol. 2. Richard Bentley, London, p. 5.

93. Robinson, J. H., 1904, *Readings in European History*, vol. 1. Ginn and Company, Boston, p. 319.

94. Ibid.

95. *Catholic Encyclopedia*, 1913, Merit, vol. 10. The Encyclopedia Press, New York, p. 202.

96. Gibbon, E., 1912, *The History of the Decline and Fall of the Roman Empire*, Chapter 58, edited by J. B. Bury, vol. 6. Methuen & Co., London, p. 280.

97. *Encyclopædia Britannica*, Eleventh Edition, 1910, Crusades, vol. 7. Cambridge University Press, New York, p. 524.

98. Schaff, P., 1907, *History of the Christian Church*, Third Edition, vol. 5, part 1, *The Middle Ages, from Gregory VII, 1049, to Boniface VIII, 1294*. Charles Scribner's Sons, New York, p. 221.

99. *Encyclopædia Britannica*, Eleventh Edition, 1910, Crusades, vol. 7. Cambridge University Press, New York, p. 526.

100. Mackay, C., 1841, *Memoirs of Extraordinary Popular Delusions*, vol. 2. Richard Bentley, London, p. 11.

101. *Encyclopædia Britannica*, Eleventh Edition, 1910, Crusades, vol. 7. Cambridge University Press, New York, p. 527.

102. Ibid., p. 528.

103. Thorndike, L., 1917, *The History of Medieval Europe*. Houghton Mifflin Company, Boston, p. 316.

104. Schaff, P., 1907, *History of the Christian Church*, Third Edition, vol. 5, part 1, *The Middle Ages, from Gregory VII, 1049, to Boniface VIII, 1294*. Charles Scribner's Sons, New York, p. 240.

105. Ibid., p. 239.

106. *Encyclopædia Britannica*, Eleventh Edition, 1910, Crusades, vol. 7. Cambridge University Press, New York, p. 529.

107. Schaff, P., 1907, *History of the Christian Church*, Third Edition, vol. 5, part 1, *The Middle Ages, from Gregory VII, 1049, to Boniface VIII, 1294*. Charles Scribner's Sons, New York, p. 241.

108. Munro, D. C., 1903, Christian and Infidel in the Holy Land, in *Essays on the Crusades*. Fox, Duffield, New York, p. 7.

109. Robinson, J. H. (editor), 1904, *Readings in European History*, vol. 1. Ginn and Company, Boston, p. 426.

110. Ibid.

111. Ibid., p. 427.

112. Ibid., p. 428.

113. *Encyclopædia Britannica*, Eleventh Edition, 1910, Crusades, vol. 7. Cambridge University Press, New York, p. 524–552.

114. Thorndike, L., 1917, *The History of Medieval Europe*. Houghton Mifflin Company, Boston, p. 323.

115. *Encyclopædia Britannica*, Eleventh Edition, 1910, Crusades, vol. 7. Cambridge University Press, New York, p. 546.

116. Schaff, P., 1907, *History of the Christian Church*, Third Edition, vol. 5, part 1, *The Middle Ages, from Gregory VII, 1049, to Boniface VIII, 1294*. Charles Scribner's Sons, New York, p. 221.

117. *Encyclopædia Britannica*, Eleventh Edition, 1910, Crusades, vol. 7. Cambridge University Press, New York, p. 547.

118. Ibid., p. 549–550.

119. Thorndike, L., 1917, *The History of Medieval Europe*. Houghton Mifflin Company, Boston, p. 416.

120. Reinach, S., 1904, *The Story of Art Throughout the Ages, an Illustrated Record*. Charles Scribner's Sons, New York, p. 107.

121. Gimpel, J., 1983, *The Cathedral Builders*, translated by Teresa Waugh. Michael Russell Publishing Ltd., Wiltshire, England, p. 7.

122. van der Meulen, J., 1985, Gothic Architecture, in *Dictionary of the Middle Ages*, vol. 5, edited by Joseph R. Strayer. Charles Scribner's Sons, New York, p. 580.

123. Frothingham, A. L., 1915, *A History of Architecture*, vol. 3. Doublebay, Page & Company, Garden City, New York, p. 9.

124. *Encyclopædia Britannica*, Eleventh Edition, 1910, Architecture, vol. 2. Encyclopædia Britannica Company, New York, p. 396.

125. Ibid., p. 397.

126. Harvey, J., 1950, *The Gothic World, 1100–1600. a Survey of Architecture and Art*. B. T. Batsford Ltd., London, p. 2.

127. Frothingham, A. L., 1915, *A History of Architecture*, vol. 3. Doublebay, Page & Company, Garden City, New York, p. 7.

128. Ibid., p. 4–5.

129. Harvey, J., 1950, *The Gothic World, 1100–1600. a Survey of Architecture and Art*. B. T. Batsford Ltd., London, p. 1.

130. Pacey, A., 1992, *The Maze of Ingenuity*, Second Edition. MIT Press, Cambridge, Massachusetts, p. 5.

131. Harvey, J., 1950, *The Gothic World, 1100–1600. a Survey of Architecture and Art*. B. T. Batsford Ltd., London, p. 2.

132. Ibid.

133. Thorndike, L., 1917, *The History of Medieval Europe*. Houghton Mifflin Company, Boston, p. 419.

134. Frothingham, A. L., 1915, *A History of Architecture*, vol. 3. Doublebay, Page & Company, Garden City, New York, p. 21.

135. Shelby, L. R., 1964, The Role of the Master Mason in Mediaeval English Building. *Speculum*, no. 3, vol. 39, p. 388.

136. Taylor, A. J., 1950, Master James of St. George. *The English Historical Review*, no. 257, vol. 65, p. 452.

137. Shelby, L. R., 1964, The Role of the Master Mason in Mediaeval English Building. *Speculum*, no. 3, vol. 39, p. 388.

138. Frothingham, A. L., 1915, *A History of Architecture*, vol. 3. Doublebay, Page & Company, Garden City, New York, p. 9.

139. Taylor, A. J., 1950, Master James of St. George. *The English Historical Review*, no. 257, vol. 65, p. 433.

140. Ibid., p. 448.

141. Shelby, L. R., 1964, The Role of the Master Mason in Mediaeval English Building. *Speculum*, no. 3, vol. 39, p. 394.

142. *Encyclopædia Britannica*, Eleventh Edition, 1910, Architecture, vol. 2. Encyclopædia Britannica Company, New York, p. 397.

143. Pacey, A., 1992, *The Maze of Ingenuity*, Second Edition. MIT Press, Cambridge, Massachusetts, p. 1.

144. Ibid., p. 8.

145. Frothingham, A. L., 1915, *A History of Architecture*, vol. 3. Doublebay, Page & Company, Garden City, New York, p. 13.

146. Gimpel, J., 1983, *The Cathedral Builders*, translated by Teresa Waugh. Michael Russell Publishing Ltd., Wiltshire, England, p. 32.

147. Thorndike, L., 1917, *The History of Medieval Europe*. Houghton Mifflin Company, Boston, p. 424.

148. Reinach, S., 1904, *The Story of Art Throughout the Ages, an Illustrated Record*. Charles Scribner's Sons, New York, p. 110.

149. Newhouse, E. L. (editor), 1992, *The Builders. Marvels of Engineering*. National Geographic Society, Washington, D.C., p. 247.

150. *Encyclopædia Britannica*, Eleventh Edition, 1910, Architecture, vol. 2. Encyclopædia Britannica Company, New York, p. 398.

151. Reinach, S., 1904, *The Story of Art Throughout the Ages, an Illustrated Record*. Charles Scribner's Sons, New York, p. 109–110.

152. Ibid., p. 108.

153. Haskins, C. H., 1957, *The Renaissance of the 12th Century* (first published in 1927 by Harvard University Press, Cambridge, Massachusetts). Meridian Books, New York, p. 32.

154. Ibid., p. 127.

155. Ibid., p. 32.

156. Ibid., p. 360.

157. Ibid., p. 79.

158. Ibid., p. 81.

159. Haskins, C. H., 1927, *Studies in the History of Medieval Science*, Second Edition. Harvard University Press, Cambridge, p. 253.

160. Haskins, C. H., 1957, *The Renaissance of the 12th Century* (first published in 1927 by Harvard University Press, Cambridge, Massachusetts). Meridian Books, New York, p. 345.

161. Rashdall, H., 1895, *The Universities of Europe in the Middle Ages*, vol. 1. Oxford at the Clarendon Press, Oxford, p. 33.

162. Ibid.

163. Ker, W. P., 1955, *The Dark Ages* (first published in 1904 by William Blackwood and Sons, Edinburgh). Thomas Nelson and Sons, London, p. 118.

164. Rashdall, H., 1895, *The Universities of Europe in the Middle Ages*, vol. 1. Oxford at the Clarendon Press, Oxford, p. 36.

165. Ibid., p. 35.

166. Munro, D. C., 1897, *The Attitude of the Western Church toward the Study of the Latin Classics in the Early Middle Ages* (reprinted from vol. 8, American Society of Church History). Knickerbocker Press, New York? p. 189.

167. Ibid., p. 188.

168. Ker, W. P., 1955, *The Dark Ages* (first published in 1904 by William Blackwood and Sons, Edinburgh). Thomas Nelson and Sons, London, p. 133.

169. Munro, D. C., 1897, *The Attitude of the Western Church toward the Study of the Latin Classics in the Early Middle Ages* (reprinted from vol. 8, American Society of Church History). Knickerbocker Press, New York? p. 186.

170. Ibid.

171. Sandys, J. E., 1903, *A History of Classical Scholarship*. Cambridge at the University Press, Cambridge, p. 485.

172. Munro, D. C., 1897, *The Attitude of the Western Church toward the Study of the Latin Classics in the Early Middle Ages* (reprinted from vol. 8, American Society of Church History). Knickerbocker Press, New York? p. 191.

173. Ibid., p. 193.

174. Ibid., p. 187.

175. Ibid., p. 193–194.

176. Haskins, C. H., 1957, *The Renaissance of the 12th Century* (first published in 1927 by Harvard University Press, Cambridge, Massachusetts). Meridian Books, New York, p. 93–126.

177. Ibid., p. 107.

178. Taylor, H. O., 1914, *The Mediaeval Mind*, Second Edition, vol. 1. Macmillan, London, p. 294.

179. *Encyclopædia Britannica*, Eleventh Edition, 1911, Universities, vol. 27. Encyclopædia Britannica Company, New York, p. 751.

180. Wallace, W. A., 1982, Aristotle in the Middle Ages, in *Dictionary of the Middle Ages*, vol. 1, edited by Joseph R. Strayer. Charles Scribner's Sons, New York, p. 460.

181. Taylor, H. O., 1914, *The Mediaeval Mind*, Second Edition, vol. 1. Macmillan, London, p. 33–34.

182. Poole, R. L., 1884, *Illustrations of the History of Medieval Thought and Learning*. Williams and Norgate, London, p. 168.

183. Haskins, C. H., 1927, *Studies in the History of Medieval Science*, Second Edition. Harvard University Press, Cambridge, p. 223.

184. Aristotle, 1906, *The Nicomachean Ethics of Aristotle*, Book 6, Chapter 3, Tenth Edition, translated by F. H. Peters. Kegan Paul, Trench, Trübner & Co., Ltd., London, p. 185 (1139b).

185. Ibid.

186. Schaff, P., and Schaff, D. S., 1907, *History of the Christian Church, vol. 5, part 1, The Middle Ages, from Gregory VII, 1049, to Boniface VIII, 1294*. Charles Schribner's Sons, New York, p. 598.

187. St. Anselm, 1903, *Proslogium; Monologium; an Appendix in Behalf of the Fool by Gaunilon; and Cur Deus Homo*, translated by Sidney Norton Deane. Open Court, Chicago, p. 1.

188. Adelard of Bath, 1998, Questions on Natural Science, in *Adelard of Bath, Conversations with his Nephew*, translated and edited by Charles Burnett. Cambridge University Press, Cambridge, p. 103.

189. Adelard of Bath, 1998, On the Same and the Different, in *Adelard of Bath, Conversations with his Nephew*, translated and edited by Charles Burnett. Cambridge University Press, Cambridge, p. 3.

190. Adelard of Bath, 1998, Questions on Natural Science, in *Adelard of Bath, Conversations with his Nephew*, translated and edited by Charles Burnett. Cambridge University Press, Cambridge, p. 83.

191. Ibid., p. 209.

192. Adelard of Bath, 1998, On the Same and the Different, in *Adelard of Bath, Conversations with his Nephew*, translated and edited by Charles Burnett. Cambridge University Press, Cambridge, p. 25.

193. Haskins, C. H., 1927, *Studies in the History of Medieval Science*, Second Edition. Harvard University Press, Cambridge, p. 38.

194. *Encyclopædia Britannica*, Ninth Edition, 1890, Abelard, vol. 1. R. S. Peale & Co., Chicago, p. 35.

195. Rashdall, H., 1895, *The Universities of Europe in the Middle Ages*, vol. 1. Oxford at the Clarendon Press, Oxford, p. 42.

196. Ibid., p. 56.

197. Abelard, P., 1922, *Historia Calamitatum, the Story of My Misfortunes*, translated by Henry Adams Bellows. Thomas A. Boyd, Saint Paul.

198. Ibid., p. 1.

199. Ibid., p. 1–2.

200. Ibid., p. 2.

201. Ibid., p. 3.

202. *Encyclopædia Britannica*, Ninth Edition, 1890, Abelard, vol. 1. R. S. Peale & Co., Chicago, p. 34.

203. Vaughan, R. G., 1871, *The Life & Labours of S. Thomas of Aquin*, vol. 1. Longmans & Co., London, p. 153.

204. Gilson, E., 1955, *History of Christian Philosophy in the Middle Ages*. Random House, New York, p. 153.

205. Taylor, H. O., 1914, *The Mediaeval Mind*, Second Edition, vol. 2. Macmillan, London, p. 369.

206. Ibid.

207. Cram, R. A., 1922, Introduction, in *Historia Calamitatum, the Story of My Misfortunes*, translated by Henry Adams Bellows. Thomas A. Boyd, Saint Paul, p. xi.

208. Ibid.

209. Schaff, P., and Schaff, D. S., 1907, *History of the Christian Church, vol. 5, part 1, The Middle Ages, from Gregory VII, 1049, to Boniface VIII, 1294*. Charles Schribner's Sons, New York, p. 595.

210. Abelard, P., 1922, *Historia Calamitatum, the Story of My Misfortunes*, translated by Henry Adams Bellows. Thomas A. Boyd, Saint Paul, p. 5.

211. Gilson, E., 1955, *History of Christian Philosophy in the Middle Ages*. Random House, New York, p. 154.

212. Rashdall, H., 1895, *The Universities of Europe in the Middle Ages*, vol. 1. Oxford at the Clarendon Press, Oxford, p. 50.

213. *Encyclopædia Britannica*, Ninth Edition, 1890, Abelard, vol. 1. R. S. Peale & Co., Chicago, p. 34.

214. Adams, H., 1913, *Mont-Saint-Michel and Chartres*. Houghton Mifflin, Boston, p. 300.

215. McCabe, J., 1901, *Peter Abelard*. G. P. Putnam's Sons, New York, p. 82.

216. Norton, A. O. (editor), 1909, *Readings in the History of Education, Mediaeval Universities*. Harvard University, Cambridge, p. 19.

217. Ibid., p. 20.

218. Ibid., p. 20–21.

219. Vaughan, R. G., 1871, *The Life & Labours of S. Thomas of Aquin*, vol. 1. Longmans & Co., London, p. 168–169.

220. Abelard, P., 1922, *Historia Calamitatum, the Story of My Misfortunes*, translated by Henry Adams Bellows. Thomas A. Boyd, Saint Paul, p. 6.

221. Ibid., p. 9.

222. Ibid., p. 10.

223. Ibid., p. 11.

224. Ibid., p. 13.

225. Ibid.

226. *Encyclopædia Britannica*, Ninth Edition, 1890, Abelard, vol. 1. R. S. Peale & Co., Chicago, p. 34.

227. Abelard, P., 1922, *Historia Calamitatum, the Story of My Misfortunes*, translated by Henry Adams Bellows. Thomas A. Boyd, Saint Paul, p. 14.

228. Adams, H., 1913, *Mont-Saint-Michel and Chartres*. Houghton Mifflin, Boston, p. 289.

229. Schaff, P., and Schaff, D. S., 1907, *History of the Christian Church, vol. 5, part 1, The Middle Ages, from Gregory VII, 1049, to Boniface VIII, 1294*. Charles Schribner's Sons, New York, p. 611.

230. Vaughan, R. G., 1871, *The Life & Labours of S. Thomas of Aquin*, vol. 1. Longmans & Co., London, p. 161–162.

231. Abelard, P., 1922, *Historia Calamitatum, the Story of My Misfortunes*, translated by Henry Adams Bellows. Thomas A. Boyd, Saint Paul, p. 14.

232. Bible, King James Version, Proverbs 16:18.

233. Vaughan, R. G., 1871, *The Life & Labours of S. Thomas of Aquin*, vol. 1. Longmans & Co., London, p. 162.

234. Abelard, P., 1922, *Historia Calamitatum, the Story of My Misfortunes*, translated by Henry Adams Bellows. Thomas A. Boyd, Saint Paul, p. 14.

235. Ibid., p. 15.

236. Ibid., p. 16.

237. Ibid.

238. Ibid.

239. Ibid., p. 17.

240. Ibid.

241. Ibid., p. 16.

242. Ibid., p. 18.

243. Ibid., p. 19.

244. Ibid., p. 20.

245. Ibid.

246. Ibid., p. 21.

247. Ibid.

248. Ibid., p. 29.

249. Ibid.

250. Ibid., p. 30.

251. Ibid.

252. Ibid., p. 31–32.

253. Ibid., p. 32.

254. *Encyclopædia Britannica*, Ninth Edition, 1890, Abelard, vol. 1. R. S. Peale & Co., Chicago, p. 34.

255. Abelard, P., 1922, *Historia Calamitatum, the Story of My Misfortunes*, translated by Henry Adams Bellows. Thomas A. Boyd, Saint Paul, p. 34.

256. *Encyclopædia Britannica*, Ninth Edition, 1890, Abelard, vol. 1. R. S. Peale & Co., Chicago, p. 34.

257. Ibid.

258. Abelard, P., 1922, *Historia Calamitatum, the Story of My Misfortunes*, translated by Henry Adams Bellows. Thomas A. Boyd, Saint Paul, p. 44.

259. Graves, F. P., 1914, *A History of Education*. Macmillan, New York, p. 54.

260. Ibid., p. 53.

261. Ibid.

262. Vaughan, R. G., 1871, *The Life & Labours of S. Thomas of Aquin*, vol. 1. Longmans & Co., London, p. 168.

263. Abelard, P., 1922, *Historia Calamitatum, the Story of My Misfortunes*, translated by Henry Adams Bellows. Thomas A. Boyd, Saint Paul, p. 46.

264. Ibid., p. 52.

265. *Oxford English Dictionary*, Online Version, Draft Revision, September, 2008.

266. Bible, John 16:7.

267. *Encyclopædia Britannica*, Ninth Edition, 1890, Abelard, vol. 1. R. S. Peale & Co., Chicago, p. 35.

268. Abelard, P., 1922, *Historia Calamitatum, the Story of My Misfortunes*, translated by Henry Adams Bellows. Thomas A. Boyd, Saint Paul, p. 61–62.

269. *Encyclopædia Britannica*, Ninth Edition, 1890, Abelard, vol. 1. R. S. Peale & Co., Chicago, p. 35.

270. Abelard, P., 1922, *Historia Calamitatum, the Story of My Misfortunes*, translated by Henry Adams Bellows. Thomas A. Boyd, Saint Paul, p. 64.

271. Ibid., p. 65.

272. Ibid., p. 73.

273. Ibid., p. 74.

274. *Encyclopædia Britannica*, Ninth Edition, 1890, Abelard, vol. 1. R. S. Peale & Co., Chicago, p. 35.

275. *Encyclopædia Britannica*, Eleventh Edition, 1911, Universities, vol. 27. Encyclopædia Britannica Company, New York, p. 752.

276. Taylor, H. O., 1914, *The Mediaeval Mind*, Second Edition, vol. 2. Macmillan, London, p. 89.

277. Hugh of St. Victor, 1991, *The Didascalicon of Hugh of St. Victor*, Book 1, Chapter 11, translated by Jerome Taylor. Columbia University Press, New York, p. 58.

278. Ibid., Book 2, Chapter 1, p. 83.

279. Ibid., Book 2, Chapter 20, p. 74.

280. Taylor, H. O., 1914, *The Mediaeval Mind*, Second Edition, vol. 2. Macmillan, London, p. 93.

281. Ibid.

282. Ibid., p. 201.

283. Ibid., p. 403.

284. Poole, R. L., 1884, *Illustrations of the History of Medieval Thought and Learning*. Williams and Norgate, London, p. 222.

285. John of Salisbury, 1955, *The Metalogicon of John of Salisbury*, Prologue, translated by Daniel D. McGarry. University of California Press, Berkely and Los Angeles, p. 5.

286. Knowles, D., 2006, John of Salisbury, in *Encyclopedia of Philosophy*, Second Edition, vol. 4, edited by Donald Borchert. Macmillan Reference, Detroit, p. 844.

287. John of Salisbury, 1955, *The Metalogicon of John of Salisbury*, Book 1, Chapter 2, translated by Daniel D. McGarry. University of California Press, Berkely and Los Angeles, p. 12.

288. Ibid., Book 2, Chapter 3, p. 78.

289. Ibid., Book 2, Chapter 6, p. 84.

290. Ibid., Book 3, Chapter 4, p. 167.

291. Turnbull, H. W. (Editor), 1959, *The Correspondence of Isaac Newton*, vol 1. Cambridge University Press, London, p. 416.

292. John of Salisbury, 1955, *The Metalogicon of John of Salisbury*, Book 3, Chapter 4, translated by Daniel D. McGarry. University of California Press, Berkely and Los Angeles, p. 167.

293. Lindberg, D. C., 1978, The Transmission of Greek and Arabic Learning to the West, in *Science in the Middle Ages*, edited by David C. Lindberg. University of Chicago Press, Chicago, p. 52–53.

294. Haskins, C. H., 1927, *Studies in the History of Medieval Science*, Second Edition. Harvard University Press, Cambridge, p. 3.

295. Lindberg, D. C., 1978, The Transmission of Greek and Arabic Learning to the West, in *Science in the Middle Ages*, edited by David C. Lindberg. University of Chicago Press, Chicago, p. 52.

296. Wallace, W. A., 1982, Aristotle in the Middle Ages, in *Dictionary of the Middle Ages*, vol. 1, edited by Joseph R. Strayer. Charles Scribner's Sons, New York, p. 460.

297. Grant, E., 1977, *Physical Science in the Middle Ages*. Cambridge University Press, Cambridge, p. 13.

298. Lindberg, D. C., 1978, The Transmission of Greek and Arabic Learning to the West, in *Science in the Middle Ages*, edited by David C. Lindberg. University of Chicago Press, Chicago, p. 58.

299. Adelard of Bath, 1998, On the Same and the Different, in *Adelard of Bath, Conversations with his Nephew*, translated and edited by Charles Burnett. Cambridge University Press, Cambridge, p. 69–71.

300. Burnett, C. S. F., 1989, Translation and Translators, Western European, in *Dictionary of the Middle Ages*, vol. 12, edited by Joseph R. Strayer. Charles Scribner's Sons, New York, p. 137.

301. Ibid., p. 139.

302. Ibid.

303. Crombie, A. C., 1963, *Medieval and Early Modern Science*, Second Edition, vol. 1. Harvard University Press, Cambridge, Massachusetts, p. 35.

304. Lindberg, D. C., 1978, The Transmission of Greek and Arabic Learning to the West, in *Science in the Middle Ages*, edited by David C. Lindberg. University of Chicago Press, Chicago, p. 59.

305. Gibbon, E., 1909, *The History of the Decline and Fall of the Roman Empire*, Chapter 52, edited by J. B. Bury, vol. 6. Methuen & Co., London, p. 30.

306. Haskins, C. H., 1927, *Studies in the History of Medieval Science*, Second Edition. Harvard University Press, Cambridge, p. 12.

307. Ibid., p. 17–18.

308. Richler, B. Z., 1989, Translation and Translators, Jewish, in *Dictionary of the Middle Ages*, vol. 12, edited by Joseph R. Strayer. Charles Scribner's Sons, New York, p. 135.

309. Haskins, C. H., 1927, *Studies in the History of Medieval Science*, Second Edition. Harvard University Press, Cambridge, p. 8.

310. Sarton, G., 1927, *Introduction to the History of Science*, vol. 1. Carnegie Institution, Washington, DC, p. 670.

311. Struik, D. J., 2008, Gerbert, in *Complete Dictionary of Scientific Biography*, edited by Charles Gillispie, vol. 5. Cengage Learning, New York, p. 365.

312. Clagett, M., 2008, Adelard of Bath, in *Complete Dictionary of Scientific Biography*, edited by Charles Gillispie, vol. 1. Cengage Learning, New York, p. 61.

313. Haskins, C. H., 1927, *Studies in the History of Medieval Science*, Second Edition. Harvard University Press, Cambridge, p. 10.

314. Clagett, M., 2008, Adelard of Bath, in *Complete Dictionary of Scientific Biography*, edited by Charles Gillispie, vol. 1. Cengage Learning, New York, p. 63.

315. Grant, E. (editor), 1974, *A Source Book in Medieval Science*. Harvard University Press, Cambridge, Massachusetts, p. 35.

316. Lindberg, D. C., 1978, The Transmission of Greek and Arabic Learning to the West, in *Science in the Middle Ages*, edited by David C. Lindberg. University of Chicago Press, Chicago, p. 66.

317. Sarton, G., 1927, *Introduction to the History of Science*, vol. 2, part 1. Carnegie Institution, Washington, DC, p. 338.

318. Haskins, C. H., 1927, *Studies in the History of Medieval Science*, Second Edition. Harvard University Press, Cambridge, p. 15.

319. Lemay, R., 2008, Gerard of Cremona, in *Complete Dictionary of Scientific Biography*, edited by Charles Gillispie, vol. 15. Cengage Learning, New York, p. 188.

320. Ibid., p. 189.

321. *Encyclopedia of World Biography*, Second Edition, 2004, Alfonso X, vol. 1. Gale, Detroit, p. 150.

322. Dreyer, J. L. E., 1953, *A History of Astronomy from Thales to Kepler* (first published in 1906 by Cambridge University Press as *History of the Planetary Systems from Thales to Kepler*). Dover, New York, p. 272.

323. Ibid., p. 273.

324. *Encyclopædia Britannica*, Eleventh Edition, 1911, Alphonso, vol. 1. Encyclopædia Britannica Company, New York, p. 735.

325. Lindberg, D. C., 1978, The Transmission of Greek and Arabic Learning to the West, in *Science in the Middle Ages*, edited by David C. Lindberg. University of Chicago Press, Chicago, p. 67.

326. Haskins, C. H., 1927, *Studies in the History of Medieval Science*, Second Edition. Harvard University Press, Cambridge, p. 156.

327. *Encyclopædia Britannica*, Eleventh Edition, 1911, Sicily, vol. 25. Encyclopædia Britannica Company, New York, p. 31–32.

328. Ibid., p. 32.

329. Ibid., p. 33.

330. Ibid.

331. Ibid.

332. Lindberg, D. C., 1978, The Transmission of Greek and Arabic Learning to the West, in *Science in the Middle Ages*, edited by David C. Lindberg. University of Chicago Press, Chicago, p. 67.

333. Minio-Paluello, L., 2008, Michael Scot, in *Complete Dictionary of Scientific Biography*, edited by Charles Gillispie, vol. 9. Cengage Learning, New York, p. 361.

334. *Encyclopædia Britannica*, Eleventh Edition, 1911, Sicily, vol. 25. Encyclopædia Britannica Company, New York, p. 34.

335. Minio-Paluello, L., 2008, Michael Scot, in *Complete Dictionary of Scientific Biography*, edited by Charles Gillispie, vol. 9. Cengage Learning, New York, p. 362.

336. Haskins, C. H., 1927, *Studies in the History of Medieval Science*, Second Edition. Harvard University Press, Cambridge, p. 283.

337. Ibid., p. 288–289.

338. Ibid., p. 296.

339. Haskins, C. H., 1922, Science at the Court of Emperor Frederick II. *The American Historical Review*, no. 4, vol. 27, p. 672.

340. Haskins, C. H., 1957, *The Renaissance of the 12th Century* (first published in 1927 by Harvard University Press, Cambridge, Massachusetts). Meridian Books, New York, p. 345.

341. Rashdall, H., 1895, *The Universities of Europe in the Middle Ages*, vol. 1. Oxford at the Clarendon Press, Oxford, p. 350.

342. Haskins, C. H., 1957, *The Renaissance of the 12th Century* (first published in 1927 by Harvard University Press, Cambridge, Massachusetts). Meridian Books, New York, p. 345.

343. Haskins, C. H., 1927, *Studies in the History of Medieval Science*, Second Edition. Harvard University Press, Cambridge, p. 144.

344. Lindberg, D. C., 1978, The Transmission of Greek and Arabic Learning to the West, in *Science in the Middle Ages*, edited by David C. Lindberg. University of Chicago Press, Chicago, p. 71.

345. Minio-Paluello, L., 2008, James of Venice, in *Complete Dictionary of Scientific Biography*, edited by Charles Gillispie, vol. 7. Cengage Learning, New York, p. 65–66.

346. Wallace, W. A., 1982, Aristotle in the Middle Ages, in *Dictionary of the Middle Ages*, vol. 1, edited by Joseph R. Strayer. Charles Scribner's Sons, New York, p. 461.

347. Lindberg, D. C., 1978, The Transmission of Greek and Arabic Learning to the West, in *Science in the Middle Ages*, edited by David C. Lindberg. University of Chicago Press, Chicago, p. 73–74.

348. Minio-Paluello, L., 2008, Moerbeke, William of, in *Complete Dictionary of Scientific Biography*, edited by Charles Gillispie, vol. 9. Cengage Learning, New York, p. 435.

349. Ibid., p. 436.

350. Ibid., p. 436–437.

351. Ibid., p. 437.

352. Lindberg, D. C., 1978, The Transmission of Greek and Arabic Learning to the West, in *Science in the Middle Ages*, edited by David C. Lindberg. University of Chicago Press, Chicago, p. 74.

353. Gilson, E., 1955, *History of Christian Philosophy in the Middle Ages*. Random House, New York, p. 220.

354. Ibid., p. 403.

355. Aristotle, 1923, *Meteorologica* (*Meteorology*), Book 1, Chapter 14, translated by E. W. Webster. Oxford at the Clarendon Press, London, p. 353a.

356. Gilson, E., 1955, *History of Christian Philosophy in the Middle Ages*. Random House, New York, p. 645.

357. Ibid., p. 225.

358. Thorndike, L., 1914, Roger Bacon and Experimental Method in the Middle Ages. *The Philosophical Review*, no. 3, vol. 23, p. 277.

359. Rashdall, H., 1895, *The Universities of Europe in the Middle Ages*, vol. 1. Oxford at the Clarendon Press, Oxford, p. 355.

360. Ibid.

361. Vaughan, R. G., 1871, *The Life & Labours of S. Thomas of Aquin*, vol. 1. Longmans & Co., London, p. 402–403.

362. Norton, A. O. (editor), 1909, *Readings in the History of Education, Mediaeval Universities*. Harvard University, Cambridge, p. 45.

363. Rashdall, H., 1895, *The Universities of Europe in the Middle Ages*, vol. 1. Oxford at the Clarendon Press, Oxford, p. 356.

364. Vaughan, R. G., 1871, *The Life & Labours of S. Thomas of Aquin*, vol. 1. Longmans & Co., London, p. 403.

365. Norton, A. O. (editor), 1909, *Readings in the History of Education, Mediaeval Universities*. Harvard University, Cambridge, p. 45–46.

366. Gilson, E., 1955, *History of Christian Philosophy in the Middle Ages*. Random House, New York, p. 404.

367. Norton, A. O. (editor), 1909, *Readings in the History of Education, Mediaeval Universities*. Harvard University, Cambridge, p. 46.

368. Grant, E. (editor), 1974, *A Source Book in Medieval Science*. Harvard University Press, Cambridge, Massachusetts, p. 42.

369. Rashdall, H., 1895, *The Universities of Europe in the Middle Ages*, vol. 1. Oxford at the Clarendon Press, Oxford, p. 358.

370. Grant, E. (editor), 1974, *A Source Book in Medieval Science*. Harvard University Press, Cambridge, Massachusetts, p. 44.

371. Schaff, P., and Schaff, D. S., 1907, *History of the Christian Church, vol. 5, part 1, The Middle Ages, from Gregory VII, 1049, to Boniface VIII, 1294*. Charles Scribner's Sons, New York, p. 592.

372. Sarton, G., 1931, *Introduction to the History of Science*, vol. 2, part 2. Carnegie Institution of Washington, Washington, DC, p. 935.

373. Van Steenberghen, F., 2008, Siger of Brabant, in *Complete Dictionary of Scientific Biography*, edited by Charles Gillispie, vol. 12. Cengage Learning, New York, p. 428.

374. Gilson, E., 1955, *History of Christian Philosophy in the Middle Ages*. Random House, New York, p. 389–390.

375. Maurer, A., 2003, Boethius of Sweden (Dacia), in *New Catholic Encyclopedia*, Second Edition, vol. 2. Gale, Detroit, p. 457.

376. Boethius of Dacia, 1987, *On the Supreme Good, On the Eternity of the World, On Dreams*, translated by John F. Wippel. Pontifical Institute of Mediaeval Studies, Toronto, 47.

377. Dunphy, W., 1988, Siger of Brabant, in *Dictionary of the Middle Ages*, vol. 11, edited by Joseph R. Strayer. Charles Scribner's Sons, New York, p. 285.

378. Gilson, E., 1955, *History of Christian Philosophy in the Middle Ages*. Random House, New York, p. 398.

379. Ibid.

380. Ibid.

381. Wallace, W. A., 1982, Aristotle in the Middle Ages, in *Dictionary of the Middle Ages*, vol. 1, edited by Joseph R. Strayer. Charles Scribner's Sons, New York, p. 463.

382. Grant, E. (editor), 1974, *A Source Book in Medieval Science*. Harvard University Press, Cambridge, Massachusetts, p. 46.

383. Ibid., p. 48–49.

384. Ibid.

385. Aristotle, 1939, *On the Heavens* (*De Caelo*), Book 1, Chapter 8, translated by W. K. C. Guthrie. William Heinemann, London, p. 75 (277b).

386. Ibid., Book 1, Chapter 8, p. 73 (276b).

387. Grant, E. (editor), 1974, *A Source Book in Medieval Science*. Harvard University Press, Cambridge, Massachusetts, p. 48.

388. Grant, E., 1962, Late Medieval Thought, Copernicus, and the Scientific Revolution. *Journal of the History of Ideas*, no. 2, vol. 23, p. 200.

389. Lindberg, D. C., 1992, *The Beginnings of Western Science*. University of Chicago Press, Chicago, p. 243.

390. Gilson, E., 1955, *History of Christian Philosophy in the Middle Ages*. Random House, New York, p. 399.

391. Rashdall, H., 1895, *The Universities of Europe in the Middle Ages*, vol. 1. Oxford at the Clarendon Press, Oxford, p. 362.

392. Wallace, W. A., 1982, Aristotle in the Middle Ages, in *Dictionary of the Middle Ages*, vol. 1, edited by Joseph R. Strayer. Charles Scribner's Sons, New York, p. 463.

393. Rashdall, H., 1895, *The Universities of Europe in the Middle Ages*, vol. 1. Oxford at the Clarendon Press, Oxford, p. 363.

394. Grant, E. (editor), 1974, *A Source Book in Medieval Science*. Harvard University Press, Cambridge, Massachusetts, p. 47.

395. Haskins, C. H., 1957, *The Renaissance of the 12th Century* (first published in 1927 by Harvard University Press, Cambridge, Massachusetts). Meridian Books, New York, p. 368.

396. Rashdall, H., 1895, *The Universities of Europe in the Middle Ages*, vol. 1. Oxford at the Clarendon Press, Oxford, p. 5.

397. Marrou, H. I., 1964, *A History of Education in Antiquity*, translated by George Lamb. Mentor, New York, p. 447.

398. Ibid., p. 448.

399. Rashdall, H., 1895, *The Universities of Europe in the Middle Ages*, vol. 1. Oxford at the Clarendon Press, Oxford, p. 27.

400. Marrou, H. I., 1964, *A History of Education in Antiquity*, translated by George Lamb. Mentor, New York, p. 443.

401. Ogg, F. A. (editor), 1908, *A Source Book of Mediaeval History*. American Book Company, New York, p. 88–89.

402. Marrou, H. I., 1964, *A History of Education in Antiquity*, translated by George Lamb. Mentor, New York, p. 449.

403. Lindberg, D. C., 1978, The Transmission of Greek and Arabic Learning to the West, in *Science in the Middle Ages*, edited by David C. Lindberg. University of Chicago Press, Chicago, p. 53.

404. Marrou, H. I., 1964, *A History of Education in Antiquity*, translated by George Lamb. Mentor, New York, p. 244.

405. Rashdall, H., 1895, *The Universities of Europe in the Middle Ages*, vol. 1. Oxford at the Clarendon Press, Oxford, p. 35.

406. Ibid., p. 36.

407. Ibid., p. 38.

408. Lindberg, D. C., 1978, The Transmission of Greek and Arabic Learning to the West, in *Science in the Middle Ages*, edited by David C. Lindberg. University of Chicago Press, Chicago, p. 53.

409. Graves, F. P., 1914, *A History of Education*. Macmillan, New York, p. 19.

410. Ibid., p. 18.

411. Ibid., p. 25.

412. *Encyclopædia Britannica*, Eleventh Edition, 1910, Carolingians, vol. 5. Cambridge University Press, Cambridge, p. 381.

413. Graves, F. P., 1914, *A History of Education*. Macmillan, New York, p. 26.

414. Bryce, J., 1920, *The Holy Roman Empire*. Macmillan, London, p. 49.

415. Ogg, F. A. (editor), 1908, *A Source Book of Mediaeval History*. American Book Company, New York, p. 113.

416. Graves, F. P., 1914, *A History of Education*. Macmillan, New York, p. 27.

417. Ogg, F. A. (editor), 1908, *A Source Book of Mediaeval History*. American Book Company, New York, p. 145.

418. Ibid., p. 146.

419. Rashdall, H., 1895, *The Universities of Europe in the Middle Ages*, vol. 1. Oxford at the Clarendon Press, Oxford, p. 76.

420. Walsh, J. J., 1920, *Medieval Medicine*. A. & C. Black, Ltd., London, p. 42.

421. Ibid., p. 40.

422. Ibid., p. 39.

423. Ibid., p. 48–49.

424. Ibid., p. 50.

425. Rashdall, H., 1895, *The Universities of Europe in the Middle Ages*, vol. 1. Oxford at the Clarendon Press, Oxford, p. 80.

426. Lindberg, D. C., 1978, The Transmission of Greek and Arabic Learning to the West, in *Science in the Middle Ages*, edited by David C. Lindberg. University of Chicago Press, Chicago, p. 61–62.

427. McVaugh, M., 2008, Constantine the Africa, in *Complete Dictionary of Scientific Biography*, edited by Charles Gillispie, vol. 3. Cengage Learning, New York, p. 393.

428. Rashdall, H., 1895, *The Universities of Europe in the Middle Ages*, vol. 1. Oxford at the Clarendon Press, Oxford, p. 78.

429. Ibid., p. 83.

430. Ibid., p. 85.

431. Ibid., p. 94.

432. *Encyclopædia Britannica*, Eleventh Edition, 1911, Universities, vol. 27. Encyclopædia Britannica Company, New York, p. 750.

433. *Encyclopædia Britannica*, Eleventh Edition, 1911, Justinian I. Encyclopædia Britannica Company, New York, p. 598.

434. Rashdall, H., 1895, *The Universities of Europe in the Middle Ages*, vol. 1. Oxford at the Clarendon Press, Oxford, p. 111.

435. Taylor, H. O., 1914, *The Mediaeval Mind*, Second Edition, vol. 2. Macmillan, London, p. 410.

436. *Encyclopædia Britannica*, Eleventh Edition, 1911, Roman Law, vol. 23. Encyclopædia Britannica Company, New York, p. 576.

437. *Encyclopædia Britannica*, Eleventh Edition, 1911, Universities, vol. 27. Encyclopædia Britannica Company, New York, p. 750.

438. Rashdall, H., 1895, *The Universities of Europe in the Middle Ages*, vol. 1. Oxford at the Clarendon Press, Oxford, p. 8.

439. Taylor, H. O., 1914, *The Mediaeval Mind*, Second Edition, vol. 2. Macmillan, London, p. 413.

440. Ibid., p. 410.

441. Rashdall, H., 1895, *The Universities of Europe in the Middle Ages*, vol. 1. Oxford at the Clarendon Press, Oxford, p. 7.

442. Ibid., p. 152.

443. Ibid., p. 163.

444. *Encyclopædia Britannica*, Eleventh Edition, 1911, Universities, vol. 27. Encyclopædia Britannica Company, New York, p. 748.

445. Thorndike, L., 1917, *The History of Medieval Europe*. Houghton Mifflin, Boston, p. 389.

446. Rashdall, H., 1895, *The Universities of Europe in the Middle Ages*, vol. 1. Oxford at the Clarendon Press, Oxford, p. 277.

447. Ibid., p. 278.

448. Ibid., p. 289.

449. Ibid., p. 290.

450. Ibid.

451. Ibid., p. 294.

452. Ibid.

453. Taylor, H. O., 1914, *The Mediaeval Mind*, Second Edition, vol. 2. Macmillan, London, p. 415.

454. Rashdall, H., 1895, *The Universities of Europe in the Middle Ages*, vol. 1. Oxford at the Clarendon Press, Oxford, p. 300.

455. Ibid., p. 302.
456. Ibid., p. 312.
457. Ibid., p. 309.
458. Rashdall, H., 1895, *The Universities of Europe in the Middle Ages*, vol. 2, part 2. Oxford at the Clarendon Press, Oxford, p. 324.
459. Ibid., p. 326.
460. Ibid., p. 345.
461. Ibid., p. 329.
462. Ibid., p. 349.
463. Ibid.
464. Ibid., p. 378.
465. Rashdall, H., 1895, *The Universities of Europe in the Middle Ages*, vol. 1. Oxford at the Clarendon Press, Oxford, p. 324.
466. Taylor, H. O., 1914, *The Mediaeval Mind*, Second Edition, vol. 2. Macmillan, London, p. 417.
467. Ibid., p. 418.
468. Ibid., p. 412.
469. Rashdall, H., 1895, *The Universities of Europe in the Middle Ages*, vol. 1. Oxford at the Clarendon Press, Oxford, p. 150.
470. Taylor, H. O., 1914, *The Mediaeval Mind*, Second Edition, vol. 2. Macmillan, London, p. 413.
471. Pachter, H. M., 1951, *Magic into Science. the Story of Paracelsus*. Henry Schuman, New York, p. 26.
472. Vaughan, R. G., 1871, *The Life & Labours of S. Thomas of Aquin*, vol. 1. Longmans & Co., London, p. 374–376.
473. Taylor, H. O., 1914, *The Mediaeval Mind*, Second Edition, vol. 2. Macmillan, London, p. 414.
474. Thatcher, O. J. (editor), 1907, *The Library of Original Sources*, vol. 4. University Research Extension, New York, p. 357.
475. Ibid., p. 357–358.

Chapter 5.

1. Sarton, G., 1931, *Introduction to the History of Science*, vol. 2, part 2. Carnegie Institution of Washington, Washington, DC, p. 954.
2. Thorndike, L., 1923, *A History of Magic and Experimental Science*, vol. 2. Columbia University Press, New York, p. 597.
3. *Encyclopædia Britannica*, Eleventh Edition, 1910, Aquinas, Thomas, vol. 2. Encyclopædia Britannica Company, New York, p. 250.
4. McInerny, R., 1982, Aquinas, St. Thomas, in *Dictionary of the Middle Ages*, vol. 1, edited by Joseph R. Strayer. Charles Scribner's Sons, New York, p. 353.
5. Vaughan, R. G., 1871, *The Life & Labours of S. Thomas of Aquin*, vol. 1. Longmans & Co., London, p. 1.
6. Ibid., p. 6.
7. *Oxford English Dictionary*, 2008, Draft Revision Dec. 2008, Online Version.
8. Vaughan, R. G., 1871, *The Life & Labours of S. Thomas of Aquin*, vol. 1. Longmans & Co., London, p. 9–10.
9. McInerny, R., 1982, Aquinas, St. Thomas, in *Dictionary of the Middle Ages*, vol. 1, edited by Joseph R. Strayer. Charles Scribner's Sons, New York, p. 353.
10. *Encyclopædia Britannica*, Eleventh Edition, 1910, Dominicans, vol. 8. Encyclopædia Britannica Company, New York, p. 402.
11. Ibid., p. 403.
12. Ibid.
13. Vaughan, R. G., 1871, *The Life & Labours of S. Thomas of Aquin*, vol. 1. Longmans & Co., London, p. 99.
14. Ibid., p. 100.
15. Ibid., p. 103.
16. Ibid.
17. Ibid., p. 104.
18. Ibid.
19. Ibid., p. 105.
20. Ibid., p. 107.
21. Ibid., p. 108.

22. Ibid.
23. Ibid., p. 109.
24. Ibid., p. 110–111.
25. Ibid., p. 113.
26. Ibid., p. 114.
27. Wallace, W. A., 2008, Aquinas, Saint Thomas, in *Complete Dictionary of Scientific Biography*, edited by Charles Gillispie, vol. 1. Cengage Learning, New York, p. 196.
28. Sarton, G., 1931, *Introduction to the History of Science*, vol. 2, part 2. Carnegie Institution of Washington, Washington, DC, p. 939.
29. Ibid., p. 935.
30. Wallace, W. A., 1982, Aristotle in the Middle Ages, in *Dictionary of the Middle Ages*, vol. 1, edited by Joseph R. Strayer. Charles Scribner's Sons, New York, p. 462.
31. Weisheipl, J. A.,1982, Albertus Magnus, in *Dictionary of the Middle Ages*, vol. 1, edited by Joseph R. Strayer. Charles Scribner's Sons, New York, p. 127.
32. Sarton, G., 1931, *Introduction to the History of Science*, vol. 2, part 2. Carnegie Institution of Washington, Washington, DC, p. 935.
33. Thorndike, L., 1923, *A History of Magic and Experimental Science*, vol. 2. Columbia University Press, New York, p. 535.
34. Ibid., p. 539.
35. Ibid., p. 546–547.
36. Thorndike, L., 1914, Roger Bacon and Experimental Method in the Middle Ages. *The Philosophical Review*, no. 3, vol. 23, p. 287.
37. Thorndike, L., 1923, *A History of Magic and Experimental Science*, vol. 2. Columbia University Press, New York, p. 587.
38. Ibid., p. 583.
39. Grant, E. (editor), 1974, *A Source Book in Medieval Science*. Harvard University Press, Cambridge, Massachusetts, p. 547.
40. Thorndike, L., 1923, *A History of Magic and Experimental Science*, vol. 2. Columbia University Press, New York, p. 584.
41. Vaughan, R. G., 1871, *The Life & Labours of S. Thomas of Aquin*, vol. 1. Longmans & Co., London, p. 119.
42. *Encyclopædia Britannica*, Eleventh Edition, 1910, Aquinas, Thomas, vol. 2. Encyclopædia Britannica Company, New York, p. 251.
43. Ibid.
44. Vaughan, R. G., 1871, *The Life & Labours of S. Thomas of Aquin*, vol. 1. Longmans & Co., London, p. 124–125.
45. Ibid., p. 315–316.
46. Schaff, P., and Schaff, D. S., 1907, *History of the Christian Church, vol. 5, part 1, The Middle Ages, from Gregory VII, 1049, to Boniface VIII, 1294*. Charles Scribner's Sons, New York, p. 663.
47. Ibid., p. 664.
48. McInerny, R., 1982, Aquinas, St. Thomas, in *Dictionary of the Middle Ages*, vol. 1, edited by Joseph R. Strayer. Charles Scribner's Sons, New York, p. 353.
49. Ibid., p. 354.
50. Ibid.
51. Wallace, W. A., 2008, Aquinas, Saint Thomas, in *Complete Dictionary of Scientific Biography*, edited by Charles Gillispie, vol. 1. Cengage Learning, New York, p. 197.
52. *Encyclopædia Britannica*, Eleventh Edition, 1910, Aquinas, Thomas, vol. 2. Encyclopædia Britannica Company, New York, p. 251.
53. Schaff, P., and Schaff, D. S., 1907, *History of the Christian Church, vol. 5, part 1, The Middle Ages, from Gregory VII, 1049, to Boniface VIII, 1294*. Charles Scribner's Sons, New York, p. 665.
54. Aquinas, T., 1952, Summa Theologica, Treatise on God, Question 1, Article 1, translated by the Fathers of the English Domincan Province, *Great Books of the Western World*, vol. 19. William Benton, Chicago, p. 3.
55. Ibid.
56. Ibid., Treatise on God, Question 1, Article 2, p. 4.
57. Ibid., Treatise on God, Question 1, Article 5, p. 5.

58. Ibid., Treatise on God, Question 1, Article 6, p. 6.

59. Gilson, E., 1955, *History of Christian Philosophy in the Middle Ages*. Random House, New York, p. 398.

60. *Encyclopædia Britannica*, Eleventh Edition, 1910, Anselm, vol. 2. Encyclopædia Britannica Company, New York, p. 82.

61. Ibid.

62. St. Anselm, 1903, *Proslogium; Monologium; an Appendix in Behalf of the Fool by Gaunilon; and Cur Deus Homo*, translated by Sidney Norton Deane. Open Court, Chicago, p. 7.

63. *Encyclopædia Britannica*, Eleventh Edition, 1910, Anselm, vol. 2. Encyclopædia Britannica Company, New York, p. 82.

64. Grant, E., 2001, *God and Reason in the Middle Ages*. Cambridge University Press, Cambridge, p.36–37.

65. St. Augustine, 1887, On Christian Doctrine, Book 2, Chapter 40, Paragraph 60, translated by J. F. Shaw, in *A Select Library of Nicene and Post-Nicene Fathers*, vol. 2, *St. Augustine's City of God and Christian Doctrine*, edited by Philip Schaff. Charles Scribner's Sons, New York, p. 554.

66. *Encyclopædia Britannica*, Eleventh Edition, 1911, Scholasticism, vol. 24. Encyclopædia Britannica Company, New York, p. 347.

67. Ibid., p. 346.

68. Aquinas, T., 1952, Summa Theologica, Treatise on God, Question 2, Article 3, translated by the Fathers of the English Domincan Province, *Great Books of the Western World*, vol. 19. William Benton, Chicago, p. 12–13.

69. Aristotle, 1941, *Metaphysics*, Book 12, Chapter 7, translated by W. D. Ross, in *Basic Works of Aristotle*. Random House, New York, p. 879 (1072a).

70. Russell, B., 1945, *A History of Western Philosophy*. Simon and Schuster, New York, p. 462.

71. Taylor, H. O., 1914, *The Mediaeval Mind*, Second Edition, vol. 2. Macmillan, London, p. 425.

72. Aquinas, T., 1952, Summa Theologica, Treatise on the Angels, Question 50, Article 1, translated by the Fathers of the English Domincan Province, *Great Books of the Western World*, vol. 19. William Benton, Chicago, p. 269.

73. Ibid., Treatise on the Angels, Question 50, Article 2, p. 270.

74. Ibid., Treatise on the Angels, Question 50, Article 3, p. 272.

75. Ibid., Treatise on the Angels, Question 50, Article 4, p. 273.

76. Ibid., Treatise on the Angels, Question 50, Article 5, p. 274.

77. Ibid., Treatise on the Angels, Question 52, Article 3, p. 280.

78. Ibid., Treatise on the Angels, Question 53, Article 3, p. 283.

79. Ibid., Treatise on the Angels, Question 59, Article 3, p. 308.

80. Ibid., Treatise on the Angels, Question 59, Article 4, p. 309.

81. Russell, B., 1945, *A History of Western Philosophy*. Simon and Schuster, New York, p. 461.

82. Aquinas, T., 1952, Summa Theologica, Supplement to the Third Part, Treatise on the Resurrection, Question 80, Article 4, translated by the Fathers of the English Domincan Province, *Great Books of the Western World*, vol. 20. William Benton, Chicago, p. 959.

83. Vaughan, R. G., 1872, *The Life & Labours of S. Thomas of Aquin*, vol. 2. Longmans & Co., London, p. 916.

84. Ibid., p. 917.

85. Ibid.

86. Ibid., p. 919.

87. *Encyclopædia Britannica*, Eleventh Edition, 1910, Aquinas, Thomas, vol. 2. Encyclopædia Britannica Company, New York, p. 250.

88. Vaughan, R. G., 1872, *The Life & Labours of S. Thomas of Aquin*, vol. 2. Longmans & Co., London, p. 924.

89. Bible, King James Version, Song of Solomon 7:10–7:13.

90. Schaff, P., and Schaff, D. S., 1907, *History of the Christian Church, vol. 5, part 1, The Middle Ages, from Gregory VII,*

1049, to Boniface VIII, 1294. Charles Schribner's Sons, New York, p. 661.

91. Thorndike, L., 1923, *A History of Magic and Experimental Science*, vol. 2. Columbia University Press, New York, p. 597.

92. Grant, E. (editor), 1974, *A Source Book in Medieval Science*. Harvard University Press, Cambridge, Massachusetts, p. 47.

93. Schaff, P., and Schaff, D. S., 1907, *History of the Christian Church, vol. 5, part 1, The Middle Ages, from Gregory VII, 1049, to Boniface VIII, 1294*. Charles Schribner's Sons, New York, p. 662.

94. *Encyclopædia Britannica*, Eleventh Edition, 1910, Christianity, vol. 6. Encyclopædia Britannica Company, New York, p. 288.

Chapter 6.

1. Thorndike, L., 1914, Roger Bacon and Experimental Method in the Middle Ages. *The Philosophical Review*, no. 3, vol. 23, p. 271.

2. Whewell, W., 1858, History of the Inductive Sciences, Third Edition, vol. 1. D. Appleton, New York, p. 245.

3. Mackay, C., 1841, *Memoirs of Extraordinary Popular Delusions*, vol. 3. Richard Bentley, London, p. 35.

4. Thoms, W. J. (editor), 1858, *Early English Prose Romances*, Second Edition, vol. 1. Nattali and Bond, London, p. 248.

5. Sandys, J. E., 1914, Roger Bacon in English Literature, in *Roger Bacon Esssays*, edited by A. G. Little. Oxford University Press, London, p. 366.

6. Thorndike, L., 1914, Roger Bacon and Experimental Method in the Middle Ages. *The Philosophical Review*, no. 3, vol. 23, p. 278.

7. Ibid., p. 290.

8. Ibid., p. 294.

9. Ibid., p. 292.

10. Ibid., p. 294–295.

11. Ibid., p. 295.

12. Aristotle, 1941, *Metaphysica* (*Metaphysics*), Book 1, Chapter 1, translated by W. D. Ross, in Basic Works of Aristotle. Random House, New York, p. 689–690 (981a).

13. Aristotle, 1941, *Analytica Posteriora* (*Posterior Analytics*), Book 2, Chapter 19, translated by A. J. Jenkinson, in Basic Works of Aristotle. Random House, New York, p. 185 (100a).

14. Aristotle, 1939, On the Heavens (*De Caelo*), Book 3, Chapter 7, translated by W. K. C. Guthrie. William Heinemann, London, p. 313–315 (306a).

15. Aristotle, 1923, *Meteorologica* (*Meteorology*), Book 2, Chapter 3, translated by E. W. Webster. Oxford at the Clarendon Press, London, p. 358b.

16. Aristotle, 1912, *De Generatione Animalium* (*On the Generation of Animals*), Book 3, Chapter 10, translated by Arthur Platt, in *The Works of Aristotle Translated into English*, vol. 5, edited by J. A. Smith and W. D. Ross. Oxford University Press, London, p. 760b.

17. Bible, King James Version, Romans 1:20.

18. Thorndike, L., 1923, *A History of Magic and Experimental Science*, vol. 1. Columbia University Press, New York, p. 162.

19. Ibid.

20. Sarton, G., 1954, *Galen of Pergamon*. University of Kansas Press, Lawrence, p. 48, 59.

21. Thorndike, L., 1923, *A History of Magic and Experimental Science*, vol. 1. Columbia University Press, New York, p. 157.

22. Pines, S., 1963, What Was Original in Arabic Science? in, *Scientific Change, Historical Studies in the Intellectual, Social and Technical Conditions for Scientific Discovery and Technical Invention, from Antiquity to Present*, edited by A. C. Crombie. Heinemann, London, p. 195.

23. al-Biruni, 1879, *The Chronology of Ancient Nations*, Preface, translated by C. Edward Sachau. William H. Allen, London, p. 3.

24. Gilson, E., 1955, *History of Christian Philosophy in the Middle Ages*. Random House, New York, p. 642.

25. Adelard of Bath, 1998, On the Same and the Different, in *Adelard of Bath, Conversations with his Nephew*, translated and edited by Charles Burnett. Cambridge University Press, Cambridge, p. 25.

26. Ibid., p. 27.

27. Moody, E. A., 1958, Empiricism and Metaphysics in Medieval Philosophy. *The Philosophical Review*, no. 2, vol. 67, p. 155.

28. Bryce, J., 1920, *The Holy Roman Empire*. Macmillan, London, p. 204.

29. Ibid.

30. McVaugh, M., 2008, Frederick II of Hohenstaufen, in *Complete Dictionary of Scientific Biography*, edited by Charles Gillispie, vol. 5. Cengage Learning, New York, p. 147.

31. Haskins, C. H., 1922, Science at the Court of the Emperor Frederick II. *The American Historical Review*, no. 4, vol. 27, p. 691–692.

32. Ibid., p. 689–690.

33. Ibid., p. 688.

34. Ibid.

35. Ibid., p. 687.

36. Ibid.

37. Ibid., p. 686.

38. Ibid.

39. Ibid.

40. Ibid.

41. Ibid.

42. Thorndike, L., 1914, Roger Bacon and Experimental Method in the Middle Ages. *The Philosophical Review*, no. 3, vol. 23, p. 285.

43. Ibid., p. 288.

44. Adelard of Bath, 1998, On the Same and the Different, in *Adelard of Bath, Conversations with his Nephew*, translated and edited by Charles Burnett. Cambridge University Press, Cambridge, p. 25.

45. Aquinas, T., 1952, Summa Theologica, Treatise on Man, Question 84, Article 6, translated by the Fathers of the English Domincan Province, *Great Books of the Western World*, vol. 19. William Benton, Chicago, p. 448.

46. McVaugh, M., 2008, Arnald of Villanova, in *Complete Dictionary of Scientific Biography*, edited by Charles Gillispie, vol. 1. Cengage Learning, New York, p. 290.

47. Thorndike, L., 1914, Roger Bacon and Experimental Method in the Middle Ages. *The Philosophical Review*, no. 3, vol. 23, p. 289.

48. Hackett, J., 2008, Bacon, Roger, in *Complete Dictionary of Scientific Biography*, edited by Charles Gillispie, vol. 19. Cengage Learning, New York, p. 143.

49. Little, A. G., 1914, Introduction on Roger Bacon's Life and Works, in *Roger Bacon Esssays*, edited by A. G. Little. Oxford University Press, London, p. 1.

50. Crowley, T., 1950, *Roger Bacon, the Problem of the Soul in his Philosophical Commentaries*. Editions de l'Institut superieur de philosophie, Louvain, p. 19.

51. Bridges, J. H., 1914, *The Life & Work of Roger Bacon*. Williams & Norgate, London, p. 18.

52. Crowley, T., 1950, *Roger Bacon, the Problem of the Soul in his Philosophical Commentaries*. Editions de l'Institut superieur de philosophie, Louvain, p. 19.

53. Bridges, J. H., 1914, *The Life & Work of Roger Bacon*. Williams & Norgate, London, p. 146–147.

54. Crowley, T., 1950, *Roger Bacon, the Problem of the Soul in his Philosophical Commentaries*. Editions de l'Institut superieur de philosophie, Louvain, p,. 21.

55. Crombie, A. C., 2008, Robert Grosseteste, in *Complete Dictionary of Scientific Biography*, edited by Charles Gillispie, vol. 5. Cengage Learning, New York, p. 551.

56. Stevenson, F. S., 1899, *Robert Grosseteste, Bishop of Lincoln*. Macmillan, London, p. 47.

57. Crombie, A. C., 1953, *Robert Grosseteste and the Origins of Experimental Science 1100–1700*. Oxford at the Clarendon Press, Oxford, p. 10.

58. Ibid., p. 54.

59. Ibid., p. 84–85.

60. Aristotle, 1941, Analytica Priora (Prior Analytics), Book 1, Chapter 7, translated by A. J. Jenkinson, in *Basic Works of Aristotle*. Random House, New York, p. 76 (29b).

61. Heath, T. L., 1956, *The Thirteen Books of Euclid's Elements*, Second Edition, vol. 1 (first published in 1908 by Cambridge Univ. Press). Dover, New York, p. 136.

62. Aristotle, 1941, De Generatione et Corruptione (On Generation and Corruption), Book 2, Chapter 10, translated by Harold H. Joachim, in *Basic Works of Aristotle*. Random House, New York, p. 525 (336a).

63. Crombie, A. C., 1953, *Robert Grosseteste and the Origins of Experimental Science 1100–1700*. Oxford at the Clarendon Press, Oxford, p. 88.

64. Ibid., p. 86.

65. Ibid., p. 85.

66. Ptolemy, C., 1952, The Almagest, Book 3, Chapter 4, translated by R. Catesby Taliaferro, in *Great Books of the Western World*, vol. 16. William Benton, Chicago, p. 93.

67. Stevenson, F. S., 1899, *Robert Grosseteste, Bishop of Lincoln*. Macmillan, London, p. 50.

68. Bridges, J. H., 1914, *The Life & Work of Roger Bacon*. Williams & Norgate, London, p. 147.

69. Crombie, A. C., 1953, *Robert Grosseteste and the Origins of Experimental Science 1100–1700*. Oxford at the Clarendon Press, Oxford, p. 139.

70. Stevenson, F. S., 1899, *Robert Grosseteste, Bishop of Lincoln*. Macmillan, London, p. 51.

71. Ibid.

72. Ibid., p. 43.

73. Hackett, J. M. G., 1983, Bacon, Roger, in *Dictionary of the Middle Ages*, vol. 2, edited by Joseph R. Strayer. Charles Scribner's Sons, New York, p. 35.

74. Crowley, T., 1950, *Roger Bacon, the Problem of the Soul in his Philosophical Commentaries*. Editions de l'Institut superieur de philosophie, Louvain, p, 28.

75. Bridges, J. H., 1914, *The Life & Work of Roger Bacon*. Williams & Norgate, London, p. 149.

76. Ibid., p. 25.

77. Little, A. G., 1914, Introduction on Roger Bacon's Life and Works, in *Roger Bacon Esssays*, edited by A. G. Little. Oxford University Press, London, p. 3.

78. Wallace, W. A., 1973, Experimental Science and Mechanics in the Middle Ages, in *Dictionary of the History of Ideas*, edited by P. P. Wiener, vol. 2. Charles Scribner's Sons, New York, p. 197.

79. Titus Lucretius Carus, 1743, *Of the Nature of Things*, Book 6, vol. 2. Daniel Brown, London, p. 303.

80. Pliny the Elder, 1857, *The Natural History of Pliny*, translated by John Bostock and H. T. Riley, book 36, chapter 25, vol. 6. Henry G. Bohn, London, p. 355.

81. Ibid.

82. Petrus Peregrinus, 1904, *The Letter of Petrus Peregrinus on the Magnet*, translated by Brother Arnold. McGraw, New York, p. xvi.

83. Ibid., p. 8.

84. Ibid., p. 10–11.

85. Ibid., p. 11.

86. Ibid., p. 12.

87. Ibid., p. 25.

88. Ibid., p. 31.

89. White, L., 1962, *Medieval Technology and Social Change*. Oxford at the Clarendon Press, Oxford, p. 89.

90. Ibid., p. 87–88.

91. Ibid., p. 130–131.

92. Grant, E., 2008, Peter Peregrinus, in *Complete Dictionary of Scientific Biography*, edited by Charles Gillispie, vol. 10. Cengage Learning, New York, p. 533.

93. Ibid., p. 534.

94. Bridges, J. H., 1914, *The Life & Work of Roger Bacon*. Williams & Norgate, London, p. 22.

95. Ibid., p. 21–22.

96. Bacon, R., 1928, *The Opus Majus of Roger Bacon*, vol. 2, translated by Robert Belle Burke. University of Pennsylvania Press, Philadelphia, p. 630.

97. Ibid.

98. Thorndike, L., 1923, *A History of Magic and Experimental Science*, vol. 1. Columbia University Press, New York, p. 170.

99. Bridges, J. H., 1914, *The Life & Work of Roger Bacon*. Williams & Norgate, London, p. 24.

100. Ibid., p. 20.

101. Crowley, T., 1950, *Roger Bacon, the Problem of the Soul in his Philosophical Commentaries*. Editions de l'Institut superieur de philosophie, Louvain, p. 29–31.

102. Bridges, J. H., 1914, *The Life & Work of Roger Bacon*. Williams & Norgate, London, p. 16–17.

103. the date for Bacon's entry into the Franciscan order is given as 1257 by Crowley (1950, p. 32). Bridges (1914, p. 17) cites a range of 1245–1250.

104. *Encyclopædia Britannica*, Eleventh Edition, 1910, Bonaventura, Saint. Encyclopædia Britannica Company, New York, p. 198.

105. Gilson, E., 1955, *History of Christian Philosophy in the Middle Ages*. Random House, New York, p. 726.

106. *Encyclopædia Britannica*, Eleventh Edition, 1910, Bonaventura, Saint. Encyclopædia Britannica Company, New York, p. 197.

107. Little, A. G., 1914, Introduction on Roger Bacon's Life and Works, in *Roger Bacon Esssays*, edited by A. G. Little. Oxford University Press, London, p. 7.

108. Bridges, J. H., 1914, *The Life & Work of Roger Bacon*. Williams & Norgate, London, p. 26.

109. Grant, E. (editor), 1974, *A Source Book in Medieval Science*. Harvard University Press, Cambridge, Massachusetts, p. 50.

110. Crowley, T., 1950, *Roger Bacon, the Problem of the Soul in his Philosophical Commentaries*. Editions de l'Institut superieur de philosophie, Louvain, p. 56.

111. Bridges, J. H., 1914, *The Life & Work of Roger Bacon*. Williams & Norgate, London, p. 83–93.

112. Bacon, R., 1900, *The Opus Majus of Roger Bacon*, vol. 1, edited and translated by John Henry Bridges. Williams and Norgate, London, p. cxv.

113. Bacon, R., 1928, *The Opus Majus of Roger Bacon*, vol. 1, translated by Robert Belle Burke. University of Pennsylvania Press, Philadelphia, p. 404.

114. Ibid., p. 403.

115. Ibid., p. 276.

116. Little, A. G., 1914, Introduction on Roger Bacon's Life and Works, in *Roger Bacon Esssays*, edited by A. G. Little. Oxford University Press, London, p. 24.

117. Bridges, J. H., 1914, *The Life & Work of Roger Bacon*. Williams & Norgate, London, p. 85.

118. Thorndike, L., 1923, *A History of Magic and Experimental Science*, vol. 2. Columbia University Press, New York, p. 628.

119. Bacon, R., 1900, *The Opus Majus of Roger Bacon*, vol. 1, edited and translated by John Henry Bridges. Williams and Norgate, London, p. cxiii.

120. Bridges, J. H., 1914, *The Life & Work of Roger Bacon*. Williams & Norgate, London, p. 88.

121. Bacon, R., 1928, *The Opus Majus of Roger Bacon*, vol. 2, translated by Robert Belle Burke. University of Pennsylvania Press, Philadelphia, p. 615.

122. Ibid., p. 616.

123. Ibid., p. 625.

124. Ibid., p. 623–624.

125. Crowley, T., 1950, *Roger Bacon, the Problem of the Soul in his Philosophical Commentaries*. Editions de l'Institut superieur de philosophie, Louvain, p. 36.

126. Ibid., p. 37.

127. Little, A. G., 1914, Introduction on Roger Bacon's Life and Works, in *Roger Bacon Esssays*, edited by A. G. Little. Oxford University Press, London, p. 10.

128. accounts differ. Crowley (1950, p. 37) maintained that "the *Opus Majus* was not even planned when Pope Clement's letter reached Bacon." On the contrary, Thorndike (1923, vol. 2, p. 624) concluded that "the *Opus Majus*…was practically finished, if not already sent, when the papal mandate of 1266 reached Bacon.".

129. Little, A. G., 1914, Introduction on Roger Bacon's Life and Works, in *Roger Bacon Essays*, edited by A. G. Little. Oxford University Press, London, p. 11.

130. Ibid.

131. Bacon, R., 1928, *The Opus Majus of Roger Bacon*, vol. 1, translated by Robert Belle Burke. University of Pennsylvania Press, Philadelphia, p. 36.

132. Ibid., p. 4.

133. Ibid., p. 20.

134. Ibid., p. 23–24.

135. Burtt, E. A., 1932, *The Metaphysical Foundations of Modern Physical Science*, Revised Edition. Kegan Paul, Trench, Trubner & Co., Ltd., London, p. 64.

136. Bacon, R., 1928, *The Opus Majus of Roger Bacon*, vol. 1, translated by Robert Belle Burke. University of Pennsylvania Press, Philadelphia, p. 116.

137. Smith, D. E., 1914, The Place of Roger Bacon in the History of Mathematics, in *Roger Bacon Esssays*, edited by A. G. Little. Oxford University Press, London, p. 167.

138. Ibid.

139. Lindberg, D. C., 1997, Roger Bacon on Light, Vision, and the Universal Emanation of Force, in *Roger Bacon & the Sciences, Commemorative Essays*, edited by Jeremiah Hackett. Leiden, New York, p. 266.

140. Bacon, R., 1928, *The Opus Majus of Roger Bacon*, vol. 1, translated by Robert Belle Burke. University of Pennsylvania Press, Philadelphia, p. 311.

141. Grant, E., 1977, *Physical Science in the Middle Ages*. Cambridge University Press, Cambridge, p. 62–63.

142. Woodward, D., and Howe, H. M., 1997, Roger Bacon on Geography and Cartography, in *Roger Bacon & the Sciences, Commemorative Essays*, edited by Jeremiah Hackett. Leiden, New York, p. 206.

143. Bacon, R., 1907, On Experimental Science, in *The Library of Original Sources*, vol. 4, edited by Oliver Joseph Thatcher. University Research Extension, New York, p. 369.

144. Ibid., p. 369–370.

145. Thorndike, L., 1923, *A History of Magic and Experimental Science*, vol. 1. Columbia University Press, New York, p. 158.

146. Bacon, R., 1928, *The Opus Majus of Roger Bacon*, vol. 1, translated by Robert Belle Burke. University of Pennsylvania Press, Philadelphia, p. 273, 398, 401–402.

147. Ibid., p. 401–402.

148. Bacon, R., 1928, *The Opus Majus of Roger Bacon*, vol. 2, translated by Robert Belle Burke. University of Pennsylvania Press, Philadelphia, p. 633.

149. Lindberg, D. C., 1997, Roger Bacon on Light, Vision, and the Universal Emanation of Force, in *Roger Bacon & the Sciences, Commemorative Essays*, edited by Jeremiah Hackett. Leiden, New York, p. 267.

150. Ibid., p. 243.

151. Hackett, J., 2008, Bacon, Roger, in *Complete Dictionary of Scientific Biography*, edited by Charles Gillispie, vol. 19. Cengage Learning, New York, p. 147.

152. Lindberg, D. C., 1997, Roger Bacon on Light, Vision, and the Universal Emanation of Force, in *Roger Bacon & the Sciences, Commemorative Essays*, edited by Jeremiah Hackett. Leiden, New York, p. 270.

153. Bacon, R., 1928, *The Opus Majus of Roger Bacon*, vol. 2, translated by Robert Belle Burke. University of Pennsylvania Press, Philadelphia, p. 629–630.

154. Hall, A. R., 1956, A Note on Military Pyrotechnics, in *A History of Technology*, vol. 2, edited by Charles Singer. Oxford University Press, London, p. 377.

155. Goodrich, L. C., and Feng, C-S., 1946, The Early Development of Firearms in China. *Isis*, no. 2, vol. 36, p. 123.

156. Hall, A. R., 1956, Military Technology, in *A History of Technology*, vol. 2, edited by Charles Singer. Oxford University Press, London, p. 726.

157. Taylor, H. O., 1914, *The Mediaeval Mind*, Second Edition, vol. 2. Macmillan, London, p. 538.

158. White, L., 1962, *Medieval Technology and Social Change*. Oxford at the Clarendon Press, Oxford, p. 134.

159. *Encyclopædia Britannica*, Eleventh Edition, 1910,

Bacon, Roger, vol. 3. Encyclopædia Britannica Company, New York, p. 154.

160. Coulton, G. G. (editor and translator) 1929, *Life in the Middle Ages*, Second Edition, vol. 2 (first published as *A Medieval Garner* in 1910 by Constable, London). Cambridge University Press, Cambridge, p. 56.

161. Ibid.

162. Ibid.

163. Ibid. p. 56–57.

164. Ibid., p. 59–60.

165. Ibid., p. 60.

166. Ibid., p. 60–61.

167. Sarton, G., 1931, *Introduction to the History of Science*, vol. 2, part 2. Carnegie Institution, Washington, DC, p. 953.

168. Ibid., p. 954.

169. *Encyclopædia Britannica*, Eleventh Edition, 1911, Nicholas IV, vol. 19. Encyclopædia Britannica Company, New York, p. 650.

170. Grant, E. (editor), 1974, *A Source Book in Medieval Science*. Harvard University Press, Cambridge, Massachusetts, p. 45–50.

171. Bridges, J. H., 1914, *The Life & Work of Roger Bacon*. Williams & Norgate, London, p. 31.

172. Hackett, J. M. G., 1983, Bacon, Roger, in *Dictionary of the Middle Ages*, vol. 2, edited by Joseph R. Strayer. Charles Scribner's Sons, New York, p. 35.

173. *Encyclopædia Britannica*, Eleventh Edition, 1910, Bacon, Roger, vol. 3. Encyclopædia Britannica Company, New York, p. 154.

174. Crowley, T., 1950, *Roger Bacon, the Problem of the Soul in his Philosophical Commentaries*. Editions de l'Institut superieur de philosophie, Louvain, p. 69.

175. Hackett, J., 2008, Bacon, Roger, in *Complete Dictionary of Scientific Biography*, edited by Charles Gillispie, vol. 19. Cengage Learning, New York, p. 142.

176. Bridges, J. H., 1914, *The Life & Work of Roger Bacon*. Williams & Norgate, London, p. 34.

Chapter 7.

1. White, L., 1940, Technology and Invention in the Middle Ages. *Speculum*, no. 2, vol. 15, p. 151.

2. Cardwell, D. S. L., 1972, *Turning Points in Western Technology*. Science History Publications, New York, p. 4.

3. Drower, M. S., 1954, Water-Supply, Irrigation, and Agriculture, in *A History of Technology*, vol. 1, edited by Charles Singer. Oxford University Press, London, p. 539.

4. Jope, E. M., 1956, Agricultural Implements, in *A History of Technology*, vol. 2, edited by Charles Singer. Oxford University Press, London, p. 83.

5. White, L., 1962, *Medieval Technology and Social Change*. Oxford at the Clarendon Press, Oxford, p. 41–42.

6. Pliny the Elder, 1856, *The Natural History of Pliny*, translated by John Bostock and H. T. Riley, book 18, chapter 48, vol. 4. Henry G. Bohn, London, p. 62.

7. Jope, E. M., 1956, Agricultural Implements, in *A History of Technology*, vol. 2, edited by Charles Singer. Oxford University Press, London, p. 88.

8. White, L., 1962, *Medieval Technology and Social Change*. Oxford at the Clarendon Press, Oxford, p. 53–54.

9. Ibid., p. 43.

10. *Encyclopædia Britannica*, Eleventh Edition, 1910, Harrow, vol. 13. Cambridge University Press, New York, p. 27.

11. Jope, E. M., 1956, Agricultural Implements, in *A History of Technology*, vol. 2, edited by Charles Singer. Oxford University Press, London, p. 94.

12. *Encyclopædia Britannica*, Eleventh Edition, 1910, Harrow, vol. 13. Cambridge University Press, New York, p. 27.

13. White, L., 1962, *Medieval Technology and Social Change*. Oxford at the Clarendon Press, Oxford, p. 43–44.

14. Gies, F., and Gies, J., 1994, *Cathedral, Forge, and Waterwheel*. HarperCollins, New York, p. 47.

15. Gimpel, J., 1976, *The Medieval Machine*. Holt, Rinehart and Winston, New York, p. 33.

16. White, L., 1962, *Medieval Technology and Social Change*. Oxford at the Clarendon Press, Oxford, p. 61.

17. Ibid., p. 62.

18. Jope, E. M., 1956, Agricultural Implements, in *A History of Technology*, vol. 2, edited by Charles Singer. Oxford University Press, London, p. 91.

19. Gimpel, J., 1976, *The Medieval Machine*. Holt, Rinehart and Winston, New York, p. 36–37.

20. White, L., 1962, *Medieval Technology and Social Change*. Oxford at the Clarendon Press, Oxford, p. 57.

21. Gimpel, J., 1976, *The Medieval Machine*. Holt, Rinehart and Winston, New York, p. 34.

22. Goodchild, R. G., and Forbes, R. J., 1956, Road and Land Travel, in *A History of Technology*, vol. 2, edited by Charles Singer. Oxford University Press, London, p. 527.

23. White, L., 1962, *Medieval Technology and Social Change*. Oxford at the Clarendon Press, Oxford, p. 66–68.

24. Diodorus Siculus, 1814, *The Historical Library of Diodorus the Sicilian*, Book 2, Chapter 3, vol. 1, translated by G. Booth. W. M'Dowall for J. Davis, London, p. 139.

25. White, L., 1962, *Medieval Technology and Social Change*. Oxford at the Clarendon Press, Oxford, p. 71.

26. Gimpel, J., 1976, *The Medieval Machine*. Holt, Rinehart and Winston, New York, p. 52.

27. Cato, Marcus Porcius, 1913, De Agricultura, in *Roman Farm Management*, translated by "A Virginia Farmer." Macmillan, New York, p. 42.

28. White, L., 1962, *Medieval Technology and Social Change*. Oxford at the Clarendon Press, Oxford, p. 72.

29. Gimpel, J., 1976, *The Medieval Machine*. Holt, Rinehart and Winston, New York, p. 40.

30. Ibid., p. 43.

31. Forbes, R. J., 1956, Food and Drink, in *A History of Technology*, vol. 2, edited by Charles Singer. Oxford University Press, London, p. 108.

32. Forbes, R. J., 1956, Power, in *A History of Technology*, vol. 2, edited by Charles Singer. Oxford University Press, London, p. 593–595.

33. Gies, F., and Gies, J., 1994, *Cathedral, Forge, and Waterwheel*. HarperCollins, New York, p. 33.

34. Forbes, R. J., 1956, Power, in *A History of Technology*, vol. 2, edited by Charles Singer. Oxford University Press, London, p. 596.

35. Vitruvius, 1960, *The Ten Books on Architecture*, Book 10, Chapter 5, translated by Morris H. Morgan (first published in 1914 by Harvard University Press, Cambridge, Massachusetts). Dover, New York, p. 294.

36. Forbes, R. J., 1956, Power, in *A History of Technology*, vol. 2, edited by Charles Singer. Oxford University Press, London, p. 596–599.

37. Gies, F., and Gies, J., 1994, *Cathedral, Forge, and Waterwheel*. HarperCollins, New York, p. 115.

38. Ibid.

39. Strabo, 1856, *The Geography of Strabo*, Book 12, Chapter 3, Paragraph 30, vol. 2, translated by H. C. Hamilton and W. Falconer. Henry G. Bohn, London, p. 306.

40. Forbes, R. J., 1956, Power, in *A History of Technology*, vol. 2, edited by Charles Singer. Oxford University Press, London, p. 598.

41. Ibid., p. 599.

42. White, L., 1962, *Medieval Technology and Social Change*. Oxford at the Clarendon Press, Oxford, p. 82.

43. Forbes, R. J., 1956, Power, in *A History of Technology*, vol. 2, edited by Charles Singer. Oxford University Press, London, p. 602.

44. Suetonius, C. T., 1906, *The Lives of the Twelve Caesars*, Vespasian, Paragraph 18. George Bell & Sons, London, p. 457.

45. Forbes, R. J., 1956, Power, in *A History of Technology*, vol. 2, edited by Charles Singer. Oxford University Press, London, p. 605.

46. White, L., 1962, *Medieval Technology and Social Change*. Oxford at the Clarendon Press, Oxford, p. 85.

47. Gies, F., and Gies, J., 1994, *Cathedral, Forge, and Waterwheel*. HarperCollins, New York, p. 113.

48. Gimpel, J., 1976, *The Medieval Machine*. Holt, Rinehart and Winston, New York, p. 10.

49. Ibid., p,. 12.

50. White, L., 1962, *Medieval Technology and Social Change*. Oxford at the Clarendon Press, Oxford, p. 84.

51. Ibid., p. 40.

52. Ibid., 84.

53. Gimpel, J., 1976, *The Medieval Machine*. Holt, Rinehart and Winston, New York, p. 66–67.

54. Ibid., p. 46–47.

55. Ibid., p. 68.

56. Gies, F., and Gies, J., 1994, *Cathedral, Forge, and Waterwheel*. HarperCollins, New York, p. 114.

57. Forbes, R. J., 1956, Power, in *A History of Technology*, vol. 2, edited by Charles Singer. Oxford University Press, London, p. 610–611.

58. Gille, B., 1956, Machines, in *A History of Technology*, vol. 2, edited by Charles Singer. Oxford University Press, London, p. 653.

59. White, L., 1940, Technology and Invention in the Middle Ages. *Speculum*, no. 2, vol. 15, p. 153.

60. Gille, B., 1956, Machines, in *A History of Technology*, vol. 2, edited by Charles Singer. Oxford University Press, London, p. 652.

61. Gies, F., and Gies, J., 1994, *Cathedral, Forge, and Waterwheel*. HarperCollins, New York, p. 117.

62. Gimpel, J., 1976, *The Medieval Machine*. Holt, Rinehart and Winston, New York, p. 23.

63. Forbes, R. J., 1956, Power, in *A History of Technology*, vol. 2, edited by Charles Singer. Oxford University Press, London, p. 616–620.

64. White, L., 1962, *Medieval Technology and Social Change*. Oxford at the Clarendon Press, Oxford, p. 87–88.

65. Hill, D., 1984, *A History of Engineering in Classical and Medieval Times*. Open Court, La Salle, Illinois, p. 225.

66. Price, D. J., 1957, Precision Instruments. to 1500, in *A History of Technology*, vol. 3, edited by Charles Singer. Oxford University Press, London, p. 556.

67. Hill, D., 1984, *A History of Engineering in Classical and Medieval Times*. Open Court, La Salle, Illinois, p. 224.

68. Price, D. J., 1957, Precision Instruments. to 1500, in *A History of Technology*, vol. 3, edited by Charles Singer. Oxford University Press, London, p. 602.

69. Drachman, A. G., 2008, Ctesibius, in *Complete Dictionary of Scientific Biography*, vol. 3. Charles Scribner's Sons, Detroit, p. 491.

70. Vitruvius, 1960, *The Ten Books on Architecture*, Book 9, Chapter 8, translated by Morris Hicky Morgan (first published by Harvard University Press in 1914). Dover, New York, p. 274.

71. Cicero, Marcus Tullius, 1775, *Of the Nature of the Gods, in Three Books*, Book 2. T. Davies, London, p. 134.

72. Hill, D., 1984, *A History of Engineering in Classical and Medieval Times*. Open Court, La Salle, Illinois, p. 224–225.

73. Needham, J., 1959, *Science and Civilisation in China*, vol. 3. Cambridge University Press, Cambridge, p. 363.

74. Ibid., p. 363–366.

75. Usher, A. P., 1954, *A History of Mechanical Inventions*, Revised Edition. Harvard University Press, Cambridge, Massachusetts, p. 189.

76. Thorndike, L., 1941, Invention of the Mechanical Clock about 1271 AD. *Speculum*, no. 2, vol. 16, p. 242.

77. Hill, D., 1984, *A History of Engineering in Classical and Medieval Times*. Open Court, La Salle, Illinois, p. 243.

78. Cardwell, D. S. L., 1972, *Turning Points in Western Technology*. Science History Publications, New York, p. 14.

79. e.g., see the illustration in. Gies, F., and Gies, J., 1994, *Cathedral, Forge, and Waterwheel*. HarperCollins, New York, p. 212.

80. Usher, A. P., 1954, *A History of Mechanical Inventions*, Revised Edition. Harvard University Press, Cambridge, Massachusetts, p. 207.

81. Ibid., p. 197.

82. Ibid., p. 195.

83. Ibid., p. 197.

84. Lloyd, H. A., 1957, Mechanical Timekeepers, in *A History of Technology*, vol. 3, edited by Charles Singer. Oxford University Press, London, p. 652.

85. Usher, A. P., 1954, *A History of Mechanical Inventions*, Revised Edition. Harvard University Press, Cambridge, Massachusetts, p. 209.

86. Cardwell, D. S. L., 1972, *Turning Points in Western Technology*. Science History Publications, New York, p. 18.

87. Lloyd, H. A., 1957, Mechanical Timekeepers, in *A History of Technology*, vol. 3, edited by Charles Singer. Oxford University Press, London, p. 653.

88. Ibid., p. 656.

89. Ibid., p. 656–657.

90. Usher, A. P., 1954, *A History of Mechanical Inventions*, Revised Edition. Harvard University Press, Cambridge, Massachusetts, p. 210.

91. Lloyd, H. A., 1957, Mechanical Timekeepers, in *A History of Technology*, vol. 3, edited by Charles Singer. Oxford University Press, London, p. 662–663.

92. Bos, H. J. M., 2008, Huygens, Christiaan, in *Complete Dictionary of Scientific Biography*, edited by Charles Gillispie, vol. 6. Charles Scribner's Sons, Detroit, p. 598.

93. White, L., 1962, *Medieval Technology and Social Change*. Oxford at the Clarendon Press, Oxford, p. 1–38.

94. Herodotus, 1910, *The History of Herodotus*, Book 3, Chapter 64, translated by George Rawlinson (1812–1902), vol. 1 (first published in 1858). J. M. Dent & Sons, New York, p. 241–242.

95. Polybius, 1889, *The Histories of Polybius*, Book 3, Chapter 117, vol. 1, translated by Evelyn S. Shuckburgh. Macmillan and Co., London, p. 273.

96. White, L., 1962, *Medieval Technology and Social Change*. Oxford at the Clarendon Press, Oxford, p. 14.

97. Xenophon, 1857, On Horsemanship, in *Xenophon's Minor Works*, Chapter 8, Paragraph 8, translated by J. S. Watson. Henry G. Bohn, London, p. 290.

98. Jope, E. M., 1956, Vehicles and Harness, in *A History of Technology*, vol. 2, edited by Charles Singer. Oxford University Press, London, p. 556.

99. Dien, A. E., 1986, The Stirrup and Its Effect on Chinese Military History. *Ars Orientalis*, vol. 16, p. 33.

100. De Camp, L. S., 1960, Before Stirrups. *Isis*, no. 2, vol. 51, p.159–160.

101. Dien, A. E., 1986, The Stirrup and Its Effect on Chinese Military History. *Ars Orientalis*, vol. 16, p. 33.

102. Ibid., p. 35.

103. Jope, E. M., 1956, Vehicles and Harness, in *A History of Technology*, vol. 2, edited by Charles Singer. Oxford University Press, London, p. 557.

104. De Camp, L. S., 1960, Before Stirrups. *Isis*, no. 2, vol. 51, p.159.

105. *Encyclopædia Britannica*, Eleventh Edition, 1911, Maurice, vol. 17. Encyclopædia Britannica Company, New York, p. 909.

106. White, L., 1962, *Medieval Technology and Social Change*. Oxford at the Clarendon Press, Oxford, p. 21.

107. Jope, E. M., 1956, Vehicles and Harness, in *A History of Technology*, vol. 2, edited by Charles Singer. Oxford University Press, London, p. 557.

108. Contamine, P., 1984, *War in the Middle Ages*, translated by Michael Jones. Basil Blackwell, Oxford, p. 179.

109. White, L., 1962, *Medieval Technology and Social Change*. Oxford at the Clarendon Press, Oxford, p. 2.

110. Gies, F., and Gies, J., 1994, *Cathedral, Forge, and Waterwheel*. HarperCollins, New York, p. 57–58.

111. Ibid., p. 62.

112. White, L., 1962, *Medieval Technology and Social Change*. Oxford at the Clarendon Press, Oxford, p. 13.

113. Gies, F., and Gies, J., 1994, *Cathedral, Forge, and Waterwheel*. HarperCollins, New York, p. 55.

114. Reynolds, R. L., 1961, *Europe Emerges*. University of Wisconsin Press, Madison, p. 158–162.

115. Boissonnade, P., 1987, *Life and Work in Medieval Europe*, translated by Eileen Power (first published in 1927 by A. A. Knopf in New York and by Routledge & K. Paul in London). Dorset Press, New York, p. 115.

116. Hall, A. R., 1956, Military Technology, in *A History of Technology*, vol. 2, edited by Charles Singer. Oxford University Press, London, p. 707–720.

117. Vitruvius, 1960, *The Ten Books on Architecture*, Book 10, Chapters 10 and 11, translated by Morris Hicky Morgan (first published by Harvard University Press in 1914). Dover, New York, p. 303–308.

118. Reynolds, R. L., 1961, *Europe Emerges*. University of Wisconsin Press, Madison, p. 173.

119. Chevedden, P. E., et al., 1995, The Trebuchet. *Scientific American*, no. 1, vol. 273, p. 66.

120. Hall, A. R., 1956, Military Technology, in *A History of Technology*, vol. 2, edited by Charles Singer. Oxford University Press, London, p. 724.

121. Chevedden, P. E., et al., 1995, The Trebuchet. *Scientific American*, no. 1, vol. 273, p. 68.

122. Contamine, P., 1984, *War in the Middle Ages*, translated by Michael Jones. Basil Blackwell, Oxford, p. 103–104. In converting to metes, I have assumed the "feet" given here are "French feet," with one French foot equal to 0:3248 meters. The *Oxford English Dictionary* (Second Edition, 1989) defines a *toise* as equivalent to 1:949 meters.

123. assuming a density for packed and compressed soil of 1,500 kilograms per cubic meter, based on data in. Lal, R. (Editor), 2006, *Encyclopedia of Soil Science*, Second Edition, vol. 1. CRC Press, Boca Raton, Florida, p. 192.

124. Chevedden, P. E., et al., 1995, The Trebuchet. *Scientific American*, no. 1, vol. 273, p. 67.

125. Contamine, P., 1984, *War in the Middle Ages*, translated by Michael Jones. Basil Blackwell, Oxford, p. 103.

126. Ibid., p. 104.

127. Ibid., p. 104–105.

128. Hall, A. R., 1956, Military Technology, in *A History of Technology*, vol. 2, edited by Charles Singer. Oxford University Press, London, p. 727.

129. Chevedden, P. E., et al., 1995, The Trebuchet. *Scientific American*, no. 1, vol. 273, p. 69.

130. Hall, A. R., 1956, A Note on Military Pyrotechnics, in *A History of Technology*, vol. 2, edited by Charles Singer. Oxford University Press, London, p. 377.

131. White, L., 1962, *Medieval Technology and Social Change*. Oxford at the Clarendon Press, Oxford, p. 98.

132. Thucydides, 1942, The Peloponnesian War, Book 2, Chapter 77, translated by Benjamin Jowett (1817–1893), in *The Greek Historians*, vol. 1. Random House, New York, p. 668.

133. *Encyclopædia Britannica*, Eleventh Edition, 1910, Greek Fire, vol. 12. Cambridge University Press, New York, p. 492.

134. Ibid., p. 492–493.

135. Gies, F., and Gies, J., 1994, *Cathedral, Forge, and Waterwheel*. HarperCollins, New York, p. 61.

136. Hall, A. R., 1956, Military Technology, in *A History of Technology*, vol. 2, edited by Charles Singer. Oxford University Press, London, p. 726–727.

137. *Encyclopædia Britannica*, Eleventh Edition, 1910, Arms and Armour, vol. 2. Encyclopædia Britannica Company, New York, p. 590.

138. Hall, A. R., 1957, Military Technology, in *A History of Technology*, vol. 3, edited by Charles Singer. Oxford University Press, London, p. 348.

139. Ibid., p. 350–351.

140. Ibid., p. 352–353.

141. *Encyclopædia Britannica*, Eleventh Edition, 1910, Gun, vol. 12. Cambridge University Press, New York, p. 717.

142. Ibid.

143. Ibid., p. 718.

144. White, L., 1962, *Medieval Technology and Social Change*. Oxford at the Clarendon Press, Oxford, p. 100.

145. Gies, F., and Gies, J., 1994, *Cathedral, Forge, and Waterwheel*. HarperCollins, New York, p. 73.

146. Mott, L. V., 1991, *The Development of the Rudder, 100–1600 AD. a Technological Tale*. MS Thesis, Texas A&M University, College Station, p. iii.

147. *Encyclopædia Britannica*, Ninth Edition, 1890, Shipbuilding, vol. 21. Henry G. Allen, New York, p. 823.

148. Gies, F., and Gies, J., 1994, *Cathedral, Forge, and Waterwheel*. HarperCollins, New York, p. 76.

149. White, L., 1962, *Medieval Technology and Social Change*. Oxford at the Clarendon Press, Oxford, p. 132.

150. Singer, C., Price, D. J., and Taylor, E. G. R., 1957, Cartography, Survey, and Navigation to 1400, in *A History of Technology*, vol. 3, edited by Charles Singer. Oxford University Press, London, p. 523.

151. Petrus Peregrinus, 1904, *The Letter of Petrus Peregrinus on the Magnet*, translated by Brother Arnold. McGraw, New York, p. 29.

Bibliography

Abelard, P. 1922. *Historia Calamitatum, the Story of My Misfortunes*. Trans. Henry Adams Bellows. Saint Paul: Thomas A. Boyd.

Adams, F. D. 1954. *The Birth and Development of the Geological Sciences* (first published in 1938 by William & Wilkins, Baltimore). New York: Dover.

Adams, H. 1913. *Mont-Saint-Michel and Chartres*. Boston: Houghton Mifflin.

Adelard of Bath. 1998. *Adelard of Bath, Conversations with his Nephew*, trans. and ed. by Charles Burnett. Cambridge: Cambridge University Press.

Aelianus, Claudius. 1665. *Claudius Aelianus his Various History*. Trans. Thomas Stanley. London: Thomas Dring.

Ambah, F. S. 2008. Saudi Women See a Brighter Road on Rights. *Washington Post*, January 31.

Anawati, G. C. 1974. Philosophy, Theology, and Mysticism. In *The Legacy of Islam*, Second Edition. Ed. Joseph Schacht and C. E. Bosworth. London: Oxford at the Clarendon Press.

_____. 2008. Hunayn Ibn Ishaq Al-Ibadi, Abu Zayd. In *Complete Dictionary of Scientific Biography*. Ed. Charles Gillispie. New York: Cengage Learning.

Anonymous. 1895. Prolegomena, Sketch of the Life and Works of Saint Basil. In *A Select Library of Nicene and Post-Nicene Fathers of the Christian Church, Second Series*. Ed. Philip Schaff and Henry Wace, vol. 8, *St. Basil, Letters and Select Works*. New York: The Christian Literature Company.

_____. 2005. Martin Lings—Obituary. *Times* (London), May 25.

Antoninus, Marcus Aurelius. 1875. *The Thoughts of the Emperor M. Aurelius Antoninus*. Trans. George Long, Second Edition. London: George Bell.

Appian. 1913. *The Civil Wars*. Trans. Horace White. In *Appian's Roman History*, vol. 3. London: William Heinemann.

Aquinas, T. 1952. *Summa Theologica, Supplement to the Third Part, Treatise on the Resurrection*. Trans. the Fathers of the English Dominican Province. In *Great Books of the Western World*, vol. 20. Chicago: William Benton.

_____. 1952. *Summa Theologica, Treatise on God*. Trans. the Fathers of the English Province. *Great Books of the Western World*, vol. 19. Chicago: William Benton.

Archimedes. 2002. *The Works of Archimedes*. Ed. T. L. Heath, first published as *The Works of Archimedes* (1897, Cambridge Univ. Press) and *The Method of Archimedes* (1912, Cambridge Univ. Press). Mineola, New York: Dover.

Aristotle. 1885. *The Politics of Aristotle*. Trans. Benjamin Jowett. London: Oxford at the Clarendon Press.

_____. 1906. *The Nicomachean Ethics of Aristotle*, Tenth Edition. Trans. F. H. Peters. London: Kegan Paul, Trench, Trübner.

_____. 1910. *Historia Animalium (History of Animals)*. Trans. D'Arcy Wentworth Thompson. In *The Works of Aristotle Translated into English*, vol. 4. Ed. J. A. Smith and W. D. Ross. London: Oxford University Press.

_____. 1912. *De Generatione Animalium (On the Generation of Animals)*. Trans. Arthur Platt. In *The Works of Aristotle Translated into English*, vol. 5. Ed. J. A. Smith and W. D. Ross. London: Oxford University Press.

_____. 1923. *Meteorologica (Meteorology)*. Trans. E. W. Webster. London: Oxford at the Clarendon Press.

_____. 1939. *On the Heavens (De Caelo)*. Trans. W. K. C. Guthrie. London: William Heinemann.

_____. 1941. *Analytica Posteriora (Posterior Analytics)*. Trans. A. J. Jenkinson. In *Basic Works of Aristotle*. New York: Random House.

_____. 1941. *Analytica Priora (Prior Analytics)*. Trans. A. J. Jenkinson. In *Basic Works of Aristotle*. New York: Random House.

_____. 1941. *De Generatione et Corruptione (On Generation and Corruption)*. Trans. Harold H. Joachim. In *Basic Works of Aristotle*. New York: Random House.

_____. 1941. *Metaphysica (Metaphysics)*. Trans. W. D. Ross. In *Basic Works of Aristotle*. New York: Random House.

Armstrong, K. 1994. *A History of God*. New York: Alfred A. Knopf.

Arnaldez, R. 2008. Ibn Rushd. In *Complete Dictionary of Scientific Biography*. Ed. Charles Gillispie, vol. 12. New York: Cengage Learning.

_____. 2009. Ibn Rushd, in, *Encyclopedia of Islam*, Second Edition. Ed. P. Bearman et al. Brill Online, accessed April 14, 2009.

al-Athir, Ibn. 2006. *The Chronicle of Ibn al-Athir for The Crusading Period*. Trans. D. S. Richards, vol. 13 of *Crusade Texts in Translation*. Burlington, Vermont: Ashgate.

Averroes. 1954. *Averroes' Tahafut al-Tahafut (The Incoherence of the Incoherence)*. Trans. Simon Van Den

Berg, vol. 1 and 2. Cambridge: University of Cambridge Press for the Gibb Memorial Trust.

_____. 1961. *On the Harmony of Religion and Philosophy*. Trans. George F. Hourani, E. J. W. Gibb Memorial Series, New Series 21. London: Luzac & Co. for the Trustees of the E. J. W. Gibb Memorial.

Avicenna. 1951. *Autobiography*. Trans. Arthur J. Arberry. In *Avicenna on Theology*. London: John Murray.

_____. 1951. On Prayer. Trans. Arthur J. Arberry. In *Avicenna on Theology*. London: John Murray.

_____. 1951. On the Nature of God. Trans. Arthur J. Arberry. In *Avicenna on Theology*. London: John Murray.

_____. 1951. Predestination. Trans. Arthur J. Arberry. In *Avicenna on Theology*. London: John Murray.

Baas, J. H. 1889. *Outlines of the History of Medicine and the Medical Profession*. Trans. H. E. Handerson. New York: J. H. Vail.

Bacon, R. 1900. *The Opus Majus of Roger Bacon*. Ed. by John Henry Bridges. London: Williams and Norgate.

_____. 1907. On Experimental Science. In *The Library of Original Sources*. Ed. Oliver Joseph Thatcher. University Research Extension, New York.

_____. 1928. *The Opus Majus of Roger Bacon*. Trans. Robert Belle Burke. Philadelphia: University of Pennsylvania Press.

Bakewell, C. M. 1907. *Source Book in Ancient Philosophy*. New York: Scribner's.

Barnard, H. C. 1922. *The French Tradition in Education*. Cambridge Univ. Press.

Becker, C. H. 1913. The Expansion of the Saracens. In *Cambridge Medieval History*, vol. 2, *The Rise of the Saracens and the Foundation of the Western Empire*. Ed. H. M. Gwatkin and J. P. Whitney. New York: Macmillan.

Bevan, A. A. 1913. Mahomet and Islam. In *Cambridge Medieval History*, vol. 2, *The Rise of the Saracens and the Foundation of the Western Empire*. Ed. H. M. Gwatkin and J. P. Whitney. New York: Macmillan.

al-Biruni. 1879. *The Chronology of Ancient Nations*. Trans. C. Edward Sachau. London: William H. Allen.

_____. 2003. *Alberuni's India* (first published in 1888 by K. Paul, Trench, Trübner & Co., London). Delhi, India: Low Price Publications.

Boethius of Dacia. 1987. *On the Supreme Good, On the Eternity of the World, On Dreams*. Trans. John F. Wippel. Toronto: Pontifical Institute of Mediaeval Studies.

Boilot, D. J. 2009. al-Biruni. In *Encyclopedia of Islam*, Second Edition. Ed. P. Bearman et al. Brill Online, accessed April 10, 2009.

Boissonnade, P. 1987. *Life and Work in Medieval Europe*. Trans. Eileen Power (first published in 1927 by A. A. Knopf in New York and by Routledge & K. Paul in London). New York: Dorset Press.

_____. 2002. *Life and Work in Medieval Europe* (first published in 1927 by A. A. Knopf, New York). New York: Dover.

Bond, G., et al. 2001. Persistent Solar Influence on North Atlantic Climate During the Holocene. *Science*, no. 5549, vol. 294.

Bornkamm, G. 1971. *Paul*. Trans. D. M. G. Stalker. New York: Harper & Row.

Bos, H. J. M. 2008. Huygens, Christiaan. In *Complete Dictionary of Scientific Biography*. Ed. Charles Gillispie, vol. 6. Detroit: Scribner's.

Böwering, G. 1985. Islam, Religion. In *Dictionary of the Middle Ages*. Ed. Joseph R. Strayer. New York: Scribner's.

Bowman, S. 2003. Twelfth-Century Jewish Responses to Crusade and Jihad. In *Crusaders, Condottieri, and Cannon: Medieval Warfare in Societies Around the Mediterranean*. Ed. Donald J. Kagay and L. J. Andrew Villaion. Leiden: Brill.

Brehaut, E. 1912. An Encyclopedist of the Dark Ages, Isidore of Seville. *Studies in History, Economics, and Law*, vol. 48, no. 1. New York: Columbia University.

Bridges, J. H. 1914. *The Life & Work of Roger Bacon*. London: Williams & Norgate.

Broecker, W. S. 2001. Was the Medieval Warm Period Global? *Science*, no. 5508, vol. 291.

Browne, E. G. 1906. *A Literary History of Persia*. New York: Scribner's.

Bryce, J. 1920. *The Holy Roman Empire*. London: Macmillan.

Burckhardt, J. L. 1829. *Travels in Arabia*. London: Henry Colburn.

_____. 1831. *Notes on the Bedouins and Wahabys*. London: Henry Colburn and Richard Bentley.

Burkhart, R. L. R. 1942. The Rise of the Christian Priesthood. *The Journal of Religion*, vol. 22, no. 2.

Burnett, C. S. F. 1989. Translation and Translators, Western European. In *Dictionary of the Middle Ages*. Ed. Joseph R. Strayer. New York: Scribner's.

Burton, R. F. (translator). 1894. *The Book of the Thousand Nights and a Night*. London: H. S. Nichols.

Burtt, E. A. 1932. *The Metaphysical Foundations of Modern Physical Science*, Revised Edition. London: Kegan Paul, Trench, Trubner.

Bury, J. B. 1955. *The Idea of Progress* (first published in 1920 by MacMillan, London). New York: Dover.

Butterfield, H. 1965. *The Whig Interpretation of History* (first published in 1931 by G. Bell and Sons, London). New York: W. W. Norton.

_____. 1973. Christianity in History. In *Dictionary of the History of Ideas*. Ed. Philip P. Wiener. New York: Scribner's.

Caldwell, W. 1913. The Doctrine of Satan: I. In the Old Testament. *The Biblical World*, no. 1, vol. 41.

de Camp, L. S. 1960. Before Stirrups. *Isis*, no. 2, vol. 51.

Cardwell, D. S. L. 1972. *Turning Points in Western Technology*. New York: Science History Publications.

Carlyle, T. 1840. *On Heroes, Hero-Worship and the Heroic in History*. New York: Frederick A. Stokes.

Catholic Encyclopedia. 1910. New York: Encyclopedia Press.

_____. 1911. New York: Encyclopedia Press.

_____. 1913. New York: Encyclopedia Press.

Cato, Marcus Porcius. 1913. De Agricultura. In *Roman Farm Management*. Trans." "A Virginia Farmer." New York: Macmillan.

Chevedden, P. E., et al. 1995. The Trebuchet. *Scientific American*, no. 1, vol. 273.

Cicero, M. T. 1899. *De Officiis* (*On Duties*). Trans. George B. Gardiner. London: Methuen.

_____. 1775. *Of the Nature of the Gods, in Three Books.* London: T. Davies.

Clagett, M. 2008. Adelard of Bath. In *Complete Dictionary of Scientific Biography*. Ed. Charles Gillispie. New York: Cengage Learning.

Clapham, M. 1957. Printing. In *A History of Technology*. Ed. Charles Singer. London: Oxford University Press.

Constable, P. 2009. Afghan Law on Women Brings Societal Conflict onto World Stage. *Washington Post*, April 5.

Contamine, P. 1984. *War in the Middle Ages*. Trans. Michael Jones. Oxford: Basil Blackwell.

Cook, M. A. 1974. Economic Developments. In *The Legacy of Islam*, Second Edition. Ed. Joseph Schacht and C. E. Bosworth. London: Oxford at the Clarendon Press.

Cosmas Indicopleustes. 1897. *Christian Topography*. Trans. J. W. McCrindle. London: Hakluyt Society.

Coulton, G. G. (editor and translater) 1929, *Life in the Middle Ages*, Second Edition (first published as *A Medieval Garner* in 1910 by Constable, London). Cambridge: Cambridge University Press.

Cram, R. A. 1922. Introduction. In *Historia Calamitatum, the Story of My Misfortunes*. Trans. Henry Adams Bellows. Saint Paul: Thomas A. Boyd.

Creasy, E. S. 1908. *The Fifteen Decisive Battles of the World from Marathon to Waterloo*, Everyman's Library Edition. New York: E. P. Dutton.

Crombie, A. C. 1953. *Robert Grosseteste and the Origins of Experimental Science 1100–1700*. Oxford: Oxford at the Clarendon Press.

_____. 1963. *Medieval and Early Modern Science*, Second Edition. Cambridge, Massachusetts: Harvard University Press.

_____. 1995. *The History of Science, from Augustine to Galileo*, Second Edition. New York: Dover.

_____. 2008. Robert Grosseteste. In *Complete Dictionary of Scientific Biography*. Ed. Charles Gillispie. New York: Cengage Learning.

Crossan, J. D. 1991. *The Historical Jesus*. San Francisco: Harper.

Crowley, T. 1950. *Roger Bacon, the Problem of the Soul in his Philosophical Commentaries*. Louvain: Editions de l'Institut superieur de philosophie.

Curtius, E. R. 1990. *European Literature and the Latin Middle Ages*, translated from German by Willard R. Trask. Princeton, New Jersey: Princeton University Press.

Cyprian. 1844. *The Epistles of S. Cyprian*. Oxford: John Henry Parker.

David-Neel, A. 1932. *Magic and Mystery in Tibet*, First Edition. New York: Claude Kendall.

Dawson, J. B. 1928. Avicenna: the Prince of Physicians. *The Medical Journal of Australia*, vol. 2.

Day, C. 1922. *A History of Commerce*. New York: Longmans, Green, and Co.

Derry, T. K., and Williams, T. I. 1993. *A Short History of Technology, From the Earliest Times to A. D. 1900* (first published in 1960 by Oxford University Press). New York: Dover.

Descartes, R. 1649. *A Discourse of a Method for the Well Guiding of Reason, and the Discovery of Truth in the Sciences*. London: Thomas Newcombe.

Dien, A. E. 1986. The Stirrup and Its Effect on Chinese Military History. *Ars Orientalis*, vol. 16.

Digeser, E. D. 1998. Lactantius, Porphyry, and the Debate Over Religious Toleration. *Journal of Roman Studies*, vol. 88.

Diodorus Siculus. 1814. *The Historical Library of Diodorus the Sicilian*. Trans. G. Booth. London: W. M'Dowall for J. Davis.

Diogenes Laërtius. 1905. *The Lives and Opinions of Eminent Philosophers*. Trans. C. D. Yonge. London: George Bell.

Doane, T. W. 1884. *Bible Myths and Their Parallels in Other Religions*, Third Edition. New York: J. W. Bouton.

Donner, F. M. 1985. Islam, Conquests of. In *Dictionary of the Middle Ages*. Ed. Joseph R. Strayer. New York: Scribner's.

Drachman, A. G. 2008. Ctesibius. In *Complete Dictionary of Scientific Biography*. Detroit: Scribner's.

Drake, S. 1995. *Galileo at Work, His Scientific Biography* (first published by the University of Chicago Press in 1978). New York: Dover.

Dreyer, J. L. E. 1953. *A History of Astronomy from Thales to Kepler* (first published in 1906 by Cambridge University Press as *History of the Planetary Systems from Thales to Kepler*). New York: Dover.

Drower, M. S. 1954. Water-Supply, Irrigation, and Agriculture. In *A History of Technology*. Ed. Charles Singer. London: Oxford University Press.

Dufour, P. S. 1685. *The Manner of Making Coffee, Tea, and Chocolate*. London: William Crook.

Duhem, P. 1913. Physics. In *The Catholic Encyclopedia*. New York: The Encyclopedia Press.

Dunphy, W. 1988. Siger of Brabant. In *Dictionary of the Middle Ages*. Ed. Joseph R. Strayer. New York: Scribner's.

Encyclopedia of World Biography, Second Edition. 2004. Detroit: Alfonso X. Gale.

Eusebius. 1845. The Life of the Blessed Emperor Constantine. In *The Greek Ecclesiastical Historians of the First Six Centuries of the Christian Era*. London: Samuel Bagster.

_____. 1851. *Ecclesiastical History*. Trans. C. F. Cruse. London: Henry G. Bohn.

F. A. D. 1902. Mendel's Theory of Heredity. *Nature*, no. 1719, vol. 66.

Fairbanks, A. 1898. *The First Philosophers of Greece*. London: Kegan Paul, Trench, Trübner.

Fakhry, M. 1970. *A History of Islamic Philosophy*. New York: Columbia University Press.

al-Faruqi, M. J. 2004. Sufism and the Sufi Orders. In *Encyclopedia of the Modern Middle East and North Africa*, 2nd Edition. Ed. Philip Mattar. New York: Macmillan Reference.

Fisher, G. J. 1883. Abu Ali El-Hosein Ibn-Abdallah Ibn Sina, Commonly Called Avicenna. *Annals of Anatomy and Surgery*.

Folland, C. K., Karl, T. R., and Vinnikov, K. Y. A. 1990. Observed Climate Variations and Change, in *Climate Change, The IPCC Scientific Assessment*. Ed. J.

T. Houghton, G. J. Jenkins, and J. J. Ephraums. Cambridge: Cambridge University Press.

Forbes, R. J. 1956. Food and Drink. In *A History of Technology*. Ed. Charles Singer. London: Oxford University Press.

_____. 1956. Power. In *A History of Technology*. Ed. Charles Singer. London: Oxford University Press.

Formigari, L. 1973. Chain of Being. In *Dictionary of the History of Ideas*. Ed. Philip P. Wiener. New York: Scribner's.

Frazer, J. G. 1900. *The Golden Bough*, Second Edition. New York: Macmillan.

Freind, J. 1727. *The History of Physick; From the Time of Galen, to the Beginning of the Sixteenth Century*, Second Edition, Corrected. London: J. Walthoe.

Frothingham, A. L. 1915. *A History of Architecture*. Garden City, New York: Doubleday, Page.

al-Ghazali. 1917. *The Rescuer from Error*. In *The Sacred Books and Early Literature of the East*. Ed. Charles F. Horne. New York: Parke, Austin, and Lipscomb.

_____. 1997. *The Incoherence of the Philosophers*. Trans. Michael E. Marmura. Provo, Utah: Brigham Young Press.

Gibbon, E. 1909. *The History of the Decline and Fall of the Roman Empire*. Ed. J. B. Bury. London: Methuen.

Gies, F., and Gies, J. 1994. *Cathedral, Forge, and Waterwheel*. New York: HarperCollins.

Gille, B. 1956. Machines. In *A History of Technology*. Ed. Charles Singer. London: Oxford University Press.

Gilson, E. 1955. *History of Christian Philosophy in the Middle Ages*. New York: Random House.

Gimpel, J. 1976. *The Medieval Machine*. New York: Holt, Rinehart and Winston.

_____. 1983. *The Cathedral Builders*. Trans. Teresa Waugh. Wiltshire, England: Michael Russell Publishing Ltd.

Goldston, R. 1979. *The Sword of the Prophet*. New York: Dial Press.

Goldziher, I. 1981. The Attitude of Orthodox Islam Toward the" "Ancient Sciences." In *Studies on Islam*. Ed. and trans. Merlin L. Swartz. New York: Oxford University Press.

Goodchild, R. G., and Forbes, R. J. 1956. Road and Land Travel. In *A History of Technology*. Ed. Charles Singer. London: Oxford University Press.

Goodrich, L. C., and Feng, C-S. 1946. The Early Development of Firearms in China. *Isis*, no. 2, vol. 36.

Grant, E. (editor). 1974. *A Source Book in Medieval Science*. Cambridge, Massachusetts: Harvard University Press.

Grant, E. 1962. Late Medieval Thought, Copernicus, and the Scientific Revolution. *Journal of the History of Ideas*, no. 2, vol. 23.

_____. 1977. *Physical Science in the Middle Ages*. Cambridge: Cambridge University Press.

_____. 2001. *God and Reason in the Middle Ages*. Cambridge: Cambridge University Press.

_____. 2007. *A History of Natural Philosophy*. Cambridge: Cambridge University Press.

_____. 2008. Peter Peregrinus. In *Complete Dictionary of Scientific Biography*. Ed. Charles Gillispie. New York: Cengage Learning.

Graves, F. P. 1914. *A History of Education*. New York: Macmillan.

Greenwood, T. 1858. *A Political History of the Greek Latin Patriarchate*, Books III, IV, & V. London: C. J. Stewart.

Gregory I. 1911. *The Dialogues of St. Gregory*. London: Philip Lee Warner.

Gregory Nazianzen. 1894. Orations. In *A Select Library of Nicene and Post-Nicene Fathers of the Christian Church*. Ed. Philip Schaff and Henry Wace, vol. 7. New York: The Christian Literature Company.

Guillaume, A. 1931. Philosophy and Theology. In *The Legacy of Islam*, First Edition. Ed. T. Arnold, and A. Guillaume, London: Oxford University Press.

Hackett, J. M. G. 1983. Bacon, Roger. In *Dictionary of the Middle Ages*, vol. 2. Ed. Joseph R. Strayer. New York: Scribner's.

Hackett, J. 2008. Bacon, Roger. In *Complete Dictionary of Scientific Biography*. Ed. Charles Gillispie, vol. 19. New York: Cengage Learning.

Hall, A. R. 1956. A Note on Military Pyrotechnics. In *A History of Technology*, vol. 2. Ed. Charles Singer. London: Oxford University Press.

_____. 1956. Military Technology. In *A History of Technology*, vol. 2. Ed. Charles Singer. London: Oxford University Press.

Hamel, G. 1990. *Poverty and Charity in Roman Palestine, First Three Centuries C.E.* Berkeley: University of California Press.

Hands, A. R. 1968. *Charities and Social Aid in Greece and Rome*. Ithaca, New York: Cornell University Press.

Harvey, J. 1950. *The Gothic World, 1100–1600: A Survey of Architecture and Art*. London: B. T. Batsford.

Haskins, C. H. 1922. Science at the Court of Emperor Frederick II. *The American Historical Review*, no. 4, vol. 27.

_____. 1927. *Studies in the History of Medieval Science*, Second Edition. Cambridge: Harvard University Press.

_____. 1957. *The Renaissance of the 12th Century* (first published in 1927 by Harvard University Press, Cambridge, Massachusetts). New York: Meridian Books.

Heath, T. L. 1956. *The Thirteen Books of Euclid's Elements*, Second Edition, vol. 1 (first published in 1908 by Cambridge Univ. Press). New York: Dover.

Heaton, H. 1936. *Economic History of Europe*. New York: Harper & Brothers.

Henig, R. M. 2000. *The Monk in the Garden*. New York: Houghton Mifflin.

Henninger, J. 1981. Pre-Islamic Bedouin Religion. In *Studies on Islam*, translated and edited by Merlin L. Swartz. New York: Oxford University Press.

Herodotus. 1910. *The History of Herodotus*, vol. 1 (first published in 1858). Trans. George Rawlinson. New York: J. M. Dent.

Hesiod. 1920. *Works and Days*. In *Hesiod, the Homeric Hymns and Homerica*, with an English translation by Hugh G. Evelyn-White. London, William Heinemann.

Hill, D. 1984. *A History of Engineering in Classical and Medieval Times*. La Salle, Illinois: Open Court.

Hinde, A. 2003. *England's Population, a History Since the Domesday Survey*. London: Hodder Arnold.

Hippocrates. 1846. On the Art of Medicine. In *The Writings of Hippocrates and Galen*. Trans. John Redman Coxe. Philadelphia: Lindsay and Blakiston.

_____. 1846. On the Nature of Man. In *The Writings of Hippocrates and Galen*. Trans. John Redman Coxe. Philadelphia: Lindsay and Blakiston.

_____. 1886. *The Genuine Works of Hippocrates*, vol. 2. Trans. Francis Adams. New York: William Wood and Company.

_____. 1950. *The Medical Works of Hippocrates*. Trans. John Chadwick and W. N. Mann. Springfield, Illinois: Charles C. Thomas.

_____. 1950. The Nature of Man. Trans. J. Chadwick, and W. N. Mann. In *The Medical Works of Hippocrates*. Springfield, Illinois: Charles C. Thomas.

Hippolytus. 1868. *The Refutation of All Heresies*. In *Ante-Nicene Christian Library*. Ed. Rev. Alexander Roberts and James Donaldson, vol. 7, *Hippolytus, Bishop of Rome*, vol. 1. Edinburgh: T. & T. Clark.

Hitti, P. K. 1968. *The Arabs: A Short History* (first published in 1948 by Macmillan, London). New York: St. Martin's Press.

Hugh of St. Victor. 1991. *The Didascalicon of Hugh of St. Victor*. Trans. Jerome Taylor. New York: Columbia University Press.

Hutton, W. H. 1913. Gregory the Great. In *The Cambridge Medieval History*. Ed. H. H. Gwatkin and J. P. Whitney, vol. 2. New York: Macmillan.

Hyman, A., and Walsh, J. J. 1967. *Philosophy in the Middle Ages*. New York: Harper & Row.

Ibn Ishaq (died c. 768). 1967. *The Life of Muhammad* (first published in 1955 by Oxford University Press, London). Trans. Alfred Guillaume. Karachi, Pakistan: Ameena Saiyid, Oxford University Press.

Ibn Khaldun. 1958. *The Muqaddimah, an Introduction to History*. Trans. Franz Rosenthal, vol. 3, Bollingen Series 43. Princeton, New Jersey: Princeton University Press.

Ierley, M. 1984. *Charity for All: Welfare and Society, Ancient Times to the Present*. New York: Praeger.

Institoris, H., and Sprenger, J., 1928, *Malleus Maleficarum*. Trans. Montague Summers. London: J. Rodker.

Irenaeus. 1903. *Against Heresies*. In *The Ante-Nicene Fathers, vol. 1, The Apostilic Fathers with Justin Martyr and Irenaeus*. Ed. Alexander Roberts and James Donaldson. New York: Scribner's.

Iskandar, A. Z. 2008. Ibn Sina (Medicine). In *Complete Dictionary of Scientific Biography*. Ed. Charles Gillispie, vol. 15. New York: Cengage Learning.

John of Salisbury. 1955. *The Metalogicon of John of Salisbury*. Trans. Daniel D. McGarry. Berkeley and Los Angeles: University of California Press.

Jolivet, J., and Rashed, R. 2008. Al-Kindi, Abu Yusuf Ya'qub Ibn Ishaq Al-Sabbah. In *Complete Dictionary of Scientific Biography*, vol. 7. Ed. Charles Gillispie. New York: Cengage Learning.

Jope, E. M. 1956. Agricultural Implements. In *A History of Technology*, vol. 2. Ed. Charles Singer. London: Oxford University Press.

_____. 1956. Vehicles and Harness. In *A History of Technology*, vol. 2. Ed. Charles Singer. London: Oxford University Press.

Josephus, F. 1987. *The Antiquities of the Jews*. In *The Works of Josephus*. Trans. William Whiston. Peabody, Massachusetts: Hendrickson Publishers.

_____. 1987. *The Life of Flavius Josephus*. In *The Works of Josephus*. Trans. William Whiston. Peabody, Massachusetts: Hendrickson Publishers.

_____. 1987. *The Wars of the Jews*. In *The Works of Josephus*. Trans. William Whiston. Peabody, Massachusetts: Hendrickson Publishers.

Juvenal. 1918. Satire 10, *The Vanity of Human Wishes*. In *Juvenal and Perseus*. Trans. G. G. Ramsay. London: William Heinemann.

_____. 1918. Satire 6, *The Ways of Women*. In *Juvenal and Perseus*. Trans. G. G. Ramsay. London: William Heinemann.

al-Juzjani. 1951. Biography of Avicenna. Trans. Arthur J. Arberry. In *Avicenna on Theology*. London: John Murray.

Kennedy, E. S. 2008. Al-Biruni. In *Complete Dictionary of Scientific Biography*. Ed. Charles Gillispie, vol. 2. New York: Cengage Learning.

Ker, W. P. 1955. *The Dark Ages* (first published in 1904 by William Blackwood and Sons, Edinburgh). London: Thomas Nelson and Sons.

Knowles, D. 2006. John of Salisbury. In *Encyclopedia of Philosophy*, Second Edition, vol. 4. Ed. Donald Borchert. Detroit: Macmillan Reference.

Koran, 1861. Trans. John Medows Rodwell. London: Williams and Norgate.

Krey, A. C. 1921. *The First Crusade, the Accounts of Eye-Witnesses and Participants*. Princeton: Princeton University Press.

Kunitzsch, P. 2003. The Transmission of Hindu-Arabic Numerals Reconsidered. In *The Enterprise of Science in Islam, New Perspectives*. Ed. Jan P. Hogendijk and Abdelhamid I. Sabra. Cambridge, Massachusetts: MIT Press.

Lactantius. 1871. *The Divine Institutes*. In *Ante-Nicene Christian Library*, vol. 21, *The Works of Lactantius*, vol. 1. Ed. Alexander Roberts and James Donaldson. Edinburgh: T. & T. Clark.

Lamb, H. H. 1982. *Climate, History and the Modern World*. London: Methuen.

Landes, D. S. 1969. *The Unbound Prometheus*. Cambridge: Cambridge University Press.

Lane-Poole, S. 1894. *The Mohammadan Dynasties*. Westminster (London): Archibald Constable.

Lecky, W. E. H. 1897. *History of European Morals*, Third Edition, Revised, vol. 1. New York: D. Appleton.

Lemay, R. 2008. Gerard of Cremona. In *Complete Dictionary of Scientific Biography*. Ed. Charles Gillispie, vol. 15. New York: Cengage Learning.

Lindberg, D. C. 1978. The Transmission of Greek and Arabic Learning to the West. In *Science in the Middle Ages*. Ed. David C. Lindberg. Chicago: University of Chicago Press.

_____. 1992. *The Beginnings of Western Science*. Chicago: University of Chicago Press.

_____. 1997. Roger Bacon on Light, Vision, and the Universal Emanation of Force. In *Roger Bacon & the Sciences, Commemorative Essays*. Ed. Jeremiah Hackett. New York: Leiden.

Lings, M. 1983. *Muhammad, His Life Based on the*

Earliest Sources. Inner Traditions, Rochester, Vermont.

Little, A. G. 1914. Introduction on Roger Bacon's Life and Works. In *Roger Bacon Essays.* Ed. A. G. Little. London: Oxford University Press.

Livius, T. 1850. *The History of Rome*, Books Twenty-Seven to Thirty-Six. Trans. Cyrus Edmonds. London: Henry G. Bohn.

Lloyd, G. E. R. 1970. *Early Greek Science: Thales to Aristotle.* New York: W. W. Norton.

Lloyd, H. A. 1957. Mechanical Timekeepers. In *A History of Technology*, vol. 3. Ed. Charles Singer. London: Oxford University Press.

Lyell, C. 1892. *Principles of Geology*, Eleventh Edition, vol. 1. New York: D. Appleton.

Macculloch, J. A. 1902. *Comparative Theology.* London: Methuen.

MacDonald, D. B. 1899. The Life of al-Ghazali, with Especial Reference to His Religious Experiences and Opinions. *Journal of the American Oriental Society*, vol. 20.

Mackay, C. 1841. *Memoirs of Extraordinary Popular Delusions.* London: Richard Bentley.

Macmurray, J. 1939. *The Clue to History.* New York: Harper & Brothers.

Maimonides, M. 1956. *Guide for the Perplexed.* Trans. M. Friedlander (Second Revised Edition, first published in 1904 by Routledge & Kegan Paul). New York: Dover.

Makdisi, G. 1981. *The Rise of Colleges, Institutions of Learning in Islam and the West.* Edinburgh: Edinburgh University Press.

Margoliouth, D. S. 1905. *Mohammed and the Rise of Islam*, Third Edition. New York: G. P. Putnam's.

Marrou, H. I. 1964. *A History of Education in Antiquity.* Trans. George Lamb. New York: Mentor.

Masood, E. 2005. Women at Work. *Nature*, vol. 433.

Maurer, A. 2003. Boethius of Sweden (Dacia). In *New Catholic Encyclopedia*, Second Edition, vol. 2. Detroit: Gale.

McCabe, J. 1901. *Peter Abelard.* New York: G. P. Putnam's.

McCrindle, J. W. 1897. Introduction. In *Christian Topography.* London: Hakluyt Society.

McInerny, R. 1982. Aquinas, St. Thomas. In *Dictionary of the Middle Ages*, vol. 1. Ed. Joseph R. Strayer. New York: Scribner's.

McVaugh, M. 2008. Arnald of Villanova. In *Complete Dictionary of Scientific Biography.* Ed. Charles Gillispie, vol. 1. New York: Cengage Learning.

_____. 2008. Constantine the African. In *Complete Dictionary of Scientific Biography.* Ed. Charles Gillispie, vol. 3. New York: Cengage Learning.

_____. 2008. Frederick II of Hohenstaufen. In *Complete Dictionary of Scientific Biography.* Ed. Charles Gillispie, vol. 5. New York: Cengage Learning.

Meyerhof, M. 1931. Science and Medicine. In *The Legacy of Islam* (First Edition). Ed. T. Arnold, and A. Guillaume. London: Oxford University Press.

_____. 1935. Thirty-Three Clinical Observations by Rhazes. *Isis*, no. 2, vol. 23.

Milton, J. 1667. *Paradise Lost. A Poem Written in Ten Books.* London: Peter Parker.

Minio-Paluello, L. 2008. James of Venice. In *Complete Dictionary of Scientific Biography.* Ed. Charles Gillispie, vol. 7. New York: Cengage Learning.

_____. 2008. Michael Scot. In *Complete Dictionary of Scientific Biography.* Ed. Charles Gillispie, vol. 9. New York: Cengage Learning.

_____. 2008. Moerbeke, William of. In *Complete Dictionary of Scientific Biography.* Ed. Charles Gillispie, vol. 9. New York: Cengage Learning.

Mommsen, T. E. 1942. Petrarch's Conception of the "Dark Ages." *Speculum*, no. 2, vol. 17.

Mommsen, T. 1996. *A History of Rome Under the Emperors.* London: Routledge.

Montague, F. C. (editor). 1903. *Critical and Historical Essays Contributed to the Edinburgh Review by Lord Macaulay* (Essay on Lord Bacon, July, 1837). New York: G. P. Putnam's.

Moody, E. A. 1958. Empiricism and Metaphysics in Medieval Philosophy. *The Philosophical Review*, no. 2, vol. 67.

Mooney, J. 1896. The Ghost-Dance Religion and the Sioux Outbreak of 1890. In *Fourteenth Annual Report of the Bureau of Ethnology*, Part 2. Washington: U. S. Government Printing Office.

Moore, T. G. 1995. *Global Warming: A Boon to Humans and Other Animals.* Hoover Institution Essays in Public Policy No. 61. Stanford, California: Stanford University.

Mott, L. V. 1991. *The Development of the Rudder, 100–1600 AD: a Technological Tale.* MS Thesis, Texas A&M University, College Station.

Motzki, H. 2004. Hadith. In *Encyclopedia of Islam and the Muslim World*, vol. 1. Ed. Richard C. Martin. New York: Macmillan Reference.

Muir, W. 1858. *The Life of Mahomet and History of Islam, to the Era of the Hegira.* London: Smith, Elder.

_____. 1892. *The Caliphate, Its Rise, Decline, and Fall*, Second Edition. London: Religious Tract Society.

Munro, D. C. 1897. *The Attitude of the Western Church toward the Study of the Latin Classics in the Early Middle Ages* (reprinted from vol. 8, American Society of Church History). New York: Knickerbocker Press.

_____. 1903. Christian and Infidel in the Holy Land. In *Essays on the Crusades.* New York: Fox, Duffield.

Nasr, S. H. 1992. *Science and Civilization in Islam* (first published in 1968 by Harvard University Press, Cambridge, Massachusetts). New York: Barnes & Noble.

Needham, J. 1959. *Science and Civilisation in China*, vol. 3. Cambridge: Cambridge University Press.

Newhouse, E. L. (editor). 1992. *The Builders: Marvels of Engineering.* Washington, D.C.: National Geographic Society.

Norton, A. O. (editor). 1909. *Readings in the History of Education, Mediaeval Universities.* Cambridge: Harvard University.

Nutton, V. 2004. *Ancient Medicine.* London: Routledge.

Ogg, F. A. (editor). 1908. *A Source Book of Mediaeval History.* New York: American Book.

Oldfield, A. 1865. On the Aborigines of Australia. *Transactions of the Ethnological Society of London*, New Series, vol. 3.

O'Leary, D. L. 1948. *How Greek Science Passed to the Arabs.* London: Routledge and Kegan Paul.

Oman, C. W. C. 1885. *The Art of War in the Middle Ages, A. D. 378–1515.* London: B. H. Blackwell.

Omar Khayyam. 1896. *Rubaiyat of Omar Khayyam,* Twenty-Sixth American Edition, Poem 71. Trans. Edward Fitzgerald. Boston: Houghton, Mifflin.

Pacey, A. 1992. *The Maze of Ingenuity,* Second Edition. Cambridge, Massachusetts: MIT Press.

Pachter, H. M. 1951. *Magic into Science: the Story of Paracelsus.* New York: Henry Schuman.

Pedersen, J., et al. Madrasa. In *Encyclopedia of Islam,* Second Edition. Ed. P. Bearman et al. Brill Online.

Petrus Peregrinus. 1904. *The Letter of Petrus Peregrinus on the Magnet.* Trans. Brother Arnold. New York: McGraw.

Phillips, W. D. 1985. *Slavery from Roman Times to the Early Transatlantic Trade.* Minneapolis: University of Minnesota Press.

Pickthall, M. M. 1977. *The Meaning of the Glorious Qur'an, Text and Explanatory Translation.* New York: Muslim World League, U.N. Office.

Pines, S. 1963. What Was Original in Arabic Science? In *Scientific Change, Historical Studies in the Intellectual, Social and Technical Conditions for Scientific Discovery and Technical Invention, from Antiquity to Present.* Ed. A. C. Crombie. London: Heinemann.

_____. 2008. Al-Razi, Abu Bakr Muhammad Ibn Zakariyya. In *Complete Dictionary of Scientific Biography.* Ed. Charles Gillispie, vol. 11. New York: Cengage Learning.

Pirenne, H. 1948. *Medieval Cities, Their Origins and the Revival of Trade.* Trans. Frank D. Halsey. Princeton: Princeton University Press.

Plato. 1937. Symposium. In *The Dialogues of Plato,* vol. 1. Trans. Benjamin Jowett. New York: Random House.

_____. 1937. *The Republic.* In *The Dialogues of Plato,* vol. 1. Trans. Benjamin Jowett. New York: Random House.

Plautus. 1852. *Trinummus (Three Pieces of Money).* In *The Comedies of Plautus,* vol. 1. Trans. Henry Thomas Riley. London: Henry G. Bohn.

Plessner, M. 1974. Science, The Natural Sciences and Medicine. In *The Legacy of Islam,* Second Edition. Ed. Joseph Schacht and C. E. Bosworth. London: Oxford at the Clarendon Press.

Pliny the Consul. 1809. *The Letters of Pliny the Consul.* Trans. William Melmoth, vol. 2. Boston: E. Larkin.

Pliny the Elder. 1855. *The Natural History of Pliny.* Trans. John Bostock and H. T. Riley, vol. 1. London: Henry G. Bohn.

Plutarch. 1952. Marcellus. In *The Lives of the Noble Grecians and Romans.* Trans. John Dryden. *Great Books of the Western World,* vol. 14. Chicago: William Benton.

_____. 1952. Pericles. In *The Lives of the Noble Grecians and Romans,* Trans. John Dryden. *Great Books of the Western World,* vol. 14. Chicago: William Benton.

Polybius. 1889. *The Histories of Polybius.* Trans. Evelyn S. Shuckburgh. London: Macmillan and Co.

Poole, R. L. 1884. *Illustrations of the History of Medieval Thought and Learning.* London: Williams and Norgate.

Pope, A. 1907. Essay on Man. In *The Poetical Works of Alexander Pope.* Ed. Adolphus William Ward. London: Macmillan.

Popper, K. 1966. *The Open Society and Its Enemies,* Fifth Edition. Princeton, New Jersey: Princeton University Press.

Porphyry. 1823. *On Abstinence from Animal Food.* In *Select Works of Porphyry.* Trans. Thomas Taylor. London: Thomas Rodd.

Price, D. J. 1957. Precision Instruments: to 1500. In *A History of Technology.* Ed. Charles Singer. London: Oxford University Press.

Ptolemy, C. 1952. *The Almagest.* Trans. R. Catesby Taliaferro. In *Great Books of the Western World,* vol. 16. Chicago: William Benton.

Rahman, F. 2005. Islam: an Overview. In *Encyclopedia of Religion,* Second Edition. Ed. Lindsay Jones, vol. 7. Detroit: Macmillan Reference.

Rashdall, H. 1895. *The Universities of Europe in the Middle Ages,* vol. 1. Oxford: Oxford at the Clarendon Press.

al-Razi. 1848. *A Treatise on the Small-Pox and Measles.* Trans. William Alexander Greenhill. London: Sydenham Society.

Reinach, S. 1904. *The Story of Art Throughout the Ages, an Illustrated Record.* New York: Scribner's.

Reynolds, R. L. 1961. *Europe Emerges.* Madison: University of Wisconsin Press.

Richler, B. Z. 1989. Translation and Translators, Jewish. In *Dictionary of the Middle Ages,* vol. 12. Ed. Joseph R. Strayer. New York: Scribner's.

Rist, J. M. 1965. Hypatia. *Phoenix,* no. 3, vol. 19.

Robinson, J. H. (editor). 1904. *Readings in European History,* vol. 1. Boston: Ginn and Company.

Rogers, K. M. 1966. *The Troublesome Helpmate.* Seattle: University of Washington Press.

Russell, B. 1945. *A History of Western Philosophy.* New York: Simon and Schuster.

Sabra, A. I. 1988. Science, Islamic. In *Dictionary of the Middle Ages,* vol. 11. Ed. Joseph R. Strayer. New York: Scribner's.

Sachau, C. E. 1879. Preface. In *The Chronology of Ancient Nations.* London: William H. Allen.

Sachau, E. C. (translator and editor). 2003. *Alberuni's India* (first published in 1888 by K. Paul, Trench, Trübner & Co., London). Delhi, India: Low Price Publications.

St. Ambrose. 1896. *Duties of the Clergy.* In *A Select Library of Nicene and Post-Nicene Fathers of the Christian Church, Second Series,* vol. 10, *St. Ambrose Select Works and Letters.* Ed. Philip Schaff and Henry Wace. New York: The Christian Literature Company.

St. Anselm. 1903. *Proslogium; Monologium; an Appendix in Behalf of the Fool by Gaunilon; and Cur Deus Homo.* Trans. Sidney Norton Deane. Chicago: Open Court.

St. Athanasius. 1892. On the Incarnation of the Word. In *A Select Library of Nicene and Post-Nicene Fathers, Second Series,* vol. 4, *St. Athanasius, Select Works and Letters.* Ed. Philip Schaff and Henry Wace. New York: The Christian Literature Society.

St. Augustine. 1887. *On Christian Doctrine.* Trans. J. F.

Shaw. In *A Select Library of Nicene and Post-Nicene Fathers*, vol. 2, *St. Augustine's City of God and Christian Doctrine*. Ed. Philip Schaff. New York: Scribner's.

St. Basil. 1895. Letter 14. In *A Select Library of Nicene and Post-Nicene Fathers of the Christian Church, Second Series*. Ed. Philip Schaff and Henry Wace, vol. 8, *St. Basil, Letters and Select Works*. New York: The Christian Literature Company.

St. Hilary. 1902. *On the Trinity*. In *A Select Library of Nicene and Post-Nicene Fathers, Second Series*, vol. 9. Ed. Philip Schaff and Henry Wace. New York: Scribner's.

Saliba, G. 1983. Biruni. In *Dictionary of the Middle Ages*, vol. 2. Ed. Joseph R. Strayer. New York: Charles Scribner's Sons.

Sandys, J. E. 1903. *A History of Classical Scholarship*. Cambridge: Cambridge at the University Press.

_____. 1914. Roger Bacon in English Literature. In *Roger Bacon Essays*. Ed. A. G. Little. London: Oxford University Press.

Sarton, G. 1927. *Introduction to the History of Science*, vol. 1. Washington, DC: Carnegie Institution.

_____. 1931. *Introduction to the History of Science*, vol. 2. Washington, DC: Carnegie Institution.

_____. 1954. *Galen of Pergamon*. Lawrence: University of Kansas Press.

Schaff, P. 1859. *History of the Christian Church, A. D. 1–311*. New York: Charles Scribner.

_____. 1884. *History of the Christian Church*, Revised Edition, *Ante-Nicene Christianity, A. D. 100–325*. Edinburgh: T. & T. Clark.

_____. 1884. *History of the Christian Church*, vol. 3, Nicene and Post-Nicene Christianity A. D. 311–600. New York: Scribner's.

_____. 1885. *History of the Christian Church*, vol. 4, *Medieval Christianity A. D. 590–1073*. New York: Scribner's.

_____. 1907. *History of the Christian Church*, Third Edition, vol. 5, part 1, *The Middle Ages, from Gregory VII, 1049, to Boniface VIII, 1294*. New York: Scribner's.

Seneca, Lucius Annaeus. 1786. *The Epistles of Lucius Annaeus Seneca*, Epistle 90, vol. 2. London: W. Woodfall.

Shelby, L. R. 1964. The Role of the Master Mason in Mediaeval English Building. *Speculum*, no. 3, vol. 39.

Singer, C. 1956. Epilogue: East and West in Retrospect. In *A History of Technology*, vol. 2. Ed. Charles Singer. London: Oxford University Press.

_____., Price, D. J., and Taylor, E. G. R. 1957. Cartography, Survey, and Navigation to 1400. In *A History of Technology*, vol. 3. Ed. Charles Singer. London: Oxford University Press.

Smith, D. E. 1914. The Place of Roger Bacon in the History of Mathematics. In *Roger Bacon Essays*. Ed. A. G. Little. London: Oxford University Press.

_____, and Karpinski, L. C. 1911. *The Hindu-Arabic Numerals*. Boston and London: Ginn.

Socrates Scholasticus. 1890. *Ecclesiastical History*. In *A Select Library of Nicene and Post-Nicene Fathers, Second Series*, vol. 2. Ed. Philip Schaff and Henry Wace. New York: The Christian Literature.

Stevenson, F. S. 1899. *Robert Grosseteste, Bishop of Lincoln*. London: Macmillan.

Stock, B. 1978. Science, Technology, and Economic Progress in the Early Middle Ages. In *Science in the Middle Ages*. Ed. David C. Lindberg. Chicago: University of Chicago Press.

Strabo. 1856. *The Geography of Strabo*, vol. 2. Trans. H. C. Hamilton and W. Falconer. London: Henry G. Bohn.

Struik, D. J. 2008. Gerbert. In *Complete Dictionary of Scientific Biography*. Ed. Charles Gillispie, vol. 5. New York: Cengage Learning.

Suetonius, C. T. 1906. *The Lives of the Twelve Caesars*, Julius Caesar. London: George Bell.

al-Suhrawardy, A. A. 1999. *The Sayings of Muhammad*. Secaucus, New Jersey: Citadel Press.

Sulpitius Severus. 1894. *Life of St. Martin*. In *A Select Library of Nicene and Post-Nicene Fathers of the Christian Church, Second Series*. Ed. Philip Schaff and Henry Wace, vol. 11. New York: The Christian Literature.

Tacitus. 1942. *Annals*. In *The Complete Works of Tacitus*. Trans. Alfred John Church and William Jackson Brodribb. New York: Modern Library.

Ta-k'un, W. 1952. An Interpretation of Chinese Economic History. *Past and Present*, no. 1, vol. 1.

Taylor, A. J. 1950. Master James of St. George. *The English Historical Review*, no. 257, vol. 65.

Taylor, H. O. 1914. *The Mediaeval Mind*, Second Edition, vol. 1. London: Macmillan.

Tertullian. 1868. *Against Marcion*. In *Ante-Nicene Christian Library*, vol. 7, *Tertullianus Against Marcion*. Ed. Alexander Roberts and James Donaldson. Edinburgh: T. & T. Clark.

_____. 1869. *Ad Martyras*. In *Ante-Nicene Christian Library*. Ed. Rev. Alexander Roberts and James Donaldson, vol. 11, *The Writings of Tertullian*, vol. 1. Edinburgh: T. & T. Clark.

_____. 1869. *Apologeticus*. In *Ante-Nicene Christian Library*. Ed. Rev. Alexander Roberts and James Donaldson, vol. 11, *The Writings of Tertullian*, vol. 1. Edinburgh: T. & T. Clark.

_____. 1869. *Apology*. In *Ante-Nicene Christian Library*. Ed. Rev. Alexander Roberts and James Donaldson, vol. 11, *The Writings of Tertullian*, vol. 1. Edinburgh: T. & T. Clark.

_____. 1869. *On Female Dress*. In *Ante-Nicene Christian Library*. Ed. Rev. Alexander Roberts and James Donaldson, vol. 11, *The Writings of Tertullian*, vol. 1. Edinburgh: T. & T. Clark.

_____. 1870. *De Anima (On the Soul)*. In *Anti-Nicene Christian Library*, vol. 15, *The Writings of Tertullian*, vol. 2. Ed. Alexander Roberts and James Donaldson. Edinburgh: T. & T. Clark.

_____. 1870. *On Exhortation to Chastity*. In *Ante-Nicene Christian Library*. Ed. Rev. Alexander Roberts and James Donaldson, vol. 18, *The Writings of Tertullian*, vol. 3. Edinburgh: T. & T. Clark.

_____. 1870. On *Prescription Against Heretics*. In *Anti-Nicene Christian Library*. Ed. Alexander Roberts and James Donaldson, vol. 15, *The Writings of Tertullian*, vol. 2. Edinburgh: T. & T. Clark.

_____. 1903. *Apology*. In *The Ante-Nicene Christian Fa-*

thers, vol. 3, *Latin Christianity: Its Founder, Tertullian*. Ed. Alexander Roberts and James Donaldson. New York: Scribner's.

Thatcher, O. J. (editor). 1907. *The Library of Original Sources*, vol. 4. New York: University Research Extension.

Thoms, W. J. (editor). 1858. *Early English Prose Romances*, Second Edition, vol. 1. London: Nattali and Bond.

Thorndike, L. 1914. Roger Bacon and Experimental Method in the Middle Ages. *The Philosophical Review*, no. 3, vol. 23.

_____. 1917. *The History of Medieval Europe*. Boston: Houghton Mifflin Company.

_____. 1923. *A History of Magic and Experimental Science*, vol. 2. New York: Columbia University Press.

_____. 1941. Invention of the Mechanical Clock about 1271 AD. *Speculum*, no. 2, vol. 16.

Thucydides. 1942. *The Peloponnesian War*. Trans. Benjamin Jowett. In *The Greek Historians*, vol. 1. New York: Random House.

Titus Lucretius Carus. 1743. *Of the Nature of Things*, , vol. 2. London: Daniel Brown.

Trimpi, H. P. 1973. Demonology. In *Dictionary of the History of Ideas*, vol. 1. Ed. Philip P. Wiener. New York: Charles Scribner's Sons.

Turnbull, H. W. (Editor). 1959. *The Correspondence of Isaac Newton*, vol. 1. London: Cambridge University Press.

Usher, A. P. 1954. *A History of Mechanical Inventions*, Revised Edition. Cambridge, Massachusetts: Harvard University Press.

Ussher, J. 1658. *The Annals of the World Deduced from the Origin of Time*. London: E. Tyler.

van der Meulen, J. 1985. Gothic Architecture. In *Dictionary of the Middle Ages*, vol. 5. Ed. Joseph R. Strayer. New York: Scribner's.

Van Steenberghen, F. 2008. Siger of Brabant. In *Complete Dictionary of Scientific Biography*. Ed. Charles Gillispie, vol. 12. New York: Cengage Learning.

Vaughan, R. G. 1871. *The Life & Labours of S. Thomas of Aquin*, vol. 1. London: Longmans & Co.

de Vaux, C. 1931. Astronomy and Mathematics. In *The Legacy of Islam*, First Edition. Ed. T. Arnold, and A. Guillaume. London: Oxford University Press.

Vitruvius. 1960. *The Ten Books on Architecture*. Trans. Morris Hicky Morgan (first published by Harvard University Press in 1914). New York: Dover.

von Humboldt, A. 1848. *Kosmos, a General Survey of the Physical Phenomena of the Universe*, vol. 2. London: Hippolyte Bailliere.

Wallace, W. A. 1973. Experimental Science and Mechanics in the Middle Ages. In *Dictionary of the History of Ideas*. Ed. P. P. Wiener, vol. 2. New York: Scribner's.

_____. 1982. Aristotle in the Middle Ages. In *Dictionary of the Middle Ages*, vol. 1. Ed. Joseph R. Strayer. New York: Scribner's.

_____. 2008. Aquinas, Saint Thomas. In *Complete Dictionary of Scientific Biography*. Ed. Charles Gillispie, vol. 1. New York: Cengage Learning.

Walsh, J. J. 1920. *Medieval Medicine*. London: A. & C. Black.

Walzer, R. 1967. Early Islamic Philosophy. In *The Cambridge History of Later Greek and Early Medieval Philosophy*. Ed. A. H. Armstrong. Cambridge: Cambridge at the University Press.

Warmington, E. H. 2008. Posidonius. In *Complete Dictionary of Scientific Biography*. Ed. Charles Gillispie, vol. 11. New York: Cengage Learning.

Watt, G. 1907. *The Wild and Cultivated Cotton Plants of the World*. London: Longmans, Green.

Watt, W. M. 1987. Muhammad. In *Dictionary of the Middle Ages*, vol. 8. Ed. Joseph R. Strayer. New York: Scribner's.

Weiling, F. 1991. Historical Study. Johann Gregor Mendel, 1822–1884. *American Journal of Medical Genetics*, vol. 40.

Weisheipl, J. A.,1982, Albertus Magnus. In *Dictionary of the Middle Ages*, vol. 1. Ed. Joseph R. Strayer. New York: Scribner's.

Wells, H. G. 1921. *The Outline of History*, Third Edition. New York: Macmillan.

Whewell, W. 1858. History of the Inductive Sciences, Third Edition, vol. 1. D. New York: Appleton.

White, A. D. 1909. *A History of the Warfare of Science with Theology in Christendom*, vol. 1 and 2. New York: D. Appleton.

White, L. 1940. Technology and Invention in the Middle Ages. *Speculum*, no. 2, vol. 15.

_____. 1962. *Medieval Technology and Social Change*. Oxford: Oxford at the Clarendon Press.

Whitehead, A. N. 1967. *Science and the Modern World* (first published in 1925 by Macmillan, New York). New York: Free Press.

Whittaker, T. 1911. *Priests, Philosophers and Prophets*. London: Adam and Charles Black.

Williams, M. 1885. *Religious Thought and Life in India*. London: John Murray.

Woodward, D., and Howe, H. M. 1997. Roger Bacon on Geography and Cartography. In *Roger Bacon & the Sciences, Commemorative Essays*. Ed. Jeremiah Hackett. New York: Leiden.

Wright, C. A. 2004. Food: Coffee. In *Encyclopedia of the Modern Middle East and North Africa*. Ed. Philip Mattar, vol. 2. New York: Macmillan Reference.

Wright, O. 2008. Al-Farabi, Abu Nasr Muhammad Ibn Muhammad Ibn Tarkhan Ibn Awzalagh. In *Complete Dictionary of Scientific Biography*. Ed. Charles Gillispie, vol. 4. New York: Cengage Learning.

Xenophon. 1857. On Horsemanship. In *Xenophon's Minor Works*. Trans. J. S. Watson. London: Henry G. Bohn.

Xenophon. 1898. Oeconomicus. In *Xenophon's Minor Works*. Trans. J. S. Watson. London: George Bell.

Yavetz, Z. 1988. *Slaves and Slavery in Ancient Rome*. New Brunswick, New Jersey: Transaction Books.

Zwemer, S. M. 1920. *The Influence of Animism on Islam*. New York: Macmillan.

Index